To Sarah Ward
and
Ningkun and Yikai, who know

EDWARD A. GARGAN

China's Fate

A People's Turbulent Struggle with Reform and Repression 1980–1990

DOUBLEDAY

NEW YORK LONDON TORONTO SYDNEY AUCKLAND

PUBLISHED BY DOUBLEDAY
a division of Bantam Doubleday Dell Publishing Group, Inc.
666 Fifth Avenue, New York, New York 10103

DOUBLEDAY and the portrayal of an anchor with a dolphin
are trademarks of Doubleday, a division
of Bantam Doubleday Dell Publishing Group, Inc.

"The Echo" and "A Blank" by Bei Dao and translated by Bonnie S. McDougall reprinted from the *Bulletin of Concerned Asian Scholars* (vol. 16, no. 3, July–Sept. 1984) and from *Contemporary Chinese Literature: An Anthology of Post-Mao Fiction and Poetry*, Michael S. Duke, ed. (New York and London: M. E. Sharpe, 1985) with the permission of and copyright © by the Bulletin of Concerned Asian Scholars, Inc.

Excerpt from "It's Not That I Can't See" by Cui Jian from *Seeds of Fire* by Geremie Barmé and John Minford. Copyright © 1988 by Geremie Barmé and John Minford. Reprinted by permission of Hill & Wang, a division of Farrar, Straus & Giroux, Inc.

Library of Congress Cataloging-in-Publication Data

Gargan, Edward A.
China's fate: a people's turbulent struggle with reform
and repression 1980–1990/Edward A. Gargan.—1st ed.
p.   cm.
Includes index.
1. China—Politics and government—1976–   I. Title.
DS779.26.G36   1991
951.05′8—dc20   90-38760
CIP

ISBN 0-385-26320-1

ACKNOWLEDGMENTS

THIS BOOK would not have appeared without the labors of Paul Golob and Herman Gollob, the editors who made the manuscript intelligible. Flip Brophy made the book happen in the first place. The Council on Foreign Relations awarded me the Edward R. Murrow Fellowship, which gave me the time and support to write in peace. And lastly, Sarah Ward weathered China, me, and the book; what more could one ask?

CONTENTS

CONTENTS

AUTHOR'S NOTE

CHINA'S CURRENCY is denominated in units called *yuan*, the value of which has dropped considerably during the 1980s. From 1978 to 1981, a U.S. dollar fluctuated between 1.49 and 1.71 yuan. In January 1981, the yuan was fixed at 1.53 to the dollar. On January 1, 1985, the yuan was devalued to 2.80 to the dollar, and then again on October 30, 1985, to 3.2 to the dollar. On July 5, 1986, the yuan was fixed at 3.7 to the dollar where it remained until December 1989, when a new rate of 4.7 to the dollar was established. Chinese currency is issued in two forms, *renminbi*, or "People's Money," which is used by the Chinese people, and *waihuijuan*, or "Foreign Exchange Certificates," the scrip used by foreigners inside the country. Although nominally the two types of currency are of equivalent value, because renminbi are not convertible to foreign exchange, the Foreign Exchange Certificates are actually worth more, about double the value of renminbi by the end of the decade, on the black market.

China measures the area of farmland in units called *mou*, a traditional land measure of area. Historically the size of a mou varied from province to province, but today, a mou is about one sixth of an acre. A mou is further subdivided into tenths of a mou, units that are called *fen*.

For the most part throughout this book, I have used the conventional pinyin system of romanization for Chinese proper and place names. In the chapter on Lolam village however, I have used a romanization system approximating the Cantonese dialect spoken in the region for the spelling of names and locales. I have done this because I feel it is important to emphasize the regional disparities in China; in Lolam no one speaks or understands the north standard dialect of Chinese, commonly called Mandarin. In respect for the people of Lolam, and to reflect accurately the sounds of their language, I have eschewed the use of pinyin in discussing their lives.

Finally, in order to protect the identity of people who are still in China and who spoke with me candidly about their thoughts and feelings, I have changed the names of some people. For those informants who are either in exile or have been imprisoned, I have used their proper names.

INTRODUCTION

HISTORY IS PEOPLED SPARSELY with men or women whose ideas, whose actions, whose writings transcend the petty concerns of everyday life, whose life's work is of such rarity, of such originality that one stands aside in awe. For most of us, rare are the occasions when we brush such greatness. One early spring day in 1988, I did.

A friend called me that morning and asked if I would like to accompany him to see his friend Shen Congwen. To most Americans, indeed to most Chinese, the name means nothing. For four decades of Communist rule, Shen's name has been rarely heard. In the United States, even the most widely read individuals can muster up only a handful of common Chinese names, none of them Shen's.

But for me, it was a moment to savor. Simply put, Shen Congwen is the greatest Chinese writer of this century.

I picked up my friend at his home and we drove to the southern edge of the original old city of Beijing. I talked excitedly about the visit, about Shen's reputation and his work, with which I was somewhat familiar. Shen was born in 1902 near a town called Fenghuang in western Hunan, a remote, wild area populated by the fiercely independent Miao minority. I had visited Fenghuang the previous year, in large part to visit the land and the people Shen had written about. I walked the streets of Fenghuang, a town largely untouched by modernization, a town of cobbled streets and watchtowers, of wood houses balanced precariously on frail scaffolding over the Tuo River, where the Miao women wear enormous headdresses of gauzy black cloth and heavy silver jewelry that clinks when they walk. I knocked on the door of the house where Shen had written as a young man, and peered into the dark shed that was the study where he first put brush to paper.

Shen's work, embedded in the folklore and customs of western Hunan, is of such density and obscurity that it defies easy access. From the exuberant if undisciplined poetry of his early years, which explores nature and sexual life, to the short dramas —one-act farces—that skewer modern social conventions, to the thickly textured mature novels that chronicle the culture of the Miao under siege by the dominant Chinese, Shen continually grappled with life's fundamentals. In the words of his American biographer, Jeffrey C. Kinkley, Shen sought "to frame universal questions of life and death, love and sexuality, permanence and change. . . . Ultimately, he conveyed a sense of his country folk as a moral community sitting in judgment of modern China."

Unlike many of his contemporaries, Shen never embraced the ideological constraints on intellectual life that were essential for accommodation with the emerging Communist movement in the 1930s and 1940s. Nonetheless, Shen refused to flee his country when it became apparent that Mao Zedong and his armies would succeed in wresting China from the hopelessly corrupt Kuomintang of Chiang Kai-shek. Within four years of the Communist triumph, however, Shen was informed by his Shanghai publisher that his books were to be burned and the printing plates smashed. In the words of the devoted Communist intellectual Guo Moruo, Shen was nothing more than a "reactionary pornographer."

After 1949, Shen never again wrote fiction, devoting himself instead to studies of lacquerware, Chinese costume, and folk art. He was repeatedly denounced by the party, sent to political indoctrination courses, and later forced to scrub latrines. And though the 1980s brought relaxed controls on intellectual life, Shen's advanced age inhibited his ability to work, and he told friends he could never really return to fiction.

I tried for years to find Shen's works in the bookstores of

Beijing, without success. Invariably I was met with blank stares from clerks who either had never heard of Shen, or had only the dimmest recollection of his work, but no volumes of his writings were to be found. Moreover, Shen is omitted from two post-Mao compilations, both entitled *The History of Modern Chinese Literature*, as well as the *Dictionary of Chinese Authors*, issued in 1979. A twelve-volume edition of his collected oeuvre published in Guangzhou between 1982 and 1985 was unavailable everywhere I looked. Only in Hong Kong could I find any of Shen's collected essays, novels, or poetry. At various times in the 1980s, Shen's name was murmured in the West in connection with the Nobel Prize for Literature, his work compared, for ease of apprehension, with that of William Faulkner.

So as my friend and I parked amid a procession of domino-like cement apartment buildings in southern Beijing, my excitement was palpable. We were met at the door of the apartment by Shen's wife, Zhang Zhaohe. "He's just getting up," she told us. "He'll be in shortly." My friend shooed me into the book-lined living room of the apartment, a spacious three-bedroom flat that had been bestowed on Shen by the government a few years earlier in belated and (it seemed to many) grudging recognition of his literary stature. My friend whispered to me that Shen was in declining health, and that I should be prepared.

After a few minutes, Shen appeared at the entrance to the living room, supported at the elbow by his son, who steered him to a stuffed armchair. Shen sat down shakily, but his eyes twinkled behind thick glasses. He had suffered a small stroke earlier in the year and did not have full control of his hands, which shook slightly. He resembled, in a way, an owl of great age, his eyes somehow larger behind the lenses of his glasses, his cheeks a bit cherubic. My friend asked Shen how his health was.

Shen laughed weakly and, in the guttural dialect of his western Hunan, he simply replied, "Not so good, as you can see." My friend joked with Shen about mutual friends and the conversation skated lightly over the condition of writing in Beijing. I asked Shen if he read many of the newer writers, young authors who had risen to notice since Mao's death.

"It's hard to read now," he said, struggling with the words. "Zhaohe has to read for me." I explained to Shen that I had been to his hometown and that I had visited his old home. "Ah," he sighed, "and how is it, Fenghuang?" I told him that I thought it still resonated with traces of the culture he had written about, that Miao culture, especially in the hills away from the town, endured despite the efforts of the Chinese government to suppress it. He nodded slightly as I talked.

I reminded him of passages he had written of Fenghuang, passages that were fresh in my mind as I walked the streets of his home town.

"At sunset or dusk," Shen wrote, "if you climb a height in that town which stands impressively alone surrounded by mountains, gazing at the ruined forts near and far, you can still conjure up a faint picture of the past when bugles, drums, and torches raised an alarm . . . everything is fast changing and progressing; this progress is putting an end to all past misunderstandings and vendettas. . . . There are various different local authorities, the highest being deities, the next officials with below them the village heads and the attendants of spirits who practice magic. The people here are honest and law-abiding, believing in spirits and afraid of officials."

I wondered aloud whether it was so different today. Shen just sighed.

It was not, I should say, a full and vibrant conversation. Shen was hobbled by the frailties of his years and declining health. I explained that his works were very difficult to find in China, and he nodded wearily. "Go get them something," he whispered to his wife, who pulled two volumes from a bookshelf. His hands trembled too much to write, so Zhaohe penned Shen's name in each of our volumes. And that was all. A month later, on May 11, 1988, my friend called to tell me that Shen had died. The obituary of Shen I wrote appeared in *The New York Times* the next day. It took four days before the Chinese press noted Shen's passing, at less length than did the distant New York newspaper.

Shen's fate—the effort to erase his memory from the Chinese mind, his anonymous life under the People's Republic and his death unmourned in China, my encounter with him—is in many ways what this book is about. It is not about Shen himself, of course. Rather, it is about a China where Shen's fate was not only possible, but inevitable. It is a book that describes a changing China and an immutable China, a China not exhilarated by change but instead wracked by the uncertainties and conflicts provoked by the erosion of political and economic verities.

Throughout the 1980s, America's popular imagination was fired by a China that seemed to be becoming just like us. Enthusiastic accounts in newspapers and magazines, as well as the innumerable volumes trumpeting China's transition from socialist darkness to capitalist light—after all, the opening of a three-story Kentucky Fried Chicken outlet on the corner of Tiananmen Square could imply no less, could it?—reassured readers that all was right in China.

But what happened to Shen Congwen, his honorable intellectual self-exile, his refusal even in the eighties to return to a compromised writing, suggests deeply troubling currents coursing through the China that captivated even casual observers for ten years. The wondrous demonstrations for democracy and economic change that swept China in the spring of 1989, ending in the butchery on Beijing's streets on June 4, were but the most visible and tragic manifestations of China's intellectual, social, and political inner turmoil.

China's immense size, its linguistic complexities, its regional fragmentation all combine to daunt genuine understanding. China's equally immense and mostly obdurate bureaucracy, with which the foreign journalist is constantly fencing, conspires to restrict access, to limit knowledge, to pervert comprehension. Yet beacons of clarity and truth exist: men like Shen Congwen.

WHEN MAO ZEDONG DIED in Beijing on the warm late-summer day of September 9, 1976, there was little of which he should genuinely have been proud. Three decades earlier, he had climbed to the top of the Gate of Heavenly Peace, where tourists now pay eight dollars each to visit, and talked about China's rising up on the stage of world history, and of his intention to turn the country into a land of socialist equality. There had been other socialist thinkers in China, others who had worked with China's vast peasantry to improve their condition, but Mao alone displayed both the skill to mold them into a rural revolution and the discipline to endure the years of hardship needed to win.

There was, to be sure, genuine grief in China when news of the Chairman's death filtered down to the streets of Beijing, and into other cities and then into the impoverished countryside. But today, a decade and a half later, many people say that the tears they shed were tears of relief. That may well be true, but there remains a lingering, and now a romanticized, affection for the man who created the People's Republic of China. Occasionally, one can see a copy of Mao's little red book, a compendium of the great man's aphorisms and trinket-wisdom, on an office windowsill or in the corner of a small bookcase in someone's home, a visible remnant of the decade of rage and destruction that ended with his death.

Looking at their lives on the day of Mao's death, the Chinese people could see little improvement in their standard of living from prerevolutionary days. In the countryside, peasants still lived in mud-walled houses, large families were packed into small huts with thatched roofs. They ate rice, a few vegetables, meat rarely. Like their parents and grandparents before them, they possessed one set of clothes, perhaps two, if they were fortunate. Their children went to school sporadically, if at all. They tilled collective fields with tools and, in wealthier areas, with water buffaloes owned by the commune on which they lived, a social order deemed by Mao and the most radical of his colleagues to be the genuine expression of socialism.

In the cities, life was not much better. Rudimentary industries chugged along irregularly, producing trucks or plastic buckets, blue padded Mao jackets or electric motors. State shops, food markets, and department stores had little on their shelves. Cities like Beijing had become a mix of rapidly deteriorating prerevolutionary neighborhoods and deplorably constructed gray cement slab apartment blocks. City dwellers were lucky to have a radio, let alone a television. Schooling was somewhat more regular than in the countryside, although the universities were still struggling to recover from Mao's policy of shipping professors to distant rural villages to "learn from the peasants."

Politically, China was in total disarray. Fealty to celluloid notions of revolution—to the worship of Mao himself—displaced a national commitment to grow enough food for the country to eat, to manufacture basic consumer goods, to improve the miserable conditions of people's lives. There was no law, no restraints on the police, no courts, no appeal procedures, no justice in any Western sense of the word. Indeed, since the inception of the People's Republic, people had been arrested, executed, banished to labor camps at the mere word of a Communist Party official. People who wrapped garbage in newspaper sheets printed with Mao's picture were arrested. A politically incorrect utterance led to public criticism at the least, and more often to the loss of one's job, or arrest. Reading anything that did not praise the great man, even one of China's classical novels, much less a work of foreign origin, courted imprisonment. Libraries across China were looted, books burned, the tangible historical record of a once-great civilization amputated in chunks. Willful ignorance became a badge of political honor.

China's social structure, the sinews that hold any society together, was disintegrating steadily. Familiar handholds—tradition, religion, the family, work, play—were all under assault, both for their resonances with pre-1949 society and for their purported corruption since. Children were asked to spy on and denounce their parents for supposed political transgressions. Couples were sundered, as husbands and wives were scattered to villages or towns thousands of kilometers apart. Children were stripped of their parents' names. An illiterate duck farmer who earned money raising his own flock was denounced as a capitalist while an opera singer was forced to shovel manure. Local party tyrants tortured and murdered with impunity.

This was the China Mao left his successors. Although Mao had designated Hua Guofeng, a dull-witted Hunanese who had thrived in the political hysteria of the Cultural Revolution, to assume the chairmanship of the Chinese Communist Party, the turmoil within the party was so intense that there was no certainty as to who would genuinely lead the nation. At the time of Mao's death, there were thousands of party members, including former senior leaders who had participated in the revolutionary wars against the Japanese and Chiang Kai-shek, who were toiling on farms or in factories, men who had been purged from power during the Cultural Revolution of 1966 to 1976. During the last decade of his life, Mao had seized upon the virulent conviction that the party itself had petrified, that it had become mired in a sludge of bureaucratic, self-serving patronage and interests inimical to revolutionary purity. In response, he did the simplest thing he could: he destroyed the party.

The president of Beijing University was made to parade

through his campus with a paper dunce's cap on his head. Peng Zhen, the mayor of Beijing who had obediently murdered tens of thousands of his city's citizens for counterrevolutionary activities in the 1950s, was denounced in the nation's newspapers. The president of China, Liu Shaoqi, was dragged from his home inside the leadership's guarded compound of Zhongnanhai and thrown into prison, where he died writhing on the floor in his own excrement. Another member of the leadership, Deng Xiaoping, was also shipped to the countryside to labor.

The party organizations that ran cities, factories, neighborhoods, hospitals, schools were abolished, replaced by "revolutionary committees" manned by people who had demonstrated their revolutionary commitment and enthusiasm, character traits which largely consisted in exhibiting a fevered and vociferous devotion to Mao. Governance at the national level, to the extent that it existed at all, was overseen by Zhou Enlai, the country's prime minister and the man who remained Mao's closest associate following his ascension to power. Zhou, who has often been characterized as China's gray eminence and its most impressive statesman, did keep particular elements of the government running. China's nuclear engineers and physicists continued to churn out atomic weapons in an atmosphere undisturbed by political turbulence; the Forbidden City, home for centuries to Chinese emperors and one of humanity's great architectural and artistic treasures, was preserved; visiting foreign dignitaries were entertained in lavish style at the Great Hall of the People. Zhou, it is generally argued, kept a few thin strands of the government intact, protected many purged party leaders from more savage treatment, and managed to present at least a facade of Chinese dignity and reasonableness, despite what was transpiring around him—achievements many Chinese came to see as implicitly anti-Maoist, and which became the source of their virtual veneration of Zhou.

Indeed, in many Chinese homes today, particularly in the cities, hangs a framed picture of Zhou, austere in a gray Mao suit, his right arm bent at the elbow. To be sure, such a picture is a token of affection for the man, but it is also a symbol of muted opposition to the destruction of the country wrought by Mao. In reality, however, many of the people displaying such pictures of Zhou often participated in at least some of the political upheaval of the time. There was often simply no alternative to waving the little red book, or attending public criticisms of rightists, bourgeois revisionists, enemies of the people. It is only with embarrassment and great reluctance that most Chinese today will admit their role, however small, in the political hysteria of the Cultural Revolution. The professor of philosophy who now favors tweed jackets and knit ties may very well have been a propagandist for Mao's wife, Jiang Qing, who was the ideological and cultural czar of China. The librarian who now quietly sorts books may have led her fellow Red Guards in raiding the homes of writers and burning "bourgeois" literature.

A month after Mao died, a small coterie of purged army and party leaders led a lightning coup d'état, arresting Jiang Qing and her associates, who were quickly dubbed "the Gang of Four." As unofficial accounts of her arrest have it, Jiang, the woman who had tyrannized the minds of her countrymen, who had her enemies murdered and had destroyed the lives of imagined rivals from decades past, urinated on herself when green uniformed soldiers placed handcuffs on her wrists. At her trial four years later, she displayed her disdain for her accusers, denouncing them for their betrayal of Mao and the revolution.

Elsewhere in the country, in the days and weeks following the arrest of the Gang of Four, the new leadership moved rapidly to quell unrest over Jiang's arrest. The leaders in Shanghai, which had been a hotbed of Cultural Revolution radicalism, heatedly debated whether to capitulate to the new order or to fight for the principles, such as they were, of the revolution. Bullied by Beijing and, finally, resigned to the defeat of the Cultural Revolution, they abdicated their positions and accepted the emergence of the new leadership in Beijing, nominally headed by Hua Guofeng. Behind the scenes, still not visible, was Deng Xiaoping, a man Mao had regarded at times with admiration but always with suspicion.

Deng, a tough, chain-smoking bridge player, was born in Sichuan Province in 1904, seven years before the collapse of the Qing dynasty. In the early 1920s, when Chinese students were first being sent abroad to learn from the West, he studied in Lyons, where he organized Chinese students and joined the infant Chinese Communist Party in 1924. Upon his return to China, he served in a series of increasingly important military posts during the guerrilla wars against Chiang Kai-shek, most frequently as the political commissar of military units. It was Deng who led the final mopping up of Chiang's forces in 1949 and 1950 before returning to Beijing, where he was appointed vice-premier, a post he held until the Cultural Revolution. When that cataclysm engulfed the country, Deng was stripped of all his posts, denounced as China's "number two capitalist roader" ("number one" being the soon-to-be murdered president of the country, Liu Shaoqi), and banished to the countryside. In 1973, he resurfaced as vice-premier, a post he managed to retain until April 1976, when he was again purged from his positions following the violent suppression of a memorial protest honoring the recently deceased prime minister, Zhou Enlai.

Establishing control over the military and civilian organizations that ostensibly administered the country was the first priority for the coup leaders. Reasserting the primacy of the Communist Party was the second. Party authority, largely obliterated by the violent forces of the Cultural Revolution of 1966 to 1976 on the one hand and discredited in the eyes of many Chinese, on the other, was, in the eyes of the new leadership, the key to righting the ship of state. Without the party, it would not be possible to salvage the country from the mayhem into which it had sunk. The party was therefore rebuilt, its authority reestablished. The revolutionary committees that ran cities and towns, factories and communes, were abolished and party committees imposed in their place. Party secretaries, the functionaries chosen to oversee party committees, became plant managers, city mayors, university administrators, bank supervisors. In short, the party became, once again, the central apparatus of administration and control, directing and shaping the course of Chinese life. But for Deng Xiaoping and the men he turned to for support, reconstituting the party was hardly enough.

DETERMINED BOTH to obliterate Mao's legacy and to create a new model for modernization, Deng and his colleagues and supporters were determined to houseclean the Communist Party itself. Methodically, Deng ousted Hua from the chairmanship of the party and awarded all the senior posts in the party and government to his own supporters. Hua's backers, for the most part, were dismissed or demoted. Deng rehabilitated hundreds of former party leaders who had once been provincial secretaries, governors, university presidents, heads of important party organs. Many of those who returned were in their seventies, men who had fought alongside Deng and Mao to defeat the Japanese and then Chiang Kai-shek's Kuomintang army. Deng also turned to others who were a bit younger, men who had demonstrated skills in rejuvenating provincial economies or in rebuilding the party. Two of these men, Zhao Ziyang and Hu Yaobang, were at the core of Deng's plans for remaking China, not as Mao had anticipated, but as a nation at ease with the West, a nation strong economically and militarily, a nation no longer mired in Third World poverty.

Eschewing the grandiose title of party chairman as well as the formal stewardship of the party as its general secretary, Deng nonetheless established himself as the central repository of power—power enhanced by the allegiance of the army, by the loyalty of rehabilitated party officials, and, perhaps most important, by a vision of a sweeping new economic order for his country. Deng argued forcefully and persuasively within the party's leadership that the old approaches to economic development had failed. The Soviet-style planning of the 1950s had rescued China from the chaos of war and revolution, but little more. Maoist notions of accelerated economic growth based on fantastic conceptions of utopian egalitarianism and continuous revolution had set China back, not forward. Deng sought as well a definitive end to the political anarchy of the Cultural Revolution, a stability eagerly embraced by his fellow victims of that period and ensured by a vigorous assertion of the party's preeminence in Chinese life.

Deng's proposals, initially set forth and approved by his colleagues in 1979, called for a fundamental restructuring of China's economy. At the top of Deng's list of economic changes were his ideas on agriculture: the country's farmers, the vast population of China's heartland, were to be given back their land. Each family would be given fields to till as it saw fit, to survive or fail on the basis of its own efforts, not those of a larger collective or commune. At the same time, farmers would be paid a free market price for the portion of their grain that they sold to the state. The free market price, in turn, would be largely determined by permitting the proliferation of free markets, not only for grain, but for vegetables, fruits, meats, poultry, eggs; indeed, anything grown or raised on the farm, at prices determined by the push and pull of supply and demand.

To many of Deng's colleagues, this not merely smacked of capitalism, it *was* capitalism. Deng replied brusquely that what would matter in the future was the effectiveness of a policy, not its ideological coloration. His oft-cited precept that the mouse-catching abilities of a cat were always more important than the tint of its fur became the convenient riposte to orthodox nay-sayers. In time, the extraordinary success of his policy, the dramatic leap in agricultural production and productivity, spoke for itself. This single step marked a decisive rupture with the past, at once underscoring the failures of Maoism and setting China on an apparently irreversible new course.

Deng and the two men he chose to implement and develop his broad policies, Hu and Zhao, also laid the groundwork for reviving other facets of the moribund economy, from large industry to the manufacture of consumer goods. They urged that private enterprise be permitted once again; that individuals be given the opportunity to strike out on their own, to set up workshops, factories, or stores, and become rich in the process. The state's industries, horrendously inefficient, bureaucratic behemoths, were told to reform themselves, to adopt new management styles, to pay attention to profits and losses. More radically, Hu and Zhao suggested that the country's work force be stimulated, not by the slogan-mongering of the past, but by financial and material incentives. Again, some of Deng's colleagues bridled. Introducing bonuses in the factories, they insisted, would create schisms in the work force that would undermine class solidarity. Deng again rebuffed them.

For urbanites, most of whom worked in factories or in state-run organizations, ministries, or institutions, Deng and his allies saw the need for a rapid increase in the standard of living. Market forces soon brought an ever-expanding cornucopia of foodstuffs; what lagged behind were consumer goods, household appliances, modern clothing. Deng encouraged the rapid growth of consumer-goods manufacturing, both by the state and by the private sector, the latter responding to demand, the former to the orders of central planners. Over the course of the decade, automatic clothes-washing machines rapidly replaced washboards, televisions augmented radios. Refrigerators and pocket cameras and portable electric pianos, mini-skirts and blue jeans—a plethora of products—poured into urban department stores and shops. Private restaurants and bars took root, offering better food, drink, and service than their slovenly state-owned counterparts.

Finally, Deng ordered a major reversal of China's approach to the world. Shedding the armor of xenophobia, Deng declared that foreigners would be welcome in China, as tourists, investors, traders, teachers. China, he lectured his colleagues in the Politburo, had much to learn from the rest of the world, particularly the West and Japan. China's obsessive concern for secrecy was to be slowly relaxed; the country had much to gain by becoming more open. Foreign investors stormed the gates of Beijing, offering deals on everything from hamburgers to airplanes, shampoo to automobiles. Tourists arrived by jumbo jet and luxury cruise ship, more every year, until by the end of the decade China was earning $2.2 billion a year from tourism.

Even more, Deng insisted that China's best and brightest study abroad, go out into the world to learn and absorb the science and technology, arts and letters of the West. Only in this way, Deng counseled, did China stand a chance of recovering the decades lost to Maoism. And they went, by the thousands at first, by the tens of thousands later. The children of China's leadership went, led by Deng Zhifang, the son of the supreme leader. The children of China's farmers and factory workers went too. By the end of the decade, more than forty thousand Chinese were enrolled in American universities alone. Those who returned brought back new attitudes about the world, about life, about what Chinese society could be. And as the decade wore on, these new ideas flooded into the country in the shape of books, movies, and magazines. Eyes long closed were opened as the Chinese learned that the world is not a malevolent, decaying place intent on crushing China. Rather, it was a vibrant, complex, tremendously different universe, where some people lived lives of unimaginable luxury and opportunity, especially in the West and Japan. As one Chinese friend told me, half in jest but revealingly, nonetheless, "We won World War II, right? Japan lost. Look at us now."

These images of the outside world, clichéd and idealized

though they were, helped remold the worldview of many Chinese, both urban and rural. Moreover, as relatives from Hong Kong, the United States, Europe, and, toward the end of the decade, Taiwan, brought new values and ideas along with their Rolex watches and Gucci pumps, the message of this world became patently clear to most Chinese—communism has failed me, communism has failed China. Deng's more conservative colleagues did not fail to bring such developments to his attention, developments Deng did not dismiss, for he was deeply and thoroughly committed to the Chinese Communist ideology of authoritarian rule. But he chose, for the most part, to rely on his subordinates—men like Hu, Zhao, and the men they gathered around them—to preserve the ideological spirit of communism, only sporadically leaning on his increasingly elderly, and more ideologically hard-line, contemporaries.

Like Mao, Hu Yaobang, born in 1915, was a native of Hunan Province, a heritage many Chinese believed responsible for his pungent wit and evident unconcern in later life for formality in party affairs. Hu had earned his revolutionary stripes in the hills of China with Mao's armies, and he went on to head the party's youth wing and, in 1956, to become the youngest, and at four feet nine, the shortest member of the Central Committee. It was in the party's Youth League that Hu built a large following among the post-1949 generation of party members. Like most senior party officials, Hu was felled by the Cultural Revolution, reappearing only in 1972 in an obscure post. Hu's colleague in the 1980s, Zhao Ziyang, was born to landlord parents in Henan Province in 1919. He attended high school in Kaifeng and Wuhan before joining the party in 1938. Unlike Deng or Hu, Zhao concerned himself mostly with rural reform activities in areas occupied by Mao's armies. After 1949, he worked primarily in the southern province of Guangdong. He too was victimized by the Cultural Revolution, but reappeared in 1971 as party secretary of Inner Mongolia. He returned to Guangdong the following year, and remained there until 1976, when he was sent to Sichuan to rebuild the province's agriculture.

Throughout the 1980s, rumbles among China's intelligentsia, vocal unhappiness over party-imposed strictures on intellectual, artistic, and political expression, were heard periodically. At times, these rumblings built into extraordinary displays of discontent, public demonstrations of displeasure over unyielding party control over important facets of life and the slowness of change. Each time, the party responded aggressively. Visible dissidents were jailed, louder voices silenced, liberal ideas labeled heretical. Deng and, more frequently, his aging colleagues periodically warned of the public's (and in particular, the intelligentsia's) crumbling faith in the ideological tenets of communism. Free markets did not mean capitalism, and did not imply a need for Westernized notions of democratic government, Deng decreed. Individual ownership of land, private enterprise, and stock markets did not erode, but enhanced, the march toward socialism. The dominance of the Communist Party was, he maintained, unassailable.

Pushed by his protégés, particularly Zhao and Hu, Deng agreed to some limited steps toward political and governmental reform: the creation of a rudimentary legal system, and permission of modest expressions of criticism. The National People's Congress, a body of appointed delegates who robotically confirm party policy as government program, was given a tentative shove toward independence; some members were even allowed to cast negative votes from time to time. Great fanfare was accorded a decision to introduce a civil service system for government employees designed so that competence, rather than nomination by the party, was the central criterion for employment.

China was changing. Indeed, by May 1989, there had been extraordinary transformations in the country's economy and society, most of which would have been unthinkable only a decade earlier. Prostitutes brazenly cruised hotels in Guangzhou and Shanghai. Private banks, patently illegal, flourished. Superstitious beliefs—homage to earth gods, faith in fortune-tellers, and reverence for geomancy—resurfaced in an atmosphere of declining Communist Party influence. Crime, from theft to murder, bribery to kidnapping, increased. Shackled by bureaucratic, jealous party officials, the private sector, which was the fastest growing segment of the economy, responded with the grease of bribery. Corruption spread like unchecked cancer, to the point that nothing could be done without passing money from hand to hand.

Throughout the decade, the grumbling of hard-line opponents about the pace and direction of change was audible. Periodic clampdowns on writers and artists, on newspapers and hemlines, were visible signs of growing dissension within the inner sanctums of the Communist Party. These spasms of repression were largely ignored in the West, which tended to see them as aberrations rather than symptoms of mounting political and social crisis. Even though these tensions were apparent in society, and we reporters simply had to travel the country, to talk to the people, to see the evidence of it, the tensions within the leadership were only dimly visible. Inner party documents hinting at the depth of unhappiness among hard-liners occasionally surfaced; party officials and some higher-level Chinese journalists from time to time described the simmering discontent.

Finally, in January 1987, after more than a month of student protests in cities across the country, the hard-liners struck what they hoped was a knockout blow to the apparently relentless transformation of Chinese society and economy: they forced Deng Xiaoping's handpicked party leader, Hu Yaobang, to resign. Hu's departure did not, however, prove to be enough. Six months of intellectual repression were followed, inevitably it seemed, by a renewal of debate about where China was headed, by a reinvigorated devotion among the country's entrepreneurs to the expansion of the private economy and to the continuing deterioration of the party's claim on universal truth. The culmination of these conflicting forces, led, inexorably, toward Tiananmen Square on June 4, 1989.

IN JULY 1986, I was driving into Uganda's Lowero Triangle, where Milton Obote had slaughtered three hundred thousand people before being driven from the country six months earlier. I drove past pyramids assembled from skulls and leg bones, past gutted tanks and burned villages. It was a chilling experience. The car radio was tuned to the local Kampala station. After a while, the news came on and only half-distractedly did I hear the news reader announce "*The New York Times* correspondent in Peking, China, has been arrested for espionage . . ." I found it amusing that the travails of one of my colleagues, in this case John Burns, should be of any concern to Ugandan radio. I didn't give the report another thought.

Some weeks later (by this time, John had served six days in a

State Security Bureau jail, after which he was expelled from the country), the foreign editor of *The Times* called me in Nairobi and told me that I had been chosen as the paper's next Beijing correspondent. The announcement was not a complete surprise, for at some point, I knew, I would be posted to China. Before joining *The Times*, I had studied modern Chinese history at the University of Wisconsin, where I received a master's degree. I left Madison to pursue doctoral work in medieval Chinese history at the University of California at Berkeley, where I spent four years plumbing sixth-century ghost stories, Tang poetry, neo-Confucian philosophy, Song urban history—the *appareil* of scholarship. Because I either lacked the talent or was simply lured by the less cloistered ambience of journalism, I left Berkeley in 1979 to take a job fetching coffee for editors at *The Times*. In this humble role, I was to learn the ropes of big-time journalism while somehow dazzling the editors with the writing I did between coffee runs. In time, perhaps because I never learned that a "regular" coffee in New York City means "with milk," I was made a reporter on the paper's metropolitan staff. There, I was expected to continue dazzling editors so that someday I would earn a place on the foreign staff of *The Times*, which generally is thought of as a pinnacle of American journalism. In 1985, I was dispatched to Africa, a continent I came to love.

When the call came to go to China, I was delighted. If only because I had spent so many years studying the country's history, I felt I should at some point in my journalistic career attempt to grapple with its contemporary manifestation. Barely had John Burns been deported before I found myself touring the streets of Beijing, my head full of classical history, my eyes absorbing its modern expression. Within a few days of wandering the city, I realized that the culture I had studied was fast slipping away. As I scanned shop signs, neighborhood blackboards, even the city-minted street signs, I realized that China could not even write its own language: many, many of the signs were filled with wrongly written ideograms. China was being decisively reshaped; I set out to find out how.

SO WHY BEGIN this book with Shen Congwen? Because Shen's failure to flourish in the 1980s runs like a stubborn weed through the plastic garden watered by the Communist Party.

Here and there, flowers bloomed, but it was always the weeds, the Shen Congwens, that were whacked at, dug away at, or, worse, ignored. Shen is important to me because I cannot think of China, of how it has changed—and more important, how it has not—without reflecting upon his fate. I will permit Shen to speak the words that inform the rest of this book.

"I worship vitality and love freedom. I extol the plucky and the strong of heart. Any person who is vigorous in his actions or spirit—who doesn't jockey for petty advantage or care about material gain and public prestige—if he can stiffen his backbone and go his own way, straight as a ramrod, then I can accept him as a friend, as a man. No matter that what he knows is different from what I know, that his political ideology is opposite to mine, or that his religious beliefs and mine are in conflict. I love this kind of person. I respect him. He might be a little wild, or a little crude, but only people like him stand behind great accomplishments and great literary works. He'll fail sometimes, then try again. In fact he'll stumble often. But he'll get up immediately."

Part I

The Idea of China

. . . and so I ran wild all day, looking around, listening and smelling about. Though at that time unable to put into words the smell of a dead snake, of rotten grass, the butcher's body, or the kiln where bowls were burnt after rain, I could easily recognize each. The cry of bats, the sigh of an ox when a butcher cut its throat, the hiss of a big yellow-throated snake hiding in a hole in the fields, the faint plopping of fish jumping in the river at night, all sounded quite distinctive and I remembered them clearly. So when I went home at night I used to have endless extraordinary dreams. Even now, nearly twenty years later, these dreams often disturb my sleep and carry me back to the void of my "past," carry me into a world of fantasy . . .

SHEN CONGWEN, 1932

ONE

China in the Mind of America

IN THE DAYS after tanks and armored personnel carriers thundered into Beijing, slaughtering the city's residents and its students, I spent some time helping the Irish embassy round up wayward citizens so they could be evacuated from China. One afternoon, I guided Brendan Ward, a third secretary at the embassy, through the rubble of the capital toward the train station. Irish flags were plastered on the rear windows of our white Toyota, although we did not delude ourselves that the illiterate troops from Manchuria casually waving AK-47s at our car knew or cared what the Irish tricolor was. Nor was I terribly reassured by the Irish passport in my hip pocket (although I was raised in America, I am a citizen of both Ireland and the United States), a document that provided security more psychological than real.

After maneuvering into the parking lot of the train station, mostly empty save for a few hardy bicycle rickshaw drivers, we charged into the throng inside looking for a red-haired Irish girl who had telephoned an SOS and her description to the embassy the day before. The station, a grotesque edifice identified by an

3

illuminated red sign in Mao Zedong's calligraphy, was sardined with travelers, more than the usual complement that engenders its normal pandemonium. Fearful out-of-town students, hoping to slip home inconspicuously, huddled in corners on their bedrolls, assiduously ignoring the world around them. Rustic farmers from the boondocks who had been caught in the mayhem of May and June drifted, dazed, through the hall. Uniformed and plainclothes police wove through the hall, checking documents, scrutinizing everyone who passed.

I made for the first-class waiting room, where foreigners usually waited for trains, a cavernous chamber only slightly less chaotic and claustrophobic than the plebeian waiting rooms outside. This hall too was jammed, with foreigners and Chinese alike. The benches and chairs were crammed, the terra-cotta floor virtually impassable, with backpacks and suitcases piled waist-high everywhere. Chinese officials were stuffed next to world-wandering hippies, recumbent on bedrolls tucked against well-worn knapsacks. Clumps of middle-aged tourists looked worried—some, even frightened. After burrowing through the mass of international humanity, I located the Irish girl and her traveling companion, and Brendan and I prepared to hustle them to the car and the relative safety of the embassy.

Around us, there was a din of conversation in English. "What should we do?" "Where should we go?" "Is the Trans-Siberian running?" "When is the next train to Canton?" "Should we call our embassy?" The questions spilled from a clot of older American tourists, mostly women in their late fifties or early sixties.

"What are you doing here?" I asked one of them, my voice betraying some astonishment at their evident nonchalance toward the swirl around them.

"Well, we're trying to get to Xian," one replied. "We haven't seen the terra-cotta army."

"Don't you know what has happened here?" I asked, somewhat incredulously. "Don't you know what's going on in Xian?"

"A little," she answered. "Anyway, we've decided we should see the terra-cotta soldiers. We'll be safe in Xian. Everything will be all right."

After we had shepherded our charges to the embassy, I reflected on this woman's comments and found that there was far more to her words than the banalities of ignorance and willfulness. She brought to her conviction the simple certainties with which Americans for nearly two decades have lacquered their views of China and of things Chinese.

China, in the American mind, is a land steeped in three or four millennia of culture, culture which in some obscure way has shadowed and molded the reality of China under communism. The Chinese are polite. They revere their elders and children. They have always been a hierarchical, ordered society. They are natural acrobats. They are concerned about saving face. They are natural capitalists. China is mysterious, a vast land filled with archaeological treasures, ancient culture, and exotic cuisine.

I have heard each of these characterizations from the mouths of Americans, some of whom are highly educated and reasonably worldly. These perceptions proliferated and reinforced each other, particularly over the course of the 1980s, a decade that saw Americans troop through China by the hundreds of thousands, swept in polished buses from glass-sheathed hotels to archaeological sites, from acrobatic circuses to the Great Wall. Polite, deferential tour guides with glib, and often inaccurate, historical anecdotes smiled inscrutably at bizarre questions, nodding assent to middle-American convictions about the way the Chinese really are. And so the Americans returned home, even more sure of themselves about China; after all, they had been there. Real Chinese people had talked to them.

THIS WARM GLOW that visitors brought back from China was an emotion that was fueled by American policy toward China, and in turn generated substantial support for that policy, which was fixed almost immutably during the Nixon administration. Henry A. Kissinger, the President's national security adviser, crafted the opening to Beijing like a city planner moving neighborhoods around according to lofty notions of balance and proportion. Kissinger's elegant and illuminating description of the overtures to China, and the subsequent waltz of seemingly antagonistic partners is, in the final analysis, an essay on the cynicism of power.

Kissinger described the China that he visited in 1971 (bringing Richard Nixon in tow the following year) as a "beautiful, and to us, mysterious land." It was not, however, as elusive as Kissinger has made out. China in 1971 was a land of torment and ideological hysteria, of persecution, imprisonment, exile and death. In his memoirs, Kissinger contends that little of China's internal situation was clear to policy planners at the White House. To be sure, American television cameras may not have been there to record China's nightmare, but the tide of refugees who flooded into Hong Kong were recounting tales of the unending horror; of families wrenched apart, of starvation, of executions, of relentless indoctrination campaigns. Were those eyewitnesses inadequate, perhaps the mutilated bodies of Chinese floating onto Hong Kong's beaches, washed from the Pearl River and Guangdong Province, might have suggested something about the country. China in 1971 was a land neither beautiful nor mysterious.

I have no way of knowing whether Kissinger's professions of ignorance about China in the throes of the Cultural Revolution were genuine, or born of a disingenuousness beholden to his larger purposes. Neither matters much, because, as he himself made clear, geopolitical archetectonics relies on building blocks of many shapes and sizes. China's abhorrent domestic policies were irrelevant in a world where China's international positioning was everything. Zhou Enlai's masterful handling of Kissinger, and Zhou's agile and enduring intellect, persuaded Kissinger, not that China was a nice place, but that he was dealing with a hard-nosed government whose antagonism to the Soviet Union was compatible with American policy and that, inescapably, there were grounds for nurturing a relationship between the two nations. More, Kissinger's propensity to indulge public fantasies about China were used deftly to fuel the American people's curiosity for the unknown, ensuring domestic support and even enthusiasm for his China initiative.

What was critical to Henry Kissinger, and to Richard Nixon, was global strategy, and China was part of that strategy. Cordial relations with China edged Moscow off-balance; friendly relations with China exerted even stronger pressure. The relationship between Beijing and Washington blossomed on this foundation, based increasingly on areas of agreement on world affairs, a consensus reached for different reasons, but a consensus nonetheless. As Kissinger observed, China was well served by a strong and united NATO faced off against Eastern Europe and the Soviet Union, a position no different from Washington's. In the wake of the Vietnam War, China's incipient antagonism toward Hanoi flowered as the Vietnamese progressively strengthened their ties to Moscow, an antagonism viewed with pleasure in Washington. And the lurking threat to China of a rearmed Japan dissipated somewhat in the folds of a security treaty with the United States, and with Japan's obsession with becoming an economic, not a military, superpower.

Only after the Cultural Revolution was ended and Deng Xiaoping had reappeared as the strongman within the leadership, however, did the relationship between Beijing and Washington really prosper. Formal diplomatic relations were established, displacing an arrangement of liaison offices. In the wake of formal recognition, the network of interests and opportunities proliferated like wild poppies. The American intelligence community hurried to take advantage of the closer ties that brought a new proximity to the Soviet Union, and won Chinese concurrence to establish secret electronic listening posts directed at the Russian heartland. American news correspondents, for the first time since the establishment of the People's Republic, were permitted to set up bureaus in Beijing. And American business, salivating at the prospect of one billion customers, stormed into Beijing offering deals on everything from banks to boilers, Coca-Cola to computers, Colonel Sanders to Mickey Mouse. Never was there a market like this, or so American executives thought.

The prevailing sentiment, from corporate board rooms to the State Department, was that the United States needed China. American business needed new markets, and American policymakers needed geopolitical levers to pull. Contacts between the United States and China expanded rapidly. Tens of thousands of Chinese students poured into American universities, sometimes to read poetry, but more often to study engineering or physics, to "drink foreign ink," as they put it. Cultural exchanges blossomed. The United States got Ming and Qing dynasty paintings from the Forbidden City, panda bears and energetic acrobats; China got *Little House on the Prairie,* the Juilliard School Orchestra and Rambo. Bloomingdale's in New York City held unabashed promotions of Chinese products and themes. Qingdao, home port of China's North Sea Fleet, welcomed a task force of American naval ships, the first since 1949. China was the "in" spot for tourists. As the decade wore on, the river of American visitors to China became a tidal wave, and, while tourists made up the bulk of the wave, phalanxes of American executives, from bankers to car makers, lawyers to coal miners, lined up outside the doors of Chinese ministries and government offices like latter-day Henry Hills.

Many American businessmen, and they were men almost exclusively, were driven to clinch "a China deal" for their company, an accomplishment that assumed obsessive dimensions in corporate boardrooms. A China deal had something no hard-nosed venture in South Korea or Brazil could ever have; it had allure. China was, in the minds of these executives, a bottomless reservoir of cheap labor, a country starved for modern technologies, a market so vast that it was difficult to contemplate. But it was not enough to sell to the Chinese; anyone could do that. What was important was to set up business in China. Some were successful; many more floundered. One of those who came was Babcock and Wilcox, a company that makes everything from steam-driven generators to nuclear power plants. Babcock signed a deal to manufacture boilers. Under its agreement with the Chinese, Babcock agreed to assume complete control of Beijing Boiler Works, a concern that had not made money since the day it opened twenty years earlier, and to reengineer the plant so that it could begin producing 250-megawatt boilers, the sort used in municipal power plants. In the long run, the hope was that the factory would export its products and begin earning some foreign exchange, the only financial inducement for Babcock's investment. The firm sent a man named Irl R. Hicks to make it work.

FOND OF BOTH baseball hats and the flat-voweled frank talking of his native South Dakota, Irl Hicks is a gruff, thickset man who knows his business. He knows boilers; how to make them, how to sell them. He assumed that when Babcock and Wilcox entered into a joint venture agreement with a Chinese boiler maker he would be sent to do what he does best. It was a rougher road than he first thought. "China was somewhere on the other side of the map," Hicks told me as we walked through the plant on the west side of Beijing one fall day in 1987. "Nixon had come here in 1970 or something. That's all I knew. Basically, all they said was, 'Go to China. Good luck.' "

I spent time with Hicks, touring his plant, listening to his good-natured grumbles. The catalogue of his problems was thick and dense: there weren't any technical drawings when he arrived the first day—the Chinese considered them "extra"; the factory floor was crammed with six hundred beds, which he promptly had dumped in the scrap yard; the workers staged a wildcat strike, heaving bricks through the factory's windows, when he introduced a wage system that accounted for skill and seniority and included steep performance bonuses; the city held up the connecting of electricity and water lines to the factory; and, Hicks said with characteristic bluntness, the factory was "a dump." In the end, though, Hicks said, he'd managed to get the plant running more like an American factory, including turning it into a profit-making venture. Of course, the profits were in *renminbi,* the unconvertible domestic Chinese currency and therefore essentially useless. Still, Hicks thought the Babcock venture was as successful as possible; at least he was making money on paper.

Hicks's and Babcock's experience in China, one that only marginally approached the heady expectations of American investors, is indeed considered a success. More often, American investors, as well as their European counterparts, have taken a drubbing at the hands of the Chinese. Typical, perhaps, were the exertions of a fellow I met from Ohio, who suggested that his name not be used in the hopes that he might someday actually make some money. He was involved in a joint venture with a Beijing company to manufacture files, the sort used to hone wood planks and the rough edges of steel pipes. "I've been here five years and I'm yet to make a penny," he said. When I asked him why, he laughed. "Seventy percent of our files don't meet quality standards and are returned to us," he said. "Seventy percent." Why not just give up and leave? "I've set up plants all over the world," he answered. "I've made money for my company everywhere. I'm damn well not leaving here until we do this right. I mean, this isn't a high-technology product we're talking here."

Even those that turn profits often do so only in renminbi, which does nothing to bolster the corporate balance sheets in the United States. Indeed, most American companies refuse to discuss the profitability of their China operations, primarily because the visions of gold proved to be little more than a vaporous mirage. Still, the companies would show up in Beijing, sign a deal, and hold a press conference celebrating things such as "the first joint venture to manufacture kryptonite tennis rackets."

Once, amid this procession of American executives, a gaggle of movie studio executives from Gulf + Western arrived and sold the Chinese the distribution rights for some movies, including the classic tear-jerker *Love Story.* At the press conference, the studio executives gushed self-congratulatory verbiage about being the first American movie company to strike a deal with the Chinese; "historic" was the favored adjective of the day. Of course, it turned out they weren't the first Hollywood types to do business in Beijing, but their Chinese partners made no effort to disabuse them of these illusions in their moment of international glory. Then I asked the Americans whether they would actually be making any money from the deal. At first they refused to answer the question, citing the confidentiality of contracts. Finally, when the skepticism of the assembled journalists seemed likely to dampen the self-induced glow in which they were basking, one of the executives said that yes, they would be making money. After the press conference, I called around town to check with some people and, of course, it turned out that all the money they would make was to be in renminbi. After all, Chinese moviegoers don't pay for theater tickets in U.S. dollars.

American business horror stories began circulating like plot summaries of morbid television soap operas. Mats Engstrom, the chairman of (the decidedly non-Sinitic) Tsar Nicoulai, a gourmet food company in San Francisco, bemoaned his fate over drinks with me one evening in a Beijing hotel in 1988. Engstrom had signed an agreement with the Chinese to harvest and pack caviar along the Manchurian-Soviet border, a region normally off-limits to foreigners. His business, he explained, was severely circumscribed by the seasonality of sturgeon egg-laying. Knowing this, the Chinese regularly extorted more and more money from him to ensure a smooth-running operation. One year, Engstrom said, he bought two Jeep Cherokees from an AMC joint venture assembly plant in Beijing, and flew them up to the border to use on the project. When the cars arrived, the Chinese insisted that he give the Jeeps to them and then charged him one hundred dollars a month to rent them back. "What could I do?" Engstrom asked. "We had to move the caviar. We had to get it packed and onto the plane." He flipped through photographs of the People's Liberation Army cargo plane he chartered to fly his caviar out of the northern wilderness. "They are never satisfied, these Chinese. They want your last drop of blood."

Engstrom and hundreds of other investors have learned that they have little recourse when their Chinese partners suddenly renege on signed deals, insist on new contract provisions, impose new surcharges for various services, or fail to provide promised employees. In 1986, aware that China was rapidly earning a reputation as an undependable place to do business, the Chinese leadership enacted a series of proposals intended to smooth the way for foreign investors. It did little good. In June 1987, Jerome A. Cohen, an American lawyer with vast experience in China and a man widely known for his sympathetic attitude toward Chinese business practices, and Stuart J. Valentine wrote a devastating critique of China's treatment of foreign investors, an analysis they presented to Chinese officials and a copy of which found its way onto my desk in Beijing.

Cohen and Valentine waved a fistful of red flags at American businesses looking at China. First, they argued, China remained uncertain of its political direction in the wake of the previous year's huge student protests and the shake-up of the Communist Party's leadership. Indeed, in the two years since Cohen and Valentine made their observations, China has descended into still greater political instability and its future course is even more unsure, a prospect few people thought possible at the time. More specifically, they said, companies could expect difficulties in repatriating profits, given China's tight control over foreign exchange. They went on to tell American business that it should be prepared to pay exorbitant fees and charges as well as Tokyo-level prices for accommodation for managers based in China. And despite the Chinese government's insistence that it encouraged foreign investment, American business should be aware that contract provisions were frequently ignored, that government officials often interfered in the running of joint

11

ventures, that taxes were arbitrarily determined, and that, in the end, there was no legal recourse for the foreign investor.

"Until now," Cohen and Valentine wrote, "there has been a widespread belief in China that a foreign company is fair game for any costs and that no matter how many it is loaded down with it will nevertheless be able to earn a profit and retain its enthusiasm for China." The prevalence of hidden costs for labor, utilities, land use and raw materials, and the imposition of new rules and regulations even after the signing of a contract conspired to undermine hopes of a profit-making enterprise. And, in the end, Cohen and Valentine wrote, there is nothing the foreign investor can do: "In practice, contracts concluded with Chinese entities lack legal enforceability."

Chinese trade and investment officials have routinely insisted that China still has a long way to go in remedying such problems. "We are still learning," they say. "We are feeling our way. You cannot expect too much too fast." But in fact these blandishments are less explanations than efforts to resist the reforms necessary to make foreign investments work. Indeed, there are substantial reserves of hostility within the Communist Party bureaucracy to the foreign investors stampeding into China. Maoist notions of self-reliance still resonate among a considerable segment of the party's leadership as well as the faithful. Foreigners, as all Chinese are taught, humiliated and subjugated China in the past, something that will never be permitted again.

THAT ATTITUDE, combined with the country's essential backwardness, has undermined efforts to reintegrate Western-trained students into the work force. Physicists with degrees from major American universities return to primitive laboratories, engineers come back with training that meshes poorly with Chinese industry, and managers come home with iconoclastic ideas about how to run companies. One of the most ambitious educational programs, sponsored by the State University of New York at Buffalo, is a two-year curriculum conducted partly at a new management center in Dalian and partly in Buffalo to train Chinese MBAs. Begun with the best of intentions—to provide China with the core of a competent managerial work force—the program has foundered on the shoals of ingrained prejudices against foreign training, intransigent bureaucracies, and an underdeveloped economy.

Li Xiaoyan, a generous-sized young man with a trip-hammer laugh, personifies the conflicts created when the good intentions of foreigners collide with the limits of China's ability to change. Li graduated from the Buffalo program, as accomplished as any American MBA, but he told me one afternoon in 1987 that he was beginning to regret "drinking foreign ink."

"Everyone said we would be the central pillar of Chinese talent. We thought we had a great future. So did our American professors. It didn't work out that way." Li massaged his kneecaps as he talked, sipping occasionally from a cup of black coffee that sat on the side table next to him. He spoke with a mixture of fondness and irony of the Buffalo program, perhaps the most competitive higher educational training in China. In 1984, the Chinese government conducted a nationwide search for possible candidates for the program. Altogether, four hundred and forty students and promising young low-ranking officials sat for the entrance examination. Li was one of only forty people finally accepted, none of whom were the children of high officials, a rare occurrence in a land where official nepotism is boundless. "They couldn't have done the work," Li said, contempt scuffing his words.

Before being accepted by the Buffalo program, Li had already weathered China's political upheavals. During the Cultural Revolution, he was shipped to Inner Mongolia, retribution exacted for his parents' having fled to the decadence of Hong Kong. Although Li fell in love with the desolate reaches of Mongolia and still speaks nostalgically of his years there—"I rode horses every day, lived in a yurt. We rounded up sheep, lassoed horses. I was a cowboy"—he retained a yearning for more substantial intellectual nourishment, despite a political climate that disparaged learning. "I smuggled books to Mongolia to study English," he recounted. "I took a radio to listen to the Voice of America. Of course I had to do that in secret. I didn't waste my time. I studied every day." In 1973, as some universities were resuming classes for the first time since the onset of the Cultural Revolution in 1966, Li was admitted to the second class at Beijing University, where he specialized in applied mathematics. After he graduated, he was assigned to the

Institute of Geophysics, a discipline with which he said he was only casually familiar. When the opportunity came to leave the institute, he was elated.

The Buffalo program was unlike any university program in China. "I thought the work was very difficult," he explained. "Time was very limited. There was lots of homework. The psychological pressures were tremendous." Li finished the eighteen months in Dalian and then, along with his classmates, completed his last semester at the Buffalo campus. While in Buffalo, he participated in a local bank's management training program, where he studied the way computers were used to manage the bank's resources. In December 1986, Li and his fellow students returned to China, enthusiastic about their accomplishments, confident that they had much to offer their country. It was not to be.

Nearly all the students found that their previous employers, state companies for the most part, were uninterested in the students' new learning. Some of the students found no jobs at all. "The State Economic Commission helped set up this program," Li said. "But they said they weren't responsible for us getting jobs. In China, if the government doesn't help, you can't get a job."

I asked Li what happened to his classmates. "Nearly everybody went back to the same jobs they had before because their work units paid for their plane tickets," he replied. "Nobody could get good jobs."

And what, I asked, had become of him? A visible unhappiness descended on Li. "I wanted to get into business. I speak English and have management skills. I started looking for work. I went to many companies but they didn't know what an MBA was. They said, 'If you want to work here you can be a translator.' One day I went to the Bank of China and wanted to contact the personnel department. But the guard wouldn't let me in. He said I didn't have a letter of introduction."

Li's problems were shared by his classmates. Liu Zhongtian, nicknamed "Shotgun" by his Chinese colleagues, returned to the factory where he had worked before attending the Buffalo program. He tried to transfer to another job, but his factory refused. The factory manager lectured Liu, "Since I've provided the funds for you to study abroad, I certainly can afford to keep

14

you now that you're back. You don't believe me? Watch me keep you here for twenty years. Who says your talents aren't being used? Last time, when visitors from Mauritania came here, their translator was useless. Next time, you'll be the translator."

Another student, Yu Changbin, was assigned to a manual labor job by his factory. Rued Yu, "Traditional things are strong in China. The existing quality of our enterprises and the cultural level of our workers cannot live up to the management methods learned in an MBA program."

Word of the failings of the Buffalo program spread across China's universities like a wind-whipped brush fire and was picked up by the spunky newspaper *China Youth News*, which wrote a series of articles describing the difficulties of the Buffalo graduates. The visibility of the program and the utter contempt with which most of its graduates were treated triggered concern among some Chinese leaders, including Prime Minister Li Peng, who promised that appropriate jobs would be found for the new MBAs.

After much hunting, Li Xiaoyan finally found employment with the China Metals and Minerals Export Corporation, where he was assigned to conduct a feasibility study of whether the corporation should build a hotel in Mexico. "I guess I'm using ten percent of what I learned," Li said to me, chuckling a bit mournfully at his fate. "And because I'm new, I have no seniority. I get paid eighty-two yuan a month. Most people my age get ninety-seven yuan. I want to use my skills as much as possible, but in the Chinese system this degree means nothing."

Li's fate and that of his colleagues reflect almost pristinely the constraints on China's modernization efforts, and illuminate the unease with which much of China views the world outside. At the same time, the generosity and goodwill of the sponsors of the Buffalo program, their almost missionary zeal to impart the wisdom of the West, betray the unsullied optimism and, in some measure, the unstudied ignorance of Americans in China. China's backwardness—economic, technological, institutional, educational—is so profound that it conditions much of how the country responds to the world. The glitziness of China's big-city hotels seen by foreigners does much to disguise this backwardness, and the apparent sophistication of the Chinese who host foreign business delegations veils the chasm between China's aspirations to join the modern world and the obstacles that stand in the way.

Foreign companies have sold China hundreds of millions of dollars in sophisticated equipment such as assembly lines, computers, and research equipment, technology purchased to buttress the country's march into the twentieth century. Yet vast quantities of it are ill-used or even stand idle. An American physician I knew in Shanghai told me that the hospital where he spends most of his time has the world's most advanced equipment for testing for the presence of forty-seven drugs in a patient's blood.

"The problem," he said, his evident frustration chewing at him, "is that only two of the drugs are available in China." Similarly, the surgeons at his hospital are intent on learning advanced techniques for heart bypass surgery. "Instead of doing the routine and more needed surgery to correct congenital heart defects in children, they're doing this. Why? Because we do it in the West." In Shenyang, the capital of Liaoning Province in the northeast, the main hospital has two CAT-scan machines. The problem is that no one in the hospital knows how to operate them. Everywhere in China, imported machinery lies rusting in factory storage yards, or is misused. An Italian engineer who spent a great deal of time in China installing million-dollar plastic injection molding machines told me that many of his products were idled because they were not maintained and broke down after only a few months. "This is not sophisticated technology," he complained to me one night after spending a week trying to restart one of his machines in a factory near Nanjing. "But it's too sophisticated for China."

IN SIMILAR FASHION, the ideas and methods of people like Li Xiaoyan are ill-suited for the inflexible bureaucracies of China's industrial and commercial enterprises. None of the principles imbued in Li and his classmates—a riveting regard for efficiency, productivity, profitability, flexibility—none of these are particularly relevant to the officials, mostly Communist Party members, who run China's factories, mines, banks, and trading companies. When Liu Zhongtian's boss told him his MBA was worthless and that he could serve as translator the next time the factory was visited by a delegation of Mauritanians, it was not a reprimand to

an over-ambitious, arrogant yuppie. It was an entrenched antagonism toward new ideas, toward foreign ideas. It is an attitude
shared by much of this country's officialdom, one grounded in
the political heritage of the People's Republic. As eagerly as new
and foreign ideas are embraced by China's younger generation,
they are just as deeply distrusted by the older generation—the
generation that rules.

In the wake of the December 1986 student demonstrations, I
visited Chen Zhongjing, an influential member of the hard-line
wing of the Communist Party. I had first met Chen at a reception
at the residence of the American ambassador, Winston Lord,
and I arranged with Chen to visit him at the Institute of Contemporary International Relations, where he was the director. I
drove over to the institute, on the far western edge of Beijing,
with Jim Mann, a colleague from the *Los Angeles Times.* The importance of this institute was immediately apparent when we
were stopped by a pistol-toting member of the People's Armed
Police at the gate. We were greeted by Chen at the entrance of
the institute, a dull, vaguely modern building that seemed
strangely empty.

Chen, who had earned his revolutionary stripes as one of
Mao's most trusted spies inside the Kuomintang army, ushered
us into a reception room along with several younger men, some
of whom took notes on our conversation and none of whom said
a word during our visit. Chen forcefully steered the conversation through subjects that concerned him, especially his concern
about Japanese military policy, before reflecting on China's relationship with the outside world.

"There are unhealthy tendencies in society," he lectured us,
"especially among officials. They are all very lazy in their thinking."

What, we asked, was he getting at?

"What China needs," he responded, "what we need, is to
emphasize self-reliance. We cannot rely on foreigners. Take hotels, for example. We should not rely on joint-venture hotels
with foreigners. The Chinese can build and manage hotels. It's
not enough to say we lack experience. This is related to the
mood of the country. We should not be lazy and rely on foreigners. The open door policy does not mean that we cannot rely on
ourselves."

17

Chen's little speech echoed, not unconsciously, it seemed to me, the Maoist belief in self-reliance which for so long sustained Chinese socialism, particularly after the break with Moscow in 1959. More, Chen's prominence within the senior councils of government suggested that there was rather widespread sympathy for this point of view. Our discussion wound down with Chen assuring us that no matter what, Sino-American relations were basically sound. As he left the institute, I was amused to see this exponent of Chinese self-reliance step into a new black Mercedes.

There is, of course, no single Chinese attitude toward the outside world. What university students believe, their parents often do not. The manager of a television factory looks at the foreign presence in China differently from a foundry worker in a steel mill in Shenyang. And most important for the direction of China's approach to the world, there are radically divergent views within the Communist Party leadership itself over the shape of China's interaction with the world, particularly with the West.

One of the critical failings in American policy toward China has been a persistent inability or unwillingness to perceive these different strands of thought and ideology within the party, and to assess accurately their strengths. American policymakers have too easily believed that the benefits they perceive in Sino-American relations are viewed similarly by the entire Chinese leadership, of whatever ideological stripe. Because first and foremost Washington's maturing relationship with China is aimed at influencing the Soviet Union, ideological debates within the Chinese Communist Party are essentially of little concern. As a result, American policymakers often have tended to misread signs of impending political upheaval and to dismiss as inconsequential internal crackdowns on dissent—so much so that Washington has tacitly tolerated abhorrent behavior by the Chinese, both domestically and internationally.

A decade ago, when Deng Xiaoping promulgated the policy of *kaifang*, or openness to the world beyond China's borders, he had a very clear idea of what he expected. "No matter to what degree we open up to the outside world and admit foreign capital," Deng told the Italian journalist Oriana Fallaci in August 1980, "its relative magnitude will be small and it can't affect our

18

system of socialist public ownership of the means of production. Absorbing foreign capital and technology and even allowing foreigners to construct plants in China can only play a complementary role to our effort to develop the socialist productive forces. Of course, this will bring some decadent capitalist influences into China. We are aware of this possibility; it's nothing to be afraid of. . . . We intend to acquire advanced technology, science, and management skills to serve our socialist production."

Washington and much of the Western world understood this to mean that China was prepared to embark on the road to modernization, one that would lead toward an economic and political order that would gradually mirror that of the West. As much as Americans were dazzled by Chinese culture, or what they perceived Chinese culture to be, there was, among many Americans, including policymakers in Washington, an almost primordial urge to turn the Chinese into Americans. Chinese students were allowed to flood into the United States—forty thousand were attending American universities by the end of 1988—because they would return to their country touched by the values and ideals of Americans. Kentucky Fried Chicken opened its first outlet in China, on the edge of Tiananmen Square a nine-iron shot away from the mausoleum housing Mao's body. "Kekou-Kele," or Coca-Cola, in bright red cans and tuck-waisted bottles, became everyday sights on the streets of many cities. Boeing 747s daubed with the five-star Chinese red flag ferried tourists across the Pacific, and Cadillac Fleetwood limousines carried the well-heeled visitors around the capital in New York style. China, American officials told us all, was changing.

AMONG THE PRINCIPAL CHEERLEADERS for this remarkable apparent transformation of China was the third American ambassador to Beijing, Winston Lord, and his wife, Bette Bao Lord, a novelist who has written about Chinese family life.

One sunny June day in 1988, the Lords drove through Beijing, a crisp American flag snapping from a chrome strut on the right front fender of their black Cadillac. The car sailed through the gates of Beijing University, purred past the university library and glided to a stop near a grove of scholar trees. In their shade, a bronze statue of Cervantes gazed down on a clump of students who milled about purposefully; heated conversations could be heard here and there.

The Lords alighted from their automobile and strolled over to the spot where Beijing University students convened irregular colloquia to discuss political and social issues. The ambassador and his wife plopped onto a thin blanket of newspapers. Lord began by extolling American values, as well as that country's failings; its hopes and its dreams. His wife translated while he was cheerleading for enhancing Sino-American relations.

Abruptly, a student raised his hand and in hard-clipped Mandarin asked Lord why he thought there was a future for such a relationship given China's fundamental commitment to communism.

Lord seemed taken aback by the bluntness of the question. A country's political system, Lord retorted, is irrelevant. The only issue, he explained, "is, do they exhibit peaceful policies or aggressive policies? This is more important to us than their specific ideology. It's true we have values in our society and we are concerned about human rights. But we respect other countries and do not try to impose our values. We try to improve relations with all countries, including Communist ones. But it is easier to do that with a country like China that is not threatening anyone, than with the Soviet Union. We look at how a country performs on the world stage rather than at its ideology."

For these Beijing University students, it was a first lesson in Kissingerian geopolitics. Afterward, a student who had listened to Lord said to me, "What he's really saying is that it doesn't make a difference if our government puts us in jail here, or prevents us from saying what we want, prevents democracy from being realized." The following year, this student went on to participate in the occupation of Tiananmen Square. He knew, because he had heard it from the American ambassador, that the voices for democracy there could expect no succor from the United States.

I talked at length with Lord on several occasions in 1988, exploring his perceptions of the United States' objectives toward China and how they were elaborated in policy terms. Lord spoke with considerable authority, more, perhaps, than any of his predecessors, because he had accompanied Henry Kissinger on that first secret trip, as well as on the subsequent public visits to Beijing that marked the beginning of relations between the People's Republic and the United States.

"I was struck by the drama, both personal and historical," Lord said of the first voyage to China as we talked in his second-floor office at the American embassy. "I scooped up some Chinese soil and brought that home, just some rocks and pebbles. I think we understood very well their motivations and therefore receptivity to having a new relationship with us. So I think we understood their sense of isolation and their concern about geopolitical encirclement by the Soviet Union and its friends; the fact that you had the invasion of Czechoslovakia, the Brezhnev doctrine, the clashes on the border with Vietnam in sixty-nine, the fact that they'd been totally isolated from most countries because of the xenophobia of the Cultural Revolution, and the fact that they took the long view. It was obvious that we were not going to invade China. So we had pretty well figured out they had an interest in resuming ties, for geopolitical reasons, primarily, and later on down the pike, perhaps for economic, scientific, cultural, and other reasons.

"What we did not understand very well was what was happening in China. We did not understand, and in fact the whole world did not recognize, the tragic dimensions of the Cultural Revolution. So we knew, obviously, it was an authoritarian regime and [we knew about] the rampages of the Red Guards. But I don't think we realized how terrible that experience was. It wasn't really revealed to the world at that point. Nor did we fully appreciate the tensions within the Chinese leadership. We were not aware of the struggle between Lin Biao and Mao and Zhou Enlai." This was a reference to the purported 1971 coup attempt staged by Mao's chosen successor, Lin Biao, which, according to official Chinese accounts, ended with Lin's escape from China and his death when his plane crashed in Mongolia. Nonetheless, the Kissinger mission succeeded. But the principles of geopolitical accommodation, to use Lord's characterization, have continued to be the dominant thread in the fabric of the two countries' relationship.

That accord, Lord argues, has lent American policy toward China broad support within Congress and, to the extent that it cares, among the American public. "The relationship is very important because it's a quarter of the world's people, an ancient civilization," he continued. "They're already a major power. They're going to be even more of a major power in the next century. I think the reason there is general consensus is first, everyone recognizes the importance of China in geopolitical terms, in terms of easing tensions in Asia, and also in balancing the Soviet Union; not in any crude anti-Soviet way—we're both trying to improve relations with the Soviets—it's just a lot easier for us to compete with the Soviets when we have a friendly relationship with China. Then there are the economic benefits, trade, investment already accruing to us with the potential of even greater benefits in the future, [and] the cultural benefits of engaging this ancient civilization, the scientific benefits. I think there is a recognition that these are in the U.S. interest and are not controversial."

As we talked, direct American investment in China was edging toward $4 billion and annual bilateral trade had surged past $14 billion. Cultural exchanges had blossomed, and the Chinese were eagerly sopping up all the technology and scientific learning the United States provided. But, Lord explained, it was the mushrooming business contacts that formed a central element of Washington's objectives: "The more commercial, investment, and trade ties that we can set up between our two countries, the more that the overall political relationship can develop and help in the strategic orientation of China toward the West."

Both in my conversations with Lord and in the regular briefings provided by the embassy's senior officers, it became clear that these objectives—the geopolitical stratagems aimed at Moscow and the desire to reorient China politically and economically—shadowed the embassy's, and hence the Administration's, understanding of China. Analysis became beholden to the policy desires, both of the Reagan administration and its ambassador to China, so much so that these objectives effectively sapped any real initiative on Washington's part, allowing Beijing virtually free rein in its dealings with the United States.

It became clear in the wake of nationwide student protests in the winter of 1986–87 that the embassy was adrift in its interpretation of China's political scene. Beginning in Hefei, the capital of Anhui Province and the home of the University of Science and Technology, student demonstrations swept across China. These protests (which will be discussed further in Chapter Twelve) covered a range of issues, from conditions on campuses to political democracy, and provoked a fierce response from Deng Xiaoping and the hard-liners within the Communist Party. It also led to the dismissal of Hu Yaobang, the party's general secretary and a leading advocate of political and intellectual liberalization. The first serious indication that the American embassy was off-balance in its perspective came during a briefing for foreign correspondents on the afternoon of January 16, only hours before Hu Yaobang's dismissal was announced on national television. As we sat in a semicircle, the embassy's senior officers told us that if Hu was dismissed, something I had already reported as an accomplished fact in that morning's newspaper, he would certainly "be given some kind of party position appropriate to his position." The mounting campaign of ideological terror and repression, already felt acutely among the capital's artists and intellectuals, constituted, in the words of one political officer, no more than "an ideological chill."

"The conservatives have been active in ideological matters," this senior embassy officer maintained, "but they have not been given the right to interfere in the real world." Regardless of what happened in the short term, we were told, China's basic course toward restructuring the centrally planned economy and toward establishing a polity grounded in law and government institutions would continue unhindered. What I and some of my colleagues found remarkable about this performance was the unwillingness, or inability, of the embassy to contemplate the possibility that there was a genuine threat of political instability and of potential truncation or reversal of China's program of change. In fact, as some of us suspected and we all later learned, the seeds of reversal were being sown as we spoke.

As if to emphasize this point, Secretary of State George Shultz came through Beijing on a whirlwind Asian trip in March 1987 during a time of severe intellectual repression. At a press conference, Shultz was asked whether the crackdown of recent months hinted at underlying tensions that could derail China's efforts to clamber out of socialist backwardness. Shultz replied unequivocally. "China is on a irrevocable course of modernization," he declared. "Modernization means openness . . . one [opening is] to the outside world and the other is an opening inside."

It would be unfair to suggest that American diplomats should have foretold with absolute precision the course China would take, but their uncritical acceptance of the Chinese leadership's declarations that all was well, that the program of economic and political reform would be pursued, and their fervent hope that it would, inhibited a more realistic appraisal of China's prospects. The campaign of intellectual terror that followed Hu's dismissal, a campaign that ran its course by late summer of 1987, was viewed not as a glimpse at the soul of the Chinese Communist Party but as an aberrant convulsion triggered by the whims of a coterie of unhappy old men. Indeed, in one of our conversations, Lord referred to Yang Shangkun, who then held a senior post on the military commission, as "a warm, open person." Yang, it turned out, was the man who would oversee the slaughter of Beijing's citizens on June 3 and 4 two years later.

In October 1987, the Communist Party held its Thirteenth Congress, and a new Politburo and Standing Committee were announced. Already, the wing of the party supporting the continuation and acceleration of economic reform, led by Zhao Ziyang, was in retreat; the new standing committee was solidly hard-line, with Zhao and his supporter Hu Qili outnumbered by Li Peng, Yao Yilin, and Qiao Shi. But, once again, the American embassy insisted that China's basic direction remained unaltered. Winston Lord expressed this view in another briefing for American correspondents two months later. "My only view is that the general principles of reform and openness remain," the ambassador told us. Assaying the new Standing Committee, he declared, "There is no general disagreement on the fundamental direction, only on the pace of reform. On the whole, this is a plus for the reforms and opening."

I then asked Lord and his colleagues what they made of Qiao Shi's ascent to the Standing Committee and his new job as watchdog over Hu Qili in the party's secretariat. We were all astonished to hear Lord announce that "Qiao Shi, frankly, is a total unknown." Perhaps unknown to the American diplomats, but several Asian and European diplomats had already fingered Qiao Shi as a contender to succeed Deng as the party's senior leader.

Lord went on to assure us that Sino-American relations were sound, despite the reshuffle at the top of the party. "The basic relationship is in solid shape," he said. "The geopolitical dimension remains crucial." Then, just as he finished speaking, an aide hurried to his side and whispered in his ear. Lord hastily excused himself and dashed from the room. We learned later that evening that he had been summoned to the Foreign Ministry, where he was issued a stinging protest over a congressional resolution denouncing China's human rights abuses in Tibet.

Still, the message we were being given, and the message we were expected to report in the pages of our newspapers, was that despite its occasional difficulties China had settled down once again on its march toward modernity. We were told that China would never retreat from its overall aim of creating a new economic order; that personnel changes, even at the top, were incidental to the thrust of national policy; and, finally, that China's role in the world, its essentially responsible foreign policy, warranted American friendship.

In fact, none of this was true. The economic problems confronting the country had encouraged the elderly, hard-line members of the leadership to eviscerate systematically Zhao Ziyang's economic programs. The personnel changes we were witnessing reflected the beginning of this shift away from economic reform. And, more important, at least to the stated position of the United States, China was persisting in international behavior that directly challenged American interests.

For some time, Beijing had been shipping Silkworm missiles to Iran, sometimes directly from Chinese arms warehouses, other times through North Korea. Washington repeatedly explained to the Chinese leadership that it found this policy unacceptable, and the Chinese just as often retorted that the United States was in no position to lecture them on arms sales. Moreover, the Chinese insisted that they never sold missiles to the Iranians in the first place. The United States responded by showing Chinese officials satellite intelligence photographs of Silkworms being unloaded at Iranian docks. Still the shipments continued.

Unable to persuade the Chinese to halt the missile sales, the Reagan administration announced, with considerable public fanfare, that it was suspending its consideration of liberalizing the rules restricting high-technology equipment exports to China. The sanctions were described by the Administration as a forceful response to China's irresponsible international behavior. In reality, however, the sanctions had absolutely no impact on China's ability to continue purchasing high-technology equipment. "There really wasn't any effect in the first place," said an American businessman in Beijing who marketed computers to the Chinese. "One effect might have been to deny export licenses. That didn't happen. There weren't any sanctions. There never were."

Strangely, even though the sanctions were official Administration policy, no one at the American embassy would discuss them on the record. A few cynical businessmen suggested over beers one night that the reason was that the sanctions had no effect on China at all. Three months later, the so-called sanctions were quietly lifted, even though, as Lord told American reporters in a briefing, "There is still material going to both sides." A disenchanted diplomat in the American embassy told me that many of the younger officers had dubbed Washington's policy toward China "preemptive capitulation."

The Reagan administration and later the Bush administration remained equally diffident toward Beijing's ferocious response to the series of Tibetan pro-independence demonstrations that convulsed Lhasa, Tibet's capital, and to a lesser extent the town of Shigatse. These protests, which began in October 1987, were the first public expression of anti-Chinese sentiment there since Chinese troops occupied Tibet in 1959, subduing a revolt for independence and forcing the Dalai Lama into exile. As the dimensions of Chinese repression of the protests became apparent, there were mild public remonstrances from the Reagan administration, but no words of condemnation, no expressions of outrage comparable to those directed at human rights abuses in Poland after the banning of Solidarity in 1981, or toward the governments of Nicaragua, Afghanistan, or Vietnam.

In March 1989, after another bloody suppression of Tibetan Buddhist monks and nuns marching for Tibetan independence in Lhasa, the U.S. State Department issued an ambiguous statement that ascribed no blame to Beijing and in fact failed even to mention China by name. "We deplore the violence, and particularly the use of weapons, that has apparently resulted in numerous deaths and injuries," said department spokesman Charles E. Redman, reading from a prepared statement. "We believe the interests of all parties would be best served by the restoration of calm and resumption of efforts to address the legitimate concerns of the inhabitants of Tibet." My colleague Elaine Sciolino reported that when President George Bush briefed the Senate leadership that same month on his trip to China, he said that he and the Chinese had "agreed to disagree" on Tibet. But, she reported, "A senior White House official assured the senators in the meeting that China's objectives regarding human rights are the same as those of the United States."

China's continuing repression of the Tibetan people suggests that this cannot really be the case. Such comments are inevitable, however, as the Reagan and Bush administrations have pursued a China policy that precludes human rights considerations. My colleagues and I raised this question repeatedly with Winston Lord during his tenure in Beijing, and he forthrightly explained that the larger imperatives of Sino-American relations overshadowed human rights issues. "There are many interests you have to weigh," Lord told me during a visit to his office. "You have to look at trends, and not just take a snapshot. You have to decide what is effective and not just what makes you feel good. It seems to me there's no question that China is performing much better in the area of human rights than it did ten or fifteen years ago, and I believe it's performing much better than the Soviet Union, even with the recent improvements in the Soviet Union."

As Winston Lord put it in a speech to the Foreign Correspondents Club in Beijing, "How do you balance off projecting your own values without interfering in the domestic affairs of another government? Human rights has to be part of our policy toward China, but it is not our only objective. We have to balance it off with our other goals."

THOSE OTHER GOALS, encapsulated in the talismanic formulation "geopolitics," became sharply etched in the wake of the massacre on Beijing's streets and in Tiananmen Square on June 3 and 4, 1989. On June 3, President Bush declared that "I deeply deplore the decision to use force against peaceful demonstrators and the consequent loss of life." But the same day, Secretary of State James A. Baker observed, "It would appear that there may be some violence being used here on both sides,"

27

referring to both the soldiers armed with assault rifles and the
unarmed civilians. What was being reported on television sets
across the world was very simply the Chinese army massacring
the citizens and students of Beijing.

On June 5, Bush stepped in front of reporters at the White
House and announced that he was suspending weapons exports
to China and military visits between the two countries. He also
decreed that Chinese students studying in the United States
could extend their visas. He announced no diplomatic or economic sanctions against China. On June 7, army troops in open-
backed trucks, chanting in Orwellian unity, "The army loves the
people; the people love the army," and snipers positioned
across Jianguomenwai Avenue fired hundreds of armor-piercing
bullets into a diplomatic compound, many of the rounds aimed
at the apartments of American military attachés.

The following day, four days after the Tienanmen Square
massacre, Bush defended his moderate response to the brutal
suppression of the democracy movement. "Some have suggested to show our forcefulness that I bring the American ambassador back. I disagree with that one hundred and eighty
degrees. Some have suggested—well, you gotta go full sanctions
on the economic side. I don't want to cut off grain. I think that
would be counterproductive and would hurt the people." Nonetheless, Bush insisted, "We can't have totally normal relations
unless there's a recognition . . . of the validity of the students'
aspirations."

The President was asked whether he had misjudged Deng
Xiaoping, a man he had frequently described as his "good
friend." Bush cautioned reporters that it was not clear that Deng
had in fact been responsible for the army's assault on
Tiananmen Square. "Let's not jump to conclusions as to how
individual leaders in China feel when we aren't sure of that," he
said. To those of us in Beijing who had witnessed the army's
attack and had received leaks of Deng's actions in the days
leading up to the massacre, such a statement seemed preposter-
ous. Hours later, publicly driving home his responsibility for the
slaughter, Deng appeared on national television vigorously ap-
plauding army officers for their victories in suppressing what
China's propaganda apparatus was now calling a "counterrevolutionary rebellion."

Finally, on June 20, after nearly three weeks of manhunts, sweeping arrests, and executions in China, the Bush administration announced a series of measures designed to express American indignation over the massacre. Among the actions announced by the White House were a suspension of "high-level contacts" with the Chinese, a ban on military sales, and the postponement of new loans to China by international agencies such as the World Bank. The United States, acting together with its allies, did pressure the World Bank to suspend $780 million in loans. But in fact it was only when the Administration "sensed that the ground under Mr. Bush was eroding" in the face of such overwhelming pressure from Congress (in the words of Thomas L. Friedman of *The New York Times*) that the President decided to take any action at all. Any further steps, he said, would be taken only if the situation in China deteriorated.

Almost immediately, though, the Administration had begun looking for ways to ease or remove the sanctions it had imposed, even as Congress was pressing for stronger actions. On July 7, Secretary of State Baker announced that it was waiving the sanctions for the Boeing Company so that it could go ahead with a $200 million sale of four airplanes to China. Congressman Tom Lantos deplored the decision, expressing his concern "that there are powerful forces in this country that are ready to do business with China irrespective of what Chinese human rights are." The State Department explained that although the navigation equipment on the Boeing aircraft was on the list of banned military equipment, its use in a civilian airliner warranted the waiver. "Our decision is in keeping with the President's intent not to disrupt nonmilitary commercial trade," the department spokesman said. Conveniently ignored, however, was the fact that China's civilian airliners, many manufactured by Boeing and MacDonnell Douglas, were used to airlift into Beijing the troops who had assaulted the capital's citizenry on June 3 and 4. The new American ambassador, James Lilley, placed his imprimatur on the Sino-American commercial relations by appearing at a signing ceremony for a land deal between MGM and the Chinese in the port city of Tianjin.

Despite the ban on high-level government-to-government contacts, Bush's national security adviser, Brent Scowcroft, and Deputy Secretary of State Lawrence S. Eagleburger secretly visited Beijing in July to see the Chinese leaders. They made a second, also secret trip in December, this time raising wineglasses in toasts to Chinese Foreign Minister Qian Qichen in an effort, as Scowcroft put it, "to reduce the negative influence of irritants in the relationship."

As for the impact of the sanctions on military sales, the perception in Washington was that they had no effect whatsoever on China's military purchases. Jim Mann of the *Los Angeles Times* was told by an Asian diplomat in Washington that "virtually all the military equipment they wanted to sell had either already gone or won't be ready for several years. And they will grant special exceptions for the rest." Indeed, Administration officials told Mann that the "prevailing view" at the White House was that the American television networks had presented an unrepresentative and skewed view of the events on Tiananmen Square, a remark that echoed eerily the position of the Chinese government itself.

Even as the Administration rolled back its thin blanket of sanctions, the Chinese government continued its murderous repression. The first round of arrests and executions were trumpeted on national television; the young victims, their faces swollen from beatings, were shown being dragged into police interrogation rooms under the glare of television lights. The immediate storm of international outrage did nothing to diminish the pace of arrests and executions. Instead, according to Amnesty International, the repression simply moved away from public view, away from the prying eyes of the Western press. For the Bush administration, intent on resuming business as usual with the Chinese, repression in the shadows was repression that could be ignored.

What has become clear over the course of the decade is that American policy toward China is, in effect, no policy. By intoning the mantra of geopolitics, successive American administrations have stripped themselves of any substantive flexibility in dealing with China. Geopolitical considerations, married to an unwarranted and unsubstantiated faith in China's march toward Western ideals of modernization, both economic and political, have rendered the American government powerless to respond to Chinese atrocities. American policy is anchored to fears of international imbalance, of lost opportunities for American business, of "losing" China. What is equally clear to those of us who have lived in China is that the Chinese leadership has adroitly exploited those fears, openly playing the foreigners off against one another, openly restoring normal relations with the Soviet Union—for sound foreign policy reasons, to be sure, but also with the knowledge that it would make Washington more compliant. In September 1989, George Bush's brother Prescott, a representative of an investment company, hurried to Beijing to cut some deals with the Chinese. As he told *The Wall Street Journal*, "We aren't a bunch of carrion birds coming to pick the carcass. But there are big opportunities in China, and America can't afford to be shut out. We don't want to lose the market to the Japanese, the Germans, or anyone else."

China, a country mired in political instability and economic backwardness, has persuaded the American government and a collection of academic China experts supporting its position that it is indispensable to the United States. In fact, the converse is true: China needs American capital, American technology, American grain, American managerial expertise. China did not encourage foreign investment because international business was looking for new markets and investment opportunities. China did not seek out men like Irl Hicks because Babcock and Wilcox needed a boiler plant in Beijing. China did not turn to the World Bank for billions of dollars in loans because the bank was short of nations needing developmental assistance. China did not send tens of thousands of students to study in the United States because of empty classrooms in American universities.

Many countries treat their citizenry in the most horrific fashion. In most instances, the civilized world brands these nations outcasts, cutting them off from the comfort of international respectability and assistance. China, though, is different. It is different because it has persuaded the United States that it should be treated differently. For the people of China who ended the decade under the most rigorous repression since the Cultural Revolution, however, the haste with which the United States hurriedly returned to normal relations with the leadership in Zhongnanhai gives them little room for hope. Democracy, they know, will come despite the United States, not because of it.

31

TWO

Losing the Faith

SHAOSHAN, wedged between hills dense with China fir, is a dusty, quiet village in Hunan Province. It is also where Mao Zedong was born in December 1893. During the Cultural Revolution, it was transformed into the Lourdes of China, inundated by millions of Red Guards, soldiers, young workers, travelers seeking inspiration from ground on which Mao walked when he was young. I went to Shaoshan in April 1987 to see what had become of this shrine a decade after Mao's death.

The central square was ghostly empty the day I arrived, save for a few souvenir sellers gathered around an arthritically gnarled scholar tree. A solitary farmer, a wooden plow balanced on his shoulder, whacked the flanks of his water buffalo with a reed switch as he and his beast plodded across the sunlit pavement toward a distant paddy field. I ambled over to the tree, where a couple of drowsy young women in large-brimmed sun hats dozed behind folding metal tables on which were scattered a few crimson Mao buttons, some palm-sized statues of Buddha, and a small box of crucifixes on fragile chains—an eclectic reliquary. I fingered a few buttons, dropped a few aluminum coins on the table, and made off with a nicely crafted button of Mao's face painted on a slice of bamboo.

A tree-shaded macadam road winds toward the house where Mao was born. Along the road, like carnival barkers, a few young men and women urge passersby to stop and shoot a proffered air gun at a line of bright balloons floating on the still water of a sectioned paddy field. In the early spring heat, though, declinations are met with quiet shrugs. The house, actually a reconstruction of the original structure, is pristine ocher adobe, its size reflecting the modest affluence of Mao's father, who had owned a good amount of the fertile land of Shaoshan. More souvenir tables line the uphill pathway to the house, and a few dilapidated buses lumber to a stop and disgorge Chinese day tourists taking in the local historical sights. The tourists chatter away, hurrying more, it seems, to take snapshots of their friends than perspectives of the Mao family manse.

A tour guide mechanically recites the history of Mao's early life as she treads from room to room. A hand gesture here: "This is the bedroom of Chairman Mao's parents. They were very hard-working peasants." A nodded head there: "This is for cooking pig's feet. In the winter, the family used to sit around the fire pit to keep warm." The guide glances out the window toward a stagnant pond in front of the house. "Chairman Mao swam in this pond when he was young." And, I am told, "Chairman Mao began to work in the fields when he was six. When he was between fourteen and fifteen he stopped going to school and worked at home and learned the basic skills of farming to stay in contact with working people." In reality, Mao's father, with whom he fought violently, forced the young man to stay home to help with the farm until the young Mao, against his father's wishes, reenrolled in school to continue his studies.

Across the pond from the house is a clump of tumbledown cement buildings, one of which proclaims that it is the "Mao Family Restaurant," a sort of local "Mom's Place." A tarred pathway leads into the hill off to the right, winding past shimmering, water-logged paddies to a modern cast-cement pavilion hidden in the trees on the hilltop, its roof freshly painted with a red and gold dragon and phoenix. Two granite slabs mark the graves of Mao's parents. Scratched onto the tombstones is rough graffiti: "Liu Xiaolin was here."

In the village center, there is a rambling and now sparsely visited museum of Mao's life, or, rather, of the currently acceptable rendition of his life. Room after room is filled with photographs of Mao during the years of revolution; photographs of important party documents and letters; memorabilia of the Long March, the caves of Yanan. Most of the museum's space is taken up with displays from the years before the establishment of the People's Republic; there are only small, innocuous photographs from the devastating years of the Great Leap Forward, during which perhaps thirty million people starved to death, or from the Cultural Revolution. I inquired of my guide, Wu Dawei, an unctuous functionary of the local party propaganda department, why there were no photographs of Jiang Qing, Mao's wife, who was serving a life sentence in prison for her role in the Cultural Revolution. Unruffled, he informed me that "Pictures of Jiang Qing were not put up because they were not relevant to Mao's life." The museum, he reminded me, "is devoted to the merits of Mao Zedong in history," a comment that unintentionally explained why so little of the museum's wall space was given over to Mao's years in power.

Outside the museum, I bought a few more Mao buttons and commented to the young woman at the folding table beneath the plane tree that they were proving harder to find. "Oh yes," she said, "they made the buttons here in Shaoshan, but they stopped a long time ago. There aren't so many about these days." I asked her where the old button factory was, and she told me how to get to what was now called the Shaoshan Arts and Crafts Factory, on the edge of the village. My guide was consternated by my request that we go to the factory, something that had not been suitably arranged beforehand, but I insisted, and he capitulated when it became apparent that I would go with or without him.

While Wu Dawei hurried off to find a factory official, I was deposited in the factory's reception room, which I shared with a twelve-foot-tall, gleaming white plastic statue of the Chairman. Wu finally returned and introduced me to a man named Pang Wengqing, who announced that he was the director of the factory's office (roughly, the chief of the clerical staff). He was, like many officials, not unfriendly, but not helpful either.

My intent was simply to learn what had happened to an enterprise that had been created solely to promote the glorification of Mao Zedong and how the factory had responded to the new economic climate in the decade since the end of the Cultural Revolution. The answer, it soon became apparent, was that it had not. After offering me the ritual cup of tea, Pang said that the factory was built in 1967 explicitly to produce Mao badges, a product it churned out at an annual rate of more than one million until just a few weeks after Mao died in 1976. In 1974, in a move toward product diversification, the factory had also begun producing tea boxes adorned with the Chairman's picture.

"There's only several hundred badges left now," Pang explained. "When we finally run out there won't be any more." He spun me through the factory, a decrepit series of dirty, garbage-strewn buildings that were oddly empty of workers. In one of the factory buildings, more a workshop, there were stacks of crude plastic buckets, and in a corner a group of six or seven women sat on low stools carving off the excess plastic left on each bucket from the molding process. In the central courtyard of the enterprise, huge rusting machines, drill presses, and motors slowly sank into flourishing weed patches. Pang claimed that there were two hundred and forty workers at the factory, but altogether I saw no more than about thirty people on the premises.

I asked Pang to show me the storeroom where the final trove of Mao buttons was kept, but he demurred, claiming that the keeper of the keys was not at work on that day and he himself had no idea where the key was. "We are almost out of them anyway," he interjected. "By the beginning of next year it will be impossible to buy any Mao buttons." He was plainly irritated by my idiosyncratic interest in the buttons and was relieved when I decided to leave. Mao, it seemed, was best forgotten now that plastic buckets were the order of the day.

Standing once again in village square, which was actually paved as a parking lot for buses, it was hard to imagine platoons of Red Guards, their eyes glazed by the holiness of their pilgrimage, marching into Shaoshan under flapping red banners to proclaim their revolutionary faith. A boy and girl on a red motorcycle shot by, the girl's ponytail floating behind her on the wind as she hugged the boy in sunglasses, who cranked the machine's throttle, the whine of the engine rattling hollowly against the bald concrete face of the Mao museum and the pillared post office. A day later, when I was in the provincial capital of Changsha, I chatted with a man named Wen Huikang, who had once worked as a guide at the Mao family house. I nudged him to talk about the fervor of those days, to conjure up the emotions that flowed so easily then.

"Well," he answered, not completely comfortable with my urgings, "I was a guide in Mao's house. I worked all day, except to eat and sleep."

I asked Wen to describe a typical day. "It was very difficult," he replied, "because it was eight hours a day without stopping. You had to carry a thermos of water with you because you could never stop for a second. There were problems if you had to go to the bathroom. People were lining up outside the door for four or five hours waiting to get in, and then they only had ten minutes in the house. The Red Guards all wanted to push in, and there was usually tremendous commotion. I said the same things over and over again, I don't know how many times, tens of thousands of times—'Here's Chairman Mao's bedroom. The photograph over his bed was taken in 1914'—that sort of thing. If you spoke slowly, the Red Guards would get angry at you and accuse you of not loving Mao Zedong. They said the same thing if you spoke too quickly, too. At the peak, there were fifty-six thousand people a day walking through the house."

Wen paused in his monologue and fiddled with a chrome ballpoint pen. "Well, we had the cult of Chairman Mao then. That's over with now. That sort of thing seems a long time ago. It doesn't seem as important now, does it?"

Yet, just a couple of years later, after the slaughter of unarmed demonstrators in Beijing—bloodshed that gripped the attention of the world—there was an officially sponsored resurgence of interest in Shaoshan, in China's revolutionary heritage and in the place where it all began.

IT WAS this sustaining, if mindless, faith that Deng Xiaoping and the new party leadership sought to reinvent in the early 1980s. During the Cultural Revolution, even Marx and Lenin had been shunted aside, and Mao Zedong Thought, as the collected writings and wisdom of the Chairman were known, became the central creed by which the nation lived. Pigs were raised according to principles divined from this new catechism; rice was planted, steel blasted, planes flown, operas composed, and novels written. Lin Biao, one of the greatest Chinese Communist guerrilla generals during the revolutionary wars, and the man who dreamed up the little red book, described Mao Zedong Thought as "a spiritual atom bomb of infinite power." The image of millions of grinning Red Guards parading through Tiananmen Square, waving their vermilion plastic-covered copies of the little missal, became overly familiar in the West; indeed, for many Americans, this was their only image of China, apart from the Great Wall.

After this decade of political hysteria and social instability, not to mention virtual economic collapse, China's Communist Party sought to reestablish itself and, more important, its credibility with the Chinese people. There was no doubt in the minds of the new party leadership that no matter how scarred the party was, it would nevertheless continue to rule. The dilemma faced by the party was dangerous in its simplicity. If it were formally proclaimed that Mao himself was primarily responsible for wrecking the country, then the Communist Party and everything it purported to stand for would be exposed as irredeemably bankrupt. On the other hand, if the party declared that Mao had merely been duped by those around him, that he really had not precipitated the cataclysmic Cultural Revolution, then the party would be exposed as irredeemably deranged. Deng himself controlled the formal evaluation of Mao and that of the Communist Party, and he made it clear that Mao was not going to be jettisoned; the costs were just too great.

"On no account," Deng said in a candid discussion with some members of the Central Committee in October 1980, "can we discard the banner of Mao Zedong Thought. To do so would, in fact, be to negate the glorious history of our party. . . . What we have achieved cannot be separated from the leadership of the Chinese Communist Party and Comrade Mao Zedong. It is precisely this point that many of our young people don't sufficiently understand." He went on, in an extraordinary display of intellectual contortionism, to explain that the party's new leaders, who had toppled Mao's widow and her allies, had actually acted in accordance with the principles of Mao Zedong Thought.

"Who achieved all this?" he asked his colleagues. "Is it not the generation educated in Mao Zedong Thought? . . . When we write about his mistakes, we should not exaggerate, for otherwise we shall be discrediting Comrade Mao Zedong, and this would mean discrediting our party and our state."

Finally, in 1981, five years after Mao's death and after bitter debate within the newly coalescing leadership, the party published a document, elliptically titled "Resolution on Certain Questions in the History of Our Party Since the Founding of the People's Republic of China," that condemned the Cultural Revolution, praised the Communist Party for correctly resolving the "mistakes" of that era, and graded Mao's legacy as 70 percent good and 30 percent bad. Although Deng and the rest of the senior leadership recognized that the lingering effects of the Cultural Revolution could not be eradicated simply by issuing documents, they did feel that the party had been refitted and put back on course. The party's reputation, Deng believed, would not hinge on the catastrophes of the past, but on his newly instituted economic programs, which, if successful, would encourage even greater confidence in the party.

Deng was wrong on both counts. Many people, especially those in academia and the arts who had been viciously persecuted during the Cultural Revolution, would never again hold the party in the esteem they once did; time and again, the party had committed such grotesque atrocities that it could never be relied on to design and implement beneficial policies for the country. Poets had been forced to scrub pigsties for composing verses romantic rather than revolutionary; violinists were beaten to death for having played Mozart; farmers were made to chant Maoist slogans as they replanted rice shoots; professors were jailed for having James Joyce on their bookshelves. These artists and intellectuals were exhausted by the repression, murder, starvation, and instability precipitated by a succession of party mandarins.

But for the great majority of Chinese who did not number themselves within the elite of the intelligentsia, disillusionment with the party came not from contemplation of past injustices but from the party's growing irrelevance to their lives. Deng

Xiaoping was convinced that the new economic policies would produce new respect for the Communist Party by finally spurring substantial economic development, but in the countryside, towns, and cities where these policies encouraged a reliance on individual initiative, the party became at worst an obstruction to accelerating economic growth, and at best an archaic curiosity from a retreating history.

Even so, party membership jumped by more than a third, to forty-eight million members by the decade's end, but the party's role in Chinese society and the structure of its beliefs were increasingly at odds with the demands of economic reform. Hints of this discord appeared as early as 1982, when General Secretary Hu Yaobang spoke to the Twelfth Party Congress.

"It is true," Hu told the delegates, "that impurities in ideology, style, and organization still exist within the party and that no fundamental turn for the better has as yet been made in our party style. In the leadership work of some party organizations, signs of flabbiness and lack of unity abound. Some primary party organizations lack the necessary fighting capacity and some are even in a state of paralysis. A small number of party members and cadres have become extremely irresponsible or seriously bureaucratic; or live a privileged life and abuse the powers entrusted to them to seek personal gain; or commit acts of anarchism and ultra-individualism in violation of party discipline; or obdurately indulge in factional activities to the detriment of the party's interests. A few party members and cadres have even sunk to corruption, embezzlement, or other malpractices, committing serious economic crimes.

"All of these phenomena," Hu noted with alarm, "have greatly impaired our party's prestige."

Over the next five years, one hundred and fifty thousand people would be thrown out of the Communist Party, some for outright criminal activity, others for their allegiance, past or present, to the Cultural Revolution, and even a few, later in the decade, for more dangerous statements challenging the very principles on which the party was founded; people like the dissident astrophysicist Fang Lizhi and the social satirist Wang Ruowang. Even the party's leadership, the alliance of aging leaders who had driven Mao's successor Hua Guofeng from power, began to split into ideological fragments. The men who had

39

originally rallied around Deng Xiaoping in an alliance of mutual self-preservation and power—people like Chen Yun, Li Xiannian, Hu Qiaomu, Deng Liqun, Yang Shangkun, all of whom had strong affinities for the Stalinist centralized economic planning of the 1950s—expressed increasing disillusionment with the progress of Deng's economic reform programs. Deng's support came less and less from his contemporaries, those old revolutionaries who had worked side by side with Mao Zedong, and more and more from the next generation of leaders, men like Hu Yaobang, who ran the party, and Zhao Ziyang, who, as prime minister, ran the government.

These battles within the leadership invariably filtered into the public consciousness. If the men at the top disagreed, how was the average person to know what was correct? The answer, of course, was that the average person could not know and, moreover, decided that there was no point in knowing. Ideology, that structure of political ideals and injunctions that dictate behavior, simply did not matter much any more.

Wang Zhengyun, a timid thirty-three-year-old woman, is a member of the Communist Party, and, while she says she is aware of the tumult over ideology—what it should be, what it shouldn't, and even what it is—she says she finds it easier not to think too much about such issues. She holds a minor management job at the Beijing Number One Department Store, a five-floor people's emporium that sells everything from televisions to chopsticks, from dried mushrooms to Five Sheep brand bicycles; there's even a disco on four. Although state-owned, the store boasts an array of goods far more varied than any department store in the Soviet Union and is jammed with customers every day of the week.

"In the past," Wang told me after she had ushered me into a cubbyhole office beneath the rafters of the department store, "everyone wanted to join the party. But not now. Very few people want to join." She fumbled a bit when I asked her why she had become a member, but she plugged on after a moment. "I joined in 1978; that's ten years ago now. Of course the Cultural Revolution harmed the party's reputation. But I still thought that if I joined the party I could play the role of a pioneer. I had this wish for a long time while I was in the countryside; I wanted to be a model worker."

I asked Wang if the people she worked with shared her ideal-
ism and belief in the party. She sighed. "Now, a lot of workers
have a bad attitude toward the party. People hear so much about
bureaucratism and corruption, taking bribes; it all has an influence on what people think. Many people have lost confidence in
the party. Now we have what the leaders call a commodity economy, so many people think the party has no significance for the
average person. I don't agree with that." From the window of
her office, Wang looked out at the tile rooftops and into the
perennial smog that shrouds the capital. "We still get new members, but not many. I think generally speaking most party members are good. In this department store, the hardest jobs are
filled by party members."

How, I wondered aloud, did the party's formal ideology ever
intrude into the party's work in the store? She seemed confused
by the idea. Well, I tried again, how does being a party member
contribute to the store's operation? She offered this in reply:
"After the party secretary was chosen for the store, we chose a
working group leader for the clothing department. But soon
after that, three down jackets were stolen from the store. We felt
that the group leader should be blamed, and so there was a
discussion about whether we should change the group leader.
The party committee in the store told them they must do ideological work and change the appearance that nobody cared
about the stolen coats. We decided that the salesgirls were careless, so the coats were stolen. So we changed the group leader."

Mention of neither Marx, nor Lenin, nor Mao crossed her lips.
In the retail chaos of Beijing Number One Department Store,
despite the Friday afternoon political study sessions for party
members, the party itself does little more than function as the
store's management committee. Wang's idea of good ideology
means simply a sense of responsibility for one's work, hardly a
revolutionary notion.

This trivialization of political ideas and ideals, the party leadership believes, represents a major threat to the party's vitality
and viability. The other, more serious danger, of course, is the
promulgation of political ideas and ideals that directly confront
established orthodoxy. In the former case the party is ultimately
rendered irrelevant because it ceases to have meaning in the
most quotidian sense, and in the latter the party just becomes

obsolete. From Deng Xiaoping down, members of the party's leadership, regardless of their differences in perspective, have continued to express concern about this erosion of political principles.

Deng directed the party ideologists, whom he once called "engineers of the soul," to "inspire people to work hard, set high goals for themselves, have lofty ideals and moral integrity." Deng went on to describe what he saw as the principal failings in the party's pursuit of correct theory. "It is true," Deng told his engineers, "that in the study of current problems, some comrades have deviated from the Marxist orientation. They have engaged in discussions of the value of the human being, humanism, and alienation and have only been interested in criticizing socialism, not capitalism." Deng's perceptions were in great measure accurate, if only because China's socialist record paled markedly in contrast to the thriving capitalist economies elsewhere in Asia, a comparison made with increasing regularity by Chinese economists and political thinkers.

Since the founding of China's Communist Party in 1920, political theory, and the more vulgarized rules and principles that have been codified into a formal ideology, have played a central role in the party's history. Struggles for control of the party have involved both contests of personalities and debates over ideology, with the victor using ideology to bludgeon his opponents. Mao Zedong was masterful in his ability not only to craft alliances within the party but also to elaborate in simple prose the principles on which the party, as he saw it, should develop. His knowledge of the countryside where the revolution would be made, his ruthlessness, and his charisma within the organization propelled him to the head of the party. Success in the field legitimized Mao's ideological principles, and the establishment of the People's Republic provided the national stage on which his vision would be played out.

Like other Leninist parties in the world, China's Communist Party claims to act on behalf of what it calls the masses—workers, peasants, soldiers. The party bases its claim to rule (apart from the fact that it does so by force of arms) on a fusion of Marxist, Leninist, and Maoist analyses of history and society, which together constitute a "science." The immutable laws of human progress revealed by such "scientific" analysis show that

socialism and communism must inevitably overwhelm capitalism and imperialism, much in the way April follows March.
Pushing this process along, the argument goes, is the Communist Party.

In subscribing to this rough view, China's party leadership
places extraordinary emphasis on the issue of ideology, or
rather the issue of correct ideology. Ideology may be malleable,
but it is nonetheless indispensable. (Witness Zhao Ziyang's 1987
proclamation that China is in the "initial stage of socialism," a
formula that for a time conferred a needed ideological imprima-
tur on even the most capitalist economic mechanisms.) Ideology
justifies the party's rule, establishes the guidelines for social
behavior, and fixes the limits of political debate as well as those
of intellectual discussion and exploration. Or at least that is its
goal.

In a stinging talk to the Central Committee in 1983, Deng
Xiaoping commented caustically on the crumbling of ideology's
hold over Chinese society. "For a while not long ago," he told
the party leadership, "a few comrades doubted that our society
was really socialist, that we should or could have a socialist
system, and even that our party was the party of the proletariat.
Others argued that since we were still at the socialist stage it was
only natural and correct for people to 'put money above all else.'
Things came to such a pass that most of these mistaken ideas
were published in newspapers and periodicals, and some have
still not been clarified. All this goes to show the extent of ideological confusion that existed among theoretical workers."

Four years after Deng gave that speech, I drove to the west
side of Beijing to visit a group of these theoretical workers at the
Central Committee's Party History Research Center, the place
where the authoritative version of the past is decided upon. I
was ushered into a conference room, where I was introduced to
five youngish and middle-aged researchers from the center. Because any discussion of ideology is potentially sensitive, I had
been asked to submit beforehand a list of questions or areas I
wanted to discuss, although I was not restricted in my queries or,
indeed, in any subjects I wished to pursue during our conversation. I explained in my written questions that I was most interested in eliciting an explanation of the current attitude toward
Mao Zedong Thought and in what ways it bore any relevance to

the rapidly changing Chinese economy that lay beyond the walls of the Central Committee's party school.

I was received by Zhou Cheng'en, a senior researcher at the center, a careful, deliberate man accustomed to feeling his way through conversations. I began by suggesting that there must be differences among the staff over many questions facing the party. To my mild surprise, he admitted that there were differences within the center's staff over some issues, although the disagreements were primarily petty ones. On the core question of Mao, Zhou assured me, there was universal accord.

Zhou echoed the 1981 arithmetical calculation of Mao's performance—70 percent good, 30 percent bad—but then agreed that, for the last two decades of Mao's life, it was mostly bad. "Mao sank into utopian socialism," Zhou explained to me. "We don't use the words 'turned to,' but 'sank into.' The reasons he sank into utopian socialism were many, but the main reason is that he was divorced from the idea of combining theory and practice. He paid too much attention to his own ideas, his own experiences, and was divorced from the real situation in China." Still, Zhou assured me, it was essential "to carry out correct Mao Zedong Thought."

I suggested that perhaps the demands of contemporary China were more complex than Mao's notion of politics and economic development allowed. "No," Zhou corrected me. "We are carrying out correct Mao Zedong Thought, not his errors. Regarding his mistakes, we study them and take them as a lesson. Generally speaking, what we adhere to is Mao Zedong Thought. Mao Zedong Thought is different from his own thought. Mao Zedong Thought is collective thought and we found what is correct through practice. Mao Zedong Thought does not include Mao's errors. It is called this because he is representative of the Communist Party."

This rather muddled explanation unconsciously bespeaks the confusion that grips the party so firmly. What Zhou, and the spirit of the party he represents, is attempting to promote is the idea of a Mao Zedong who was not really Mao, but some mythical personage whose fabricated essence should permeate the body and soul of Chinese life. For most Chinese who remember what the real Mao, as opposed to Zhou's Mao, was like, this conjuring does not work. It is not even working within the party.

Fealty to Mao Zedong Thought remains largely an exercise practiced in ever-narrower circles. Even Hu Yaobang, a colleague of Mao's during the revolutionary wars and a fellow Hunanese, had little use for the former chairman. Hu, who aggressively pushed Deng's reform program as general secretary of the party from 1981 to 1987, was once asked what bearing this construct known as Mao Zedong Thought had on the effort to restructure the country's economy and polity. Hu, in characteristically blunt fashion, shot back, "I think, none." Some years later, Hu's apostasy on this issue was used against him by hard-liners who demanded his dismissal as party chief in the wake of the student protests of 1986–87.

Indeed, the sad state of ideology was lamented by the *Guangming Daily* in July 1988. Revolutionary slogans, the paper noted, "can no longer inspire people's spirit as before. The influence of model heroic figures has declined. In the past period, which was full of revolutionary enthusiasm, revolutionary slogans played a great and wonderful role in inspiring and mobilizing people. People used to pay attention to every important article expounding the party's line, principles, and policies. We still have plenty of slogans, long reports, and long articles, but now the people's responses are cold."

A steady chipping away at Mao's stature occurred throughout the decade. His picture has vanished from the walls of people's houses. His *Selected Works* can be found, dusty and unsold, in official bookshops; in privately owned bookstalls, the glossy red-paper-covered works are not to be seen. I saw a copy of his little red book on the window shelf of a restorer's workshop in the Shanghai museum, but almost nowhere else during my time in China.

At Beijing University, one of the most imposing statues of Mao, a towering stone image of the Chairman as a young man, his hands clasped behind him, the folds of his coat billowing in a permanent breeze, stood outside the entrance of the main library. One night in May 1988, well past midnight, a team of workers in trucks came and toppled the statue, carting away the fractured pieces of stone in furtive silence. The next morning, as students made their way from their dormitories past the library, they saw pots of cheerful yellow chrysanthemums girding the empty pedestal. A graduate history student I knew was jubilant over the statue's removal.

"It's so wonderful," he told me a few days later. "Of course, they didn't say anything or announce it. But the fact that it's gone means a great weight has been lifted from our heads." But if Mao meant little to students on campus, what difference did a mute statue make, I asked my friend. "Symbolically, it means more freedom," he answered. "It really is the end of an era, the end of our kind of idolatry. I think everyone on campus is happy about this." School officials, pressed mercilessly by my colleagues and me for an official explanation, finally said that a small bust of Mao would be put inside the library. One year later, the bust was still not there.

More than the shards of Mao's effigy were unceremoniously lugged away that spring night; in the back of those nocturnal dump trucks went a few more fragments of a communist party whose reputation continues to erode. The party's control over the field of ideas is steadily collapsing and its claim to set the terms of China's future is being challenged. Most disturbing for the leadership is that this disintegration has begun within the ranks of the party itself, particularly through the speeches and writings of Su Shaozhi, who until recently was director of the enormously influential Institute of Marxism, Leninism, and Mao Zedong Thought, a think tank of sorts intended to provide a gloss of intellectual legitimacy to the propagation of the party's post-Cultural Revolution reformist ideology.

Su, a member of the Communist Party, is an intense, articulate man, and in recent years a familiar face at Western academic gatherings. In 1986, he delivered a speech to a conference on political reform in Beijing in which he attacked what he called the "dogmas" of party theory. Su assailed the established notion that class distinctions were evaporating in China, and argued that new notions of class were needed, including the idea that income levels were one index of analyzing society. He also insisted, in sharp contrast to the party's prevailing line, that the interests of workers were not necessarily identical to those of the peasantry or to those of the intelligentsia. But last, and most acutely, he castigated "the belief that the party leadership is almighty, with absolute power. . . . It is necessary," Su said, "to move beyond the situation in which party committees lead all and are responsible for all. . . . It is a very bad practice when party leaders act as if they are almighty, know everything, have expertise in every field: academic, theoretical, or cultural. Very often these leaders act as if they are umpires in every sphere of life. This practice is a resistant tumor inherited from feudal totalitarianism."

For the old guard—those party members who participated in the revolution in the countryside, leading up to the day when Mao mounted the Gate of Heavenly Peace to proclaim the birth of the People's Republic in 1949—Su and his like are heretics tearing away not only at Mao and the party but at Marxism and the Chinese nation itself. I became friendly with one of these elderly party stalwarts, a writer and editor named Huang Gang.

An almost stereotypically tough, grizzled man with steel-gray hair, Huang has a firm handshake and dark eyes full of conviction and good cheer. During the 1940s, he lived with Mao's revolutionaries in the caves of Yanan, where he worked as a propagandist. In contrast to those years of revolution when he felt he was being carried on the crest of history, in 1988, Huang said he felt a bit more like Don Quixote, clattering ineffectually against windmills. The tides have turned, Huang said. The old days—the good old days—are gone.

Huang invited me to his home, a typical, cookie-cutter cement apartment piled with old magazines, books, desks, and tables burdened with reams of manuscript. A critic of literature and film, he started off that day by complaining about Bernardo Bertolucci's film *The Last Emperor*.

"There's a lot of things about that production that weren't so good," he groused, picking up steam as he went on. "If something that wins an Oscar is good, then why didn't Charlie Chaplin win an Oscar? Tell me that. I think there's a couple of things about Bertolucci's movie I don't like. Take the role of the British tutor; is it supposed to mean that without British influence China would have been worse? We think the emperor was bad in many areas. We don't think the influence of the British was so good.

"The scenes of prison were not accurate, either. It wasn't that bad. And those scenes of Red Guards were not true. Given the situation Pu Yi was in, he couldn't walk around the streets like that. We think the Cultural Revolution was a total mistake, but the Bertolucci movie did not comment on it in a correct way."

Huang was warming to his theme, I could tell, because he began speaking faster, more earnestly. "A more important issue is the portrayal of the guards in prison. They were portrayed in a very, very negative light and this is not right. If the guards had been so fearsome and horrible, then the transformation of the emperor would never have happened. There is no other example in the world of an emperor being transformed into an ordinary citizen, so I suppose I should appreciate the film academy giving it an Oscar. But I don't second that choice."

Huang Gang is critical not only of foreign portrayals of China but of the avalanche of modern Chinese writing and film as well, much of which, he believes, explicitly, or more often subtly, attacks Marxism and China's socialist system. Huang insists that the goals of the revolution have been lost in a frenzy of money-making; his favorite *bête noire* is Guangdong Province, where the economy is changing most rapidly. "Marxism is crucial for those of us who study Marx and socialism," Huang argued. "The Central Committee has announced a policy of emphasizing reform and opening up to the outside world *and* emphasizing socialism. The phenomena you see in Guangdong is a result of emphasizing only one side. Of course, the people down there don't bear any responsibility; it falls to us to propagate Marxism-Leninism.

"The Communist Party," Huang went on, "requires consistency between words and deeds. There must also be close links with the masses and work with the masses, rather than seeking selfish interests. And if a party member makes a mistake, he should commit self-criticism and allow other people to criticize him. If we do all these things, then there is hope and there is a future for Marxism. The most important thing is consistency. If you make a promise you must keep it." The promises of the Communist Party and of Marxism, Huang says, are slowly being forgotten.

Huang's despair over what he sees as the party's drift from the path of pure socialism is the despair of the true believer. The revolutionary virtues of self-reliance, hard work, and thrifty living, values annealed in the hardship of revolutionary wars, are being displaced by an onslaught of consumerism, intellectual and artistic eclecticism, and distrust of the party's omnipotence. For men like Huang, the Communist Party can be the only guiding light for China, and the explosion of new attitudes, mores, approaches to daily life endanger the party's ability to impose its vision on the country.

THERE ARE OTHER PARTY MEMBERS, however, who regard the attitude of people like Huang as the tatters of a past best forgotten. For some time, I was friends with a young poet, a member of the Communist Party, who prudence demands not be identified. He is outspoken, articulate, and virulently critical of the party, but because he knows he could lose his job or perhaps even be jailed for expressing himself candidly, he suggested that his name be omitted when I wrote of our conversations. He seemed mildly surprised, even amused, by my interest in his political rather than literary attitudes and experiences. Politics and the party, he informed me, were inconsequential in his life. In time, as I prodded him to explain the apparent conflict between his membership in the party and his disdain for the organization and what it stands for, he relented. "Well, everyone my age feels this way," he said flatly. About six months before Tiananmen, he agreed to talk.

My friend, whom I will call Xiao Chen, or Little Chen (he is younger than I, and the honorific "Xiao" is one often used with affection), teaches literature and poetry at a university in Shanghai. He grew up in a small town, awakening from his childhood during the Cultural Revolution.

"I was the leader of a group of Young Pioneers at the end of elementary school," he began. "We felt very proud of ourselves then. I remember Mao's death. I remember the death of Premier Zhou. At that time, I wasn't familiar with political life in China, but I felt sad, very sorrowful at the death of Premier Zhou. Perhaps I was affected by the people around me. My father is a party member, although my mother is not. So in middle school I was not politically oriented. I didn't know much about these things.

"I wasn't accepted into the party until I graduated from the university. When I was a third-year student, all the students were advised to join. So I wrote a very, very simple report, an application. As part of this process I had to write a report on my life, so I wrote a report on my life. I forgot about it after that, but to my surprise I was accepted by the party very quickly. I think that was due to the policy of the party then, because at that time Deng Xiaoping said we should accept more intellectuals in the party. So I was accepted as a party member. But to tell the truth, I didn't like it very much. But like everybody else, I dared not refuse to join the party. How could you say that? It's dangerous. I don't like to exaggerate, it's not dangerous, but it's very bad. It might turn out to have a bad effect on your future."

Xiao Chen and I wandered through People's Park in Shanghai as he reminisced about his past, occasionally sucking noisily on a straw protruding from a bottle of orange soda. He tracked back and forth, remembering fresh details, amplifying on points he said he hadn't thought about for years. He said he didn't object to my tape recorder, which whirred away as he talked.

"You know, I didn't even attend the ceremony for newly accepted members. I was still accepted. But very soon I was considered to be one of the bad elements there, because I seldom attended political meetings for party members. I paid more attention to my work, poetry, some translations." With this bad attitude, I asked, why was he given a good job? "In the beginning, I was assigned a job at the university as a political instructor; this was in 1983. Basically that meant that you had to care about the political attitudes of the students. Actually, you're supposed to take care of everything—their ideological attitudes, their daily life, their academic work. I was supposed to talk to the students every week to find out what their problems were, what they thought of the party. Actually, I didn't do that. The students weren't very political, maybe four or five out of five hundred, that's all."

As we strolled through the park late that afternoon, the benches were crowded with couples, many nuzzling each other, indifferent to passing pedestrians eating ice cream, tugging balloons, pushing children on tricycles. Xiao Chen said he liked to come to the park because there weren't very many places in Shanghai with trees. "The head of the political instructors, our leader, she didn't have very good feelings for me because the students like me. The leaders were upset because I never lectured the students. I just played football with them. So I was criticized several times. But I've become very indifferent to that, so it doesn't matter whether they criticize me or not. I just do as I please."

I asked Xiao Chen what it was supposed to mean to be a party member. "First," he said, wagging his finger in mock admonition, "you have to love the party. To love the party means you have to agree with the party unconditionally, although that is not stated. It means you should not ask any questions as to whether the party's policies are correct or not. You just agree to the party, even though you think it is ridiculous and detest the policy. You know, I think the Chinese people are very ignorant. People like my father, he accepts the party's policies unconditionally, and all the time we argue about political issues. They just don't think, these people in China. You're not supposed to think. So that means loving the party.

"Then, love the motherland. That is, you should not say anything that is actually correct, that is actually true about the motherland. But many of us have a lot to say about the motherland, about our country, about the poverty, the lack of culture of our country, of the people. You're just supposed to say you love the country, the country is good, we have a glorious civilization, these kinds of things. That's deceiving yourself. And last, you're supposed to take part in every activity of the party; that is, meetings, continuous meetings. Nowadays there's fewer meetings, but everyone hates them. These meetings are ridiculous. There's someone in the front of the room reading documents, or something from the paper. Everybody just sits there chatting, reading, even sleeping. It's ridiculous, just reading documents. Sometimes it's just explaining something which is so obvious; for instance, 'Our party is going to take a new path and our party is going to make the country rich.' You know, that seems so stupid, but that's a fixed rule of the party."

Why, I asked, would someone join the party these days? "Well, now, nobody is interested in joining the party," he replied. "In the past, yes, we wrote applications to join the party. The reasons for that were very practical. One thing is that in the future, your assignment will be determined by the school authorities and that all depends on your personal relation with the school's leaders and also your political attitude. If you are not 'politically advanced' you will probably be assigned a bad job. Now, I don't think many Chinese feel that politics is very important. I think the people are just led around on a leash by the political leaders. They play with the people. Chairman Mao played with the people. I don't know anybody who joined the party just to realize communism."

Xiao Chen cautioned me, though, that he believed that the party still exerted tremendous influence, despite its loss of credibility among the people of his generation. "I think people are still not prepared to reject the party because of its achievements in the past, before liberation. It has changed China a great deal. That is true. The older generation is still impressed by past achievements. On the other hand, it is just because of the Chinese people's bad education, their ignorance of history, that so many terrible things have happened since liberation.

"The party is good at using language, you know. Their language is like magic. The party talks about 'the people' all the time, but it has nothing to do with real people, with living people, with ordinary people. The party is just talking about themselves. They say 'the people' own the country. But actually *they* own the country. The ordinary people, several generations live in a single room. But the party leaders, they can live in a park, or occupy any place they want, even the whole country. Those party leaders are the only capitalists in our country. They own everything.

"Our party is very clever in using different expressions. It's just rhetoric. But these words have a magic power over people." He paused. "But gradually, people will understand that the words mean nothing." Xiao Chen laughed and shook his head. "Well, not my father; he believes words and words. He really does. People like my father, they're actually peasants from the countryside and they do not know anything about other countries and they do not have a sense of democracy. So they don't feel a need for democracy. They don't have the idea of freedom of speech. For years, our country has been led by these people. I'm sure my father loves the party and he believes everything the party says. But other people, I don't know whether they believe what the party says, or just pretend."

I wondered whether, in fact, young people, simply by virtue of their generational distance from older party members like Xiao Chen's father, really did embrace ideals such as democracy and free speech, whether the student demonstrations two years earlier represented broader sentiment. Xiao Chen said he thought not. "Most young people just aren't interested in that," he said. "They are interested in making money. Some young people, or even middle-aged people, hope that China will be a country of democracy. They, like me, think this is extremely important. But it's difficult. It's difficult for party leaders to give up the things they have got from the revolution.

"I think, though, that many people think that the party is hopeless," he pushed on. "Now nobody believes in communism any more. We actually talk about this at party meetings. Nobody talks about communism anymore, except on necessary occasions; for instance, if you are speaking to a large audience."

In the wake of the student protests of the winter of 1986–87, at the height of what the party called "the campaign against bourgeois liberalization," Xiao Chen avoided party meetings, preferring instead to work on his poetry. There was in his university, indeed in all institutions, a surge in the number of required political meetings for party members. Documents explaining the campaign, the transgressions of expelled party members Fang Lizhi, Liu Binyan, and Wang Ruowang (men depicted as corrupting the thoughts of China's students), the need to support Deng Xiaoping's four cardinal principles (a quartet of bedrock beliefs enunciated by Deng in 1979 that have become the gauge by which a party member's adherence to orthodoxy is measured, these principles demand that China "keep to the socialist road," "uphold the dictatorship of the proletariat," "uphold the leadership of the Communist Party," and "uphold Marxism, Leninism, Mao Zedong Thought") were read at meetings of party members. Xiao Chen skipped all the meetings. As the semester drew to a close, the school's party secretary told Chen that he would be criticized at the public assembly marking the end of the year. "I said to the party secretary," Xiao Chen recounted, "if you criticize me, or if any of the school leaders criticize me for any reason, I will quit the school immediately. So they never said my name, they just said somebody never went to any meetings." Xiao Chen chuckled at the memory, shaking his head. "Nobody cared, nobody cared at all."

The reason Xiao Chen was so adamant that his name not be used is that he does not want his friends, fellow authors and poets, to know he is a party member. "They'll laugh at me," he confessed. "I think it's a mistake for people like me to join the party. They'll make fun of me, especially of writers or poets who are party members." At the same time, Xiao Chen said, it was impossible for him to leave the party. "I dare not," he said. "I'd probably lose my job. In recent years, being a party member is not something to be proud of, but it will affect whether you will be sent abroad, what job you will have."

Xiao Chen told me that he hadn't thought much about the party in recent years, not until our conversation. The Communist Party, he said, was not important for him, his work, or his literary friends. His lack of interest in China's central institution, while widely shared among the younger generation, people in their late twenties and thirties, is, of course, not universal. Xiao Chen, his friends, and others like them form but a fragile intellectual patina clinging to a broad and deep mass of anti-intellectualism. I heard echoes of Xiao Chen's words on campuses everywhere in China, from students and professors alike, but there are also people of his generation—factory workers, department store workers—who do believe. While the depth of that belief is often questionable, there is for many of these party members a real feeling that the only alternative to the party is chaos.

IN APRIL 1989, Hu Yaobang, the former party chief who had been in disgrace since his ouster in January 1987, died of a heart attack while attending a party meeting in Beijing. When word of his death reached campuses in Beijing and Shanghai, campuses that had been largely quiescent for the preceding two years, the students erupted in a series of huge protests aimed directly at the party. Tens of thousands of students marched the ten miles from the university district to the Zhongnanhai compound where the party leadership lives and works, at times trying to force their way through the gates, only to be pushed back by armed police.

Chants of "Down with dictatorship" and "Long live democracy" drifted over the imposing red walls of the party compound, followed by soulful renditions of the Internationale. Ranks of green-uniformed police and soldiers, shoulder to shoulder, protected the garish red-lacquered entryway (all that remains of the graceful tower gate built by the emperor Qian-long for his favorite consort, Xiangfei) from the crush of students who held a sit-down strike and called on Premier Li Peng to emerge from the party sanctuary. It was in some ways a strange protest, one that sought to defend the Communist Party of Hu Yaobang, whom the students regarded as a liberal, yet one that attacked the Communist Party of hard-liners like Li Peng and the men that deposed Hu. Although they personally advocated different approaches to certain issues, both Hu and Li would have said they belonged to the same party, recognizing the same body as exercising the "people's democratic dictatorship."

As I watched the spectacle of China's best and brightest confronting this fortress of power and authority, I thought back to a comment Xiao Chen had made before we parted at the entrance of the park in Shanghai. "What concerns me is that, in the history of China, there have always been such conflicts between political powers," he said almost sadly. "One of the results of this is that the people suffer most, the ordinary people. After the death of Deng Xiaoping, if they are lucky, the conflicts will not affect them very much. If they are unlucky, perhaps they will swing back into the darkness from which they have just come."

THREE

The Destruction of Culture

CHINA'S LEADERS in the 1980s spoke ceaselessly of doing things the Chinese way. Deng Xiaoping himself invariably mouthed the phrase "socialism with Chinese characteristics" when he talked with foreign leaders about his country's economic reform program. China's tourist industry ballyhoos millennia of culture, art, and architecture as inducements to foreign travelers. In my years in China, I continuously sought that Chineseness—what it was that was Chinese about China.

In searching for what is Chinese about China, I very consciously sought out ways of life, architecture, attitudes, behavior, habits of thinking—those fragments of daily existence that hinted at deeper links to the country's past. As I traveled the country and talked to farmers, schoolteachers, assembly-line workers, doctors of traditional medicine, I found glimpses, here and there, of resonances with traditional culture. But more frequently I saw the ravages of four decades of Communist Party rule over China, rule that was effacing much of this Chineseness.

A friend of mine, an elderly sociologist distinguished both

56

through his scholarship on Chinese popular cultures and by his broad-shouldered bearing, invited me to walk with him through Beijing over a period of several days in April 1988 to show me what remained of his China: bits of China's old culture, pieces of Beijing's past. At one time, I would have felt comfortable citing him by name, but in the climate of total repression that engulfed his country after Tiananmen, it is best that I do not. I shall simply call him Professor Ming.

The two of us ambled through narrow *hutong,* the constricted alleyways that wriggle through the last of the city's old residential areas. Professor Ming moved briskly, familiar with the warren in which we wandered. He halted in front of a pair of battered, peeling, red double doors punctuating the brick wall some eight feet high that hemmed the northern edge of the hutong. One of the doors was slightly ajar, and Professor Ming pushed it back before stepping over the worn stone sill. We skirted the *ying bi,* the screen wall behind the front door intended to keep out evil spirits, and which shields the interior from passersby on the street.

"This is what it was like one hundred years ago," said Professor Ming, his eyes plundering a U-shaped courtyard rimmed on each of three sides by a traditional single-story brick house. "There used to be lots of these old courtyard houses. This one here is a *sanhe,* with buildings on three sides of the courtyard. This particular house was built in the twenty-third year of Guangxu" (a reference to the penultimate Qing emperor, whose twenty-third year of reign was 1898).

The courtyard we were in was strung with clotheslines hung with a few white shirts and some baggy blue trousers. Earthen jars, pots of flowers, a few brooms, a jumble of clay jars, all jammed in nooks and crannies of the courtyard—the tools of life. What once must have been a garden was tramped down by the four families who now shared what had been a home to a single family decades ago. A tiny, roughly constructed one-room brick building sat in the middle of the garden, its corrugated roof held down by bricks and pipes—what is euphemistically called a "temporary building" by courtyard dwellers.

Professor Ming shooed me into the house on the west side of the courtyard, where he introduced me to an old woman. "She's a fortune-teller," he whispered in my ear as we squeezed through the doorway. Fortune-telling, along with a myriad of other traditional practices dubbed superstitious by the government, including funerary rites, the exorcism of ghosts, and magical health cures, is legally proscribed. But there are few places in China where one cannot see fortune-tellers squatting on sidewalks next to mysterious hexagram charts, waiting for customers searching for their futures. In 1986, in the course of one of the periodic campaigns against superstition, an unidentified official at the Ministry of Public Security insisted that "feudal and superstitious activities have seriously corroded people's minds, polluted social habits, and affected the healthy growth of young people." Many urban Chinese profess disbelief in such things, or at least maintain a veneer of skepticism, but there seem to be enough believers to fuel what has been a substantial surge in fortune-telling, magic, and traditional religious fervor.

"I'm seventy-eight years old," said the woman, whose frail figure was garbed in loose black cotton jacket and pants. "I've lived here a long time, thirty-six years."

Who is it that seeks her out, I asked. "Oh, a lot of people come to see me here. Usually they don't pay me, but they bring a gift of something." I asked her how people learned who she was and where she lived. "Oh, old people know where to find me," she said, a tiny smile flickering across her face. "They tell the young people where to come."

She asked a new visitor to extend his hand and she bent over it, tracing her forefinger across his palm. The old woman looked carefully at each of his fingers, turning his hand over. She then stood and examined his forehead and scalp, prodding with a finger here, a thumb there. Then she sat down. "You should not marry too soon," she began. "There's no need to hurry. You should marry later. Be patient, don't rush things. You should not marry someone from your own country. Marry a foreign girl." What about children? the visitor asked. The old woman bent over the visitor's palm. When she raised her head, she answered, "First a girl, then a boy." She nodded in satisfaction.

It was an innocuous exercise, a trivial exchange, and one that had once been a routine and undramatic part of Beijing life. The drama now is that the old woman divines in relative secrecy, a closeted sliver of Chinese culture.

We left the old fortune-teller and Professor Ming guided me

down a broader tree-lined boulevard north of the Forbidden City and into a much more spacious courtyard house. He introduced me to a middle-aged woman who invited us into a large parlor. She padded into the kitchen and returned with a teapot and cups. On the teapot's cracked enamel fading ideograms read "Long Live Chairman Mao." Professor Ming said that the woman did some fortune-telling, but was principally an adept of an obscure Daoist sect, one not authorized by the government. (Legal status is accorded only to officially sponsored religious institutions.) The woman, whose husband is a high-ranking member of China's military establishment, asked about Professor Ming's children, eyeing me from time to time until he assured her that I was a good friend. After the health of everyone's family had been established, Professor Ming asked her to explain something of her sect and its practices.

"Every year, on the fourth month of the lunar calendar, for fifteen days, there is a pilgrimage to the Miaofeng Mountain. That is the place of Wang San Nai Nai," she said. Wang San Nai Nai, or Wang Nai Nai, as she was more generally known earlier this century, was a woman who, during the Qing dynasty, restored a small temple in the far western hills of Beijing dating originally from the eleventh century. Wang Nai Nai became a patron of pilgrims to the temple because of her work, and is revered in her own right. Miaofeng Mountain traditionally has been the pilgrimage site of three Daoist female deities, one of whom, when worshipped, is regarded as beneficial in ensuring the birth of a son.

"I have struggled for many years to have Wang San Nai Nai recognized," the woman told us. "We want to build a statue to her, but the government won't allow it. The official Buddhist or Daoist associations won't recognize us. They tell us it's superstition."

"There are still pilgrimages every year," Professor Ming interjected. "Thousands of people visit Miaofeng Mountain, even though it's difficult to reach. It's the type of religious practice that was very typical in the days before communism. There used to be hundreds and hundreds of small temples in Beijing, in the hills around Beijing. And people came to pray, to give offerings, to seek blessings for the coming year, for a son, for good business. This was completely banned until after the Cultural

Revolution. Now there are official churches, even official Daoism, which of course was never constituted in any institutional sense. Daoism was always more free-spirited, more individualistic. At Miaofeng, for example, there are many types of worship, including the worship of wolves and snakes. The government wants to stop that."

The woman poured us some more tea. "The central government doesn't want us to build a statue to Wang San Nai Nai, but people in the local government there are very open to us. They say it will increase tourism, increase visits to the area. If Miaofeng is open, worship of the gods will flourish. But this will be a hard struggle."

I asked her if I could accompany her on a pilgrimage, but she shook her head furiously. "No, that won't do. It would be too dangerous. If you want to go, you should go by yourself." Professor Ming explained later that the woman's profile as leader of the sect made it too risky for her to invite foreigners. "She has enough difficulties with the authorities," he said. "She is a fervent believer." Like many popular religious movements in China, her cult is an amalgam of Buddhist and Daoist practices; the veneration of a "venerable mother" figure resonates faintly of Buddhist belief, while the rituals of incense burning and worship of animistic deities partakes dimly of Daoist traditions.

Fortune-telling and popular Daoism were fragments of daily life that no one, except the Communist Party, had ever given much thought to. They added to the complexion of Beijing in the same way teahouses, *xiangsheng* (cross-talk comedy), and classical opera did. But to the minds of party ideologues, fortune-telling and popular Daoism were shards of a discredited and corrupt feudal society, shards to be swept into dustbins. With them, too, went the teahouses. Cross-talk comedy, a traditional and extremely skillful art, has degenerated into a vulgar oral slapstick. And Beijing opera, banned during the Cultural Revolution, has been revived only to play before dwindling audiences of grandfathers and grandmothers reliving their cultural past while their children go to kung fu movies and dance halls.

Modernity is cruel, to be sure. But in China, in Beijing, the past has been pulverized, bludgeoned, needlessly and against the wisdom of some of China's most sensitive minds, into an oblivion from which it cannot be resurrected. There have been moments of liberalization during the last decade, moments when the people of China, of Beijing, have felt the hand of the state and police control lift. In those brief periods, like stubborn wildflowers sprouting through hairline cracks in concrete, China's people reacquainted themselves with some of the old ways of doing things. When the neighborhood monitors, nosy old ladies mostly, began to fade away for a time in the 1980s, many urban dwellers began playing banned games like mah-jongg, and erecting small religious shrines in their houses. But when controls were tightened, when neighborhood snoops were encouraged once again to busy themselves with other people's affairs, these older practices disappeared.

NOWHERE is the wholesale destruction of China's past, its historical achievements, so graphically evident than in the face of the country's cities, and of Beijing in particular. There is a story told, and the evidence today suggests that it is true, that when Mao and his comrades stood atop Tiananmen proclaiming the establishment of the People's Republic, the Chairman turned to Liang Sicheng, China's greatest urban planner and architect but a man whose counsel Mao ignored, and, waving his hand over the panorama of graceful yellow tile roofs, emerald-green tree tops and magnificent city walls, said that he wished to see "chimneys all over Beijing." He got his wish.

Professor Ming towed me through Beijing for several days, charting the destruction wrought on this ancient capital. We headed first for the southwest corner of the city, driving through the pall of cindery gray that had settled over Beijing, fuzzing our view of the procession of five-story concrete apartment blocks trudging south along the city's ring road. I stopped the car in a field of mud on the edge of a large construction project.

A crane swung to lift a cement bucket toward a canted fragment of brick wall jutting up from a swatch of earth bordered by roadways. The forty-foot-high piece of crumbling wall, worn, gap-toothed, supported by dark sinewy timbers exposed here and there, is among the last traces of the imposing, towered wall that once encircled this city. Stacks of new burnt-orange bricks and charcoal-gray blocks were piled around the ruin. Workers in hard hats mixed batches of batter-like cement. We watched for a while the process of refacing this remaining bit of city wall; a sort of walling off of the past.

Here, until just thirty-five years ago, stood Xibianmen, the West Wicket Gate, constructed in the mid-sixteenth century during the reign of the Ming emperor Jia Jing. Through it, merchants traveling from the western plains and mountains lugged their wares on camels for the capital's citizenry. It was one of sixteen great gates that admitted the outside world into Beijing.

This effort to fashion a new wall around the collapsing old one, to build a new West Wicket Gate to replace the razed original, is part of what many Chinese see as a feeble effort to reclaim the shreds of Beijing's past, the centuries of architectural and cultural wonders bulldozed during four decades of Communist rule. "This is not good to look at," said Professor Ming, as he maneuvered through the construction site, examining the new masonry, peering carefully at exposed sections of the old wall. He picked up a brick, turned it in his hand. "These new bricks are very common. We build houses with these. There is a phrase—*'Zheng jiu ru jiu, zheng jiu bu xin'*—which means 'Build the old like the old, don't build the old like the new.'"

The destruction of historic Beijing started almost as soon as Mao Zedong had consolidated his power over the entire mainland. It began with the decision to raze the city wall. From the beginning, there were voices of opposition. Loudest among them was the architect Liang Sicheng, the son of the early twentieth-century reformer Liang Qichao. "As plans for the new capital get under way," he wrote in May 1950, "the question of what to do with the old city wall has naturally become a problem over which many people feel concerned. . . . Only two choices are available: to preserve it or to tear it down. Some people advocate tearing down the city wall. Their reasons are that the wall is a relic of the feudal emperor; the wall obstructs traffic and limits the city's development; in tearing down the wall many bricks could be obtained and much land freed for construction.

"This," Liang retorted, "is a mistaken and childish opinion. Wasn't the Forbidden City the palace of the emperors? Nowadays, it is a people's museum. We mustn't forget that all of these remaining architectural structures are outstanding creative achievements of so many laboring people of the past. Although they once served emperors and were exclusively used by the ruling class, today they belong to the masses, and are national cultural monuments to us all." In urging the preservation of Beijing's historical and imperial edifices for their own sake, Liang was adept enough to play upon the ideological pretenses of the Communist Party by reminding his audience that it was the people, the laboring masses, who had actually done the construction work. For similar reasons, he neatly avoided the issue of who had ordered these projects and who had designed them. But Liang's views were run over roughshod, with Mao leading those who wanted to bring down the walls.

From the inception of the People's Republic, the country's leadership embarked on the wholesale razing of the most visible symbols of "feudalism" and "backwardness." The city's walls were brought down in a decade of steady destruction. The gay, colorful *pailou,* freestanding ornamental gateways that dotted streets throughout the capital, were toppled more quickly. There were, as Liang observed, many reasons offered for leveling the walls and pailou, but many thoughtful Chinese today say that an ingrained attitude of indifference—indeed, hostility— toward Beijing's architectural treasures took root in those early years.

After four decades of Communist rule, Beijing has changed. The brute forces of political upheaval, social need, explosive industrialization—all have conspired to pave over the old Beijing of temples, walls, gardens, and neighborhoods with a metropolis forested by monotonous ashen cement apartment towers, smoke-stacked factories, and leaden government buildings. Only in recent years, fueled by a realization that the city's visible heritage has all but vanished, have any gestures been made to save and rebuild. Many people believe it is too little, too late.

One man who has contemplated this destruction for decades is Hou Renzhi, one of China's most eminent geographers and now the chairman of Beijing's Committee for the Preservation of Historical Relics. I used to visit the campus frequently, and when I dropped by to see Professor Hou, he was delighted to talk about his first love, Beijing. A huge map of the capital as it looked before 1949 hangs on the wall of his living room, a city of narrow hutong, some broader streets, and, above it all, the city walls.

"By and by," said Professor Hou, "people have realized that

we have done a lot of things we shouldn't have. In the beginning, I spoke freely, but I was warned. It became a question of
your class viewpoint, how you stood on the destruction of old
things, like the city wall.

"If you see the city from the air now," he said, a tinge of
sorrow coloring his words, "it is really ugly. The old city's axis,
which ran from north to south, was changed to east and west,
with Chang'an Avenue cutting the city in half. The old city was
planned for the emperor, that is true. The new city should be
built for the people, but that doesn't mean that we have to
destroy the old.

"Liang's idea was to preserve the walls as a promenade,"
recalled Professor Hou, "like a necklace around the city." The
labor of demolishing nearly twenty-four miles of the wall, much
of it forty feet high and sixty feet thick at the base, and the
towering, multitiered gates with their curled-up eaves consumed
the labor of thousands of workers over more than a decade.
"The central government had two principles for reconstructing
Beijing," Professor Hou continued. "First, that Beijing should
be the seat of the central government. And second, that efforts
should be made to try and improve those places where the poor
lived, where there was no running water and no roads. The
second principle sounds all right, but the question was: How do
you understand it? Do you make Beijing a consumer city or a
production center? In the past, it had been a consumer center.
The new government turned it into a production center.

"They paid no attention to the natural environment, to natural resources. They built heavy industry. Why should we have
built iron and steel plants here, where there is a shortage of
resources? Why should we have built chemical works in the
western hills? This should have been a political center and a
cultural center. They preferred to build an economic center.
That's the fundamental problem. No one said this should be a
cultural center."

Even the government-owned *China Daily* conceded that ignoring Liang Sicheng had cost Beijing, and China, much. "If his far-
sighted ideas on Beijing's city planning had been appreciated by
Mao Zedong in the 1950s," the paper wrote in 1986, "or if there
had been free discussion in decision-making at the time, Beijing
would not look the way it does now. Its avenues might not be as

congested. The current traffic problems might be less serious. And the city would have looked, culturally, both modern and much more distinctive in national character, with all the ancient city walls and those exquisitely decorated old pailou and archways and many typical traditional *siheyuan* [courtyard houses] fortunately preserved instead of being destroyed."

ECONOMIC GROWTH fueled by heavy industry was a principal goal of China's new Communist government in the 1950s. When Mao Zedong came to Beijing in 1949, there were only about one hundred and fifty factories in the city, most simply handicrafts workshops inside the wall. Today, there are more than fifty-four hundred factories scattered through and girding the city. "Basically, there was no industry in Beijing at the beginning of Liberation," I was told by Chen Taifeng, the director of the industrial division of the city's planning agency. "Now we rank second behind Shanghai in industrial output."

To drive around the city's perimeter is to penetrate a swath of smoke-belching factories—chemical, electrical, machine, truck manufacture, food processing—edging the city, stretching southward from the west to the city's vast southeast industrial district of Chaoyang. Throughout the capital, older enterprises chug along as well, although, over the years, some have been moved to the outskirts of town. Industrialization brought with it the need for housing, transportation, water, and electricity. It also brought with it unparalleled pollution.

"Beijing is one of the world's cities that is facing the most serious air pollution problems," says Qu Geping, the director of China's environmental protection agency. With coal as the principal fuel for industry as well as for home heating, and with the city's streets jammed with more than four hundred thousand cars and trucks, none of which have pollution-control devices, there are many days when visibility in the city drops to a few hundred yards. According to Qu, Beijing's air is thirty-five times as polluted as London's, and sixteen times dirtier than Tokyo's. On a daily basis, the level of sulfur dioxide in Beijing's air is four times the maximum recommended by the World Health Organization. Indeed, so severe is air pollution in the country as a whole that it is the only Third World nation with a significant acid rain problem.

65

I asked Chen Taifeng, the industrial planner, whether there had been any mistakes made in locating such a concentration of factories and mills around the capital. "Some industries definitely shouldn't be in Beijing," Chen Taifeng replied. "Capital Steel Works, for one. It has played an important role in the development of the country, but if we were to set up a steel plant now, we wouldn't put it here. But since it's here, we can't get rid of it."

Factories have spread through the city, settling on tracts of land, temple plots, or the sites of long-demolished old courtyard houses, like splashes of acid on delicate lace. Large sections of old residential areas where elegant courtyard houses once stood have been flattened to make way for factory buildings or cement cube apartment blocks, what Professor Hou Renzhi calls *bing-gunr,* or ice cube buildings. From scarcely seventy thousand industrial workers in 1949, today nearly 1.8 million of the capital's 10 million residents work in factories of one sort or another. Too late, the city government has imposed zoning rules for industry. While all new factories are to be located beyond what is called the Third Ring Road, circling the outer reaches of the urban area about two miles from the city center, more than one third of Beijing's manufacturing plants still fall within the ring.

Perhaps nothing exemplifies the chaos of Beijing's attempt at planning more than the rush, which has been unrestrained in the last decade, to build housing for the city's mushrooming population. Most of the old-style living quarters in which the bulk of the population used to live, the single-story courtyard houses, were torn down to make way for apartment blocks. And almost all those courtyard houses that have survived in patches throughout the capital have had their courtyards filled with the so-called "temporary buildings," a consequence of the housing shortage that creates what often appears little better than slum conditions. Over several weeks of querying officials in Beijing, I could find no one who could tell me how many of the city's old houses had been lost to the wrecker's ball. "We don't have any solid statistics at all," admitted Chen Tongxun, an official in the city's housing department.

Planning, a staple of orthodox socialism, has been lost in the shuffle of development and politics in Beijing over the last forty years. Because every industry, government agency, and ministry, every department store and taxi company, is obligated to provide housing for its employees, apartment houses stamped from a handful of molds have been thrown up in and around the city like rows of dominoes. In the process, much of old Beijing has been ground underfoot. Driving along the Second Ring Road, a six-lane highway that circles the city where the old city wall once stood, one passes mile after mile of sullen gray apartment buildings, monuments that older Beijingers scornfully call "the second Great Wall."

A friend in the Ministry of Culture gave me a copy of a formerly *neibu*, or internal, handbook for "cultural workers," published in 1985. In language laden with the cloddish political verbiage that has become a ubiquitous feature of Chinese official prose, it described what the government planned for Beijing: "In rebuilding the old city, we should gradually change its backward appearance and limitations, and modernize it. At the same time, we must pay attention to preserving, inheriting, and carrying out the original distinctive style and superiority of the old city on the basis of the overall situation. We also want new construction to reflect the creative capacity of the people and the great achievements of the socialist motherland by demonstrating the new style of a modern socialist capital."

Peng Siqi, the deputy chief of Beijing's Cultural Relics Bureau, is deft enough to realize the incongruities in this declaration. "It's a kind of contradiction," he told me after I had read to him the previous passage. "In the past we did damage to many buildings. Many, many buildings were torn down in the fifties, sixties, and seventies. A lot has been lost. We have a lot that cannot be restored, for so many reasons. We want to preserve, but we are facing the modernization of the city, so that is a big contradiction."

I went to see Peng because I wanted to determine whether the Cultural Relics Bureau was in fact doing anything. Like many bureaucrats, Peng was able to rattle off data showing that he was doing something with his time. But when I pressed him for an example of a project his agency was working on, he became flustered. From a dusty shelf, he hauled down a large book of architectural drawings through which he leafed with obvious unfamiliarity. "We want to restore the Xiannongtan," he said, referring to the ruined Altar of Agriculture, one of the four great altars for imperial rites in Beijing. During the imperial era, the emperor was carried to the altar in a grand palanquin each spring to perform a ritual plowing of the earth as a way of expressing imperial empathy for the country's farmers and to confer his blessing upon the land.

"Nowadays, this temple is occupied by the Yucai Middle School, and there is the Taoranting Swimming Pool there as well," Peng told me as he flipped through the book of drawings. "We are still discussing how to proceed, because the school is still an important thing. One thing we want to do is set up a museum for ancient architecture. We need two million yuan to do this. But it is uncertain when it will go forward." From the unused look of the volume of plans and his but faint familiarity with it, it struck me as yet another scheme with little hope of realization.

To be sure, a handful of extraordinary sights remain in Beijing, the most stunning being the Forbidden City, the former residence of the emperor and his court. Captured in countless tourist snapshots and in cinematographic spectacles like Bertolucci's *The Last Emperor,* the Forbidden City was one of China's few architectural treasures protected by the army (at the specific direction of Zhou Enlai) during the mindless destruction of the Cultural Revolution. But it is elsewhere in the city, where fragile remnants of China's heritage decay, that one witnesses a continuing indifference to the past.

In the southwestern section of the city, near where the West Wicket Gate is being refashioned, one of Beijing's oldest pagodas stands forlornly amid smokestacks, peaked factory roofs, and low-rise brick shoe-box apartments. The Tianningsi, or Temple of Celestial Peace, was first built in A.D. 472 during the reign of Emperor Yan Xing of the Northern Wei dynasty. It was rebuilt in the fifteenth century after having been destroyed during the battles that led to the establishment of the Ming dynasty. Today, the White Cloud Pagoda, a nest of thirteen roofs soaring one hundred and ninety feet, is all that is visible of the temple from outside the front gate of the Beijing Record Factory.

When I tried to visit the pagoda, people in the neighborhood were astonished that anyone would pay attention to the structure. From the small alley where I stood, I could see the delicate upturned eaves of the temple, a few tiny bells still dangling from some of the roofs' many corners; at one time there were 3,400 small bells, and it was said that on gusty days the clanging could be heard a mile away. Old guide books to Beijing say that the pagoda contained a colossal gilded Buddha, but no one in the neighborhood had ever been to the temple, so I never learned whether the statue has survived. At the factory gate, a surly keeper informed me that visiting the pagoda was *buxing*, the generic utterance for all that is not possible in China.

It is likewise impossible to enumerate the multitude of ruined temples, razed courtyard houses, converted royal houses—to chronicle the destruction of Beijing. One day, when I was reporting a story about Chinese policy on AIDS, I interviewed an epidemiologist in ramshackle offices that had once been a Buddhist temple. My host was perturbed that my interest in AIDS waned in lieu of questions about the building in which we were sitting, only traces of its fifteenth-century grandeur still visible in the eaves and crossbeams of the roof. It was not his fault, of course, that he could report little of the structure's history, but, still, I was dispirited by the knowledge that yet another splinter of Beijing's history had been so disfigured, and was now forgotten.

Many of Beijing's older scholars have favorite projects, favorite haunts that summon up for them tangible memories of what the old city was like; the scents and hues of peonies and orchids, wisteria and lilacs that once pervaded parts of the city. But because many of these no longer exist, some of these scholars quietly lobby to have them reconstructed. Professor Hou Renzhi at Beijing University has battled to rebuild the Huitongsi, the Ancestral Temple of the Passage of Swirling Waters, which once sat on a tiny hump of an island in the northern corner of what is called the Xihai, or Western Lake. "It was all destroyed during the Cultural Revolution," Professor Hou explained. "We had no right to say anything about this then. It was just destroyed. Now, we have to rebuild the whole island, and on top of it then we will rebuild the Huitongsi."

The sprawling royal courtyard house where China's last emperor, Aisin Ghiorroh Pu Yi, lived as a boy has been taken over by the Ministry of Public Health. Inside the walled compound, whose huge brass-studded, red-beam doors open onto the now inelegantly renamed Back Lake, stubby brick buildings have been squeezed into once vast courtyards. The buildings, with their red-lacquered columns and rounded gray roof tiles, have been converted into offices and reception rooms. The compound, once one of the grandest examples of late Qing dynasty royal residential architecture, is closed to the public.

But even those magnificent sites open to the public—the Forbidden City, the Summer Palace, the Lama Temple—trouble many architectural critics and historical preservationists who are disturbed by the lack of fidelity to the original buildings. "There are simply not the old artisans," lamented Professor Hou. "They're gone; the old way of doing things is lost. Take colors, for example. In the Summer Palace, all the paintings are new, all the detailed painting in the Long Corridor is new. The problem is that the new paint is not right. It's not the same as it used to be."

Carolyn Dexter, a classics scholar and friend who lived in China for several years, recounted a conversation she once had with an official at the city's Cultural Relics Bureau. Dexter was appalled at the wholesale destruction of Beijing's imperial past and had gone to the department to search for some explanation for this assault on history. "Because we know exactly what something looked like," the cultural bureaucrat explained to Dexter, "when we rebuild it, it will be the original."

Dexter was stunned. "You don't have to be sensitive to see the difference between what is dead and what is alive. You can tell when faith produced a painting and when it's been done by someone they paid to do it. That's their approach to things, to make it the same and tell the tourists it's the original." The most monumental example of this reconstruction, of course, is the section of the Great Wall on which foreign dignitaries and tourists stroll; an exact replica of what stood there centuries before, perhaps, but it is not *the* Great Wall.

Even as some reconstruction continues, the city's—and indeed the country's—preservationists are being overwhelmed by a mounting wave of vandalism. In Xian (near the site of the Han dynasty terra-cotta army, thousands of life-size statues of imperial warriors first excavated in the 1970s), a wondrous collection of 1,095 rare memorial steles has been the target of vandals. These huge stone tablets, many as high as ten feet tall, incised with the texts of classical philosophical texts or the words of an emperor, have been designated by UNESCO as one of the world's major artistic treasures. On nearly every stele, names and messages have been scratched or chiseled into the stone, all under the inattentive eyes of the museum's guardians.

At the Summer Palace in Beijing, a rambling collection of eighteenth-century royal residences and gardens on the shores of Kunming Lake, vandalism also remains a continuing scourge. In 1860, the British Army, in a luggish display of frenzy, pillaged and burned the palace in reprisal for Chinese brutality toward captured soldiers. The Empress Dowager, unwilling and unable to address the needs of her country, squandered the dwindling resources of the nation on a new Summer Palace, what is now called the Yiheyuan. During the early years of the Cultural Revolution, the palace was severely damaged, only to be rebuilt once again. On a hillock overlooking Kunming Lake, a mid-eighteenth-century brick structure called the Wisdom Sea, decorated with countless ceramic Buddhas in greens and yellows, itself savaged during the Cultural Revolution, has been restored, only to fall prey to recurrent vandalism. The vast majority of Buddhas are now gone, their faces chipped away or the figurines chiseled from their perches entirely.

TODAY, BEIJING is among the grayest of the world's major cities. The bookshops and curio stalls, once fixtures of this city, are long gone. In a clumsy effort to re-create that ambience, the city has reconstructed an old street named after the famous (now extinct) antiquarian district Liulichang. Once a hive of narrow alleys stuffed with shops selling scroll paintings, books, jade, jewelry, lanterns, candy, porcelain, cloisonné, embroidery, and aromaed by steaming buns, noodles, and the spice of tea, the area deteriorated steadily during the first twenty years of Communist rule, finally to be torn apart completely during the Cultural Revolution.

Today, the newly crafted Liulichang is lined by buildings painted in glossy red lacquer, the eaves of their rooves overhanging the street in perfect mimicry of Qing dynasty architectural fashion. But it is a hollow street, fabricated like an American colonial lane in Disneyland; the essence of Liulichang is missing. The old men looking for calligraphy brushes, a woman searching for an ornamental hair clasp, children dashing after

71

balls, the tumult, the give and take, the joys and pains of vigorous commercial life are all gone. There are no people here now.

"Service here is intended mainly for foreigners," explained Chi Jinmin, an official who oversees the street. "All the shops deal in Chinese traditional goods such as handicrafts and reproductions of cultural relics, paintings and jewelry. Local people have little need for the articles sold there, and most cannot afford them anyway because of their low income."

I visited the street from time to time, occasionally unearthing a trove of Mao buttons from the Cultural Revolution or a book I had been looking for. But the scrolls and ceramic jars, the block prints and jade curios found on the street and sold at exorbitant prices to wide-eyed foreign tourists, are cheap, mass-produced trinkets. Truly traditional crafts are almost impossible to find any more. For example, a famous style of teapot, the delicate, tiny purple clay pots of Yixing, are simply unavailable in Beijing. Only in Macao, the Portuguese territory near Hong Kong, can good examples of the pots be purchased.

Beijing's city fathers, if they can be called that, pursued their campaign to celebrate the triumph of the capital's new face in a series of awards given in 1987 for the "top ten buildings" constructed in Beijing over the previous decade. Described by vice-mayor Zhang Baifa as "architectural breakthroughs," the buildings collectively reflect an entrenched disdain for any enduring sense of urban life.

Among the structures chosen for the bronze cup adorned with a molded bronze swallow was the city's airport terminal building, a gloomy, poorly laid out place designed less for passenger comfort than for providing hideouts for the national airline's unhelpful staff. Less than ten years old, the terminal is falling apart; its broken light fixtures dangle precariously from the ceiling, its floors are cracking and buckling, its public areas filthy. Other buildings awarded the cup included the Great Wall Sheraton Hotel, an atriumed, mirror-faced hotel topped with a revolving restaurant that doesn't, a building with the glitzy architectural genes of Atlanta or Houston. Also chosen was the new Central Television building, a mammoth edifice slathered in white tile and capped with a thirty-story saltine-box tower, which opened in early 1987. By the time the cup of excellence was bestowed upon it, the building was already crumbling around the edges. The vice-mayor, not at a loss for words to describe these additions to the capital's skyline, declared that they were "beautifully and practically designed and efficiently constructed."

IT IS NOT ONLY the architectural heritage of this city that has suffered at the hands of a government—of a Communist Party—intent upon propelling the country into the ranks of major world powers. Many older Chinese, who remember the culture of pre-Communist China, sometimes speak nostalgically of rituals and practices that have slipped away, or have been discarded in the short decades of political orthodoxy and contrived cultural expression.

My friend Professor Ming argues that the substance of daily existence has changed so dramatically under the political demands of the last four decades that the core of Chinese life has been fundamentally altered, that the soul of Beijing may have been extinguished. "The old rituals cannot be used any more," he said. "It used to be that weddings were such a part of this city's life. The bride used to be carried in a palanquin, on the shoulders of bearers. There was traditional music and a sort of parade. Now, getting married is simply a formality, signing your name. There is no ritual any more."

In great measure, Professor Ming's glum appraisal of evaporating traditional rituals is precise. I did attend several small weddings in Beijing, which, while by no means reflecting the pageant of prerevolutionary nuptial rites, were less barren of ceremony than those in the first thirty years of Communist rule. Then, as was well chronicled by foreign devotees of Maoist China, couples simply penned their names to a marriage register after their work units had given approval for the match. This austerity has eased somewhat, as economic liberalization has made spending money on family celebrations more acceptable.

A friend, a young woman I will call Xiao Tan, or Little Tan, invited me to her wedding, an invitation she sprang on me just a few days before the event. Xiao Tan, a small, cheerful woman whose parents were employed in Beijing factories, worked as a cleaner and errand-person for a government agency.

I arrived, with two other foreign friends, outside her parents' apartment building at 10 A.M. the Sunday of the event. Xiao Tan was closeted in the apartment on the uppermost floor of the four-story gray cement building awaiting the arrival of her husband, so the scattering of guests, including us foreigners, waited on the dusty courtyard outside the building. Her husband arrived in a Citroën palanquin, the car his father drove for a city taxi company, dressed in a new gray suit, white shirt, and bold maroon tie. He looked at the guests nervously, shook a few hands, and ducked into the dank hallway of the apartment building, hurrying upstairs to meet Xiao Tan and her parents. This part of the simple ceremony, greeting the parents and receiving the formal permission to carry their daughter off, occurred in private, away from the eyes of the guests.

After a time, the couple emerged from the building, Xiao Tan in a deep red satin dress, her hair curled and decorated with small flowers. Giggling and blushing, Xiao Tan held her husband's arm tightly as they hurried toward the taxi. The guests piled into other taxis and cars and followed the young couple to his parents' home, a crowded courtyard house constructed in the 1950s in one of the factory districts of the city. As we drew up before the front door, two young men set off thick ropes of firecrackers in the hutong, which gave off dense clouds of smoke and seared the summer air with cordite, to celebrate and (if tradition holds) to drive away any lurking evil spirits. As the only foreigners present, we were rushed into the house under the clicking of family cameras.

We all crowded into a cramped room that turned out to be the newlyweds' new bedroom. Xiao Tan, whose parents remained at home, as custom dictates, rushed around making sure all the guests had tea, and then, in a small ritual, unwrapped pieces of hard candy and popped one in the mouth of each guest. She told me that the couple had already signed the marriage register, the only formality required by the government. Over the bed, in a gilt frame, hung a photograph of Xiao Tan and her husband, he in his gray suit, she dressed in a full-length white wedding dress edged in lace, a white veil clinging airily to her hair. "We had that picture taken when we signed the register," Xiao Tan said, obviously delighted at the prototypical American studio wedding photo. "There's a photo shop near the registry and we went in. They have dresses and they take pictures of new couples."

Xiao Tan then hustled the dozen or so guests into a room crowded by a circular table. When we sat down, she supervised her relatives, who carried in an endless array of meticulously prepared dishes: paper-thin slices of pickled meats, expensive sea slugs, dried mushrooms, threads of pork and celery, a mammoth steamed fish with scallions and garlic—a feast so elaborate that there was no way to eat everything. As we ate, Xiao Tan and her husband circled the table, filling thimble-sized glasses with potent maotai, pushing food on their guests, but never eating. Increasingly raucous toasts were uttered, as more liquor flowed and even more food was piled upon the table.

For the couple, the wedding feast was more work than pleasure. But the event captured the happiness of the occasion, endowing it with a simple yet careful charm and ritual that hinted at past wedding ceremonies. The couple and their families, by no means wealthy people, spent several months' wages to produce so extravagant a feast and to purchase Xiao Tan's gown and her husband's suit. For the neighborhood, the rattle of firecrackers, the colorful celebration, all flavored daily life, pushing the drabness away. For their honeymoon, the couple went off to climb the seven thousand stone steps to the summit of Mount Tai, in Shandong Province, a traditional locale for newlyweds, a mountain climb that confers good fortune on the marriage. Mount Tai, one of sacred mountains of China (at least in tradition), has been a locus of Chinese religious practice for millennia; Qin Shihuangdi, the emperor who first united China, climbed the mountain in 219 B.C. The French sinologist Edouard Chavannes wrote extensively of the mountain's centrality in Chinese religious cosmology and the power it achieved as a dominant cult in Chinese popular culture: "The mountain is not only the place where gods and immortals appear; it is itself a deity . . . the source of all future lives."

This wedding rite, grounded so tentatively, so fragilely in a faint recollection of tradition, is but one facet of Chinese social relations that have dimmed under the People's Republic. Older Chinese, those who remember pre-Communist days, speak often about the disappearance of politeness, of courtesy, of the conventions of life that ease social intercourse. "Oh yes," an elderly, retired professor friend of mine said when I asked her about old Beijing, "Beijing was so formal, so polite. You know,

75

in my day this city was known as one of the most gracious capitals in the world. Not any more."

During the Cultural Revolution, the furnace in which China's past was consumed, urban manners and politeness were denounced by fervent Red Guards as affectations of the bourgeoisie, needless gestures that reflected class attitudes and background. Society would move forward smoothed by the zeal of political conviction, by the worship of Chairman Mao, and by an arrogant belief in China's mission—not by unhealthy expressions of deference. Survival during the Cultural Revolution, as the growing number of personal testimonies now tell us, meant above all an unwavering concern for self-preservation; other people could only get one in trouble; everyone else was a possible enemy. More, too, the grinding, unending hardness and spareness of life, the persistent food shortages, inadequate housing, and brutal working conditions all undermined the value of courtesy. Politesse became, not inevitably, perhaps, but inexorably, dispensable. Public politeness evaporated, not because the Chinese were told it had bad class connotations but because rudeness ensured a minimum of potentially dangerous encounters with strangers in a society of few expectations and much hardship.

The 1980s brought some fundamental changes, but the decade did not erase the loss of public cordiality in urban China. State socialism itself, as visitors to the Soviet Union will attest, encourages this indifference to manners. But in China the loss is aggravated by the memory of the courtesy that had been so integral to the well-honed popular culture of cities like Beijing. I used to visit Beijing's department stores regularly as a way of keeping track of consumer goods and prices, and in none of my visits did I witness even the most basic civil exchanges between store clerks and customers. Clerks in state-owned department stores routinely ignore customers; they are rude when asked a question and surly when they provide service.

There is not a single state-owned institution where service and politeness are the standard. Most egregious, perhaps, is the state airline, CAAC (Civil Aviation Administration of China), a company notorious for its brutish treatment of passengers. Xu Jiatun, the former chief of the Hong Kong branch of the New China News Agency and China's de facto ambassador to the

British colony, was so incensed by his treatment on one flight that he wrote to the airline denouncing its staff. Only when a copy of Xu's angry letter reached Hong Kong's voracious press did the airline announce that the staff involved in the incident would be "reeducated." I have been on many flights inside China where the flight attendants would pass around a cardboard box of stale crackers to the passengers and then retreat to the front of the plane where they ostentatiously consumed hot meals.

Rudeness is now so ingrained in Beijing that its deleterious effect on city life is troubling even to the men who run the country's propaganda apparatus. For a time in 1988, commercials instructing the citizenry to be polite were broadcast regularly after the evening news. One television spot followed a young woman around town, showing her making purchases, asking information, and with each exchange the camera dwelled on her crisp *pleases* and *thank yous*. Another commercial showed a group of young men drinking Coke in an apartment, better furnished than most in Beijing, and then tossing the can out the window, where it hit a passerby on the head. An announcer warned viewers of the dangerousness of such inconsiderate actions and urged viewers to be more aware of other people. But because all public campaigns, which are propaganda blasts designed to alter people's behavior, have become so discredited in the last four decades, China's people are largely immune to such injunctions. In any case, I detected no improvement in the way Beijing's people treated one another during the televised "politeness campaign."

I too became inured, as indeed the people of Beijing are themselves, to the absence of politesse in Chinese society. What I never accepted, and what many Beijingers who remember prerevolutionary China speak of with frustration, has been the loss of the country's gastronomic heritage. In the countryside, where life was spare—often no better than subsistence level— cooking had always been a simple affair. Indeed, starvation and brutal living conditions were often at the root of peasant uprisings and revolts. But in urban areas, among the wealthier, educated classes, China's historic love affair with food attained its greatest expression. By the end of the Qing dynasty, most major cities were honeycombed with restaurants famous for their devotion to a regional cuisine or their mastery of a single dish; duck, for instance. Even as one descended the scale of affluence, a panoply of food was available, from sidewalk stalls to pushcarts dispensing steamed buns, noodles, roasted meats, or sweet pastries.

Chinese cooking assumed its basic form around the eleventh century, during the Song dynasty. The culinary refinements and subtleties of later centuries, while elaborate and varied, were built on the foundations established during that era. At its most accomplished, Chinese cooking came to resemble an art form more than it did a daily task. But it is no longer possible in China to find the most wondrous examples of this facet of Chinese civilization. Instead, the persevering gourmet must travel to Hong Kong, to Taiwan, to San Francisco to eat as China once ate.

I scoured Beijing for restaurants, interviewed famous duck chefs, and sampled asparagus topped with fried scorpions, but found almost no restaurants that equaled the gastronomy of those in foreign cities. It is a sad statement on this lost art that the finest Chinese cuisine in Beijing is available at restaurants managed by cooks from Hong Kong or in international hotels where local cooks are trained by chefs from Taiwan. Just before leaving Beijing for the last time in June 1989, I was taken to a municipally owned restaurant just south of Qianmen by Dan Williams, a colleague from the *Los Angeles Times* who had worked in Beijing at the beginning of the decade. "Wait until you see this place," he promised me. "We ate here all the time; it's one of the best places in town."

We entered shortly after one o'clock and sat down at a linoleum-topped table littered with the scraps of a previous meal. After about ten minutes, a waitress who had been standing and chatting with her comrades, periodically glancing our way, shuffled to our table and dropped two menus on the traces of noodles, chicken bones, and spilled tea. I deferred to Dan's experience and he selected a dish of pork and vegetables, a bean curd dish, and a hot soup. The waitress took our order, leaving the table uncleaned. It seemed like an hour before the meal was served. It was, to Dan's dismay, greasy and tasteless. He also found a fly floating on the surface of his soup, a comical touch which erased the last vestiges of his nostalgia. "Was it really this bad?" he asked as we returned to the street.

There are a smattering of privately run restaurants in Beijing, one of which was famous among the foreign community for the splendor of its cuisine and the care with which the dishes were served. Carved from the living room of a back-alley house owned by the establishment's proprietors, the restaurant had but one table and served one seating for ten people. The meal, a procession of cold meats, pickled vegetables, delicately fried jumbo shrimps, strips of pork, platters of mixed mushrooms and rare, perfect duck, was unlike anything available in local Beijing restaurants; an oasis in a culinary desert. It was, though, less a meal in a restaurant than a banquet in someone's home. Beyond Beijing, especially in the south of the country, an appreciation for culinary accomplishment does endure here and there. In Shanghai, there is a restaurant in which every dish is crafted from crabmeat. In Canton, there are dim-sum houses with food as varied and delicious as any in Hong Kong. But, as many people with long experience in China often warn their friends, if you enjoy Chinese food, don't go to China.

There are, in the political iconography of modern China, scattered emblems of Chineseness—the Great Wall, the Forbidden City, the ranks of terra-cotta soldiers outside Xian—but these are little more than the visible baubles of a civilization that is being remade. Yet for Mao, and for those who followed him, the baubles have been enough, because it is not the substance, but the symbol of being Chinese that merits preservation. A profound exploration of national identity, a vivid concern for the past, serves only to muddy the certainties of ideology and to unsettle the determined march from the past. Cultures change, art vanishes, buildings crumble, memories are lost; but only in China has this process occurred with such deliberation and such thoroughness.

FOUR

The Battle for China's Soul

As STUDENTS from Beijing's colleges and universities marched to Tiananmen Square in April 1989 to mourn the death of Hu Yaobang and later to set up encampments that would remain for six weeks, they were following the example of students earlier this century who had also protested corrupt government policies. And to make sure that foreign reporters understood this link to history, we were regaled on occasion with lightning history lessons on the May Fourth Movement, the 1919 student protest in the capital that precipitated China's political modernization in this century.

China's students in 1989 were laying claim to China's past, a history of political action and dissent that they hoped would provide the succor of legitimacy to their movement. The tendrils of history, stretching forward over the decades to the paving stones of the square, strengthened the students' resolve, casting the shadows of historical truth over the faces of the country's leaders.

It was, however, not only the students who sought the defense of history to substantiate claims of legitimacy for their actions. For their part, the government and the Communist Party invoked the hallowed claims of the revolution; the overthrow of foreign domination, the rise of what the leadership refers to as "the people."

Possessing and shaping history were integral elements of the clash between student activists and an unyielding government. But the claim to China's history, and the right to understand it, did not begin on the square. Rather, it had swirled through the climate of growing intellectual dissent. Indeed, the very dismemberment of China's cultural heritage, in both material and spiritual dimensions, followed by the feeble efforts to restore past glories, reveals as well a fundamental struggle over China's identity. Like all contests in China, this contest has occurred not on the lofty plains of intellectual debate but on the battlefield of politics.

The Communist Party views China's past—its history of dynastic succession, its architectural and artistic achievement, its vast literary treasure house—as admired museum artifacts. The Communist Revolution, so the party credo goes, has successfully propelled China to a new historical stage in which the past has been vanquished. China's history is only to be scrutinized through the glass panes of the museum case, safe from touching or manipulation, but still there to reassure the present of the wonder of past glories.

And because only the party, through its "correct" understanding of history (evidenced in its revolutionary triumph), is permitted to interpret and use the past, China's history and culture have become encased in a crust of ideology and self-glorification. The carefully rebuilt Great Wall—"the only man-made object visible from the moon," Chinese tour guides enthusiastically proclaim—is a masterpiece of premodern military strategy and construction technique. Textbooks hail the exploits of early Chinese mathematicians—the derivation of pi, for example—and the achievements of astronomers like Yi Xing, the Tang dynasty monk whose work is invariably compared to that of Edmund Halley seven hundred years later. Paper, gunpowder, navigation techniques, indigenous medical therapies—all this was developed first in China, the official mythology repeats.

In what is perhaps the crassest homage to China's heritage, an

81

elderly woman named Kong Demao was appointed to an impotent yet usefully visible government body called the Chinese People's Political Consultative Conference. Kong's single qualification for membership is her bloodline; she is, seventy-seven generations removed, a direct descendant of Confucius. And just as Kong's presence in government attempts to cement the leadership's legitimacy to China's philosophical heritage, an equally transparent attempt to lay claim to China's dynastic history is visible in the appointment of Aisin Ghiorroh Pu Jie to the country's nominal legislature, the National People's Congress. Pu Jie, of course, is the brother of the last emperor, Aisin Ghiorroh Pu Yi.

Yet for many Chinese this reverence for the past, this reveling in apparent glory, sounds uncomfortably discordant when China's current condition is examined. If China was so accomplished in the past, why is it so backward today? If China was on the cutting edge of discovery centuries ago, why is it so reliant on foreign technology? If China possessed a cultural heritage of such brilliance, such sophistication and wonder, why is the country producing such thin gruel under communism?

For the last several years of the decade, the country's leading thinkers, men and women troubled by this uncomfortable paradox and the country's lack of direction, by the resurgence of hard-liners within the hierarchy of the party, by the failure of the party and the government to confront the welter of economic and political problems that were threatening the advances of the previous decade, gathered frequently to exchange views. Then in June of 1988 a six-part television series ran on national television that crystallized this paradox and challenged many of the assumptions on which China's self-identity seemed to rest. Enigmatically entitled *Heshang,* or *River Elegy,* the series sparked an intense debate, which reverberated through the remainder of the decade.

River Elegy battered the cultural and historical pieties gilded by popular parable and official mythmaking. The series, which slipped onto the national television network through what appears to have been plain inattention by the cultural watchdogs at the network, suggested that the symbolism China has created and reinforced for itself—the iconography of the dragon, the monumentalism of the Great Wall—has debased and crippled the nation. It posed the most fundamental of questions for China: Who are we? Why are we so backward? What is our future? These questions, from the Communist Party's point of view, had long since been settled. The authors of *River Elegy*, Su Xiaokang and Wang Luxiang, by contrast, insisted that these questions had been avoided under Communist rule, and that the failure to confront them was a failure for China.

The uneasy exploration of self-identity has consumed China's intellectuals for much of this century. It has been a way of examining the fate of the Chinese people, the reason for the country's woeful response to foreign exploitation and its failure to modernize. In the series, against a panorama of the Yellow River sweeping through the yellow earth plateaux of Shaanxi, a solitary voice sings a plaintive folk song, the overture of *River Elegy:*

Do you know—
Under heaven, how many bends in the Yellow River?
How many boats, on how many bends?
How many poles, on how many boats?
How many helmsmen, on how many boats, on how many
   bends, to steer the boats along?

"What are the roots of the Chinese race?" the narrator asks. "Presumably every yellow-skinned Chinese knows that the Yellow River is where the Chinese race was nurtured. So, how has this river molded our national identity? How has it historically governed our civilization? I'm afraid that this is something not everyone has contemplated. . . . At the same time, why have the Chinese chosen to worship a ferocious monster . . . the dragon?"

So sacred has the Yellow River become, that permission for two American rafters to run its course—which would have made them the first ever to do so—was refused so that a Chinese team could attempt it. In their haste, though, two rafters from the Chinese team died in the colossal rapids on the upper reaches of the Yellow River. This calamity, the narrator insists, was a tragedy ordained by a deeply rooted national insecurity.

"We should not mind that others attempt to venture out onto our Yellow River," the narrator chides. "One must not be too discouraged by losing. . . . What is most important now is to stop deceiving ourselves." In like fashion, the worship of the dragon, the imperial icon, a symbol found on silk robes sold to tourists, on teacups and the friezes of hotels, "shows that we are still living in shadow of our ancestors," the narrator argues. "It is absolutely essential to rouse ourselves from this reverie."

In another segment of *River Elegy,* the authors assault the Great Wall and the imagery and associations that have been erected around it. "It has been recognized as the only man-made structure visible from the moon. One even uses it to describe the power of China. Quite honestly, if the Great Wall were able to speak for itself, it would tell China's sons and grandsons that it is a tragic memorial created by historical destiny. There is no way it can stand for power, development, and glory; rather, it represents a nation which is closed to the rest of the world, its narrow-mindedness and its inability to protect itself, and a cowardly and weak lack of will to attack. Because it is so colossal and ancient, it has branded deeply into our national soul its boastfulness, its deceitfulness and conceit."

Other portions of *River Elegy* assail China's dynastic history, stressing the insularity of China, its inability to defend itself from invaders, its failure to capitalize on inventions like gunpowder and the compass, which brought Europeans to China's gates and led to the country's eventual humiliation. "History," the narrator says at one point, "has left us behind. . . . Even during the 1980s, people have taken an interest in Chinese culture once again. There are those who still believe that China can compare herself with the West. No wonder there are some young scholars who have said that this enormous cultural asset has turned itself into a cultural burden."

That culture, that devotion to a cultural past, at once imagined and real, has impaired China's progress. "Chinese history has always taught people to accept whatever comes along and endure it," argues Bao Zunxin, a researcher at the Chinese Academy of Social Science. "A spirit of democracy, a spirit of technology, are exactly what our nation lacks most. Without these two spirits, China's modernization is unimaginable."

The series ends with a prose poem, its rhyme scheme not verbal but thematic:

The characteristics of despotism are mysteriousness, autocracy, and willful nature.

The characteristics of democratic politics should be its
transparency, its stress on the people's will, and
technology.
We are just now stepping out of muddiness into
transparency.
We already have stepped from being sealed off into
openness.
The Yellow River must pierce the highlands of yellow earth.
The Yellow River must empty, finally, into the azure ocean.
The sorrows of the Yellow River, the hopes of the Yellow
River, constitute its greatness.
The greatness of the Yellow River may exist in building new
land between the ocean and the highlands.
When the Yellow River reaches the estuary, a great and
suffering juncture.
Here, sand churned for one thousand li will be deposited to
make new land.
Roaring, surging ocean waves will crash into the Yellow River
here.
The Yellow River must allay its dread of the ocean.
The Yellow River must maintain its course, and with it the
will and vigor it brings from the highlands.
The waters of life come from the ocean and flow back to the
ocean.
The Yellow River, after a thousand years of solitude, finally
can see the azure ocean.

And then, in final counterpoint to the opening folk song, the
voices of a man and woman sing:

We know—
Under heaven there are ninety-nine bends in the Yellow
River.
On those ninety-nine bends, there are ninety-nine boats.
On those ninety-nine boats, there are ninety-nine poles.
On those ninety-nine bends, there are ninety-nine helmsmen,
steering their boats along.

For many of China's social critics, the importance of *River
Elegy* stemmed not from its message, with which many critics
took issue, but from the sheer force with which it assaulted

Chinese consciousness. *River Elegy* insisted that China's people look at themselves and their society and that the past be seen critically, not mechanically. There had been for several years continuing conferences and discussions among the country's most prominent social critics probing precisely these issues. I sought out one of the leading members of these discussions, a middle-aged political scientist from the Academy of Social Science named Yang Baikui.

I called him at the academy one afternoon in late 1988 to arrange a time for us to talk about his ideas and work. Yang was enthusiastic; his institution was not. The watchdogs of the academy insisted on sending a note taker to our meeting, someone to keep the outspoken Yang in line. I parked my car a block from the academy, and as he hurried toward our rendezvous, Yang managed to evade the note taker. We sped off, Yang clearly cheered that the bureaucrats at the academy had lost another round in the effort to silence him. Over the following weeks, we talked at length about the looming disaster he and many of his colleagues envisioned for China.

WHEN I HAD USHERED Yang into my apartment, past the prying eyes of the elevator girls and under the gaze of secret police cameras, we settled into the sofas, he more amused than worried about the level of surveillance outside the door. I asked Yang why the issue of China's tradition had assumed such contentious dimensions, and whether the problems of Chinese society were not creatures of the political and economic system itself. Yang paused, lighting up a Marlboro filter cigarette before responding to my queries.

"This discussion of Chinese tradition actually started three years ago," he began. "Many people think that China is backward because of tradition. I would say, principally, there're several reasons for this approach. First, people have begun to think something is wrong with Mao Zedong's later thought. And second, China is still not so free in talking about ideological things. So people have started to suggest in other ways why China is backward; for example, *River Elegy*. Third, of course, people have still not found out why China is so backward. In the case of *River Elegy*, the authors suggest the main reason China is so backward is because of traditional culture. I don't agree.

86

"The main reason is the present economic and political system. The current economic and political system is not from Chinese tradition. Strictly speaking, it is from foreign countries; from the Soviet Union, from Marxism. Take public ownership, for instance. Actually, in traditional China there never was this sort of system. And our one-party system. This is not part of Chinese tradition. The state emphasizes collective interests too much. It encourages people to give up individual interests in favor of collective interests. This creates conflict between the individual and society. This has changed a bit since 1978, but it remains the old system in many places."

Yang has written frequently about the problems his country faced, and in times of relative liberalization some of his work appeared in national newspapers. I asked him to elaborate on his often-cited observation that Chinese society had become paralyzed.

"A society, if it is going to develop," Yang explained, leaning forward and puffing on his cigarette, "must have a strong motive force. As I see it, China at present lacks this strong motive force. At the moment, provincial leaders are busy going abroad and prefectural leaders are busy eating. The county and township leaders are busy gambling. Many workers at state-owned enterprises play chess and cards during working hours. A team of researchers in Beijing found that if workers work three hours a day, that would be the best we could expect. Many offices of state organs still remain the way they were in the old days—lingering over one cup of tea and a newspaper for a half a day. Many intellectuals and young students don't work hard, they just do ordinary jobs.

"To increase the number of products, the quality of products, we don't rely on initiative or efficiency. Instead, we rely on putting in more money or more foreign technology. Over this decade, our productivity efficiency increased 15 percent, but our consumption went up 284 percent. We can say that this lack of motive force is one of the most serious crises in China today."

Because of this, Yang insisted, there is no alternative for China but to move away from the idea of collectivity, the belief in Marxism so cherished by the leaders in the party.

"The experience of the past years has shown that the productivity of individually owned enterprises is much higher than in state-owned industries. If we sell state-owned things to individual ownership, production and efficiency increase on a large scale."

Yang admitted that there was, of course, no unanimity among scholars on many of these points. "One group thinks socialism has no fixed model," he continued. "Marx didn't talk about a fixed model. So ownership can be at the individual level. As I see it, though, we should move away from Marx.

"Under the present political system, people have lost many political freedoms. Politically speaking, people have no freedom to move their jobs, to move to another place. They have no freedom. Also, because of our political system, we have lost freedom of the press, to reflect public opinion. So, of course, evil things emerge—speculators, profiteering, officials taking bribes, because the press cannot report these things. As a result, people have lost their confidence and have no initiative to do their work. The other problem, of course, is the one-party system. At almost all levels, we use the appointment system; the party recommends, and someone is appointed. Some people are not qualified, but they still are given high-ranking jobs. As a result, many people who know how to manage a factory or run a store don't have a chance.

"The only way China can advance," Yang said, thumping the coffee table, "is to get rid of the one-party system. Unless we do this, China will amount to nothing. I believe that in the future, if we are successful in changing the system of ownership and creating a government of checks and balances, the Communist Party must fundamentally change their ideology.

"It is obvious that we face a crisis of authority. Deng Xiaoping's authority can only be understood in terms of traditional authority and charisma. By traditional authority, I mean power that comes from his relationships, with his colleagues, army people in the past. Charisma means that this powerful man has had many achievements. When these old leaders die, the young leaders are not going to have either charisma or traditional authority. There is, as well, an ideological crisis, both inside and outside the party. When Deng Xiaoping and Chen Yun [an elderly hard-liner who designed China's socialist economy in the 1950s] die, there will be a profusion of views."

Other social critics, while accepting Yang's conclusions as self-evident, contend that the crisis faced by China is rooted not in traditional Chinese civilization but in the culture that has emerged since 1949. One of these critics, a man I shall call Zhu Cixi, a researcher at the Academy of Social Science, finds the collapse of morality at the heart of the increasing uncertainty over self-identity. I visited Zhu at his book-lined apartment, having read several of his essays and having heard his views heatedly discussed among my friends. Zhu looks very young, although he assured me that he was older than he appeared, a circumstance that occasionally caused older academics to take him less seriously.

"The crisis of morality in China is very real," Zhu began, settling into a chair of woven rattan. A framed print of the *Mona Lisa* hung over his cluttered desk. "I feel that at the moment morality is in great disorder; that is to say, there is no standard in our society that tells us what is moral and what is not. Traditional morality has almost disappeared. By traditional morality, I mean Confucian morality. And the new tradition of morality is basically finished as well. By that, I mean the new morality since 1949—socialist morality, Communist morality. On the surface, it exists, but it is finished."

I asked Zhu to give me an example of what he meant by this. "Take the principles of collectivity," he replied; "[of] doing everything for others, not for one's own personal interest. This notion of morality was put forward just after the new government came to power. So both these traditions of morality, Confucian and Communist, have almost disappeared. The central problem is that nothing new has emerged to replace them."

Espousing what the guardians of state ideology regard as criminal heresy, Zhu argued that it was Mao himself, and the way in which the Chinese responded to him, that led to the moral debacle of the 1980s. "There was," Zhu told me, "a deification of Mao. His words, his life, all of this were worshipped. People regarded him as a god. People thought he knew everything, that he was infallible. People took him as a model of morality. When Mao asked people to do things for others, not just for themselves, people embraced his wisdom. Of course, what really was happening was that propaganda made things appear as they were not. People did not really know who Mao Zedong was and what the Communists really were.

"After the Cultural Revolution, transparency and people's awareness increased a lot. Everyone began to see what was going on. And as people began to see, they began to realize what they worshipped was not what they thought it was. They saw that the people they worshipped had done many evil things. As a result, the original morality of the revolution, Communist morality, began to disappear. As the years went by, around them, in society, people began to see corruption everywhere; not just in their immediate lives, but everywhere. People began to believe that no one adhered to morality. There developed a generalized feeling that society simply lacked any morality at all.

"I say this is a crisis of morality," Zhu continued, "because when there are no rules, there is social disorder. There is a loneliness, a hopelessness and anxiety that persists in all corners of society. Unless there are fundamental changes, there is no hope. This morality involves many things, economic and political. We have no legal system. What I feel is that no new morality has developed; principles such as individualism, democracy, determination, equality. These kind of things haven't taken form in China today."

ONE MEASURE of China's (or at least official China's) sense of confidence is the treatment of foreigners who choose to live there. The government requires them to live in foreign ghettos. Foreign journalists, the most dangerous aliens in the eyes of the government, are required to live in walled diplomatic compounds, behind gates guarded by armed sentries of the People's Armed Police. This is to prevent our Chinese friends from visiting us easily and to wall us off from the general population. For me, the only way to circumvent the security force was to drive friends like Yang Baikui through the gate so he was protected by my car, which the guards had no authority to stop.

Before the establishment of the People's Republic, many foreign concessions had restrictions on where the Chinese themselves could go. The notorious sign in the Shanghai park in the 1920s reading "No Dogs or Chinese Allowed" was frequently cited by patriotic Chinese as evidence of the inherent racism of foreigners. And they were right. The foreign community in China largely sought to prevent Chinese from intruding into their lives, even though they were in China.

Today, however, the tables have been turned. China's new masters, the Communist Party, have determined in what fashion the Chinese people will be permitted to come into contact with the contaminating influence of foreigners. Just as our residential compounds were sealed to all Chinese except those carefully screened by the Foreign Ministry, nearly all hotels where foreigners stayed were off-limits to the Beijing population. Only if I accompanied Chinese friends into a hotel were they permitted past the ever-present security guards.

On one occasion I wanted to visit a village in Guangdong Province, a part of the country where Cantonese, or one of its myriad subdialects, is spoken. I thought that it would be helpful if I were accompanied by a friend of mine who was a reporter from Hong Kong, to ease the translation problems and to provide a different, non-Western perspective. "This is not possible," I was lectured by the provincial foreign affairs office. "North and south cannot mix," the official told me, his politically lockjawed way of discriminating between Hong Kong Chinese and white foreign journalists. I went off without my friend, accompanied as usual by an official handler from the provincial foreign affairs office.

China's leaders have remarkably little confidence in their own identity as a culturally proud nation. They have even less confidence in their subjects' capacity to assert their national identity. Only in southern China, where the weight of official Beijing rests more lightly, does this frantic effort to segregate foreigners and Chinese ease. I had one memorable exchange with a bureaucrat at the Foreign Ministry (the government department charged with responsibility for foreign journalists in the country): I asked this bureaucrat, a superficially friendly but basically hostile man, why guards were posted at the gates of our compound and why they prevented our Chinese friends from coming to visit us. "Oh," he replied, "it's for your own protection." The real answer, of course, was that it was not to protect us, but to protect China. In the most vulgar sense, these regulations were enacted to restrict the flow of information from Chinese citizens to us foreigners. But in a deeper sense, this segregation revealed a deep insecurity over the ability of the new Communist culture, now enshrined as the new Chinese culture, to resist the allure of the outside world. It was, in one breath, an admission of weakness.

One of China's feistiest newspapers, at least before the slaughter of June 1989, was the *China Youth News*. In a series of thoughtful essays, the paper wrestled with the apparently conflicting demands of tradition and modernity, of Chineseness and intercourse with the world. "Tradition does not exclude modernization," the paper argued. "Japan, Singapore, Korea, and Taiwan are all more developed than we are, yet they have also retained more of their culture than we have. What is required now is an openness toward new ideas and creativity. It is no good to go to extremes and pursue Western culture or Chinese tradition." If only it were so easy.

AND SO IT IS NOT SURPRISING that the views of my friends Yang and Zhu elicited visceral reactions from hard-liners within the party, reactions that labeled their views as dangerously tainted by foreign contamination. But it was the reaction to *River Elegy* that riveted public attention. Public response to the television series was intense, both passionately approving and unrelentingly hostile. The newspaper *Wenweibao* emphasized the series's clarion call. "The purpose of the film," the paper wrote, "is meant to rouse the deaf and awaken the unhearing. It is meant to stimulate people's awareness of the reality around them."

Others, like the pseudonymous Yi Fang, writing in the *Guangming Daily*, insisted that no one in China, "including ordinary people, imagines restoring the imperial court or intends to worship the dragon. The dragon of the 1980s has no function and does not threaten the people. It can be used playfully during the lantern festival and is helpful for tourism."

The most ominous critique, however, came from Wang Zhen, one of the octogenarian leaders of the party, semiretired as vice-president of the country, who reappeared in the councils of power after the massacre on Tiananmen Square. Speaking to reporters in the remote city of Ningxia, Wang lashed out at the authors of *River Elegy*. "There is a certain television series," he said, "about our great Chinese people and our motherland's Yellow River which has not a single redeeming feature. In my opinion, this series is an insult to the Yellow River and the Great

Wall and slanders our great Chinese people and the descendants of the Yellow Emperor."

This crisis of Chinese consciousness, so allusively excavated by *River Elegy*, galvanized China's intelligentsia. Zhu's distress, and the more vigorous social and political critiques of Yang Baikui, reflected the intense ferment within intellectual circles as the country moved toward the events on Tiananmen Square. That China had lost its bearings seemed evident to many. The bankruptcy of the political establishment, of the Communist Party and of its vision for China's future, was a constant theme among the country's intelligentsia. At the same time, nostalgic yearnings for China's past, a past more mythical than real, were now revealed as little more than elaborate self-delusions. Moreover, many of these social critics, a rarefied assemblage of the country's finest and most iconoclastic thinkers, saw the crises of national identity and consciousness as pointing inexorably toward catastrophe.

Until June 1989, many of these intellectual inquiries found their way into the Chinese press. A pioneering newspaper in Shanghai, the *World Economic Herald,* rallied interest for academic conferences to examine these problems, described by the paper as the most profound facing contemporary China. There was, among the slowly emerging coterie of hard-liners within the leadership, an intense loathing of this self-examination, one grounded not in the theological simplicities of Chinese Communist ideology, but one broadly rooted in Western humanism and Western political thought.

On June 4, 1989, this all ended. There was no more questioning, no more discussion, no more debate. Instead, it was a time of arrests, imprisonment, and death. The propaganda machine, rusty from its diminished use in recent years, roared to life, handmaiden to the secret police.

River Elegy, intended to provoke discussion and critical thinking, was now portrayed as ideological poison which had encouraged the students to occupy Tiananmen Square. The national television network, which had twice broadcast the series in the summer of 1988, now declared that *River Elegy* "distorts Chinese history, entirely negates the fine traditions of Chinese culture, and vilifies the Chinese people. The essence of the film is to negate the socialist system, oppose the leadership of the Communist Party, and propagate all-round Westernization. *River Elegy* is the product of bourgeois liberalization, in collusion with the doctrine of 'peacefully transforming China' as peddled by the international reactionary forces. We should see that behind the series that there is a life-and-death struggle for the Chinese nation and the socialist system."

Beginning on August 9, two months after the Beijing massacre, the *Beijing Evening News* published a series of articles critical of *River Elegy* for one hundred and one consecutive days. Most of the articles were little more than nit-picking complaints about the series' occasionally imprecise historical references, but more often the paper assailed its interpretations of Chinese history. Typical of the level of criticism was an article that accused *River Elegy* of "an unreasonable slur on Emperor Zhu Yuanzhang," the first Ming emperor, who had ascended the throne in 1368. The point, of course, has nothing to do with the series's evaluation of Zhu Yuanzhang; it is a question of who possesses that history. That one hundred and one successive articles were published speaks eloquently of the extraordinary power with which *River Elegy* threatened the party's soul.

Of the series's authors, Wang Luxiang was arrested; his collaborator Su Xiaokang escaped to Paris. Yang Baikui, the political and economic critic, was arrested, as were more than a dozen of his colleagues at the Academy of Social Science. And, with each arrest, and each escape, China's propaganda writers became more vitriolic in their denigration of these men.

Typical was an attack on Liu Xiaobo, a young literary critic who had for several years written energetic critiques of China's political system, all of which called for a shift to a multiparty democratic state. In his writings, Liu linked the oppressive features of Marxism-Leninism with what he came to describe as traditional oriental autocracy. Liu discussed his ideas in a provocative interview in 1986 with Geremie Barmé, an Australian scholar who is one of the most prescient observers of China I know. "China is caught in a paradoxical situation: on the one hand, we lack cultural sophistication, which makes it impossible for us to experience the type of perception inherent in modern Western man. On the other hand, we Chinese are excessively vain. This gives rise to a desire to insinuate ourselves into the ranks of the world's advanced cultures. It allows us to believe that we can artificially put our culture and art on a par with the most advanced cultures on earth. The eagerness with which the Chinese yearn for a Nobel Prize for Literature or an Academy Award is part and parcel of this hypocritical approach."

Liu, and many of the iconoclasts of his generation, feel that the leg irons of history and tradition have stifled China's efforts to overcome the political constraints imposed by communism. As he told Barmé, "The inertia of the old is so great, the roots of the past so deep, it's almost impossible to guarantee that anything new you attempt will, in reality, be new. We're caught in the quagmire of the past, so everything we create is saturated with the very essence of the old."

Days after the massacre of June 4, Liu was rounded up as a key agitator behind the events of that spring.

After his arrest, the *Beijing Review,* an official weekly published in more than a dozen languages, denounced Liu and his ideas: "For his efforts since 1986, Liu Xiaobo has won the name of 'madman,' 'mad dog' and 'black horse.' " It accused him of manipulating the students on the square, of conspiring to form illegal organizations, of writing for the new student press "in order to throw dust in people's eyes and confuse their minds." Liu was but one of countless numbers of China's most creative intellects branded as enemies of socialism, enemies of the Chinese people. But what Liu and others like him had tried to do was simply to raise the question of what it means to be Chinese. He and his friends discovered just how dangerous that question really is.

Part II

The Good, the Bad, the Future

Looking out at all the high-rise buildings there
   like fields of rice and wheat,
Looking out and all I see is waves of people
   traffic in the street.
Looking left now right, front, back,
I'm so busy I can't keep track.
This 'n' that, that 'n' this
   the more I see the weirder it is.
                    CUI JIAN, rock singer, 1987

FIVE

Lolam

CHINA BEGINS IN THE VILLAGE. It is where most Chinese live. It is where the food is grown. It is where Mao Zedong made his revolution. It is also the place that has changed the most in the past decade.

In the summer of 1987, a season when southern China sags under dense heat and humidity, I drove west from Guangzhou to a village I had asked to live in for a week. I had asked the provincial authorities, whose permission was necessary, to go to a village where foreigners had never been, a village not rich but not oppressively poor either. In the minivan with me was an interpreter from the provincial foreign affairs office, someone who knew the subdialect of Cantonese spoken in the area where we were headed.

We drove for two days, past endless fields of rice and, later on, waving fields of hemp. On the afternoon of the second day, we jounced down a rutted dirt track winding off the main road, and after some time jolted to a halt outside a mud-brick building.

"Well," my interpreter sighed, obviously discomfited by the rustic tenor of life around him, "this is Lolam."

As promised, Lolam is neither the richest nor the poorest village in its county. Until a few years ago, there was not even a passable road into the village. Now an administrative agglomeration of seven natural villages—groups of houses clustered together on a swath of relatively flat terrain—Lolam is strung along a valley bottom separated by groves of creaking bamboo and diked paddy fields in gentle terraces. The hillsides rising from the sheeny water of the paddies are stubbly with growth, the dense forests of pine and China fir stripped in decades past. And with the disappearance of the forest, also gone are the swarms of wildlife, including tigers, that once roamed these hills.

I spent a week in Lolam village, living with the family of a man named Lee Seegay. I walked the dirt paths of the village, talking to the farmers, the geomancer, the members of the local Communist Party committee to learn how deeply the rural reform policies had sunk in China. Besides Lee himself (who has traveled to Guangzhou), no one in Lolam had ever seen a foreigner before, a fact that in itself bespeaks the village's fundamental provincialism.

What is happening in Lolam is, in the broadest sense, happening across China. Farmers are tilling their own land, selling their produce, building their homes, living their lives unhampered by real fear for the first time in living memory. Of course, a village in Hebei or Liaoning or Anhui would have its own customs, its own daily routines, its own tongue, different crops, a different network of relationships with urban markets and life-styles. But in nearly all provinces of China, the forces of change have settled firmly on the land.

In early summer, feathery cloud boas drape around the crests of the hills that encircle Lolam as dawn first breaks. The slowly rising sun peeks through clouds, scattering pumpkin-hued rays into the narrow valley carpeted with the iridescent green of newly sprouting rice shoots. Every morning at about six o'clock, Lee Seegay, a solidly built man with rough hands, hustles onto the second-floor balcony of his house, where a black crank telephone balances on the whitewashed cement railing. From his balcony, Lee glances distractedly at the pristine morning jelling

100

LOLAM

before him, snatches the antiquated, heavy receiver from its
cradle, and furiously spins the contraption's crank.

"Wei! Wei!" he shouts into the mouthpiece. *"Wei!"* Some
shouting later, the operator in the nearby market town answers.
After bantering with the operator through the static-choked
line, Lee is put through to one of his glass tube suppliers elsewhere in Guangdong Province. Lee, owner of one of the village's five telephones, is getting a jump on the day the way his
capitalist brethren in Hong Kong, two hundred miles to the east,
do. This morning ritual, whether it be a call to harangue a
supplier, to find parts for his trucks, or to badger a salesman
(and relative), is how Lee Seegay starts his day as Lolam's richest
man; its native son capitalist and its leader, not officially perhaps, but through an authority derived from his position and
wealth.

Elsewhere in Lee's home, a thirty-eight room extravaganza of
poured cement and tile imported from Guangzhou, his wife,
their four children, assorted brothers, sisters, and cousins are
slowly rising. The courtyard, around which the house curls,
begins to come to life as the family dogs scamper after frazzled
chickens. A small child kicks a bright yellow and orange ball
across the courtyard, unconcerned by the growing tumult
around her.

Lee swallows a cup of tea, just brewed in the dark, oil-splat-
tered kitchen off the courtyard, and wolfs down a small bowl of
rice porridge. He is no mood for talking this morning, as the
day's problems at his glass bottle plant already loom in unwelcome fashion. His factory, two low, brick buildings straddling a
thin, winding creek, churns out tens of thousands of small glass
vials, which are eagerly sought by the growing number of manu-
facturers of traditional Chinese medicines, herbs, and potions.
Although he once tilled paddy fields, Lee responded to the shift
in economic policies rapidly and flexibly, and started a factory in
this village where his family has lived for hundreds of years.

In the old days—that is, before 1980—Lolam wallowed in the
poverty that sat heavily on this area. Often there was not enough
to eat, not enough to wear, villagers remembered. Now, with
changing national policies, the village is flourishing. It is not as
wealthy as many villages far to the east in the Pearl River Delta,
where many farmers flaunt their wealth by building three- and

101

four-story houses, their facades gaudily decorated with glazed tiles in Day-Glo pinks and purples, oranges and yellows. But Lolam does have new homes. It has a school. Couples marry in splashy revelry. The dead are buried in honor, and the Lee name (nearly everyone in Lolam is surnamed Lee) is newly reverenced in the rebuilt clan hall. For the first time in history, and certainly for the first time since communism came to China, Lolam is thriving in a nutritious mix of free markets and revived tradition. And, most markedly, absent is any political tincture, any sense that a broader socialist schema charts the future.

There are tens of thousands of Lolams, and hundreds of millions of rural farmers who over the past decade have been catapulted from the most excruciating impoverishment to material well-being unimagined by their parents before them and unforeseen by even the most idealistic among China's leadership. What has occurred over the course of the last decade is, in truth, the real revolution in China, a revolution that at last brought food to the tables of virtually all Chinese and produced, for the first time in the country's history, a population of rural consumers for manufactured goods from the cities.

Lolam's history during this decade, its current accomplishments, reflects almost pristinely the course of modern Chinese politics; disasters in policy were felt tangibly here, moments of respite between misguided political campaigns enjoyed for their placidity, their return to a less-anxious normalcy. In other provinces, Jiangsu or Fujian, for instance, many farmers have begun using gasoline-powered tractors or small tillers to turn the soil of their plots. Not so in Lolam, where the water buffalo remains, as it has for centuries, the power in front of the plow. In coastal China, the forces of international commerce—the intrusion of radios, televisions, telephones, perfume, high-top sneakers, Coca-Cola—are more pronounced. Lolam, residents know, is a backwater, but it is a happier and more prosperous backwater than it has ever been.

At dinner the first night, Seegay introduced me to Fan Guanghao, a county official who had stopped by to chat. Fan is a serious man with little time for politics. Like most office workers and bureaucrats in southern China in the summertime, Fan wore a white, short-sleeved shirt with splayed collar. The deputy secretary of the Communist Party committee for the county surrounding Lolam village, Fan said he wants to make people rich, and boasts easily about the successes of recent years. He pointed with satisfaction to the fivefold increase in family income since land was parceled out to individual farmers, bringing the annual earnings of a farmer in the county up to one hundred and thirty-three dollars a year. Certainly, that is poverty by any standard, but it is not a stagnant poverty. Every year, the county's farmers earn more money from more productive rice cultivation and an ever-wider variety of cash crops. Fan thinks that there will be no return to the past.

"No matter who is in power, nobody can change this trend," Fan explained one night as we devoured a freshly killed and sautéed chicken. "Everybody says what is going on is good. In the old days, we thought of grain as the only crucial crop. Now we have many cash crops: peanuts, jute, ramie, dogbane, fruit, silkworms. We encourage cash crops and we send people to villages to show people how to grow them."

For the farmers in the county, and in China as a whole, the proliferation of different crops and greater rice production have taken place because the farmers themselves are allowed to sell their produce, much of it at free markets. Even the rice that they are required to sell to government grain dealers is sold at prices sufficient to encourage production. China's policymakers have apparently learned a major lesson that is ignored in many other Third World countries, most notably Africa; that is, if farmers are paid trivial prices for what they grow, either they won't grow or they will smuggle crops to free markets. Africa, a continent of extraordinary diversity and agricultural promise, is mired in a bog of corrupt, irrational agricultural policies intended to keep food prices low for city dwellers. China has recognized that its farmers, like farmers everywhere, will labor long and hard if they see a tangible reward for their efforts.

Most, though not all, of the families in Lolam are named Lee, a phenomenon typical in south China "lineage villages." In practice, it is the sons who stay in lineage villages, with the daughters marrying into other villages. One woman who married into Lolam, and who has been there for decades, is Chan Lapfong. She was sitting on the veranda, actually a protruding cement porch, of her new house when I walked by one evening after dinner. Like other new homes in the village, hers is fronted with a fired teal-blue brick, the back constructed of mud blocks. She was sitting on a low four-legged stool of bamboo watching a gaggle of ducks in a reed mesh pen on the edge of a paddy. She scrutinized my approach, curious at the oddity of a foreigner wandering about the village in a T-shirt and shorts. Although she never said so, I was sure that she and everyone in the village had been aware of my arrival, an event whose rarity alone dictated widespread knowledge of my comings and goings. As I approached, walking with no particular destination in mind, she invited me to join her on the porch where, after some prompting, she spoke about her life in the village, a life that had weathered the travails, and now basked in the fortunes of Lolam.

I said that I was surprised that she was not a Lee.

"Oh, I was not born here," laughed Chan, who wore the ubiquitous blue cotton tube-legged pants of a villager, a purple jacket, and a blue shirt with large white plastic buttons. Her steel-gray hair was fixed atop her head with a single, large bobby pin. "I was born in Wampo village. That's about twenty kilometers from here. But I've been here sixty years now. Now I'm more than seventy; seventy-four, actually."

As she spoke, little chicks, still fuzzy in their infancy, darted across the dirt floor of her house. Hanging from nails driven into the cement walls were framed posters of tempera paintings of idealized pagodas, mountain scenes, Chinese opera characters; posters found in rural homes across China. "When I came here, there were only six or seven families. I married into the village after being introduced to my husband by relatives. He was a farmer. My son is a village schoolteacher.

"We've always been very poor. We had very little land, never had any water buffalo. Before 1949, it was very difficult. But after 1949 was difficult too. The Great Leap Forward was very hard. People were hungry. There wasn't enough grain to eat. People died of illness in those times. If you felt hungry, you often got sick. A lot of children died of illness in those days."

Chan said that life in the village in recent years had improved for the most part. "We got land in the land reform," she said, a reference to the redistribution of land after 1949, "but it was not enough." Only since 1979, when the central government in Beijing decided to give China's farmers their own plots for their own use, have villagers actually had enough land to earn a decent living, although it took a few years before the policy of land distribution actually trickled down to Lolam. "And," she added, "in recent years, we got electricity."

As I said good-bye to Chan and walked down the valley on the ocher-colored dirt path, one of her neighbors, Lee Shaywing, waved me into his house, a mud-block structure older and less sturdy and refined than those made of the kiln-fired brick and cement block favored by his wealthier neighbors. On the wall, a large, gold-plastic-framed clock was set an hour behind Beijing time, or official Chinese time, on what Shaywing said was "sun time." His mud house, I learned, belied his financial stature. He is a typical farmer in the village, embedded in the land but eager to take advantage of changing times.

It seemed that there was a competition emerging to entertain the foreigner in Lolam. Shaywing was not to be outdone by his neighbor and he vigorously wiped off a four-legged stool before he would let me lower myself onto it.

In late middle age, Shaywing is deeply tanned from working in the fields. His wife came into the room and swooped down on their infant granddaughter, who had squatted and peed on the dirt floor of the house. I told Shaywing I was interested in how village life in China had changed in the last ten years. "The biggest change in my life has been in recent years, since about 1981," he replied, tipping his chair back on two legs against the wall of his house. Between 1981 and 1982, Lolam's land, which until then had been consolidated into a commune and farmed by the villagers collectively, was distributed to each household to use as they wished. The rule of thumb adopted by the village (and this varied from village to village in China, depending on the amount and kind of available land) was to grant three fen, or three tenths of a mou, to each family member. Everyone in Lolam, including nonfarmers like Lee Seegay, controls their own three fen of land.

"Since the policy was relaxed," Shaywing went on, "we can do more and earn more. Look at me. We've got 1.2 mou of land now. I've made an investment in the plastic factory. I've got more pigs and more chickens. In 1981, I was given my own land. About three years ago, they readjusted the land and I got more because my son got married and his wife lives here. Of course I'd like to get some more land now. I've got two water buffalo and I raise chickens, pigs, and geese. I've only got two ducks." In the days of collective farming, he said, things were much worse.

"We still don't have any tractors here," he complained. "But we can buy water buffalo at a nearby market. They're about five hundred yuan apiece, depending on what shape they're in. In the old days we got work points for our labor and got our food according to that. Nowadays, that's all done. After the harvest I will hand over part of it to the village and keep the rest, or sell it. Whatever I want." A principal source of Shaywing's income, though, is not his farming but his investment in a plastics factory, a small concern that sprang up to make caps for the vials made in Lee Seegay's factory. Shaywing scrimped, sold some pigs, borrowed from relatives, and invested one thousand yuan in the plastic cap factory, more a workshop actually than anything else. "Every year I get about a thousand yuan in income," he boasted.

Shaywing has prospered from national agricultural policy changes and from the success of his fellow villager, Lee Seegay. Many others in the village have benefited in similar fashion, including Chan, who built her house with money borrowed from Lee, and whose daughter works in Lee's vial factory.

Seegay's rising stature in the village, a prominence he displays matter-of-factly, was unmistakable to me after just a few days in Lolam. It is also a responsibility that weighs on him as his obligations to his fellow villagers multiply, whether through proffering advice, granting loans, providing jobs, or restoring the Lee clan hall. It is a position that in the prerevolutionary era was that of the dominant landlord's, and one that Communist Party cadres working in the countryside extirpated at gunpoint. From the party's point of view, the only legitimate source of authority was that of the party itself.

The all-embracing dominance of the party in the countryside has waned in the past decade with the explosive growth of free markets and what amounts to the private ownership of land. Rural industrialization, often little more than village or town workshops, but sometimes large enterprises employing hundreds of workers, has been spurred not so much through government investment as through individual or group enterprise. In this economic environment, there is little the party has to offer villagers and townspeople. In Lolam, the situation is no

different. Lee Seegay's experiences exemplify how this fundamental transformation of the countryside came about.

"When I was a child here," Seegay said one night after dinner,
a feast of fish fresh from his ponds, chicken, and newly picked
vegetables, "this village was very poor. We couldn't get clothes
to wear. It was very rare to eat pork, maybe once a month.
Normally we just ate cassava congee with very little rice. There
were about four or five landlords before the revolution. My
grandfather joined the revolutionary war and was on the Northern Expedition. My father joined the revolution in 1948. He
joined to wipe out the local bandits. Before that, he worked on
other people's land. After 1949 and in the early 1950s, the
economy was stable and everything was basically sufficient, at
least compared to before forty-nine. During the Great Leap
Forward, when I was in middle school, life was very difficult, and
during the Cultural Revolution, things were even worse.

"My father was severely criticized during the Cultural Revolution. He had been a model policeman in the countryside. But he
suffered a lot and was criticized severely. He was accused of
carrying out Liu Shaoqi's line." (Liu Shaoqi was China's first
president and was Mao Zedong's designated successor in the
early 1960s. When the Cultural Revolution descended on
China, Liu was denounced as "China's number one capitalist
roader"—Deng Xiaoping was number two—and one of the most
devastating political attacks that could be made against someone
was to accuse him of "following Liu Shaoqi's line.") "In the end,
my father was killed. I don't know who the people were who
killed him. The whole family didn't know what happened to him.
He was accused of being a special agent of Taiwan. Some people
said that he committed suicide. I don't know where my father
died. When we got the body back, he had been hit on the back of
the head.

"After my father died, I took the responsibility for my mother
and my brothers and sisters and took up farming. We lived in a
small mud-block house. Often we had to borrow rice to get
enough to eat. I was allowed to teach in the primary school
because I had graduated from senior middle school. In 1972,
the production brigade asked the higher authorities of the commune if I could become a formal teacher. But because my fa-

ther's 'problem' had not been made clear, I had to choose another way."

In the mid-seventies, when the virulence of the Cultural
Revolution appeared to be ebbing in the countryside, or at least
in more remote rural areas like Lolam, a cousin of Seegay's came
to visit from Guangzhou. As Seegay tells the story, the cousin
worked in a bottle factory in the provincial capital but thought
that a similar operation could be started in the village, one that
would benefit the villagers and perhaps Seegay himself. In those
days, there was no such thing as private enterprise. Indeed, even
the casual mention of working for personal profit, as opposed to
the collective good of the production brigade or the commune,
could entail severe public criticism, beatings, imprisonment. To
this day, one can see the faint and fading white-daubed slogans
of the Cultural Revolution on some mud walls in Lolam: one on
a shed off the main path reads, "First criticize, second work,
third take the lead."

"I was on good terms with the production brigade leader,"
Seegay continued. "I explained the plan to him, and he said okay
and let me set up the factory for the brigade. They let me be in
charge." Barely had the factory started operation when the all-
embracing righteousness of political mayhem intruded into the
village yet again. "Just when we started making money, there
was another political movement," Seegay sighed; "this time, the
'socialist line education campaign.' A campaign work team was
sent here and they objected to us expanding production. They
said that the factory was not socialist and was an underground
factory."

Political campaigns in China, particularly the Cultural Revolution, had succeeded in the countryside through a mixture of
intimidation and artificially contrived enthusiasm. Inevitably,
the failed promises of campaign leaders—China will attain communism within the decade; China will surpass Britain's standard
of living in fifteen years; a new revolutionary man will be molded
in China—eroded the will and patience of China's citizens. This
was more true in the countryside than in the cities, whose people
were captive participants in the campaigns. In rural areas, where
food production needed to continue regardless of the current
political fashion, the imperatives of farming life engendered less

tolerance for the excesses of a political sloganeering and social engineering devised in a faraway city.

For Seegay, and the production brigade, which was beginning to see the virtues of his approach, the new campaign went too far. "We'd had enough," he said. "We had signed contracts with customers and the production brigade refused to shut us down. So we stayed in business, at least for a while. But they shut us down in the end anyway. That was the policy then." Seegay, under political suspicion from the Cultural Revolution work teams and lured by a cousin's entreaties, moved to a nearby town, where he offered advice on starting a parts factory. "My brother and I went to the Wongsah commune and helped set up that factory. I wanted to prove that everything I did was not for myself. When the Cultural Revolution ended, Lolam was still very poor, very poor. Some people didn't even have enough money to buy salt. Some people came to me and asked me to run the glass factory again. I still felt that I had a lot of energy so I came back here to start the factory."

On the second morning of my stay in Lolam, he asked me to accompany him to his new factory. A narrow clay path dips away from his house, past his family's two fish ponds, to a rivulet of water that squirts through a crease in the valley floor. We skipped across two boulders, landing on another path that cuts along the top of paddy dikes to the town's access road to the world beyond. The road, little more than a dirt and gravel track wide enough to accommodate a flatbed truck, was built by Seegay when he realized he needed something better than a packed foot trail to bring in raw materials and to ship out his finished vials. In the fields, villagers were already stooped over, slicing the rice shoots with steel crescent-moon knives, stacking the tidy hourglass bundles of the shoots in piles for threshing.

Waving casually to a neighbor, Seegay turned toward his factory, which lies at the valley's end, where the hills squeeze together in great wrinkles. He paused at a flat slab of stone block, weeds sprouting between the worn stones. "That was the Guangong Temple," he said, gesturing toward the slab and field beyond. "It was destroyed in the Cultural Revolution. Now, it's just a cassava field." As he spoke there was no hint of regret in his voice, not, it seemed, because he did not mourn the temple's desecration, but because so much was destroyed that the worries of the present, and the future, were more pressing.

At the end of the main track, where it rises slightly to a squat rocky plateau, a ganglion of single-story red brick structures and steel-roofed sheds clangs and whirs with the noise of manufacturing. Seegay's office is a dimly lit brick chamber with two battered wooden desks and a crank telephone. One of his brothers was on the telephone ordering more glass tubing, the factory's principal raw material. Under the roofs of the open sheds, stands of eight-foot-tall, thin glass tubing wait for processing. Because the ends of the glass tubes constantly break, glass crunches under each footfall.

In one building, young women (most in their late teens, some in their early twenties) sit on long benches hunched over thumb-sized blue flames, over which they twist lengths of glass tube apart. Bare-handed, they deftly spin the tube segments over the flame, softening the tube's edges into a rounded lip, while other workers flatten the other end to form the vial's bottom. "Women are more skillful at doing this," Seegay informed me. "They have small hands. Their hand movements are not too fast, not too slow." In reality, it is not so much because of the size of their hands but because young women make up the bulk of the Lo-lam's surplus labor force that they work in the factory. Across much of rural China, women constitute the great majority of the workers in rural industries, while the main agricultural work, plowing and maintaining paddy dikes, is done by men. During the harvest, though, a time when rice or wheat must be taken in within a short time, both the men and the women in a household participate.

From a core of four workers, all family members, in 1980, Seegay has expanded his glass vial operation into an enterprise employing one hundred and sixty people. While he expected sales of more than three million yuan the year I visited him, he was already exploring how to expand his production capacity. "We sell the bottles all over China," he said, reeling off the names of provinces in the north, along the coast, and deep inland.

Seegay's success has infected others in the village, including the former Communist Party secretary of the village, Lee Chongwing, a man who helped stave off, at least for a time, efforts to close the fledgling bottle factory during the Cultural Revolution. Although he once wielded ultimate authority in the village as party secretary, he tacitly admits that genuine influence in Lolam flows now from economic power. Indeed, Chongwing gave up his secretaryship the previous year to open the village's first hardware store, a new wood-framed mud-block building conveniently situated on the main track through the village. On the day I visited him, he was bustling about preparing for the store's opening and, he believed, his new fortune. He proudly showed off his business license, which he got from Wongsah, the closest large town; this certificate allows him to buy wholesale from state stores.

Chongwing looks old for his fifty-seven years, the battles of the past chiseled on his visage. His face is covered with a gray stubble and his clothes are disheveled. There is a sense of loss when he talks about the village's past. "When the Cultural Revolution came along, I was told to step down," he said. "Things were very chaotic then. At that time, the policy was not as relaxed as it is now, and when we started the factory again, the work team tried to pressure me to close it down. I didn't agree. The factory earned money for the collective, and not for Mr. Lee Seegay or others. It was a good thing. But they closed the factory down anyway. Then, in 1980, I went to Mr. Lee and asked him to open the factory again. I just convinced him to come back because the village was still very poor. The policy was still not very relaxed, but I asked him to sign a contract with the production brigade to manage the factory. And he did. In 1982, the policy relaxed, so the factory became owned by Mr. Lee. We abolished the production brigade in 1984."

Chongwing said that he joined the party in the mid-1950s when a flush of enthusiasm about Mao and the party still lingered in China. The party was seen as doing good things in those days, stripping landlords of land and giving it to farmers. Joining the party gave him a chance to participate in remaking the countryside and even, by becoming party secretary, helping to lead that effort. Now he speaks of his party job overseeing the village with distaste. "The biggest problems were during the Great Leap Forward," he explained, "when we had to run the big dining halls."

Mao Zedong launched the movement known as the Great

111

Leap Forward in 1958 in an effort to propel China into the ranks of industrial nations in a matter of years; the results of this policy were the economic devastation of China and a famine that brought death by starvation to as many as thirty million people. In Lolam, as elsewhere in China, rural lands were collectivized, and all activities were organized as communal efforts. All land, animals, tools, and cooking utensils were owned by the commune. Virtually every activity within the village was dictated by the commune's leadership. Work in the fields was determined by brigade leaders. Tools that once had belonged to individual families were collected and redistributed to work teams. Families were forbidden to cook their own meals and everyone was required to eat in huge dining halls established in the village, a practice intended to instill an appreciation for the collective good as well as constitute a visible expression of genuine socialism. Not surprisingly, it was a period intensely detested by the people of Lolam.

"The farmers were really not happy about that at all," said Chongwing, who as party secretary was in charge of instituting the new order. "But they were forced to be part of this. It was all very stupid. But you couldn't object to it. You had this going on all over the country. People knew it wasn't my fault, but of course they weren't happy. They had to do everything for the collective. You couldn't do anything for yourself. Everything was up to the central authorities. We had to follow. If they said stop, we would stop. If they said go, we would go. We thought the world had gone crazy."

Chongwing has not so much abandoned the party as let it slip away. His life, and the lives of his fellow villagers, are bound up in their own concerns, their own needs and ambitions. His plunge into petty commerce reflects both disillusionment with the past and the opportunity of the present. "There're other small shops in the village," he told me. "Mine will be the fourth. But I think it will work. I've already put nearly ten thousand yuan into it to get started."

Political campaigns in China, whether in the city or the countryside, drew their energy in great measure from the emotional animosity focused on class enemies, "hidden rightists," counterrevolutionaries. The campaigns, in which Chongwing was either a leader or a participant, were no different. Lolam had its accusers and its accused, its politically pure and its politically debased. After the first land reform of the early 1950s, the handful of landlords in the village, by then elderly men, were stripped of their land and sent to work in the fields. Two decades later, it was not they but their progeny who were the targets of class rage: the orchestrated denunciations, the beatings administered in the name of revolutionary justice.

One of Lolam's victims, a slight man named Lee Yintam, stared at the ground most of the time while we talked. His story, replicated innumerable times in villages and towns, is, if anything, less horrendous than those of others singled out for attack. His survival and in a small way his economic triumph in the village today are what distinguish him. I searched him out one afternoon.

"Our family traces itself back a long way in this village," he began, sitting on a small stool in his own tiny factory. A glassless window frame allowed the wind to carry traces of freshly manured fields into the room. "My father was a landlord. He was labeled a landlord. We owned about ten mou, maybe a little more. There were a few other landlords. They owned about the same amount of land as we did. Here in Lolam the land was really very poor, so there were not any very rich people. We certainly weren't rich.

"Before liberation we lived on the other side of the valley. After that, we moved to this side and into a poorer house than before liberation. In the beginning, my father was criticized. Of course, in the beginning, criticism was much more civilized. They would just have political meetings and would criticize him there. There wasn't any violence. But in 1958, when the Great Leap came, my father was sent to labor camp. I was not yet old enough to know everything, so I didn't understand what my father did. He was just taken away. Then in 1971, my father came back. When he returned, he had bad intestinal problems that no one had treated. So he died in 1973. He was sixty-four. He never talked much about labor camp."

In China, as in other Communist societies, the political sins of the father are inevitably visited upon the son. And so Yintam was destined to suffer. "During the Cultural Revolution, I was criticized," he continued. "The reason I was criticized was that some people spread a rumor that I'd supposedly joined a counterrev-

113

olutionary organization. It was not true, but I was criticized anyway.

"I was beaten during the criticism meetings. Sometimes I was told to kneel and lower my head. I had to wear a sign that said, 'Counterrevolutionary.' In the beginning, the Wongsah commune sent a fellow who was head of the revolutionary mass organization, and he criticized many people. He was not even from this place. I was taken to Wongsah. There he beat me and forced me to say I was a member of a counterrevolutionary organization. Then I was brought back to Lolam to be criticized. I don't remember the exact date; it was long ago. But Lolam had to hold meetings to criticize me. The people here had to do it, but it was a little better than Wongsah." He uttered a thin laugh.

"There were only one or two others who were criticized in Lolam. They were accused of being part of the same counterrevolutionary organization. They were also the sons of landlords. In the early 1970s, the criticism stopped, and I went back to being a farmer."

Yintam tells his story with a certain reluctance, a hesitation universal in China when people are asked to describe what happened to them during the Cultural Revolution. For many of those who were its instigators, its enthusiasts, the events of those days are seen as mindless mistakes, the memory of which only provokes embarrassed silences. Many victims of that time prefer to forget the injustice, certain that what was taken from their lives cannot be recovered and convinced that the harshness of Chinese life does not allow for meaningful reparations. "Nobody wants to mention these things," Yintam said. "Nobody has apologized."

But the landlord's son has overcome the past, along with others in the village. As economic controls were eased, the political labels that once tarred or blessed one for life were abolished. "Because they got rid of class labels," Yintam said, "I can work. I can be a factory director. The situation is quite good now. I feel very relaxed. In a political sense, I don't have the burden of the past. I can now work as I wish."

Several years ago, Yintam and a few friends each invested one thousand yuan in a workshop to produce seals for wine and soy sauce bottles. They constructed a ramshackle building out of discarded lumber, bamboo, and mud blocks. Yintam scavenged tables and benches, purchased barrels of alcohol and other foul-smelling chemicals, and began operations. When he offered salaries of seventy-two yuan a month, a handsome wage in Lolam, he found no shortage of willing workers who, like Lee Seegay's work force, came to be made up mostly of women. The shop floor is poorly lighted and reeks of chemical and alcohol fumes. The workers sit on low, cramped benches, dipping gloved hands in vats of poison for eight hours a day. The technology is basic, the working conditions primitive. As I inhaled the vapors from the vats of chemicals, I thought that it could not have been very different from stepping back into the gloomy, odiferous workshops of early nineteenth-century England.

In the dissolution of the old economy, Chongwing, the party stalwart whose faith was lost, and Yintam, the victim who survived, are joined in a common effort to revive Lolam. From widely different viewpoints, from divergent backgrounds, they have responded to economic challenges in not dissimilar fashions. This suggests, at least in Lolam, the end of searching for universal truths set forth in distant political tracts in favor of a simpler reality: the need to subsist and the right to improve one's lot. As Low Cheunghing, the County Leader, told me one night, "In general, most people did not have enough to eat before 1979. Now, we're self-sufficient in food. A major problem has been solved."

To be sure, there are Communist Party members in Lolam, forty-nine in a village of two thousand, and five sit on the village committee, a body that from time to time functions a bit like the governing council of the town. The committee members, four men and one woman, meet on the second floor of the village granary, a barn-like stone building with massive, rough-hewn beams. In their meeting room, there are no political posters, no portraits of national party leaders, no slogans exhorting the toiling masses on to still greater efforts. A thick plank table fills the center of the room where the committee meets, when it meets, and on it there is a recent-vintage electric fan with translucent blue plastic blades. A telephone rests on a small table in the corner.

The committee members admitted quite forthrightly that the Communist Party has lost its allure; that villagers in Lolam have no real interest in the party or its doings. "There aren't any applications to join the party," acknowledged Lee Yinfuk, the thirty-five-year-old party secretary for Lolam, who took over when Lee Chongwing decided to go into the hardware business. "Frankly speaking, it's difficult getting party members. Most people are working. Women get married into other villages. I don't think anyone will join the party soon."

Not surprisingly, the party members of Lolam, like their fellow villagers, are not deeply reflective, either about their role in the village or their purpose as representatives of the party. In part, this is a natural reticence toward being completely candid with an outsider; not just a foreigner, but anyone who enters the valley, even from another village. Chan Lapfong, the elderly woman who moved from Wampo, alludes to the time it took for her to be accepted in the village, although she speaks more lightly of it now. But, beyond this, the Communist Party has lost in a very deep sense the credibility it had won through the years of the revolution and the years immediately after 1949.

Too many political campaigns and too many murders, persecutions, and abuses of village custom and tradition have soured rural Chinese on the old rallying calls, on the party that claims to have brought them a better life. Party leaders, especially those at higher levels in metropolitan offices or, even more distant, in Beijing, will publicly deny this, and deny it ferociously. No foreign observer will know what these leaders say among themselves about this patent and widespread disillusionment in the countryside, but there is virtually no place in the country where the party is esteemed. Certainly, the party's power, its ultimate control of government, is respected, but it is a conceded and most grudging respect, not one that is welcomed or enthusiastically granted.

In Lolam, the committee members hint at this by downplaying their work in the village. Indeed, in general, they suggest that the village does not really need them at all. Yinfuk paused between sentences to puff on a large bamboo pipe, a three-foot length of bamboo stalk about three inches in diameter with a small bowl for tobacco fixed to its side. "Sometimes higher authority passes documents down to us," he said, exhaling words and smoke in the same breath; "sometimes we pass things up to higher authorities." Passing the documents, which are the

116

blood in the veins of the Communist Party, is, he admits, not very time-consuming.

The single visible achievement of the village committee in recent years was to organize the construction of a small hydroelectric plant in an adjacent valley. The committee borrowed two hundred and thirteen thousand yuan from a bank in Wongsah. The plant consists of a cistern to catch water from a stream atop a hilly ridge. A single piece of four-foot diameter black pipe descends the hillside from the water tank to a compact turbine that produces between forty and sixty kilowatt-hours of electricity. Before the plant went into operation in 1986, Lolam had no electricity; now, blessed with constantly flowing mountain streams to keep the turbine spinning, the village has power twenty-four hours a day, with enough extra to sell some to the regional power grid.

Of the five committee members, only Yu Chenfong, the sole woman, does very much around the village. She never volunteered to talk about her work, and did so only when pressed. Frequently, she deferred to the men on the committee. Her work, not surprisingly, in this socially conservative village, is devoted to the problems of women and the family. As she speaks, the men on the committee fidget and shuffle their feet. They are distinctly uncomfortable talking about women and their role in the village or on the committee.

I asked Yu to give me an example of the kinds of disputes that crop up in the village. "Ah, there is this woman in the village," Yu replied, "who sometimes respects her mother-in-law and sometimes not. When this woman's in a bad mood, she will attack her mother-in-law and she will beat her children. One night about midnight, I was in bed and the husband and mother-in-law beat on my door and said [the woman] was arguing and fighting. So I got out of bed and went there and talked to her. The reason for the quarrel was that it was very late and the mother-in-law had her light on. The wife told her to shut it off, that they were wasting money. The mother-in-law said, 'Oh, it's not so much money.' The husband said they could turn it off. So there was a big argument; everyone was shouting. So I went over there and tried to talk to her. I said that the family needs unity, that we need to build up good relations among the family members and if you do that you will have wealth and good fortune.

117

This woman always listens to my words, so the next morning everything was all right."

Yu's job as family counselor was one she had before she joined the party, I learned. In fact, her willingness to mediate family fights, to help disengage battling in-laws, made her an attractive candidate for the village committee, which coveted someone who could actually do something concrete in its name. Yu's work, though, like that of other women in the village who poked their noses into their neighbors' affairs, is something the men did not want to dwell on. But it was Yu, and not the men, who spoke candidly about the changing complexion of the village.

"We're losing a lot of young men," she said. "A lot of young boys have left the village to work at other jobs. Some of them have gone into the bigger towns to work on construction projects where they can earn more money. Some have gone as far as Shenzhen to grow vegetables. Some boys are working in factories."

As Yu talked, Lee Yinsing, another committee member, butted in and described the committee's grand plans for the village, including a glass-fiber factory, a factory to make bottle caps, and expansion of the village's fruit production, particularly mandarin oranges, which fetch good prices from wholesalers at the free markets in nearby towns. He was sketchy about precisely what the committee's role would be, but, when pressed, he blurted out, "We will let the farmers do this for themselves but we will make the plan." For Lolam's farmers, though, Yinsing's remarks would be laughable. Since the farmers control the disposition of their own land and many are already intensively engaged in crop diversification, especially fruit-growing, there is not much the committee can contribute to their efforts.

Back at his house, outside the formal stiffness of the committee room, Yinsing was more effusive, more down-to-earth, less consumed by the need to present an official front. He wore a gray cotton singlet and gray cotton pants that he rolled up to his knees in a fashion seen throughout rural China. He is about sixty, he said, and is the village historian.

As he talked, he darted over to a corner and, from a dark crevice under a beam, he extracted a bundle of coarse blankets, which he laid on a low wooden table and unwrapped with great care. He lifted two old books from the moldy blankets, their yellowed pages bound with string, the traditional binding for classical texts. Turning the pages slowly, he paused to point to an illustrious name here, an ancestral locale there. In his hands, I realized, he held the sole written record of Lolam, of the Lees that made this place.

"One or two books were lost during the Cultural Revolution," he said, an unmistakable sadness creeping into his voice. "These, I hid in my house, in a hole in the ground." A worm hole in a corner of the documents attested to this. "These show that the Lees came from Zhejiang, during the Tang dynasty. It shows the five branches of the Lee clan: gold, wood, water, fire, and earth. We Lees are from the fire branch, the branch that settled in Hangzhou. In the Yuan, some Lees moved to this province." He rifled the papers until he reached a passage that seemed familiar to him, and paraphrased the cryptic classical language that was inked on the page in strong, black ideograms:

"The emperor sought men to wipe out bandits in Shaanxi Province. The emperor said, 'Whoever wipes out the bandits will become my son-in-law.' Two brothers did this; one became the emperor's son-in-law, the other became a general. These brothers had eight children. One of these children, the youngest son, was our forefather."

As with village records everywhere in China, what is told in the Lolam histories is a mixture of myth, folktales and lineage chronicles. What matters, though, is that these archives, these frail yet tangible records of a clan and region, survive. As I leafed through the pages, I saw, in a muted yet telling testimony, only chapter headings, numbered fifteen and sixteen, for the years after 1949. The pages for these chapters, for these years, were blank.

That Yinsing proudly, indeed reverently, displays these historical accounts underscores the resurgence of regard for the past as a font of values and wisdom. For three decades, Mao Zedong, the Communist Party he led, and the cultural vandals he inspired sought the systematic destruction of China's traditional heritage. To be sure, the misery in which the vast majority of Chinese peasants lived before 1949 was perpetuated in part by the successful exploitation of traditional cultural practices by rural elites, landlords, officials, regional warlords. Impoverishment and subjugation were justified, on occasions when they were ever questioned, as an integral feature of a social order dictated, for lack of a better phrase, by an imperial-Confucian hierarchy. At the same time, however, rural village life did express values and meaning through a welter of rituals, from devotion to local gods to homage to ancestors and the clan and superstitious and magical practices.

Communist political cadres working in the countryside, fueled by a grade-school Marxism and straightforward goals of social revolution, labored hard to persuade rural villagers of the uselessness of such beliefs, how the beliefs chained them to their poverty and backwardness. Fighting against unjust landlords was not enough; razing the cultural and ideological pillars of an oppressive, anachronistic system was essential. After achieving power, persuasion was less necessary. Decree, backed by the threat of force, was sufficient. During the Cultural Revolution, this assault on the past reached its apogee as political work teams of fervent Red Guards and their successors stormed through the countryside demolishing temples, smashing clan tablets, desecrating graves, melting down religious objects.

The intent was to efface millennia of accumulated tradition. It almost worked.

FOUR IDEOGRAMS—*"Lin zhi cheng xiang"*—are brushed in thick black strokes on a banner of now-fading red paper pasted above the door: "The unicorn's hooves augur auspiciousness." It is the house of Lee Waiwing, the village geomancer, Mr. Wind and Water.

Geomancy has deep roots in both classical Daoist philosophy and popular religious practice. The first known text of geomancy, or *fengshui,* dates from the fourth century, in which a man named Guo Pu discussed the most propitious locations for the graves of ancestors by balancing the cosmic forces of yin and yang as they appeared in the landscape. While geomancy never became a fixture within elite Confucian culture, it was widely practiced in rural areas—most schools of the art are named after provinces in the south—and, according to modern scholars, it was even used as a weapon by households or villages to thwart the luck of competitors.

Waiwing is eighty-one, and he approached me slowly, leaning

on a knobbed walking stick. His white hair was shaved close to his head and he had a wispy white beard that was more a handful of crinkled whiskers, and a faint mustache. His blue cotton shirt was unbuttoned, revealing a white singlet, which he wore tucked into gray cotton pants. His thin bony feet were clad in brown plastic sandals.

When Waiwing was a boy, another child, named Pu Yi, ruled China, at least nominally, as the last emperor of the Qing dynasty. Even as that dynasty disintegrated, Waiwing remembers, Lolam was untouched by the happenings in the distant northern capital. "At that time," he said, easing himself onto a four-legged wooden stool, "it was difficult to get enough grain to eat. We ate cassava and other things like wild vegetables. We also ate sweet potatoes, taro.

"I was born and raised here," Waiwing went on. "My generation is the seventeenth generation from this place. When I was eleven or twelve, my parents betrothed me to a young girl. She was from a village more than ten kilometers away, Boktou village. At that time, there were only two hundred families in the village here. I did go to school for two years. The folk teacher taught me.

"I was a farmer in the old days. I had no land. I farmed for others. I worked for the landlord Lee Jemcheung." Waiwing went on to have two sons by his bride from Boktou, and now, he said, he has two grandchildren. Then, he added, "I had four daughters. They are all married and moved out of the village."

In time, Waiwing began learning the mysteries of the wind and the water, *fengshui,* the system of knowledge that ascribes portents to dates, shapes, and geographic orientation. "The principal things I learned from others," Waiwing continued. "Other things, I learned them with my own eyes and from my own experiences." Like many Daoist and folk myths, fengshui's language and logic are elliptical and opaque, and this became evident as Waiwing sought to illumine his craft.

"According to the fengshui principle, the dragon ancestors are in Kunlun Mountain. That mountain covers 28,700 li. There are eight directions on the mountain, and there is a dragon on each direction. Five of the dragons are gone now, and three remain in China, and there are many branches, or passes, through which they exercise their power. You still feel the power

121

of the dragons. According to these branches, or paths, you have to determine what is good and what is not good. If you can see such things, then you can see where the dragon can exercise power over a place and whatever place the dragon has power over is good."

Nearly everyone in Lolam has come to visit Waiwing, to consult with this wizened man who smokes a thin reed-stemmed pipe: farmers seeking solace about future harvests, young couples hoping to fix a propitious nuptial moment, grieving relatives searching for an honorable and star-blessed site for a grave, a man who wishes to orient his new house so that fate will shine upon it.

"Yes, people who are getting married come to me," he said. "Young people ask which day is a good day to get married, which is the most fortuitous of days. Sometimes it's easy and sometimes it is difficult to determine. One has to determine these things by the lunar calendar. In these months, in this month of June, nobody gets married. June marks the half year, sundering the year in half. That is not a good sign. When there is lots of rain, it's not so good to build, to get married."

As the villagers of Lolam have begun to experience the first glimmers of improvement in their standard of living, Waiwing, rather than becoming obsolete in the invigorated economic climate, is even more in demand. "In recent years," he explained, "more and more people are building houses, so more and more people will come to see me. That is the most difficult problem, finding a suitable place to build a house."

At the root of the problem, as Waiwing sees it, is Lolam's mediocre positioning within the delicate latticework of good fortune and ill. "The fengshui in Lolam is only so-so, *yut bun,*" he said. With his long fingernail, he traces the river in the Lolam Valley on the rough board table. "The natural conditions are all right. But the stream is not straight all the way. There are many zigzags, and that is not good. Nine zigzags are best, but there are more. Also, there are too many hills and mountains and they are too steep. There are too many sharp points, too many sharp angles."

WHAT STRUCK ME, in Lolam, was the prevalence of multigenerational families living under one roof. The household of Lee

Seegay, whose newly found wealth distinguishes him substantially from his neighbors, is an almost idealized representation of how a Chinese family should live. Under his roof, in the thirty-eight rooms that stretch along the face of the carefully whitewashed two-story cement structure, live two dozen people. His mother, Lai Wahfong, the matriarch of the family, a tiny woman with jet black hair cut in a severe pageboy style and hands roughened by a life of hard work, supervises the house, which in practice means bossing around four daughters-in-law. Her four sons, each with his own living area within the house, and their wives and fifteen children, form a three-generation extended family of the sort that historically has symbolized the core of Chinese society.

The earliest philosophical texts speak poignantly of the centrality of the family within society. One of these, the *Daxue*, or Great Learning, instructs: "The ancients who wished to manifest their clear character to the world would first bring order to their states. Those who wished to bring order to their states would first regulate their families. Those who wished to regulate their families would first cultivate their person. Those who wished to cultivate their person would first rectify their mind."

This commitment and devotion to the family, at least to the formalized notion of the family, was attacked relentlessly during the Cultural Revolution as perpetuating elements of a discredited, feudal society. What was important, the Chinese were told by their political instructors, was a blind and fervent devotion to the great man, Mao Zedong, and a dedication to the greater good of the masses. In Lolam, and in countless other villages in China's countryside, the most visible evidence of this attack on the traditional belief in the family was the widespread and almost total destruction of the shrines where ancestors were honored, so-called clan halls. While many family homes, no matter how poor, had simple shrines, in strong lineage villages there were large clan halls. In Lolam there were four clan halls for different segments of the Lee clan.

Lee Waiwing, Mr. Wind and Water, remembers the day the principal clan hall in Lolam was wrecked. "It was just a simple place," he recalled, "where people put incense. The day they tore it down, I remember, I was at home. Nobody would talk about it, nobody would say anything. Everyone felt bad. But you couldn't do anything. It was not up to us. Such things are in the memory of the ancestors."

Today, Lee Seegay, as the village patron, is righting this wrong. Next to where he lives, down the bank of the slight rise on which he built his home, is an old stone and brick hall from the early part of this century, which once was the home of the village's largest landowner and some of his workers. Inside the entry area, a platform across from the main door used to be crowded with wood and stone plaques, memorials to the landlord's family. On this platform Seegay has erected a simple altar, a place to burn incense framed with two paper scrolls. In the warren of rooms that stretch to the left and right of the main hall, Seegay's more distant relatives live, not as lavishly as his family on the hill, but in a private spaciousness impossible were it not for his largesse. Seegay, whose grandparents tilled land for the old landlord, was born in this building, in a tiny room perhaps fifteen feet by ten, in which at one time his parents and their four sons lived.

Seegay's quiet rise, his aura of influence over Lolam, has been viewed with pleasure by his widowed mother. The past decade has finally brought her some comfort in the waning years of her life, comfort that the promises of socialism did not. "This village was very poor, very poor," she said. "There was not enough to wear, not enough to eat, and not enough to farm. We had to take grass and fir branches out to sell in the market; not many people wanted to buy it. We grew cassava and rice. People lived in low, mud-block houses. Rich people had very high halls, very tall houses. Now, if you are capable enough, you build very high. If you don't have the ability, you build very low. To live in a big house is good. Now we have so many rooms and so many kitchens. We really like having everyone together. It's one thousand times better than the past."

Lolam, she says in much the way any mother praises her son, has changed because of Seegay. "People say since Lee Seegay has run the factory, their lives have improved. If the factory was not run well, people would not get paid and get enough to eat. I encouraged him to run the factory. He's the eldest and he's just taken the responsibility. There's very little red-eye disease [jealousy]—the majority of people respect Seegay's ability. He gives work at the factory. At the festivals, he gives out pork."

Giving jobs, making loans, building roads, dispensing charity —all these acts, in one form or the other, are those of the prerevolutionary village heads, often the large landowner. In Lolam, Seegay's adoption of this role, made possible only by the dramatic shift in national economic policy to stress economic achievement, has made him far more important to the life of the community than are the institutions of the state, the Communist Party and its representatives. In a sense, Seegay's stature and activities mirror those of a more traditional time. At the same time, however, memories of the recent past and the knowledge that the clouds of political cataclysm could form again and wash away what has been accomplished, ensure that the worst exploitative practices of the past will not recur and that the benefits of the present are, roughly, shared in by everyone in Lolam.

For the first time in the village's history, signs of wealth are appearing: new brick houses, with soaring entry halls in the fashion of the village's prerevolutionary rich, are springing up all along the valley. Electricity and the appliances that use it are now permanent fixtures. Lee Seegay boasts Lolam's only videocassette recorder, on which he shows movies throughout the day for children who wander by and for villagers who come to visit. There are a few refrigerators in the village and a cold beer can be had at a shop across the path from the village committee offices.

In its response to these changes, Lolam has also drawn on familiar, remembered, or imagined traditions to give meaning and form to the village's resurrection. No longer is burial shameful; now the village's dead are entombed in dignity, with formal gravestones, as the dead were buried before the revolution. The local village god—*toh day bak gong,* the earth uncle—is venerated at a roadside shrine with incense and flowers. The Lee name, through the rebuilt clan hall, is honored. And a new Lee is ascendant, with the burdens and duties expected of the village's patron.

Lolam's experience can be found in villages throughout the Chinese countryside. To be sure, in rural areas closer to the coast, where commerce is vigorous, where change is more swift, there is less reliance on the comfortable and reassuring patterns of the past; economic resurrection is given meaning in other ways, often through the crude displays of wealth. But for the most part rural China has prospered in the last decade. China's farmers, China's villagers, are living their own lives and building their own futures.

SIX

Catching Mice

ON A BRILLIANTLY SUNNY Sunday afternoon in September 1988, a compact man in a gray suit strolled into Zhongnanhai, the park-like wing of the Forbidden City where China's most senior leaders now live and work—what is sarcastically refered to these days as the New Forbidden City by many Chinese. The man, Qi Wenzeng, made his way through a series of open esplanades until he reached the courtyard used by the State Council, the executive cabinet of the Chinese government.

There, in the sanctum sanctorum of Chinese communism, Qi proceeded to peddle shares of stock in the Gold Cup Automobile Company.

The moment of this occasion was noted by no less than the *People's Daily,* the official mouthpiece of the party, in a front-page article. "At 3 P.M.," the paper reported, "many people were huddled in the State Council courtyard trying to buy something new to them—stocks." There ensued, perhaps not unlike the vigorous exchanges in that arboreal setting in which the New York Stock Exchange was born, a frenetic scramble. "I want to buy five hundred yuan of stock," yelled someone. "I want two hundred," hollered another. By 5 P.M., the paper noted, "thirty thousand yuan of the stocks were sold. And for the first time, twenty-five staff members from the State Council became stock-holders."

It took a full five days before the implications of this capitalist intrusion struck home. Then, again on the front page, the *People's Daily* announced, under a headline reading "Important Correction," that "an investigation proves that no enterprise has ever been allowed to sell stocks at the State Council court-yard in Zhongnanhai, nor have any officials or staff members purchased any stocks there."

I called the offices of the *People's Daily* to see if I could sort out the conflicting accounts, but I was told that the reporter of the original article, as expected, was unavailable. I asked the anony-mous voice at the other end of the telephone line about the appearance of the correction. He informed me that "every-thing" on the front page of the newspaper was true. Well, I asked the voice, what about the original article five days earlier? "Any-thing on the front page is true," the voice replied, and hung up.

IT TURNED OUT, of course, that Qi Wenzeng had been invited into the State Council courtyard and did sell his stocks to eager government workers. The denial of Qi's activity by the *People's Daily,* and, by extension, the upper reaches of the Communist Party itself, suggests several things. First, the nonchalance of the original article implied that, at minimum, there was nothing abnormal about selling stocks to the staff of the State Council. After all, the central government had encouraged some tiny experiments with a stock market in places like Shanghai. Sec-ond, the placement of the article about Qi Wenzeng on the front page appeared to indicate that the party itself approved of this capitalist device. Third, the delay between the article and the correction meant that there was not inconsiderable discussion over what both the article and, more important, the phenome-non of Qi's salesmanship meant. But, finally, the correction itself clearly signaled both disapproval of a Communist paper extolling the virtues of capitalism and a generalized discomfort over capitalist methods themselves.

In the State Council courtyard that sun-drenched Sunday, the contradictions of China's reformist policies etched themselves as sharply as the shadows of the bronze-green cypress trees that line the winding paths of the former imperial compound. Desperate to revitalize the country's economy, during the 1980s China's leaders adopted great chunks of what is generally thought of as capitalism. Yet these leaders regularly, and with great fervor, disavow that characterization.

Again and again, the party insists that giving farmers their own land is not capitalism. Allowing farmers to sell their produce on free markets is not capitalism. Permitting innovative entrepreneurs to establish and run their own factories is not capitalism. Allowing stock markets is not capitalism. So much, indeed, is deemed not to be capitalism that in China it was often unclear what the words socialism and capitalism meant. Selling stock certificates in Zhongnanhai, for five days evidently not a capitalist exercise, turned out to be one after all.

This confusion permeates China's formal economic and political ideology. For the leadership at least, it matters whether things are draped in the red bunting of socialism. Free markets are not, in the argot of China's leaders, capitalist phenomena, but rather simply a feature of "commodity socialism." For someone who manufactures porcelain teacups in his own factory, the distinction is not only meaningless, it is irrelevant. What does matter to the private manufacturer, businessman, or trader is that the economic climate of the 1980s encouraged money-making without worrying too much about watching the political barometer in Beijing.

For much of the decade, China's leaders were exceedingly vague about what was economically permissible and what was not. Because China has only the sketchiest canon of laws, and because commercial and civil law for all practical purposes do not exist, determining what was acceptable and what was not became increasingly difficult. A melange of pronouncements from the leadership, laws and regulations promulgated by state bodies, and simple habitual practices formed the contours of legitimate economic activity. Even so, the habits of one region of China are not those of another. In Zhejiang, private banks are a way of life. In Beijing and surrounding Hebei Province, such a notion is unthinkable.

No less a figure than Deng Xiaoping has wrestled repeatedly

with this problem. "The socialist economy," Deng told a group of party theoreticians in 1979, "is based on public ownership, and socialist production is designed to meet the material and cultural needs of the people to the maximum extent possible, not exploit them. These characteristics of the socialist system make it possible for the people of our country to share common political, economic, and social ideals and moral standards. All this can never happen in a capitalist society."

Five years later, in a meeting with a group of visiting Japanese, Deng had become much vaguer in his interpretation, offering a new description of socialism that reveals the dilemmas faced by officials actually charged with devising the country's economic policies. "Some people ask why we chose socialism. We answer that we had to, because capitalism would get China nowhere." And what, Deng asked rhetorically, is socialism? "By Marxism we mean Marxism that is integrated with Chinese conditions, and by socialism we mean socialism that is tailored to Chinese conditions and has Chinese characteristics." Indeed, he explained, socialism's "superiority is demonstrated by faster and greater development of the productive forces than under the capitalist system," and socialism would "improve the people's material and cultural life." That approach has thrown open the doors, at least in the minds of many Chinese, to a belief that anything that works economically and enriches them is acceptable.

It was impossible to go anywhere in China during the last decade and not see evidence of this permissiveness. Until 1988, for example, the law of the land dictated that a privately owned factory could employ no more than eight workers. Employing more workers than that was prohibited on the murky contention that enterprises with more than eight employees constituted capitalism. The law was observed far more in the breach than in the observance. Indeed, in 1987, a government survey estimated there were two hundred and twenty-five thousand private factories with more than eight employees. Finally, in 1988, when it became apparent that such an artificial prohibition made no sense and, perhaps more important, that it was unenforceable, it was abandoned. Even the government-controlled New China News Agency, in one of its regular reports on the process of economic reform, resorted to words like "outstanding" to describe Liu Xigui, a former farmer from Liaoning Province who runs a transportation company with two hundred and forty employees and assets of 5.2 million yuan.

ONE DID NOT have to look far to find evidence of determined individual initiative, examples of gritty entrepreneurialism. One icy February, I read a spate of articles in several national Chinese newspapers about a woman in the northeastern city of Benxi who was single-handedly changing the way business was done there. Her name was Guan Guangmei. Headlines in papers across the country read, "Benxi Produces a Guan Guangmei!" (paraphrasing with transparent irony a line from an old Cultural Revolution song, "China produces a Mao Zedong") and "Inside the Guan Guangmei Phenomenon." What Guan had done was to lease most of the failing retail shops and groceries in the city and run them profitably, indeed a phenomenon in China. But there was also, as some of these newspapers noted, a strong undercurrent of criticism of this woman for embracing the ways of capitalism. After a few days of reading these articles, I was on the telephone to arrange a visit to Benxi, because it was clearly an issue of growing national concern and, equally important, it was, in this land of deep discrimination against women, a woman who was creating such a stir.

Because Chinese officialdom possesses a hummingbird's sensitivity to political currents as well as a deep-seated suspicion of and distaste for foreign journalists, my request to meet Guan Guangmei was received coolly by the authorities in Liaoning Province. I learned later that they were also unsure whether the distant drumbeat of criticism signaled Guan's impending ostracism. After some jousting over the telephone with the provincial officials, I was granted permission to travel to Benxi to see her. Ironically, attempts by an American diplomat in the provincial capital of Shenyang and by other journalists in Beijing to follow in my footsteps would be stymied by the same provincial authorities.

The train from Shenyang was poorly heated and rattled along at an agonizingly slow pace, managing the forty-five-mile run to Benxi in two hours. Benxi is a dirty, ugly place, a city of gray streets and buildings swathed in a perennial haze of smoke, ash, and dust, home to 1.4 million people. On the streets of Benxi, there was a scattering of cars, a few more trucks, and waves of the ubiquitous bicycles. It is a city that no one in China would have paid any attention to were it not for this woman, Guan Guangmei.

Driving through the city, I wondered about the aesthetic sensibilities of the people reared there, where every street assaulted the eyes. We pulled up in front of a large department store, and my handler from the provincial government escorted me to the reception room, a universal feature of all Chinese institutions.

Guan Guangmei beamed as we entered the room. She is a stocky woman with a hair-trigger smile, who favors men's gray business suits worn over more feminine embroidered flowery shirts. Her handshake was firm, authoritative; the grasp of a woman who is certain of herself and her work. She met me at the door to a reception room lined with cranberry-colored stuffed armchairs, down the hall from her office on the top floor of her six-story Dongming, or Eastern Brightness, Market. As we sank into the chairs, she introduced her right-hand man, Li Ming, a thirty-five-year-old former official in the city's Communist Party organization, whom she had craftily wooed to work for her.

Even before the customary cup of tea could be poured, Guan started lambasting her critics, some of whom had peppered newspapers with derogatory comments. The *Economic Daily*, a national newspaper that follows the progress of economic reform with reasonable care and even some objectivity, had described a wellspring of hostility toward her, principally from members of the Communist Party who felt that she was somehow undermining China's socialist edifice. Not coincidentally, the decibel level of this criticism increased sharply during a particularly vicious political campaign in early 1987 that was directed at advocates of broader rights of free expression.

"The leasing system of Guan Guangmei takes advantage of the situation to benefit herself. It has the character of exploitation," an anonymous critic declared in the *Economic Daily*. Another party member accused Guan of "playing down the role of political education." One inventive party member charged Guan with "disliking the supervision of the party," and then, for good measure, denounced her for "being good at dancing," in his mind evidently the sin of sins.

China's press is controlled to such an extent that publication of this sort of criticism generally, although not always, reflects emerging official sentiment. In times of political volatility and uncertainty, such as prevailed during the first half of 1987, I found that even the most confident of people trod more cautiously.

"Ah, these people," Guan said, shaking her head in mock weariness. "They're not used to these things so they oppose us. The people who aren't used to this are used to a sort of vague administration from above. They're used to getting paid whether they work or not, so they disagree. They think socialism means everyone should have rice to eat whether they work or not. This is a real problem. Of course I'm upset about this sort of thing. I thought I was doing the right thing. Everything I've done here is to make the reforms a success, to help make the country rich. Some people say I don't accept the party's leadership because I'm both the party secretary and the general manager. Well, my feeling is that if we follow the party line, that's following the party's leadership."

Guan offered to show me what she had done that had roused such passion. We walked down the store's back staircase to the first floor, where housewives with plastic mesh baskets maneuvered from counter to counter. Unlike most state stores, the Dongming was scrubbed clean, its old white tile counters practically sparkling. The store's salespeople wore the conventional white doctor's coats and white cotton bag hats, but their uniforms were, unlike those of workers in state stores, freshly laundered. The counters were piled with supplies: bottles of soy sauce, bags of peanuts, packages of sunflower seed, stacks of bananas, canned tomatoes and canned conch, jars of bamboo shoots and jars of peaches. At one counter more than eighty kinds of cigarettes were for sale, including the difficult to obtain Panda cigarettes, the brand favored by Deng Xiaoping.

I asked Guan what she had done to change the old ways of doing business. Two years ago, when she arrived at Dongming, she said, she turned the place upside down. She got rid of all the old managers, drastically reduced the widespread waste that was typical of the previous managers, reorganized the entire inventory system, instituted a rigorous system to evaluate the performance of her sales personnel, and, most important, raised wages through a work incentive program. "The previous leaders were no good, so I demoted them and made them workers," she said, a sharpness coming into her voice. Among the store's staff, her toughness initially provoked resistance. Guan's new system of fines for bad work and rewards for performance were unfamiliar and demanded a radical change in employees' work habits.

Jiang Xiu'e was one of the clerks whose behavior at Dongming had been notorious, her nasty tongue and manners affronting even the most hard-shelled shoppers. Guan proved less tolerant. "She told me that if I didn't change my behavior I would be heavily penalized," Jiang said. "Well, I didn't believe her at all." Jiang continued to harangue and argue with customers, but, one day, after a particularly raucous exchange with a customer, Guan slashed twenty yuan from Jiang's salary, a full 25 percent of her monthly wage. Jiang said she was astonished at Guan's action— nothing like this had ever been known to happen before. She realized then that Guan meant business. She began to mend her ways, if not because her mood changed, at least to recover her docked salary. "From that very day," Jiang said, "I began to be more cautious with customers. Finally, I began to see that customers were actually reasonable. It's strange, isn't it? Now I get the highest monthly bonus of the two hundred and twenty workers in the store."

Guan talked about her upbringing after we returned to the reception room. She was born in 1950 in a village outside Benxi, into a family of farmers. She managed to graduate from middle school during the opening years of the Cultural Revolution, and was put in charge of a production brigade of three hundred and forty workers, in part because she mouthed the expected polemics, but more, she told me, because the leaders of the commune were confident that she could get things done, even at the young age of eighteen. Three years later, she was reassigned to the pork counter at a store in Benxi, where she spent her days slicing and wrapping meat. Two and half years after that she was made a department manager. In the years that followed she moved progressively up the management ladder, receiving promotions she felt meant nothing.

"Even if you had the talent, you couldn't really do well," she explained, "because you weren't given any real power. Even as a deputy store manager, I couldn't do anything because nobody would listen to me. The leaders had no power because we had no real responsibility. This store was losing money every year. I had thought about these problems for many years. I wanted to make the store more successful but I couldn't. In 1984, the country introduced the contract system. So I bid to lease this store and the commercial administration bureau chose me. In one year, we went over the total target for three years. This is reform. I have the power to run this enterprise."

Under Guan's administration, sales increased by nearly 50 percent and profits nearly doubled in the first year. "In the past, outside leaders set the policy. While I am running the store, the manager has full power. In the past, everybody got the same wages, no matter how much they worked. Now, the more you work, the more you get. Salaries are now based on how much you sell. I have a worker here who earns two hundred and thirty yuan a month just selling cabbages"—a salary more than double the wage of the average industrial worker. "I believe if you get a system of incentives going you can save any store. This store became a success, so I started looking at other losing enterprises." Eventually, she signed leases for eight of the city's largest food stores, all of which had been running at huge losses. When I talked to Guan, they were all making money.

A shrewd businesswoman, Guan realized that her own success, most conspicuously an annual salary approaching twenty-two thousand yuan—fifty times what Deng Xiaoping himself earns—made her vulnerable to potential political attacks despite the overt support of the city government. As a good Communist and a better politician, Guan began canvasing the city's party apparatus for political allies. In 1985, she happened upon Li Ming, who was running the local Communist Party's political research bureau. Li, it turned out, was an outspoken proponent of the country's economic reforms and a sideline cheerleader for Guan herself. It did not take much persuasion to lure him from his desk at party headquarters and the ethereal realms of theory to the concrete reality of Benxi's streets.

Li told me why he teamed up with Guan. "I had seen what happened in the countryside, where there was so much progress. I figured that if we followed the Guan Guangmei model, our commercial sector would progress as well. I really believe this is the way to promote reform. I wrote a report to the city leaders explaining this, saying that this was what we should be doing, and the city leaders reaffirmed their support for her. I was interested in going to an enterprise and experimenting in a real environment. This was a way for me to be closer to real life. This is important for theorists to do. You know, in my old job I made one hundred and fourteen yuan a month as a department chief. Here I make two hundred yuan a month and, at the end of the year, Guan and I split the profits. Some people say I left my old job for the money, but they don't understand me."

He leaned over and told me a story. "One day, my old grade school teacher, a man named Wang, came into the store. He saw me and hobbled up to me and grabbed both my hands. He shook my hands so hard. And then he said to me, 'Little Li, what you are doing is right. A lot of people are opposed to you, but what you are doing is right.' "

The sotto voce campaign against Guan dissipated toward the end of the summer of 1987, especially after she was named a national model worker and had the May First Labor Award conferred upon her. Then, as if to drive a final nail in the coffin of her critics, she was named a delegate to the Thirteenth Communist Party Congress, held that fall. At that congress, in a blaze of television lights, Guan was presented to the press and the Chinese nation as a vibrant representative of the new spirit of urban reform. And more: this woman who had introduced management techniques that would be familiar to any American MBA was presented as a good Communist.

THE CLASH between China's formal insistence that it hewed unerringly to a socialist course and its evident embrace of many aspects of capitalism reached its symbolic climax in the autumn of 1986 when a gleaming Red Flag limousine bore John J. Phelan, Jr., the chairman of the New York Stock Exchange, to the Great Hall of the People. A procession of the boxy, coal-black vehicles, handmade automobiles once reserved for the likes of Mao Zedong and Deng Xiaoping, carried Phelan and a bevy of investment bankers and corporate lawyers to a symposium on American financial markets for China's senior bankers, economists, and policy advisers. As he got out of his car, Phelan could look across the street to the vast expanse of Tiananmen Square, on which squatted the columned mausoleum of the man who

denounced capitalism for "repressing the demands of the proletariat": Mao Zedong.

For those Chinese who attended Phelan's seminars, there was
no quibbling over the political complexion of the week's proceedings, no sense that welcoming some of the leading practitioners of advanced capitalism into the Great Hall of the People
smacked of ideological apostasy. Liu Hongru, a well-groomed
man who once studied in Moscow and who was deputy governor
of the People's Bank of China (roughly the equivalent of the
Federal Reserve Bank) told a group of us journalists that there
were no mysteries to the gathering. "We have to find our way
slowly, as the Chinese saying goes, by touching the stones at the
bottom of the river. To open up our financial markets is one of
the big efforts in our restructuring, but at the moment the number of securities in China is very few and we lack experience in
operating financial markets. Therefore we should aim at steady
development."

On the fingers of his left hand, Liu ticked off the changes he
foresaw for China in the coming years, including the introduction of things like stock and bond markets, currency markets, the
creation of different types of commercial paper, and short-term
notes. China's banking system also needed to be reorganized so
that it more closely resembled the central bank structure used in
the United States. "We have to experiment," said Liu. "At the
moment there are no laws governing the issuance of stocks or
bonds."

A good deal of the discussion, particularly of the more arcane
features of equity markets, appeared to whiz over the heads of
the Chinese participants. In some cases, the simultaneous trans-
lators simply buckled when pressed to translate phrases such as
"swap mechanics" and "zero coupon bonds," terms of the financial art alien to the Chinese language as it is now spoken on
the mainland. The Chinese bankers scribbled furiously, though,
intent on mastering the system that had transformed not just the
United States, but more important, the neighboring countries of
Asia—South Korea, Taiwan, Singapore, Hong Kong—into economic dynamos.

Only two years later, more than six thousand companies had
been accorded the right to issue stocks, and rudimentary markets existed in cities like Shanghai, Guangzhou, and Shenyang.

A dozen large state-owned companies had likewise issued more than two hundred million yuan in stocks by the fall of 1988. And the newspaper *Economic Information,* noting that, in the past, shareholding had been described as "a purely capitalist practice," said that the current mood had changed and the growth of securities markets were "an important measure to deepen current reforms." However, the privatization of state-owned enterprises through selling shares, akin to the privatization policies pursued by Margaret Thatcher, did not become a centerpiece of Chinese economic policy.

Experimentation at the national level during the past decade inevitably carried with it the risk of censure and setback. As a result, experimentation, like the creation of stock markets, has been limited. Reforming China's agricultural base was never conceived of as experimental; it was, from the beginning, a policy to which the leadership, by and large, was wedded. Similarly, reforming management practices in industry and permitting free markets for food products and an array of consumer goods were seen as part and parcel of the plan to revitalize the economy.

Going much further—completely deregulating all prices, selling off the country's industries to private stockholders, marketing land—these steps would bring substantial political risks. These measures would so fundamentally alter the Chinese economic landscape that no definition of socialism, no matter how flexible, could rationalize their existence. While it is foolhardy to attempt to predict Chinese policies, given the country's political instability and erratic policy shifts, it seems unlikely, as China approaches the next century, that it will abandon its instinctual trust in economic planning and central controls.

NONETHELESS, like a stubborn and growing lichen, features of capitalism eschewed at the national level are taking root and expanding down the coast and throughout Guangdong Province in the south. Mao's original idea for economic development envisaged a fairly even distribution of industry across the country. In his view, the prerevolutionary pattern of development had favored coastal cities at the expense of the hinterland. He was right; interior provinces were indeed sinkholes of poverty and underdevelopment. Mao therefore ordered factories established in all of China's provinces, regardless of rail and road links, access to raw materials or markets.

One result of this policy is that all but three of China's provinces produce automobiles or trucks. They do so in wildly different fashions, some relatively well and efficiently. Others produce what amount to hand-built vehicles at staggering cost. By the late 1970s, Deng Xiaoping and his colleagues realized that this policy made no sense. Zhao Ziyang crystallized this thinking into a schema that became known as the coastal development plan. Zhao argued that development should be accelerated along China's coast, since it is the natural contact point with the outside world, and its cities possessed more trained people than those of the interior provinces. The benefits of coastal economic expansion, Zhao concluded, would eventually seep inland. In fact, his idea, much ballyhooed in the press at the time, merely reflected the existing reality. China's coast was developing and it was doing so far faster and in a much more sophisticated fashion than inland provinces. What it was doing was becoming capitalist.

One scorching day in July 1988, I set out with Stefan Simons, the correspondent from *Der Spiegel,* down China's coast from the city of Hangzhou to sample the mood of the region. It was apparent from Chinese newspaper accounts that many areas along the coast were experiencing explosive growth, with scant regard for directives or injunctions from Beijing. This sense of independence had spawned thousands of new industries, virtually all privately owned and operated. New ways of raising money, purchasing raw materials, distributing products were being created. Trade with Taiwan, illegal in Taiwan and regulated in China, was mushrooming.

Along with this freewheeling economic activity, though, some of the side effects of capitalism, some of the social consequences of nascent affluence, were settling in along the coast. Prostitution, the scourge of cities like Tianjin, Shanghai, and Guangzhou before 1949 and effaced from the mainland by China's new Communist rulers, was once again proliferating. Similarly, homosexuality, pornography, and drug use, all banned in the climate of socialist puritanism, were said to be reappearing with a new and unrestrained vigor. And smuggling, for centuries a way of life in villages and towns along the coast, was resurgent;

gun battles between smugglers and the police were even occurring from time to time. It was, to read the Chinese press, as if the
Wild West had taken root in southeast China.

One way of tapping the pulse of the coast is through its taxi
drivers. Elsewhere in China, particularly in the north and in
inland areas, my attempts to persuade a taxi driver to leave a
city's limits usually deteriorated into a contest of wills and vocal
cords; since most taxi drivers are paid whether they drive or not,
ferrying passengers long distances is seen as more trouble than
it's worth, even if a healthy tip is added to the fare. But as we
moved south along the coast from city to city, we found no
shortage of taxi drivers willing to spend fourteen hours jousting
with tractors and trucks on narrow, winding roads. It was, I
learned, simply a matter of bargaining over the price. And, also
unlike northern China—Beijing, for instance, where road travel
by foreigners is closely monitored—there were no police check-
points along the coastal roads south of the Yangtze River.

We were headed for Wenzhou, an enclave of brash, vibrant,
unalloyed capitalism where the rules that applied elsewhere in
China were ignored or conveniently forgotten. There is no easy
way to get to Wenzhou. It has no rail links with the outside world
and there is no airport. A rattletrap steamer from Shanghai
trundles down the coast, making port in Wenzhou twenty-four
hours later. So a car seemed to be the easiest way.

China's road system is woefully inadequate; there are too few
roads for too much traffic. Because the rail system is so overbur-
dened, hundreds of thousands of small buses, most privately
owned, ply intercity roads at breakneck speeds. They fight for
room with long-distance buses and the endless stream of over-
loaded trucks that clog two-lane roads in every province. It is
impossible to travel more than a few dozen kilometers without
seeing a truck crumpled around a tree trunk or a minibus nose
down in a paddy field, skid marks tracing its trajectory from the
macadam surface above. Unlike roads in Africa, there are surprisingly few potholes. Road crews can be seen everywhere,
pounding down shoulders, painting lines occasionally, widening
roadbeds. In Beijing, there is an acute awareness that China's
current transportation system cannot support continued economic development; that it has become increasingly difficult to
move newly mined coal, harvested rice, or freshly manufactured

refrigerators. As a result, national and provincial investment in the transportation network has risen steadily.

Highway 104, the asphalt strip that runs from Hangzhou to Wenzhou, is typical of the roads in rural China. Just wide enough to permit two trucks to pass slowly, it weaves through paddy fields and into mountains, coursing through villages and towns; it is the commercial lifeline for eastern Zhejiang Province. Farmers with chugging two-wheel tractors hauling wagons of red-clay bricks creep down the edge of the road, forcing buses and cars to swerve toward oncoming traffic to pass. In patches along the road, farmers have spread their unwinnowed rice in pale amber coverlets to dry in the sun, again forcing drivers to dodge down the middle of the road. Our taxi driver maneuvered through the traffic and around the rice with a disdainful aplomb.

The driver, a tough-looking character with no evident fondness for razors or combs, had agreed to drive to Wenzhou for five hundred yuan. He said that he owned his own car, like many of the drivers in the region. "You have to pay anywhere between thirty thousand and sixty thousand yuan for a used car. But you make five thousand yuan a month. So you can usually make back your investment in the first year. It's not easy, though. You have to bribe the local tax officials not to bother you. I gave him a color television this year. As far as the police are concerned— well, every taxi driver has a friend at the police. You just go to dinner with them and you don't have any problems."

Along the road, there was ample evidence of Zhejiang's new-found affluence. New houses, two and three stories tall, of heavy stone with gray pantile roofs and turned-up eaves, sprouted from paddy fields. Gigantic bone-white semicircular stone tombs, so-called armchair tombs, were scattered like confetti on hillsides. Burial, forbidden to urban residents (where cremation is required) and disapproved of for rural folk, has reappeared as an important feature of life in much of southern China. People are spending thousands upon thousands of yuan building these memorial graves to their parents, both out of respect for the dead and as an ostentatious display of wealth.

We arrived in Wenzhou well past seven o'clock in the evening, when most Chinese cities are slowing down for the night. But Wenzhou, a city of five hundred and forty thousand people with another six million in the surrounding countryside and neighboring towns, seemed to be rousing itself. Under the spreading plane trees that line the town's main avenues, dozens upon dozens of sidewalk restaurateurs unfolded aluminum tables and portable stoves. They stacked towers of bamboo steamers crammed with meat dumplings, *jiaozi* and *xiaolongbao,* over pans of simmering water, or they whirled noodles around the inside of sizzling woks. Service started after nine o'clock, and customers would plop onto small folding stools and order a few baskets of dumplings or a plate of fried noodles. The night air was tinged with the aromas of soy sauce and rice wine. Young couples in T-shirts imprinted garishly with slogans like "Fashion Club Time," "O.K.," and "Blue Ocean" strolled hand in hand past the steaming tables.

In front of doorways to weathered plank-sided houses, older men and women reclined in deep wicker chairs, fanning themselves with heart-shaped bamboo-leaf fans and watching the street scene before them. Here and there, people would douse themselves with water from a plastic basin, a Wenzhou sidewalk shower, while large portable tape players pumped out the latest love song by Theresa Teng, a Taiwanese rock 'n' roll heartthrob. On the ring road around the town center, hundreds of stalls in an open air market teemed with customers searching for the latest fashions from Hong Kong and Taiwan. Sidewalk video games, simple color televisions linked to joystick boxes on top of folding tables, were crowded by young boys struggling for a chance to shoot down electroluminescent fighter planes. A cluster of fortune-tellers flipped over cards and muttered blandishments to superstitious customers. A man in a gray shirt walked past trailing a white horse on a frayed rope.

Wenzhou was hopping. It was teeming with life. It was not unlike some boomtowns in Asia, Thailand, the Philippines, or Taiwan. What it did not resemble very much at all was China.

Private banks are illegal in China. So, as daylight filtered through the golden-green leaves of the city's abundant trees the next morning, we headed for the offices of the Wenzhou-Lucheng City Credit Cooperative, the first bank in Wenzhou not owned by the state and now the largest of the fifty-three privately run banks in Zhejiang Province. Wenzhou was becoming known for its bemused disregard of rules that seemed to apply to the rest of China, a reputation it appeared to revel in. An

142

official of the local foreign affairs office was effusive in his plaudits for the bank, and seemed eager to arrange a meeting with the bank's chairman, Yang Jiaxing.

The candy-cane striped awnings of the bank shaded the sidewalk and entranceway where Yang Jiaxing was waiting. Of medium height and thickly built, Yang carried himself with self-assurance and authority, despite the casual open-necked white shirt and khaki pants that imparted a more leisurely air to him. We walked up two flights of stairs to his office, where he introduced Cao Wenyuan, the bank's economist. Cao, who was attired in a crisp short-sleeved white shirt that hung loosely over neatly pressed black shorts, and blue gauze knee socks, looked, with his severely parted hair, more the banker, albeit a banker on holiday. Yang passed around small cans of mango juice imported from Hong Kong.

Yang explained how the bank came into being. "We're the first private bank to open in Wenzhou. Our first day of business was November 1, 1986. Since the early 1980s there have been a lot of small private businesses and factories opening up, but the state banks would not give any credit to them. The state banks simply would not open accounts for private enterprises. So we opened our cooperative. This has broken the monopoly of the state banks. They're no longer alone under heaven." Like many things in Wenzhou, the failings and obstructionism of state institutions tend to be seen less as impediments to development than opportunities to be exploited. And what the entrepreneurs of Wenzhou find remarkable is that the rest of China does not share their perspective.

Some of this independent verve stems from Wenzhou's geographical isolation. Excised from the rest of the province by a chain of rugged mountains, Wenzhou has cultivated a sense of righteousness and purpose about its economic autonomy. Indeed, because of its relatively cloistered existence, the people of Wenzhou speak a dialect of Chinese unintelligible to anyone not from the area. In the eighteenth and nineteenth centuries, when many of the city's trades were dominated by merchants and craftsmen from Ningbo, a town in northern Zhejiang, the resident Ningbo commercial elite complained regularly about their isolation from the rest of the province and from their hometown. Today, Wenzhou runs its own affairs, and has culled both energy and resolve from this distance.

As Yang Jiaxing talked, he conveyed this tenor of untroubled confidence. "I was an electrician for a street committee factory before," he continued. "During the Cultural Revolution, I just worked. I never took part in exchanging revolutionary experiences. I never took part in political struggles. Politics weren't for me. In fact, I opened up my own electrical factory." Not only was the idea of opening one's own factory during the Cultural Revolution virtually inconceivable, even mouthing such an intention constituted counterrevolutionary behavior. Yang chuckled, a low, growling rumble, as he reflected on the insanity of those years. "There was a market for switches and motors, so we went ahead."

Only in 1986, when private businessmen began complaining regularly about the state bank's refusal to extend them credit, did Yang and a group of friends, all involved in their own private ventures, begin to think seriously about organizing a private financial institution. Cao, one of the original trio of investors, described the terrain over which they were to march. "The problem is that we don't have laws in China to deal with private individuals in banking and finance. For private enterprise now, there's no problem. But there is nothing in the law for financial institutions. In fact, it's forbidden. So even though we're in the midst of these national reforms, we ourselves have no legal standing. But, in China, we have operated before there were laws, and in China, there are sometimes laws, but you don't have to follow them. You just go on working and later the laws are changed. Just look at China's constitution, how many times that has been changed. At this point there are two alternatives. One, the state could revoke our business license. But we don't think that will happen. Or two, Wenzhou city says, we must deepen the reform, go one step farther and stay in business. That's what we expect to do."

The three original investors managed to assemble three hundred and eighteen thousand yuan in capital to start operations. Two years later, the institution had more than sixty-three million yuan in deposits. "We account for one quarter of the profits of all fifty-three private banks in the province," boasted Yang. "We provide better service than any state bank and we work

144

harder." Unlike the bureaucratically hamstrung state banks, Yang's bank is geared for the needs of its customers: it is open seven days a week, and closes for only one day a year, the Chinese New Year. Also, unlike any state office or institution in the country, the bank does not close for lunch. "If we have money at noon," Cao said, "we want it out on the street by five o'clock."

Perhaps not a typical occurrence, but indicative of the bank's attitude, was its response to the desperation of the woman who manages the Guangxia Construction Materials Market in Wenzhou. At three o'clock one afternoon, she arrived at the bank with a ticket for the five o'clock boat to Shanghai in one hand and profound anxiety on her face. "She had just found out she was short of money," Yang recalled. "She needed twenty thousand yuan to purchase materials for her business. So we had her sit down, gave her some tea, and drew up a contract. While we did this we sent someone over to her business to look over her operation quickly. Our man came back and said that everything looked all right. She had her money in one hour and made the boat." Well, I asked Yang, could not this woman have done the same thing at a state bank? He guffawed. "No way. Even one week wouldn't be enough."

Of course, the services of the Wenzhou-Lucheng City Credit Cooperative do not come free. The interest on loans is higher than at state banks, but so is the interest paid on deposits. And the rates at the bank, Yang said, change daily according to conditions in the market. He clacked away for a moment at the wooden beads on an abacus. "Today we're paying 8.64 percent for deposits of a year, and that is 20 percent higher than the state bank." For loans, the bank charges up to 19.8 percent; again, a rate determined by the demand for funds. The largest loan the bank has made to date was 19.55 million yuan. The bank's willingness to lend has also begun to nibble away at the state sector. "The rule is, we're not supposed to lend to state enterprises," Yang said, "but in reality it has happened. For example, we lent money to a state factory that makes stencils. We lent them three hundred thousand yuan. Because they were losing so much money, they had changed their management system. But there is a state regulation that state banks cannot make loans to enterprises that are losing money. So even when this stencil factory reformed itself, it was not going to survive. This factory has to buy its raw materials, a certain kind of rice paper, at one particular time of year. If it doesn't get it, it's finished. So we lent them the money. And of course they paid us back."

Yang's bank is expanding rapidly, reflecting both the vitality of Wenzhou and the institution's own flexibility. Yang said that the bank is planning for the future. "Eight people own stock in the bank right now. But we want to sell stock to another sixty or so people, to expand the capital base of the bank. But for us to do this, we have to get approval from the People's Bank of China [the country's central bank]. The cadres in the state banks are quite critical of us. The Farmers Bank and the Industrial and Commercial Bank don't like us. We're competitors, after all. The guy from the People's Bank of China doesn't like us either, but he doesn't know anything."

The city fathers do not share the antipathy of the state-run banks toward Yang and his colleagues. In 1988, they awarded the bank a plaque designating it a "New Star Enterprise." As a local official told me later, some people refer to the Wenzhou-Lucheng bank with a line from the Song dynasty poet Fan Chengda, "xuezhong songtan"—"the ones who send charcoal to those in the snow." In other words, lifesavers.

City officials lump phenomena like the Wenzhou-Lucheng Co-operative together in what they call "the Wenzhou model," their characterization of why their city has prospered. By and large, this model consists of little more than a hands-off attitude by the government. Liu Huabiao, one of the town's economic planners, sought to explain Wenzhou's success to me. "We have all types of economic structures," he said. "The main aim is to have stock companies and private companies, because these things work even if the state doesn't invest." In fact, in 1988, the state's share of the area's economic output was just 17 percent, and, in Liu's words, "it's been shrinking every year."

Neither are the city's officials concerned about the newly wealthy entrepreneurs who play an increasingly important role in the city's affairs. "What can you say if people get rich?" Liu said. "We don't get any investment from the state. It's their work. They get the raw materials, they make the products, they pay the taxes, so they get rich first. What can you say? If we had to rely on the state, we'd be finished. We asked the province for

146

help to build a good road into Wenzhou and we were told no. So
we have to build it ourselves. People here are trying anything.
There's this one guy, named Zhou, who opened a factory, hired
eight people and metal parts for engines. After he got two hundred and ninety thousand yuan, he quit the factory, took the
money and leased thirteen hundred mou of land in the mountains from the county. Now he's involved in all aspects of agriculture. He's got orchards, strawberries—very red and tasty, by
the way—vineyards, fishponds, everything possible."

There is a story, perhaps apocryphal, of a visit to Wenzhou
during the Cultural Revolution by a man named Chen Yonggui.
Chen was something of a peasant hero and a leader of a commune named Dazhai, which was portrayed as the quintessential
expression of Maoist revolutionary zeal. Enormous bumper harvests were routinely ascribed to Chen's commune, as was a
purity of political spirit and purpose. When the Cultural Revolution ended, the Communist Party admitted that it had deceived
the people of China and that all the commune's many publicized
successes were completely fraudulent. Chen, who for a time was
riding high, even rising to the post of vice-premier in the national government (and who, incidentally, was lionized by the
American author and Maoist sympathizer William Hinton), surveyed the revolutionary situation in Wenzhou and was said to
have declared, "This is capitalism." Intended as a stinging denunciation, it has since become a badge of honor in Wenzhou.

For Wenzhou, then, allegiance to the national mood has often
been little more than pretense. Huang Guohua, the blunt,
driven director of the Wenzhou Welding Equipment Works, explained how he sidestepped political problems during the Cultural Revolution. "We started our company in 1975. We put up a
sign saying we were a collective, not a private company. There
were many, many [private companies] at that time. But because
ours was a private enterprise, of course we went down the socialist road, calling ourselves a collective. Private enterprise was not
considered honorable because it had a capitalist tail. So we put
out a false nameplate." From a small factory with just seven
people, including himself, Huang now has more than one hundred and fifty people working for him and is the largest pro-
ducer of welding equipment in China.

Later on, I chatted with a local official about the welding

company and remarked on how it had erected the sign indicating that it was a collective to keep party watchdogs away. The official never batted an eyelash. "Oh, there are many enterprises like this, many. They all like to put on the socialist hat from time to time. That's just a habit. Putting on a little bit of red color is good once in a while."

In the decade since 1977, Wenzhou has witnessed a sevenfold increase in its overall industrial and agricultural output, growth dwarfing the sloth-like development in the previous three decades. Indeed, during the Great Leap Forward, from 1959 to 1961, and later during the early years of the Cultural Revolution, hunger and even some starvation were common in Wenzhou. The abject failures of an imposed socialism, weathered bitterly by Wenzhou's largely farming populace, fueled both an antipathy toward the old system and a determination to escape the poverty of the past in any way possible.

Liu Huabiao, the city planning official, capsulized the decade for me. "How did all this come into being? Because of the Wenzhou model. We started in agriculture by giving farmers land and letting them go their own way. And then we went from agriculture to industry and trade, letting people go their own way. That is the Wenzhou model." In the outlying rural districts of Wenzhou, where most of the region's population lives, there is no longer any state involvement in the economy at all. So important is industrial development to the area that only four out of every ten people now earn their living directly from agriculture. And factories are springing up so rapidly that the amount of arable land is dropping by more than one percent each year. There are now privately built condominium developments sitting on land purchased from peasants hoping to cash in on the recent land boom.

In the spring of 1990, Adi Ignatius, a colleague from *The Wall Street Journal,* visited Wenzhou and found that the long hand of Beijing's hard-liners had finally begun to touch the city. The city fathers were instructed to pay more attention to state-owned industries, and Yang Jiaxing's credit cooperative was banned from making loans to private businesses. Yang bemoaned the lash of socialism, telling Adi, "the government has its laws, and we have no choice but to follow." But while he admitted that he would buckle under to the new order, he remained unswayed in his distaste for socialism. "If Wenzhou had stressed planning," he told Adi, "it could never have developed the way it has."

DENG XIAOPING'S CALL to embrace those methods that work—those economic mechanisms that produce more food, more goods, more wealth for the Chinese nation—has not been ignored. "To get rich is glorious," a slogan bandied about in the early 1980s, has become a fact of life for a significant segment of Chinese society. The ponderous machinery of state economic planning simply has been ignored by ambitious entrepreneurs. In the meantime, an adolescent national market is maturing, nurtured by the demands of the boisterous and growing private sector.

But China's leaders have learned that genuine economic development is vastly more complex than changing sparkplugs in an engine—exchanging one economic model for another. The decision to turn to free markets, private farming, and private enterprise to rejuvenate the economy inevitably brings significant societal and political change in its wake. In the last century, Chinese political and social thinkers have wrestled with whether it was possible to adopt Western learning and techniques without endangering Confucian morals and aesthetics, an antinomy conceptualized as the dichotomy between *ti*, or essence, and *yong*, or function. Was it not possible, some of these thinkers suggested, to retain the Chinese *ti*, while carefully selecting elements of the Western *yong?* In the end, of course, Confucian values were not merely eroded, they were supplanted.

A significant wing of China's leadership, and of the party itself, rejects the notion that the economic freedoms promoted by the reform agenda of Deng Xiaoping inherently entail social and political liberalization. They see no reason why Communist Party control, at the national or local level, should not continue to be unhindered by shifts in policy that are intended simply to spur economic growth and nothing more. More, they believe that corruption, prostitution, and crime are phenomena intrinsic to the capitalist order. Others within the leadership, and, even more significantly, within the country's broad intelligentsia, see that the course China has set involves much more than mere economic tinkering; that it implies a fundamental transformation of Chinese society and polity. They view the

149

reemergence of widespread public graft, for instance, as a symptom of the pain involved in restructuring an anachronistic economic order, a symptom that will in time dissipate.

These symptoms, though, were hard to miss. They were everywhere.

SEVEN

The Demimonde

CONTINUING OUR COASTAL JOURNEY, Stefan Simons and I drove south toward Fuzhou, the capital of Fujian Province. Long considered a "front-line" province because of its proximity to Taiwan, the province had been closely watched by Beijing and has remained a cantonment for substantial numbers of troops. During the Cultural Revolution, the province, and particularly Fuzhou itself, was a hotbed of internecine warfare between contending radical factions, each professing more ardent love for Mao, the great helmsman. After the Cultural Revolution, as the rest of China's coast bolted forward economically, Fujian lagged behind, still tangled in the skein of Communist Party control. Only with the diminution of tension with Taiwan during the 1980s did the need for military alertness and severe political control finally abate.

By this time, though, the example of neighboring provinces like Zhejiang and Guangdong was spilling over Fujian's borders, triggering tardy but vigorous economic growth. Illicit contacts with Taiwan were already on the rise, particularly in the form of trade. Taiwan businessmen became a common sight at bars in Fuzhou and Xiamen, where they cut deals to buy raw materials or to sell computers assembled in Taiwan. Smuggling began to boom.

Putian, a town about midway down the Fujian coast, has historically been a Wild West town, and it took easily to the liberalized economic climate. The town soon became the locus of major smuggling operations, facilitated by the region's crafty sea captains, who maneuvered their fishing boats easily in the coves of Huaxing Bay. In 1987, one lucrative smuggling operation led to a spectacular shoot-out on the high seas.

The Japanese fondness for raw fish extends to a particular kind of eel cultivated in the Zhejiang town of Ningbo. The Chinese government has tried to monopolize the harvesting and export of these eels to Japan. In Putian, however, monopolies are meant to be broken, and a thriving and complex trade in illegal eels goes on between the Fujian town and Ningbo. The slimy black eels are shipped to Putian, where they are loaded onto offshore launches. During the night, the Chinese smugglers, their waterproof gunnysacks filled with eels, head out to sea to meet the high-powered pickup boats from Taiwan. For one full sack of eels, a smuggler can clear fifty thousand yuan.

One night in 1987, three young men in an old power launch crept out of Huaxing Bay toward open water. They were carrying two sacks of eels and stood to make a hundred thousand yuan from just this one run. As they cruised toward international waters, their running lights off, the only sound that of the warm waves of the bay lapping against their bow, a Chinese customs boat appeared from nowhere, its searchlight pinpointing them in the heaving blackness. As the boat drew up alongside the smugglers' craft, one of the young smugglers pulled a revolver from his waistband and fired at a customs official, killing him instantly. There ensued a barrage of shooting, from the young man and from the officers on the customs boat, but, miraculously, no one else was killed. The gunman's accomplices, by then thoroughly cowed, begged him to drop his gun. All three were arrested and the gunman was later executed. A friend from Putian who told me this story said that the shoot-out intimidated nobody, and that the smuggling of eels, as well as hundreds of other things, continued. "Once in a while they catch somebody, but they can never stop it," my friend said. "It's just too big."

Fuzhou mimics socialist urban development well, at least architecturally. Broad avenues are hemmed by thick, graceless concrete-block buildings. On a huge billboard across from the offices of the provincial government, its red paint flaking from age and sun, a band of white ideograms reads, "Fight for the cause of communism," neatly bordering a mammoth hammer and sickle. A huge statue of Mao, his right hand extended as if in apostolic blessing, looms over a public park. Erected at the onset of the Cultural Revolution, this statue is one of the few such remaining effigies in China's cities. But beneath this overlay of socialist propriety, a free-wheeling entrepreneurialism and commercial vigor has begun to transform Fuzhou from an economic backwater into a linchpin of coastal development.

Along with this rediscovery of unhampered economic activity, however, has come the rediscovery of capitalism's forbidden fruits, what in the minds of party ideologues are that system's inherent evils. Prostitution is, perhaps, chief among these.

"In the old days, before the Cultural Revolution, there weren't any prostitutes," a taxi driver told us as he drove us from one appointment to the next. "Now? Now there's lots. They hang around the hotels, sit alone or in twos, and their eyes wander about, up and down. They look bored. They're all girls from outside here. No one works in their own city; with all their friends and relatives that would be kind of embarrassing. Usually girls from Fuzhou go up to Wenzhou and the Wenzhou girls come down here."

The taxi driver drove up the curved ramp to the Hot Springs Hotel and Stefan and I wandered into the bar to wash twelve hours of dusty roads from our mouths. As we sat down, a young man with an ostentatious gold watch weighing down his left wrist sauntered into the room, his eyes massaging the gloomy bar the way a furrier fingers a pelt. He paused to chat in a low murmur with two young women waggling their ankles and sipping Cokes at a table before he slithered over to a black vinyl scoop chair at our table. He never looked at us; instead, his eyes cruised the room in an affected nonchalance.

"Change money?" he whispered, the accepted introductory line of all street hustlers in China. Because of the 100 percent disparity between the real value of China's currency and its officially pegged rate, there is a thriving black market for U.S. dollars, Hong Kong dollars, and the official Chinese foreign currency, so-called foreign exchange certificates.

We declined the offer, thanking him anyway.

He changed tack. "Girls?" he tried, his voice again a hoarse whisper.

"How much?" I asked.

In the leisurely way a veteran blackjack player calls for a hit, he tapped the smoked-glass topped table twice with a tapered, two inch long thumbnail. "Two hundred."

I had long wanted to interview some of China's prostitutes, both because they were being portrayed as a new social scourge and because prostitution was proving extremely resilient to periodic crackdowns by the police. But in Beijing, where the climate of political and moral rectitude is more pronounced, such efforts would have entailed unwarranted risks.

Throughout Chinese history, prostitution has remained a fundamental feature of urban life. First described in texts from the sixth century B.C., prostitution had at various times been supported by the imperial court, although, unlike Japan (where voluminous contemporaneous histories of the institution exist), Chinese texts on prostitution are rarer. In the decades before Mao assumed power, prostitution had been rampant in port cities from Tianjin to Guangzhou. Organized crime gangs operated bordellos in which young girls, driven by poverty, hunger, or desperation, sold themselves in the most degrading squalor. Opium use was rampant in these establishments and toward the end of Nationalist rule, the whorehouses had come, in a strange way, to symbolize the final degeneracy of the Chiang Kai-shek regime. When Mao's armies consolidated their hold on China's cities, one of the first tasks undertaken by the new Communist administrators was the eradication of social decadence: gambling over mah-jongg, opium smoking, and prostitution. Tens of thousands of prostitutes were shipped to labor and reeducation camps, and the personal accounts of many prostitutes were widely publicized as personal testimonies to the depravity of the previous era.

But through the 1980s, as contacts with the outside world blossomed and planeloads of tourists and business executives began flooding China's cities, some of the rigid controls over the urban populace waned. The independence needed by private entrepreneurs, the gradual strengthening of the domestic market for goods and services, and cultural infiltration from other parts of the world engendered a more laissez-faire mood in China's urban areas. Hong Kong businessmen, who arrived by the tens of thousands, expected the same services they were accustomed to in Taipei, Manila, or Bangkok. That meant good food, good hotels, and discos. It also meant prostitutes. By the mid-1980s, there was not a first-class hotel in Guangzhou that did not boast its complement of prostitutes. By the end of the decade, there were occasions when the number of hookers in the lounge at the Garden Hotel exceeded the number of guests.

Government officials rail continually about the resurgence of prostitution, but they seem unable to prevent it. Officials regularly denounce the spread of obscene publications, issue new regulations banning the sale or possession of pornography, and order the arrest of prostitutes. Even D. H. Lawrence's *Lady Chatterley's Lover* was banned in 1987, although copies of it remained available at high, black-market prices. The government's loss of control over printing plants has resulted in the proliferation of thousands of "girly magazines," torrid pamphlets on love and romance, and violent crime stories. Periodic attempts to stanch this flood of popular literature, however, do nothing to erode the selection at free-market magazine and book shops. In an unintended admission that the police are virtually powerless in this area, an official newspaper declared, "People who give pornographic video shows and allow indecent behavior during the shows are asked to confess to the police. Those who fail to do so will be punished severely."

In 1987, the police in Guangzhou said they arrested more than seven thousand prostitutes, a declaration that appears to have had no discernible impact on the trade. And there are, according to official reports, sixty-eight special prisons around the country for prostitutes. Moreover, there is little doubt that the police themselves are actively engaged in promoting prostitution, even as city officials urge them to control it. In Shenzhen, a newly created city abutting Hong Kong where special economic incentives are given foreign investors, a police sweep of ten hotels in early 1988 netted one hundred and twenty-two prostitutes and one hundred customers, among whom were Communist Party officials, Hong Kong truckers, and Shenzhen policemen. In the small town of Deqing, some one hundred miles west of Guangzhou, a peasant was executed for enticing six women into working for him as prostitutes.

The young man with the long thumbnail, who called himself Lin, told us to meet him in the bar the following night when he would bring along two of his "girls." At about six o'clock, Lin slid into the bar, one hand fingering the gold links of his watch. "Okay," he began, "you take the girls to your room now. The earlier the better. One cannon shot, okay."

Momentarily taken aback by the haste with which the pimp worked, I hesitated and said that it would be better if we talked first, and perhaps had dinner. "No no no," he insisted. "It's better to go up first, you can eat later." Then, employing the only argument that resonates meaningfully through all spectrums of Chinese society, Stefan told the pimp that there was no way we could go ahead on an empty stomach. That clinched the argument. "Okay, you eat first and then go up." Lin then told us that when we were done we should not pay the women, but pay him. We asked why, and he said that the girls would be "too embarrassed to ask us for money," so it was better that he pay them directly. That out of the way, he scurried out of the bar and then towed in two young women, a Miss Yu and a Miss Yun. Then he left, after announcing that he would see me downstairs in a couple of hours.

The women told us that they did not drink, so we went off to the hotel's restaurant, the Laughing Buddha, to eat and talk. It was, I assumed, one of the few opportunities I would have to talk with a prostitute without risking trouble for her or for me. We decided to let the two women order, since they were certainly more familiar with Fuzhou cuisine than we. I passed the menu to them. Miss Yun, a chubby woman whose manner suggested that she was less timid in the presence of a foreigner than her companion, took charge. To my surprise, though, she ordered not from the menu, but by asking the waiter what he had. It turned out that she could not read.

Miss Yu, a thin woman with frizzy hair and high cheekbones, had glossed her lips a shocking rose color. She wore a frilly, pink lace blouse and a billowy patterned cotton skirt, and seemed decidedly ill at ease. "This is my first time with a foreigner," she confessed.

"I'm twenty," she said when I began asking about her life and how she ventured into prostitution. "I was born and raised here in Fuzhou. There're ten people in my family. My father was an elementary schoolteacher and my mother worked in a hospital. My father's retired now, but my mother's still working. Me, I'm working at the long-distance bus station selling tickets. I earn one hundred yuan and some every month. It's hard work and I don't earn enough. I was assigned that job after I graduated from middle school. That was in 1986. I learned a little English there, but I've forgotten it all."

Stefan interjected and, with Germanic forthrightness, asked her why she began working as a prostitute. With a pawnshop owner's jaundiced air, she flicked a polished fingernail from her gold hoop earrings—"Three hundred"—to the lapel of her blouse—"two hundred"—to her pink plastic sandals—"nine yuan, a real bargain. I'd never wear leather shoes because they don't last. Clothes are so expensive. I need the money." Her wardrobe, indeed, was worth the equivalent of five months' salary for a skilled worker in a state factory.

Then, as an afterthought, she added, "But I only go out two or three times a week, because my mother is worried when I go out too much."

As Miss Yu talked, Miss Yun worked furiously at the array of dishes on the table, her fondness for good food evident in her gently rounded proportions. Her black hair, still wet from a shower, hung to her shoulders, and severe bangs edged her eyebrows. She wore a scoop-cut black dress, its bodice drenched in sequins. She pushed her bowl of rice away and started talking in heavily accented Mandarin.

"I'm from Xian. I was there till I was about ten, but then we moved to Fuzhou. I'm staying with my aunt now, so I speak the local dialect. But really, I prefer Xian to Fuzhou. My father was a military man but he's retired. I never did well in school, so I didn't go very far. My first job was in a restaurant and café nightclub. But the work there was simply too hard. So I switched to a hotel, where I work at the reception desk." I plied her for some rationale for her nighttime job. "We don't do this often," she said insistently. "We're not like those made-up girls sitting at

157

the bar." In other words, she thought of herself more as an amateur than a professional. Then, as an afterthought, "If my mother knew what I was doing, she would kill me."

Neither of the women expressed any concern about the police, even if they barged in when they were with a customer. "You don't have to worry because you're a foreigner," Miss Yun said, giggling. "If they scold somebody, they'll scold us. They could fine us, or pick us up. But I don't worry. It's never happened. You can always go through the back door with the police. They do it the same as anyone else. No, we're not afraid."

As dinner ended, we explained to the women that, after all, we were not interested in *war-yi-war,* or playing around with them, and gave each of them one hundred yuan for their time, an amount I dutifully entered into my expense accounts (perhaps the first time *The Times* has formally paid for a prostitute).

Outside the restaurant, pimp Lin lurked, anxious about the length of time we had spent talking. Stefan told Lin that we were not interested in taking the women upstairs. Lin, undaunted, told us we could take the women to his place, "where it's safe." We explained again that we just were not interested. He stalked off, unable, apparently, to comprehend what had gone awry.

The very banality of my conversation with the Misses Yu and Yun suggests that prostitution has become a commonplace and relatively risk-free opportunity for young women to earn significantly more money than they could in regular jobs. A friend from Fujian told me that prostitution is rampant even in the countryside, although the fees commanded by rural women are in the fifteen- to twenty-yuan range rather than the hundreds charged by city hookers. After decades of stringent social controls, the national program of economic reforms has unintentionally, but inevitably, pried open a pressure cooker of pent-up aspirations, desires, purpose. The freedom needed by a private toy maker or sweater manufacturer to operate without state interference has inexorably spilled into other spheres of Chinese life.

WITH THE GROWTH of the private economy, stark disparities in wealth have appeared once again on the Chinese mainland. For the first time in four decades, there are real millionaires who drive fancy cars, live in posh houses, and oversee manufacturing empires. More common are the merely wealthy: those individuals who run a single factory, a bus company, or a shop or restaurant, but who earn a hundred or two hundred times what an average worker does. The people who have not shared in this bounty, whose incomes have remained mired in the bog of state employment, include not just laborers, factory workers, and shop clerks, but the vast numbers of government and party bureaucrats who sit atop administrative structures in villages, towns, cities, and provinces, up through the national government itself. Millions of these bureaucrats, petty and grand, have witnessed the efflorescence of entrepreneurialism, of newly acquired wealth, of conspicuous consumption. And they have decided to cash in.

Corruption—bribery, theft, influence peddling, extortion, petty favoritism—has progressively, and relentlessly, eaten into the very marrow of Chinese society. China's forty million bureaucrats still wield the power of the "chop," the red stamp that is necessary to get anything done: to buy a plane ticket, to build a factory, to buy fertilizer, to ship manufactured goods, to have electricity or water turned on. Most Chinese quite openly assert that virtually nothing can be accomplished in China without some sort of payoff, in the form of help from a friend (or friend of a friend) or straightforward extortion. For the three decades of Communist rule, corruption was generally confined to the crafty use of *guanxi,* or connections, and use of the so-called *houmen,* or back door. During the Cultural Revolution, the children of some high officials used their connections to avoid being sent to the countryside for reeducation. A factory worker would get a better job because his brother-in-law knew the neighbor of the personnel manager. That was simply the way things got done.

But since 1980—since money has replaced politics as the currency of real power, the power to control one's own life—corruption has become an uncontrolled and uncontrollable cancer at the core of Chinese life. Chen Yun, one of China's senior leaders and a rigid, hard-line Marxist-Leninist, decried the crumbling of social discipline and control in a vitriolic speech to the party's Politburo in 1985. "The pernicious influence of capitalism and feudalism has not been reduced to a minimum," he lectured his colleagues. "Instead, some evil things that have long been extinct after Liberation have come to life again. There are now some people, including some party members, who have forsaken the socialist and Communist ideal and turned their backs on serving the people."

In a remarkable article published in mid-1988, the *People's Daily* addressed the issue bluntly: "People should prepare for a long-term struggle as corruption is an inevitable accompaniment of social progress. Corruption is caused by the coexistence of a market economy in its primitive form and the old economic, political, and cultural systems that are excessively centralized. This has produced a major breeding ground for corruption within the party." The newspaper of the People's Liberation Army even admitted that "a rather popular saying is, now that we are going in for reform, opening up and invigorating the economy, things cannot always be conducted in a good clean way without applying some 'lubrication'; otherwise, things will not go smoothly."

One of the most aggressive and iconoclastic newspapers in China, the *China Youth News,* summed up the state of the nation succinctly: "China's economy is run 40 percent by money, 30 percent by power, and 30 percent by personal connections." In 1986 alone, the government reported that 39,659 cases of corruption and bribery, in which, the paper noted, "most of the criminals were government functionaries," had been brought to the courts. But most Chinese believe that such cases represent only a fraction of the ongoing corruption within the bureaucracy. They also believe that the children of the country's senior leadership have repeatedly used their privileged positions to benefit themselves materially and that they remain beyond the purview of the law. The case most often cited by Chinese is that of Deng Pufang, the son of Deng Xiaoping.

A fervent member of the Communist Party, Pufang was a physics student at Beijing University when the Cultural Revolution exploded upon China in 1966. After his father was labeled a "capitalist despot" and purged of all his positions, Pufang was set upon by rabid Red Guards, who locked him in a university laboratory contaminated by radioactivity. In a frantic effort to save himself, Pufang leapt from the fourth-floor laboratory window, shattering his spine and paralyzing himself for life. But with the reascent of his father after 1977, Pufang, too, gained in power and influence.

Pufang organized and became the head of the China Welfare Fund for the Handicapped, an organization charged with remedying the discrimination and other problems faced by China's millions of disabled people. In fact, although it has financed rehabilitation centers, the organization has made no inroads in breaking down barriers to the disabled. I know one young woman, the daughter of a distinguished physicist and herself a promising physicist, who was paralyzed from her neck down in a car accident. Now confined to a wheelchair, she was not permitted to continue her studies, because, as she said, "They told me there were able-bodied people who could fill my place."

But it was not because of his work with the handicapped that Pufang's fame, or notoriety, blossomed. In 1984, Pufang created the Kanghua Company, later to become the Kanghua Development Corporation, a sort of investment bank and trading concern which went on to establish more than two hundred subsidiary companies across the country and in Hong Kong. Because of Pufang's family connections, Kanghua quickly became a major player in China's international economic relations, a company with its hand in deals across a wide spectrum of commerce, from farms to factories, from import-export concerns to investment banking. Pufang's Welfare Fund received some financial assistance from Kanghua, which in turn was granted an exemption from all taxation. In Hong Kong, officials of Kanghua's companies were well known for dropping Pufang's name to get tax breaks and extra export permits. Kanghua made investments in Europe and the United States, provided security for bad loans, and controlled huge amounts of rationed raw materials on the mainland. In the spring of 1988, the Japanese investment bank C. Itoh and Company granted Kanghua a concessionary loan of $1 billion.

Only in 1988, when the volume of criticism against corruption and official privileges began to reach deafening levels, was Kanghua severed from the Welfare Fund and deprived of its tax-free status. The company was also ordered to divest itself of many of its subsidiaries and to close its Hong Kong office. Deng Pufang himself, however, remained personally untouched by the crackdown.

An earlier anticorruption campaign in 1986 collapsed when it became clear that almost none of the country's senior leaders would remain untouched by scandal. As a Chinese proverb puts it, "When a man rises in power, even his dogs and roosters benefit." Zhao Ziyang's son, Zhao Sanjun, was widely known to be involved in corrupt foreign deals that brought him windfall profits. At one point, Sanjun was mixed up in importing and reselling Japanese color televisions, a product in high demand and one that could stand high price markups. Once, Sanjun was arrested for his activities, but his family connections bought his release within four hours. Not until his father was deposed in 1989 was the son brought down. His exact fate remains unknown. Charges against the daughter of longtime Politburo member Peng Zhen and the son of Hu Qiaomu, who sat on the Politburo for a time, never materialized despite the widespread knowledge that the two were deeply enmeshed in corrupt dealings with state companies. However, Ye Zhifeng, the daughter of the former commander of the country's naval forces, was sentenced to seventeen years in prison for allegedly leaking to a Hong Kong businessman "state secrets" regarding China's plans for importing foreign automobiles into the country; but her father had only made it to the Central Committee, not the Politburo.

The difficulties in prosecuting the illegal activities of the children of high-ranking officials were summed up by a small newspaper called *Market:* "Behind every big profiteer is a big protector. The children of some leaders use the cover of their parents to profiteer. Who dares to touch the tiger's ass?"

TOWARD THE END of the decade, China's papers carried reports of major instances of official malfeasance almost daily, reports intended to demonstrate government vigilance against corruption and as a warning to those engaged in such activities. From the smallest villages to the largest cities, tales of gross venality abounded. In Chengdu, the capital of Sichuan Province, the Communist Party secretary-general of the city's military district, Ning Yinghai, was found to have accepted bribes from contractors, profiteered through bulk purchases of cigarettes, and embezzled funds from military accounts. Worse still, in the words of the *Liberation Army Daily,* "He had extramarital relations with two married women and another woman, with whom he watched X-rated videos, and one of the three eventually became his live-in mate." Ning Yinghai, intoned the army newspaper, "has degenerated into a depraved person, because of corruption, speculation, and dallying with women. He was severely punished in accordance with the law and party discipline. That serves him right."

Graft has taken root across the country. In Heilongjiang Province, after a devastating forest fire consumed hundreds of square miles of forest and destroyed dozens of small villages and towns, local officials rushed out and spent the first installment of relief money from the central government on one hundred and twenty-one new cars because the roads they would have to travel on to inspect the damage were too bumpy for the old ones to traverse comfortably.

On Hainan Island, the four most senior government and party officials orchestrated a scam to import cars duty-free and then peddle the vehicles at market prices on the mainland. The general manager of the national Nonferrous Metal Import and Export Corporation in Guangdong, Ye Qi, accepted bribes worth thirty thousand dollars from Hong Kong traders as fees to close deals and siphoned off half a million dollars from the corporation's foreign bank accounts. The minister of astronautics, Zhang Jun, was caught trying to smuggle one hundred and eighty thousand color television sets into the country; he was dismissed from his position but never faced criminal charges and instead was merely given a "serious disciplinary warning." And in 1988 alone, 178 million yuan in government funds for poverty-stricken areas was either embezzled or misused, nearly 6 percent of the 3.2 billion yuan earmarked for relief in China's poorest countries.

In fact, the *People's Daily* maintained, local officials often solicited poverty funds in order to embezzle them. "Cadres in a minority of poor areas paint exaggeratedly bleak pictures of the regions under their jurisdiction in order to attract support from the state," the newspaper editorialized on its front page. "But, once this money is in their hands, all thoughts of the poor masses flee from their minds and the money is spent like water on such things as building hotels and dormitories, and on cars and banquets."

Even down on the farm, corruption is a problem. As farmers became more aggressive in their agricultural techniques, more determined to extract the highest yields possible from their tiny plots, fertilizer became a commodity like gold. Local officials in charge of the retail distribution of fertilizer cashed in on their monopoly of the market and prices skyrocketed. Officials sold fertilizer to black market dealers and even held supplies off the market so that prices would climb still further. Officials diverted truckloads of fertilizer to their relatives. So bad did the situation become in southern Hunan that upwards of one hundred and seventy thousand farmers rioted over a period of three months in the summer of 1987, looting fertilizer warehouses and attacking local officials. More than twelve farmers were shot to death by police during the riots and another eighty were injured.

Foreign investors in China, particularly Hong Kong businessmen, speak of routine demands for kickbacks, approval monies, or signing fees to complete a deal. Hong Kong businessmen generally regard such payments as the cost of doing business, and accept the fact that graft is simply a way of life in China now. I visited a factory in Guangdong that was a joint venture between the local town and a Hong Kong investor. In the parking lot of the factory, there were two gleaming Mercedes. I asked the general manager, who was in fact Chinese and not from Hong Kong, whose Mercedes they were. "Oh," he said, "our partner left them here. He said he didn't need them any more."

Western executives who do business in China are not immune to extortion either. Many American companies are pressured into accepting Chinese "interns," generally well-connected young men, to work in the home office in the United States, or to pay for the university education of the children of senior Chinese bureaucrats. Gifts of cameras, televisions, videotapes, and Sony Walkmen are commonly given by foreign executives to their Chinese partners or hosts. On the larger corporate balance sheet, such gifts are negligible. But, inexorably, they contribute to the growing pattern of bribery and extortion that clutches at the heart of all economic activity.

Less venal officials routinely divert public funds in a less covert manner. At noontime and in the evening, better restaurants in China's cities are jammed with officials eating out at the expense of their bureau, division, or government company.

Scenes of raucous officials inebriated from the powerful white liqueur that is the staple beverage at such banquets became so commonplace for a time that a storm of protest overwhelmed the newspapers. The State Council in Beijing quickly issued a regulation ordering an end to unnecessary banquets, and those deemed essential were to be restricted to *sicai yitang,* four dishes and one soup. In the numerous banquets I was compelled to attend in various parts of China, none of which I found necessary, I never attended one that restricted itself to sicai yitang.

So rampant has corruption become that many cities have set up telephone hot lines for members of the public to report instances of official wrongdoing. In Beijing, dialing 502.53.91 connects a caller with an operator at the Ministry of Supervision, who will take down details of the caller's accusations against officials. Similar systems were introduced in Shanghai, Guangzhou, and Shenzhen, all cities known for flagrant official misconduct. Despite the fanfare surrounding the creation of these systems for anonymous informing, like many things in China, there is a good deal more smoke than fire here. For decades, a similar system has existed in China's newspapers, which receive millions of letters annually from irate readers reporting on perceived wrongdoing. The *People's Daily* alone claims it gets fifty thousand such letters each month. Despite that deluge of mail, corruption has flourished like a well-watered fern.

CORRUPTION had become so pervasive by the end of the decade that it was a common topic of conversation on the street. *Xiaodao xiaoxi,* or alley talk, was filled with tales of malfeasance by officials. Coupled with the evident immunity from punishment enjoyed by leaders' children who committed crimes and engaged in corrupt activities, a surge of popular revulsion swept through China's cities.

The extent of public concern about the decay of public morals and the party's own probity was not lost on the leadership, although different elements within the leadership responded in different fashions. Zhao Ziyang, since 1987 the party's general secretary and the guiding light of the reformers within the leadership, began warning of the dangers posed by the wildfire spread of illegal activities. "There is indeed corruption among some party and government officials," Zhao told a meeting of party officials in October 1988. "If we do not take effective measures to control and overcome it, this phenomenon will spread and deepen. If we let matters drift, the new economic order will not be established; the reforms will not continue."

Zhao's alarm was well founded. He was already under heavy attack from party hard-liners, having lost two critical battles over economic policy in the previous months. The hard-liners, many of whom did not even hold formal government or party posts, were deeply distressed at the rapid erosion of public discipline and the painfully apparent decay of the party's own moral fiber. It was easy to blame Zhao, as both the architect of the economic reforms and now the party's at least titular helmsman. Zhao's sudden outspokenness on the issue, he was to learn, was too little and too late.

The hard-liners also viewed Zhao's attitude as politically expedient rather than deeply held, for Zhao and his supporters were less worried about these manifestations of criminality and moral decay than were his hard-line opponents. For much of the decade, Zhao tended to see these problems as the unfortunate detritus washed up by the process of fundamental change. In his heart, Zhao was no more enamored of graft, prostitution, embezzlement, or bribery than anyone else; he was simply preoccupied with the larger issue of China's economic transformation.

Luo Haigang, a member of one of Zhao's think tanks, did not beat around the bush in an article in a journal called *Theoretical Monthly*. Luo wrote, "People should prepare for a long-term struggle, as corruption is an inevitable accompaniment of social progress. Corruption is caused by the coexistence of a market economy in its primitive form and the old economic, political, and cultural systems that are excessively centralized. This has created a major breeding ground for corruption within the party." While Luo's analysis was unquestionably correct, it exposed the Zhaoists to relentless attacks. Hard-liners railed that the Zhaoist push toward capitalism was undermining social morality, and that their willingness to treat social ills lightly undermined the authority of the party.

Hard-liners within the leadership, people like Chen Yun, Peng Zhen, Yang Shangkun, Li Xiannian, Wang Zhen, Bo Yibo, and even Deng himself, placed enormous stock in the probity of the party. The revolution for which they fought, and to which they referred in every speech and at every public occasion, was won, in part, because it capitalized on the rampant corruption of Chiang Kai-shek's regime. If you ask anyone among the older generation in China what sticks out in their mind about the Kuomintang, they are more than likely to recall the paralyzing venality that infused the Kuomintang government. Socialist probity has become a integral part of the myth within which the Communist Party wraps itself.

I remember visiting a party official who quite forthrightly expressed his sympathy for the hard-liners within the party. He harangued me about the decline in values, the spread of pornography, the lack of respect for authority—all complaints one heard in the United States, it occurred to me, from the right wing of the Republican Party. Then, as if to drive home his point, he wagged his finger at me and said, "Look at those Kuomintang on Taiwan. They've become so rich. They've become wealthy over there. We have never become rich. That's why we're different."

For Zhao, the issue of corruption was a political minefield from which he could not, and ultimately did not, escape. Although he was correct (in the view of many Chinese economists) in his intense desire to remold China's economy, his blindness to the social consequences of his policies made him increasingly vulnerable to attacks from hard-liners disillusioned with the direction of economic reform. Not only was China becoming capitalist, it was becoming morally and politically derelict. And this they would not tolerate.

EIGHT

Only in Shanghai

DECEMBER 1986 was biting cold in Shanghai. I had flown in from Beijing to cover the latest and most serious outbreak of student demonstrations that were sweeping across China like a wind-whipped brushfire.

Students were parading through the streets of the city, shouting slogans about democracy and freedom of speech. Some carried a huge cardboard cutout of the Statue of Liberty. The central square of the city—what had been a racetrack in the days before communism—was occupied by students sitting in, holding impromptu and vigorous political seminars. The streets were jammed with gawkers; old women pushing cups of tea into the students' hands, students, in their heavily padded coats, chanting songs. It was a strange, organized chaos.

Down on the Bund, one of the most famous river roads in the world, where the gray granite monoliths of the old Hong Kong & Shanghai Bank, the Jardine, Matheson & Company, and the Chartered Bank still stand, students had surrounded the Communist Party headquarters and city hall. The iron gates were

168

chained shut, and armed police stood warily on the steps. The students shouted, chanted, sang, taunted the soldiers a bit.

And through all this—the tumult, the political excitement, the panic among the city's Communist chieftains—the rickety jazz band at the Peace Hotel played on, clanking and wheezing out big band hits from the 1940s. Only in Shanghai, I thought.

MAO ZEDONG placed his faith and his fortunes in the hands of China's peasantry. In the course of his struggles against Chiang Kai-shek and the Nationalists, the revolutionary leader learned that China's crowded cities—Beijing, Shanghai, Tianjin, Guangzhou—were places to be surrounded; cut off from the outside world and then plucked from the tree like ripe peaches. When he came to power, cities were where the government worked and where factories were built, but they were regarded as decidedly inferior to the spiritual purity of the countryside and the restorative powers of the soil.

In Mao's years in power, millions of writers, artists, teachers, what the Chinese lump together under the rubric of "intellectuals," as well as unfavored bureaucrats and Mao's political detractors, were all shipped from the cities to the countryside to remold themselves; to bathe themselves in the honest and wholesome glow exuded by China's peasantry, and to emerge as true socialist revolutionaries. This, in any case, was Mao's oft-proclaimed goal. But, like many of Mao's notions, it was based on an idealized vision of rural life no more conversant with reality than the presumed degeneration—political, cultural, moral—inherent in city life.

During Mao's reign, eight out of every ten people lived in a village or a rural town; they were the fiber of the Chinese nation. Over the last decade, all that has changed, and changed profoundly. In the short space of ten years, some two hundred million people, roughly equivalent to the entire population of the United States, have moved from the land into urban areas, dramatically and permanently altering the demographic face of China. These new urbanites, who are more likely to reside in mushrooming boomtowns than in traditional cities, sensed that opportunities were changing in the cities, just as they were down on the farm. But, instead of farming a piece of land, these new urban immigrants rushed to compete with their city cousins in

169

looking for a chance to work in a newly opened factory, a chance to pilot a shiny Toyota taxicab, to join one of the construction crews that are rapidly changing the physiognomy of China's cities, to open a small business or a sidewalk restaurant.

As in the countryside, economic life in the city had been controlled by the government in Beijing since the 1950s. Food and clothing stores were state-owned, as were herbalists' shops and trucking companies, factories and bookshops, hardware stores and restaurants. China's leadership realized, though, that revitalizing the economy could not be confined to the country-side, to the rice and wheat fields of the hinterland. Some reforms were needed in the cities; that much was acknowledged. But what those reforms should be and how deeply they should pene-trate was, and remains, a deeply divisive area of debate. People like Deng Xiaoping, Zhao Ziyang, and Hu Yaobang, the most visible of the senior leadership, were, after all, deeply commit-ted Communists. None of them was prepared to allow the nega-tion of fundamental principles of socialism or of the leadership of the Communist Party, or at least that is what they publicly proclaimed.

It was abundantly clear to any observer in 1979 that China was a century behind the developed world, technologically, educa-tionally, economically. Mao's dream of overtaking England in fifteen years had backfired catastrophically, catapulting the country into even greater distress. An obvious source of help was from abroad; from Europe, the United States, from Japan. But seeking foreign assistance, whether in the form of grants, loans, or even investment, threatened dearly held precepts about the virtues of self-sufficiency. These principles were con-ditioned in no small measure by China's unhappy historical experience with foreign powers, which in the nineteenth century had sliced off chunks of the country for their own uses.

A blizzard of questions confronted China's leaders when they looked at China's leaden cities and contemplated reform: Should private shop ownership be allowed? Should privately owned manufacturing be permitted? Could someone in private business hire workers? How would workers in the cities, all of whom were tied to assigned employment, move to private jobs? After all, the workplace, referred to by Chinese as their *danwei,* or unit, was their institutional parent: it conferred the right to live in the city; it provided housing, food coupons, and supplements; it granted permission to get married. A system of private employment would disrupt this vast scheme of social control, and social control was, in the end, a defining feature of Chinese socialism.

There were endless issues: How would private business raise money? Could private entrepreneurs borrow from state banks to establish their own companies? How would they obtain raw materials, all of which were, until then, allocated by the formidable state planning process? Could private businesses charge whatever prices they wished for their products? What system of taxation was needed for private businesses and how would these tax laws be enforced?

China was faced not simply with reforming its economy, but with rebuilding it stone by stone, with no easy schema for proceeding. At every turn, the socialist orthodoxy of the past was under siege. But the leadership recognized that a failure to move forward, an unwillingness to abandon the manifestly unworkable economy of the past, would condemn the country to permanent poverty and backwardness. After 1979, then, China's cities began reviving; slowly, tentatively. In some parts of the country, in the south and along the coast, a palpable enthusiasm greeted the new economic liberalization. Elsewhere, in places like Hunan and Shaanxi, or even Beijing and Shanghai themselves, there was more caution, more bureaucratic and political obstructionism, and there has been substantially less economic growth.

NOWHERE has the impact of migration and population growth been felt as severely as in Shanghai. This city, molded by the elbow of the mud-brown Huangpu River, emerged rebellious from the Cultural Revolution, proud of its role as the urban vanguard of that chaotic period. It also emerged impoverished, broken down, and disorganized. The city's water and sewage system was collapsing, and there were regular blackouts because of electricity shortages. There was a critical shortage of housing. Urban reform, if it was to mean anything at all, would have to take root in Shanghai or it would, China's leaders firmly believed, fail everywhere.

Shanghai is to this day an architectural relic of the era when

171

Western powers apportioned areas of the city for their own use. To the west of the Bund, along the main shopping streets, sidewalks are crammed with pedestrians: shoppers struggling with packages, people hurrying to work, tourists swept along in the tide of humanity that courses through the city. The arcades of Nanjing Road are reminiscent of British Colonial architecture around the world. In what were formerly foreign concessions, stately houses in granite or smudged sandstone sit majestically in walled, tree-shaded compounds. Today, some of these are foreign consulates, while many others are government offices and guest houses. Other compounds of brick houses with steeply pitched tile roofs punctured by chimneys and neat half-timbered gables, once the homes of Shanghai's upper-middle-class foreigners and even some wealthier Chinese, have been sliced up into shoe-box apartments. Still, with thick rosy spectacles, some avenues, on good days, have a distant tinge of Paris.

On the edge of the former French quarter, in a neat, kneaded circle, lies what was called the Chinese City, a dense jumble of dark wood-plank matchbox houses piled on top of one another, where Shanghai's indigenous population lived in the nineteenth century. Today, the streets are clean but crowded. Sidewalk merchants squatting under awnings offer a myriad of goods, from bamboo birdcages to car tires, from thick dried mushrooms to squawking ducks. Even on the coldest winter days, groups of old men, like round blue dumplings in layers of padded blue jackets, can be seen squatting on tiny wood stools in circles around low tables, playing cards or chess, smoking reed-thin pipes and chatting.

No one really knows how many people live in Shanghai, although the official estimate is over 12.5 million, more than double what it was when the first Communist troops marched into the city unopposed in 1949. Although this figure is somewhat deceptive, for only 56 percent of the population is considered truly urban (as opposed to residents who actually farm fields under the city's administration), Shanghai remains China's most densely crowded city, with nearly two thousand people per square kilometer. The next most crowded city, Tianjin, is only one third as dense. In Shanghai, generations of one family are forced by the housing shortage to inhabit tiny apartments so claustrophobic that the average Shanghainese has less than fifty square feet of living space, which is less than the floor area of an average prison cell in the United States. In the old city center, the European houses have been repeatedly subdivided in an effort to accommodate the city's exploding population. Farther out, on the rapidly expanding outskirts of the city, mile after mile of cookie-cutter cement-block apartment complexes march in ranks into the countryside and surround sprawling factories.

Shanghai is the largest industrial center in China. Its steel mills, chemical plants, machine shops, and electrical factories account for more than 8 percent of the country's industrial productivity, and except for neighboring Jiangsu, more than any single province, including Sichuan, which has a population of 100 million. One out of every four radios made in China is manufactured in Shanghai, as is one out of every ten refrigerators, one out of every seven washing machines, and one out of every five cameras. One out of every three tractors rolls off a Shanghai assembly line. But these industries, spawned during the industrialization of the 1950s, are antiquated, badly run, and unprofitable.

The city itself is a mess. Transportation is chaotic, with the streets clotted with trucks, buses, and cars moving at a pace often slower than that of the pedestrians. It is frequently impossible to telephone across town, and factories are routinely idled by electricity outages. Many small shops rely on gasoline generators that chug away on the pavement outside. Foreign investors, drawn in part by a nostalgic memory of the city's past glory, flock eagerly to Shanghai, only to find themselves mired in a swamp of red tape, official procrastination, harassment, and corruption. Every year since 1985, the city's revenues—taxes and earnings from state-owned industries—have fallen.

China's central leadership has struggled mightily to remold Shanghai. The city has weathered a procession of mayors, all with solid political credentials and all arriving with promises of great things to come, only to see them leave, frustrated by their inability to set the city right. The latest incumbent, Zhu Rongji, was a vice minister in the State Economic Commission before being dispatched in 1988 by the central government to try his hand at ordering the behemoth. A local economist puts the matter succinctly: "It is much like a strong person who has developed cancer; you can imagine what will happen if he does not get urgent and proper treatment."

I visited Shanghai frequently while in China, and each time there was a sense that the city was falling a bit further behind more aggressive cities down the coast, which were eager to cash in on the new economic opportunities. During my first visit in 1986, there was not a single international-standard hotel in town, in contrast to Beijing, Tianjin, Guangzhou, even Xian, which by any measure is a bit of a backwater. Since then, two hotels have opened, one of which, the Hilton, made the mistake of insisting on 100 percent foreign ownership; as a result, it has been the object of continued harassment by rapacious city bureaucrats miffed at not sharing in the hotel's bounty.

Shanghai's officials routinely distort facts when it suits their purposes and lie outright when distortions alone are insufficient. In most instances, these deceptions are intended to project an image of the city that bears little resemblance to reality, to smooth the hard edges of decline. Typical of this strategy are a series of remarks made in 1986 by Xiong Yongshi, an official with the Shanghai Economic Region Research Association. Xiong ladled out superlatives to describe his hometown, at one juncture characterizing Shanghai as "the crème de la crème" of Chinese cities. "It is," he said, "superior in historical traditions, psychology, concepts, and quality of its human resources." Its existing infrastructure is being "speedily improved" and its industries and financial institutions "are the most developed in the country."

But one Shanghai economist I knew angrily dismissed such palaver, and maintained that the self-delusions of people like Xiong only mask the seriousness of the city's problems. "Now it is time to pull them out of their fantasies and make them face realities," this economist said. Even the official Chinese news agency, Xinhua, has exhibited little patience for Shanghai's self-promotion. "People should change their train of thought," the news agency declared. "Now everyone is suffering poverty."

Some of Shanghai's arrogance stems from its smug confidence in its revolutionary history. The Communist Party was first organized in Shanghai by Chen Duxiu in 1920, and the first Communist Party congress was held there in July 1921. Shanghai has also regarded itself, in the era of the People's Republic, as the most politically radical city in China. The Cultural Revolution drew many of its most ardent proponents from Shanghai, some of whom rose to positions of power in China's governing councils during this decade of national turmoil and political terror. And even when the Cultural Revolution was brought to a sudden end by Mao's death, Shanghai's leaders still clung to the blood-red banner of cultural revolution, surrendering only when it became apparent that their cause was lost in Beijing.

As much as Shanghai reveled in its revolutionary credentials, its heritage as a cosmopolitan financial center in pre-Communist days was, increasingly, the vision city officials tried to re-create for visiting foreigners. Shanghai would become China's new financial center, we were told. Shanghai would become a core for new high-technology industries. Shanghai would once again be a playground for worldly travelers.

These dreams, wonderful as they were, foundered again and again on the shoals of bureaucracy so instinctual to the city's party hacks. In the dark winter of 1987, news filtered out of Shanghai that the city was besieged with an epidemic of hepatitis. In Beijing, the number of people stricken was said to be in the tens of thousands. By any measure, it was a serious health problem, and warranted a closer look. I flew down to Shanghai and interviewed city officials, health officials, doctors. I went to hospitals that were jammed with patients on beds in hallways. I interviewed people on the street all over town, and everyone seemed to have a family member who had come down with the disease. The dimensions of the epidemic seemed far greater than the figures—ten or twenty thousand cases—that had been bandied about.

But no, insisted the city officials, there were not more than ten thousand. A month later, it was revealed that the number of people who had been hospitalized with hepatitis was actually between three hundred and fifty thousand and half a million. I called a friend in the Shanghai government who had been helpful in the past, and asked her why the government had lied so baldly when I had asked about the epidemic the previous month. "You should know," she replied. "They didn't know what would happen if they gave out the correct figure. So they gave a smaller number until they had solved the problem." That's Shanghai.

· · · ·

REJUVENATING Shanghai's economy has in part focused on restructuring the city's three thousand state-owned enterprises, entities long accustomed to prodding by central planners, to guaranteed supplies and assured markets for their products. Since these industries never had control over their raw materials, the size of their work force, production targets, or the prices for their products, they never fretted about the irksome problem of profits and losses. The committees that ran the state enterprises were not trained managers but Communist Party secretaries who knew little and cared less about the intricacies of management; they were there to ensure political rectitude. This industrial structure, typical everywhere in China as the country emerged from the Cultural Revolution, was modeled on Soviet patterns of state ownership and operation. It soon became clear to many of China's leaders that to continue down the path of Soviet-style socialism would mean perpetual inefficiency and economic stagnation. To overcome this malaise, China's leaders decided to borrow from examples of industrial success around the world. They turned to the capitalist world.

Gradually, China's four hundred thousand larger state-owned industries and enterprises were told that they would no longer be subject to the dictates of some faceless planner in Beijing. Rather, managers would be given the authority to run their enterprises, and party secretaries would be restricted to a more amorphous consultative role. Furthermore, enterprises were to sign contracts with the state obligating them to meet certain production goals. This system was intended to provide incentives to industries to exceed their contracts, and hence generate profits they could retain for their own use, whether for reinvestment or for bonuses to their workers. Managers were also to be given greater flexibility in running their enterprises by allowing them to reward hardworking employees with bonuses, and to penalize those who worked badly or not at all. In some instances, workers could even be fired.

These reforms were devised precisely to shatter the so-called "iron rice bowl" system, in which workers, once employed, were guaranteed their wages regardless of performance. They were also intended to force managers to run their enterprises more efficiently and, for the first time in the history of the People's Republic, with an eye toward the company's balance sheet. And, finally, by granting more autonomy to enterprises, Beijing sought to create a national market in raw materials and finished manufactured goods, through which the forces of supply and demand would set prices, much as they do for agricultural products in the countryside.

In practice, however, the power to fire workers is rarely exercised in state-owned enterprises. Although few managers will acknowledge it openly, there remains a certain political opprobrium attached to dismissing workers. It is often simply more trouble than it is worth to fire workers, because, invariably, the party committee becomes involved and insists on holding endless meetings to "examine" the matter. Rather than undergoing the strain of actually firing a disruptive worker, harried managers usually find it easier to exile the worker to some innocuous job where he or she cannot cause too many problems.

One factory manager told me that he had finally dismissed a worker who had refused to come to work for months. "He was running his own restaurant and just never came in," this director said. "After a while there was nothing I could do. I had to fire him." But what was most amazing was not the fact that he had fired the worker. No, the factory director said; what was astonishing was the fact that the former worker turned restaurateur never even complained. "If he had complained enough, I would probably have had to take him back."

But some factory directors have used their newfound authority like a truncheon. At a diesel engine factory in Henan Province, the director, Li Zhenyan, became fed up with the factory's party secretary and fired him. "Because Comrade Song has obstructed the reforms, and does not support the factory manager, we have decided to let him go," Li said. Other directors, acting more imperiously, have been less successful. In the town of Helan, in Ningxia Province, the director of a lens-making plant fired sixteen workers who had failed to vote for him when he was elected director of the facility. The workers protested to the town government, which ordered them all reinstated.

The new system has also required significant shifts in marketing operations. "In the past, all of our products were sold only by government stores," notes Zhang Mingxu, one of the senior managers in the Hunan Rubber Factory. "Now, we decide where to sell our products. We have contracts with the state to turn

177

THE GOOD, THE BAD, THE FUTURE

over a fixed amount of taxes and profits. This year it's about thirteen million yuan. So we have to pay attention to the market when we sell our products. If certain products sell well, then we increase production of those products. If certain products don't sell well, we cut back production. As a result, the total wages we pay are affected by our sales. The manager decides on bonuses. If the company does well, we can pay the workers bonuses." Indeed, Zhang continues, the rubber factory has been "revitalized" because of the reforms imposed by the central government: "There have been major changes. Productivity has increased. We have new technology and the workers are performing better than they ever have. We have to figure out how to sell our products and where to get raw materials. I'd say we've benefited a good deal from the reforms."

By contrast, reforms in Shanghai enterprises have been less successful, so much less so that an official Chinese news report said of the city's experience with management reform, "Not much progress has been made in this regard." The leadership in Beijing, as well as Mayor Zhu, express dismay over Shanghai's recalcitrance. "Frankly speaking," the mayor told an interviewer in the summer of 1988, "the market economy in Guangzhou is much more deeply rooted." Jiang Zemin, the city's Communist Party secretary and Zhu's predecessor as mayor, even led a team of city officials to Guangdong to try and figure out why that southern province has surged past Shanghai in economic growth. Jiang never grasped what it was that made the south of China economically aggressive, but his pantomiming of the reforms won him friends among the hard-liners in Beijing, and it was he they turned to to lead the country's Communist Party after Zhao Ziyang's fall.

EVEN AS SHANGHAI GROPES toward remolding its economic infrastructure, the city has found it increasingly difficult to cope with the myriad physical and social problems that threaten to rupture the very fabric of urban life. The crush of population, insufficient and inadequate housing, bad water, sporadic electricity, crotchety public transportation, breath-stifling air pollution and occasional epidemics are not unique to Shanghai, but in Shanghai these problems are measured in extremes.

In the northwest corner of the city is an area called the Puto district, a clutter of new but already dilapidated cement apartment blocks hard by a shallow basin of rubble and miniature houses constructed of sheets of wood, beams, tar paper, bricks, and battered tin; so-called *penghu,* or shack housing. Between the houses, crooked alleyways zigzag crazily through the area. These are Shanghai's slums.

Some women from the slum houses were cooking cabbage leaves in a wok over an outdoor fire when I wandered through the area, pausing from time to time to talk to people about their lives. I stopped at one of the penghu and rapped on the plank door, which was opened by Zhang Lanying, a woman in her sixties, who invited me in. Her home consisted of one room on the level of the ground, with a dirt floor, and an identically sized alcove overhead, up a rickety ladder. Like all the people in the slum area, she was waiting for housing in one of the new apartment blocks being built nearby.

"I moved here thirty-six years ago," she told me, carefully pouring me a cup of hot water from a blackened tin kettle. "That was before Liberation. When I moved here, there were all kinds of ditches, water everywhere, and rats. I came from Jiangsu during the war, originally to look for a job. It wasn't very easy to find housing in Shanghai then. So, many people built their own houses. I built this house myself. Altogether, eight people live in my house, but we hope to get an apartment someday. I think it's better to live in a new building."

A neighbor, Xu Minggen, had poked her head in the door as we talked, curious about the commotion the presence of a foreigner was creating. "Ah," she interrupted, "welcome, welcome. Auntie Zhang is right. The new houses are good. I think it's good to live up high. Look at our houses here. We don't have any toilets; we have to cook outside. These new apartments have kitchens and toilets."

Even when the last of the Puto slums are demolished, more than four decades after communism came to Shanghai, and are replaced by ranks of apartment blocks, it will only graze the surface of the city's housing crisis. The intense demand for living space will persist well into the next century, making Shanghai but one of hundreds of major Chinese cities suffering drastic housing shortages. The demand for apartments is so acute that it affects the most basic relations among people. It is

179

common for a man's proposal of marriage to be countered with a question about his living arrangements. If the unlucky suitor has not found his own housing and still lives with his parents, his prospects for finding a bride are jeopardized significantly.

It has gotten so difficult for young couples to find housing in Shanghai that the very search for a mate is conditioned by access to an apartment. Partly as a result of this, and partly because it is not easy to meet prospective partners, institutions called *jieshao suo,* or introduction rooms, have sprung up all over town. Like dating services in the United States, the rooms are usually run by a couple of well-meaning women who make a bit of money keeping files for single people to browse through in the hope of finding a spouse. At one of these rooms, a jolly woman named Kang Weiying showed me her files, pulling at random the card of a young man named Qiu Leimeng.

"Ah, ah. You see," she said, shoving Qiu's card, with his picture attached, across the table. "He's going to have problems." Qiu had written that he lived with his parents and sister in an apartment of twenty-six square meters. "I myself am a little shy," he wrote. "I'd like a person to be a bit cute, to do housework and be tender."

Kang shook her head. "Look here," she pointed at the card. "He's only 1.55 meters tall. He's going to have a hard time. The girls all hope boys will be tall. You can only have one kid, you know, so if your husband is tall, the child will be tall. It's a kind of tradition for the women to want tall men. Mr. Qiu is not tall and doesn't have an apartment. Who will want him?"

A close friend of mine in Beijing has been married for six years, and his living circumstances are typical of urban residents, whether in the capital or in other cities in China. He, his wife, and their five-year-old son inhabit a single room perhaps fifteen feet long and twelve feet wide. The room, one of two dozen along a dimly lit corridor in a four-story cement building, is just large enough for a double bed, a simple pine two-drawer desk, a stand-up wardrobe, and a round folding table and three collapsible stools tucked in the corner. There is a single window that overlooks a paved courtyard and its solitary plane tree. My friend, his wife, and their son all share the same bed. Down the corridor, which is bitingly cold in the winter, is a common bathroom for the residents of the floor. At the midpoint of the corridor, built into the wall, are a few sinks and some cooking burners, the communal kitchen.

For years my friend complained to me, with a mixture of despair and resignation, about his cramped quarters. One night, after he had served me an elaborate meal on the folding table he squeezed between the quilt-covered bed and the desk, he lamented his failure to obtain a better apartment.

"There's nothing I can do," he told me, expressing the widely felt hopelessness of individuals tangled in the mesh of a lethargic and impersonal bureaucracy. "I've asked my unit for new housing now for the last five years. But you have to know someone. You have to have *guanxi* [connections]. I don't know anybody special. How would *you* like to live here? How can anyone live like this?

"They always tell me to wait. All I have to do is wait and then I will get an apartment. But I've waited for four years and our son is five. If I wait five more years, he will be ten. Where will he sleep then?"

My friend, like virtually every city dweller, pays a pittance for his apartment; in his case, slightly less than two dollars a month, about 3 percent of his salary. Since 1949, housing has been regarded as a fundamental social right dispensed freely or at a nominal cost by the state. This practice was deemed, from the outset of the People's Republic, as a defining and immutable feature of socialism, one copied, not incidentally, from China's neighbor, the Soviet Union.

Apartments in China are distributed by bureaucrats in city housing departments or in the state enterprises that own the buildings. As my friend observed, need bears no relation to the size of the apartment dispensed by the housing bureaucracy. My friend's wife, who is even a member of the Communist Party, did not have the right connections to wangle an apartment from officials at her workplace, a government office in Beijing. As my friend's patience with his circumstances frayed, he began actively looking for a new job, enlisting his friends to look for employers that needed office workers and who also had apartments available.

By the mid-1980s, it was apparent to policymakers in Beijing that despite an extraordinary boom in housing construction in the cities, the prevailing system of giving away the new apartments, rather than relieving the housing shortage, had in fact made the situation worse. So chaotic had the problem of housing become by 1987 that the government had no real idea of its exact extent. So, that year, Beijing conducted the first comprehensive survey of the country's housing stock and discovered that more than ten million urban homes were inadequate, that 30 percent of city housing had no indoor cooking facilities, and that 26 percent were without any piped water. Fully two thirds of city housing in China lacked an indoor lavatory. Moreover, the survey found that the average city dweller had scarcely more than six square meters of space, only a shade more than the average living space in Shanghai, supposedly the city with the most cramped living areas in the country. In addition, the government learned that three hundred and thirty thousand urban families were outright homeless.

If other sectors of the economy were to draw their strength from market forces, these policymakers asked, why should not housing benefit from a similar reliance on the push and pull of supply and demand? As logical as this query may seem, however, even broaching the issue constituted a sharp challenge to what was generally seen as an inviolable right, one grounded firmly in a perception of the state's role and the obligations of socialism toward society. Nonetheless, after bruising debate, the State Council issued a detailed plan in 1988 for reorienting the country's housing system.

The council bluntly acknowledged that "the state has spent a great deal of money on housing construction for urban residents, but urban housing problems have not been alleviated, because of official corruption and the failure to use an economic mechanism to restrain irrational demand. Partiality in housing distribution has become a serious social problem. Reform of the urban housing system is an important component of the reform of the economic structure."

Once again, the experience to which the State Council turned was that of capitalist economies; it ordered an across-the-board commercialization of the urban housing market. For the first time in the history of the socialist state, rents were to be raised, and they were to reflect, to a greater or lesser degree, the quality and amount of space being rented. The wages of urban workers were to be increased or supplemented with rent subsidy payments. In this more market-conditioned environment, urbanites seeking larger apartments would have to pay more than they had for smaller accommodations. In an even more dramatic move, vast numbers of apartments would be put up for sale, and banks would be authorized to issue long-term mortgages.

EVEN BEFORE the State Council laid out its scheme, Shanghai had begun its own experiment with housing reform; though little more than a tentative gesture, it nonetheless reflected an awareness that something had to be done. As a way of absorbing the growing savings of Shanghai residents, the government decided to sell a percentage of the city's new apartments. Of course, the prevailing credo of socialism prohibits actually selling the apartment itself, so what the city sold was the right of occupancy, a right which itself could be sold or inherited. The city government felt that families desperate enough for housing would pay for it, but, like virtually every effort to solve monumental problems in China, this one too was riddled with inequities.

Wu Xilin, a chunky woman in her fifties, is one of the few real-estate agents in Shanghai; indeed, in all China. I spoke with her in her cubbyhole office, which perhaps reflected the limited scope of her activities. Over the seven years since 1980, Wu told me, she and her colleagues had peddled a total of 4,857 apartments, and more than 1,000 of those were sold to Chinese living abroad, so-called overseas Chinese, who paid in dollars. The practice of selling apartments to people of Chinese ancestry who are citizens of other countries has become a lucrative business for many cities in China. Of course, selling apartments to foreigners (who, incidentally, must be ethnic Chinese) does nothing to resolve the domestic housing crisis.

Wu admitted that the idea of buying an apartment is a difficult psychological barrier for most city residents to overcome now, since they are accustomed to renting apartments for next to nothing. "People are aware that rent is cheaper," Wu said. "But many people don't have houses. So, if I have no house to rent I have to buy one." In 1987, Wu explained, nearly 10 percent of the new housing built in Shanghai would be sold rather than rented. The principal problem is not finding buyers, she said, but in deciding who should be allowed to buy. Because the apartments are expensive by Chinese standards, in the neighborhood of fifteen thousand yuan apiece, factories and work-places were to subsidize two thirds of the purchase price. And because of these subsidies, ultimately it falls to the employers, actually a group of petty bureaucrats, to determine who receives the subsidies, and hence the apartments.

"A lot of people want to buy houses," Wu told me, as we trudged through the mud of a new housing project on the way to visit a new apartment owner. "If all the buyers came in, they would queue from morning to night. I could sell thirty thousand apartments in one year, no problem. But with the system we have now, some of the buyers who have really serious housing problems cannot get apartments. And some of the people whose problem is not so serious, but who have lots of connections, will get apartments. Really, I don't think the housing problem in Shanghai will be solved in this way."

We walked a few blocks, some of it sidewalked, some not, to a newly erected housing project made up of ranks of six-story concrete slab buildings. The buildings were separated by stretches of raw earth littered with shards of cement and brick. We entered a building, distinguished from its neighbors only by its number, in this case "No. 6," and climbed the dark interior cement stairs. On each landing, charcoal-fired stoves blazed away, spewing soot through jerry-rigged exhaust chimneys that poked through the stairwell windows. Clothes hung to dry, cor-rugated cardboard boxes, rattan baskets filled with cabbages, bicycles, and scarred wood-paneled wardrobes cluttered the stairwell, creating an obstacle course for pedestrians. On the sixth floor, we rapped on the door of apartment 604, and were met by Song Lanying, a fifty-four-year-old woman wearing a blue plastic apron wrapped around layers of sweaters and cotton shirts.

She asked us inside and poured us tea as we chatted. I was surprised to learn that she was utterly indifferent to the fact that she was an owner rather than a renter.

"We bought this apartment last year, through my husband's factory," she said, settling into a deep armchair. "He's at work now. I used to work in an umbrella factory, but I'm retired now. We used to live in the Nanshi district in a *penghu,* a shack house. We rented a house there, one room. The person who owned the house wanted it back, so we had nowhere to live. Of course we wanted to rent but there were no apartments, so we had to buy. We preferred to rent, really."

I asked Song why, if they wanted to rent, she and her husband had taken what in China was a rather bold step, actually buying their home. Song shrugged her shoulders. "Oh, you see, in the beginning we thought we couldn't afford to buy an apartment. A lot of people handed in applications to the factory. Then the leaders decided, and we got a certificate that let us buy this apartment. Also, you have to have guanxi to get an apartment to rent these days."

I explained to Song that in New York, many people own their apartments and that it is generally believed that owners take better care of their apartments than do renters. After all, I said, using the banal logic of New York housing experts, ownership means that occupants have a greater stake in their apartment. Song waved her hand dismissively at this suggestion.

"No, it's not like that here," she said, confirming again that the wisdom of the West is not always unalloyed. "If you rent an apartment, you don't have to put out so much money at once. I don't think owning an apartment is so different. In my opinion, it's the same as renting. If I rent a house, it is also my house. I may have to live there all my life. I have to take care of that, I have to take care of this."

WANDERING DOWN NANJING ROAD one afternoon, I found myself in a shop that was selling what seemed to me to be the ultimate expression of Shanghai's quest for new approaches to old problems: easy-to-understand principles on the virtues and vagaries of property ownership and the perils of renting, on the accumulation of capital, on banking and bankruptcy. There, on a shelf behind the counter, was a Monopoly game in Chinese. It wasn't called Monopoly, of course. The manufacturer had renamed the game *Qiangshou*, or Strong Hand. But it had Park Place, or, in the off-key translation, Parking Lot. It had Get Out of Jail Free cards and the Short Line Railroad. It had dice, green houses, and red hotels. The only major difference was that the player tokens were all wheelbarrows. There were no top hats, irons, or racing cars.

"This game is a microcosm of Western society," the instructions read when I opened the box. "Now, in introducing this game to our domestic friends, we hope that in playing this game we will raise our little friends' arithmetical abilities and judgment, as well as their understanding of Western society. Buy! Sell! Increase your income! Go to jail!"

In 1988, the game sold more than two hundred thousand copies.

DESPITE THE WEIGHT of bureaucracy that sits on Shanghai, the internal strife in the city government that is only hinted at, there are instances where Shanghai seems to be trying to return to its former glory as the country's most advanced city. Central Shanghai, largely because of its heritage as a former center for foreign commerce, still has the air (albeit woefully faded) of a European city. Every street is lined with storefronts, teahouses, restaurants; sights far rarer in the impersonal grayness of Beijing.

A facet of Shanghai life I came to love was the profusion of coffeehouses, unheard of in Beijing, that have cropped up all over town. Young lovers, hand in hand, sit for hours gazing into one another's eyes, drinking, of all things, coffee. Most coffeehouses are privately owned, and the service approaches the endurable. But what distinguishes them from the large, loud, impersonal tea and dumpling joints in Beijing is that the coffeehouses provide a sense of privacy and intimacy that socialism in China had once sought to eradicate. There are dark corners where couples can nuzzle, small tables where one can read a newspaper undisturbed.

Such idiosyncrasies were not difficult to find after one had been in Shanghai for a while. My favorite discovery was China's first, and I believe only, used-car dealer. I was running around Shanghai with a Chinese friend, and she had mentioned that there was a strange business on the north side of the city that was selling cars on the open market. The reason this struck her, and me, as so peculiar is that there are almost no privately owned automobiles in this land of two-wheeled vehicles.

After some asking around, we located the place, a cavernous garage tucked down an alleyway. Lined up along the walls were about a dozen cars, some Chinese Shanghai-brand autos, a few Skodas, a couple of Polonez 1.5s, and a half a dozen Toyota Crowns, which seemed to be former taxicabs. I was obviously the first foreigner to grace the portal of the garage, and a gentleman with a Volkswagen pin on his lapel hurried over to see what my friend and I wanted. I explained that we wanted to talk about selling cars in Shanghai. He introduced himself as Shao Henian. How, precisely, I wondered, did one go about buying a car?

"First, there is bargaining," Shao said merrily. At a long table in the middle of the garage, several very animated conversations were under way, pencils dipping to scribble on lined notebooks from time to time, teacups sipped between offers and counteroffers. From the look of the discussions, some of these bargaining sessions had been under way for some time.

I told Shao that used-car dealers in the United States had unsavory reputations in the popular imagination, principally for their propensity for selling cars that drove flawlessly to the edge of the used car lot, where they promptly expired. "Oh no no no," he said, his voice rising an octave. "We have mechanics check all the cars out."

"You never sell a *ningmeng?*" I asked, using the Chinese word for lemon.

"Ningmeng?" he asked. "What is *ningmeng?*"

I explained that, in the United States, cars that seem to function well when they are bought but then tend to develop an endless series of mechanical problems are colloquially referred to as lemons.

"Ah," he nodded, "we don't sell lemons."

Only in Shanghai.

Part III

Collision

Without democracy there can be no development. Unless individual human rights are recognized, there can be no true democracy. In China, the very ABCs of democracy are unknown. We have to educate ourselves toward democracy. We have to understand that democracy is not something that our leaders can hand over to us. Democracy that comes from above is nothing but a relaxation of control. There will be an intense fight. But it cannot be avoided.

FANG LIZHI, 1987

NINE

The Other China

NOBODY EVER GOES to Tshurphu. It is on few maps, and most books on Tibet ignore the place, just an indistinct clutter of stone boulder houses and a gutted monastery a few hours from Lhasa. Perhaps, because there are thousands of Tshurphus in Tibet, it seems not so very different. But it was its very invisibility, its anonymity, its commonplace experiences, that drew me to this obscure monastery.

The Toyota Land Cruiser I had rented bucked and stalled on the rocky path that wound away into the mountains from the main road. Young boys in bare feet whacked the rumps of shaggy black yaks that dawdled along the roadside. Pierced only by a cold, neon sun, the sky arced overhead like an intense sapphire-blue parasol, pure and unblemished. My driver, a Tibetan, stoically surveyed an apparently impassable stream that gurgled in its rocky course. My interpreter, a gentle young man who lived in Dharmsala, India (the exile home of the Dalai Lama), and I began heaving stones into the water to create a track for the car. A yak-herder crouching on a knoll studied our efforts with amusement.

Carefully, the driver edged the Land Cruiser onto the boulders while we stood on the stream's opposite bank, imploring the vehicle forward with frantic arm-waving. Our driver, unperturbed, danced the car over the rocks, and we pushed on into the hills. Electricity lines, strung like fragile cobwebs through much of central Tibet, were not spun here; apart from our dusty blue vehicle, there were no signs of the twentieth century. After we jolted over the rocky trail, the road expired at the base of the ruined stone foundations of Tshurphu, a monastery built in 1185, nine years before work began on the cathedral of Chartres. Rubble filled what once were rooms of prayer, and wooden beams cantilevered at crazy angles; the fractured skeleton of the ancient monastery.

As we walked from the car, a old man, his face mapped in deep, mahogany folds, slowly walked toward us, his mouth open in a broad, toothless grin. On his head he wore a sort of Australian bush hat, the left side of the brim jauntily turned upward, and over his left shoulder, a traditional Tibetan blanket. He gave his name as Gabuk, and told us that he was seventy-three. He was a monk at Tshurphu. As he spoke not a word of Chinese, a language and people for whom he had only the greatest contempt, we conversed through my interpreter.

Gabuk waved us into his small chamber, rebuilt amid collapsed walls, its ceiling a mat of twigs and branches. A padded mat covered with a dirty quilt was in one corner. As we sat on some cushions, a young woman came in with a kettle of pungent yak butter tea, an aromatic and oily concoction that is drunk everywhere in Tibet, but one that greets the uninitiated palate with an unwelcome sourness. I sat in silence while my interpreter offered Gabuk news of Dharmsala and the Dalai Lama, the man revered as a god-king by Tibetans—news forbidden by the Chinese authorities. Gabuk bobbed his head as he listened, fingering his prayer beads, squeezing each one through his thumb and forefinger. At the mention of the Dalai Lama's name, he brought his hands together in prayer and touched his forehead, bowing slightly; the passionate devotion in his eyes was something I saw again and again in my trips to Tibet.

"It was around 1963," Gabuk began, slowly numbering the

years on his blackened prayer beads, "when they destroyed the monastery. At that time, there were more than five hundred monks. Now, there are only one hundred and thirty. The Chinese army came here and ordered the people to destroy the monastery. They ordered us to destroy it by hand. Everyone was scared. No one wanted to touch the monastery, but they knew they would be killed if they didn't. I myself never saw any monks killed. The monks just obeyed. Everyone was crying. We knew we had lost our independence."

The story of Tshurphu is not unlike those of the region's other sixty-five hundred monasteries, which were blown up, battered apart, burned, and looted by the Chinese in a frenetic effort to exterminate a religious culture incompatible with socialism, or with Han (or ethnic Chinese) culture itself. In his long life, Gabuk had lived in an independent Tibet, only to see his country occupied and then destroyed by an invading army of political zealots. His words convey, not so much despair, as an infinite sadness.

"When I see all the destruction here, I often cry," he said. "That's why I don't really like to walk through here. I was two years old when I came here to be a monk. Parents believe that if a son becomes a monk, it is very good. All this ended when the Chinese came. They burned the scriptures. All the statues were taken away by the soldiers to Beijing. They drove the monks away. I went into a village in the valley where I worked as a farmer for twenty-two years. I came back here in 1983."

The year Gabuk returned to the monastery, after he had married and had a son, work to rebuild the monastery began. Gradually, some of the older monks came back, although, as Gabuk told me, many did not. "Many monks who became farmers, or turned to business, did not return," he said. "Their lives are different now. Today, we have some young monks, although I myself don't have any students. Now we are getting some scriptures from India and some other places."

We walked out into the sunshine to watch small groups of women and monks lugging blocks of stone, piece by piece, to a wall being relaid on the old foundation. Piles of stone block, newly hewn timbers, and sand surrounded the shell of the monastery. Three young boys in maroon monks' robes scampered over the construction materials like children anywhere.

193

"Four years ago," Gabuk explained, "most interference in our religious activities stopped. We now get a little money from the government to help us rebuild the monastery, but mostly it is our own labor. Because we're so far from Lhasa, there isn't much government interference any more. The Chinese wanted to destroy Buddhism completely. I was very afraid when they first came. I never thought they'd allow us to rebuild now."

Pasted on a wall, however, an announcement from the area Communist Party branch sternly enjoined the monastery's residents: "Workers should work properly. Scriptures should be read properly." The notion that the Chinese Communist Party could pretend to dictate to the monks of Tshurphu how the scriptures should be read would be laughable, were it not so tragically revealing about China's intention to control this culture.

For a long time, I sat and watched the people of this remote place heave a stone block into place, return for another, drag it across the ground, and, grunting, hoist it into place, much the way the monastery must have first been built eight centuries ago. I wondered what the world's reaction would have been if the German occupation of France had left the cathedrals of Chartres, Reims, and Rouen in charred ruins. That, and worse, is what has happened to Tibet.

THE CHINESE are an intolerant people; their government an intolerant government. By intolerance, I mean both an unwillingness to countenance difference and a profound unease with cultural diversity within their midst. Endless essays have been written about the chauvinism of the Chinese, who ethnically are Han, a reference to the first great dynasty, and I shall not reexplore the historical roots of this trait. Rather, I prefer simply to describe what I saw: those efforts to exterminate or disembowel non-Han minority cultures.

There are many disturbing aspects of modern Chinese society, and this ongoing attempt to obliterate the few remaining fragile, indigenous cultures that trace their roots back hundreds or thousands of years is one of the most unsettling, and little discussed, facets of modern China. China's fifty-six minority groups, or nationalities, comprise about 6 percent of the nation's population of 1.1 billion, or slightly more than 60 million, people. During various periods in Chinese history, ethnic minorities have fought to retain their identity. In the early nineteenth century, Hong Xiuchuan, a Hakka (ethnic minority) from Guangxi Province, led a quasi-Christian millenarian rebellion that, for a time, seriously threatened the stability of the Qing dynasty. And in the middle of the century, the systematic discrimination by Hans against Muslims in the Yunnan, Gansu, and Shaanxi provinces triggered a bloody uprising that lasted fifteen years.

Since 1949, official rhetoric has sought to portray the country's ethnic minorities as members of a happy national family. Mounds of statistics are issued annually to demonstrate the government's commitment to the development of minority areas, some of which have been accorded a formal, although essentially meaningless, designation as "autonomous" regions or districts. In fact, those areas of China in which non-Han ethnic groups constitute a majority or a significant minority of the population are the poorest parts of the country: they have benefited the least from the past decade of economic development, they exhibit the highest rates of illiteracy, and they must endure the most oppressive and stringently authoritarian local governments.

Early in 1987, China opened a number of remote areas previously forbidden to foreigners. Among them were the western edges of Hunan, an extremely rugged, mountainous, and grindingly poor area that for centuries has been home to the Miao people. During the Ming and Qing dynasties, Miao soldiers clashed regularly with Chinese armies, developing a reputation as fearsome and durable warriors. In Western historical and anthropological literature, the Miao are often referred to as a tribal people, a designation derived largely from the tight-knit communities which, at the most primitive level, engaged in slash-and-burn agriculture as recently as the eighteenth century, and, more broadly, were a society distinctly less modern than the prevailing literate Han culture.

The major Chinese town within the region (originally a cantonment for Chinese troops) is Fenghuang, the hometown of Shen Congwen, who for nearly seven decades explored the frontier life of the Miao and Chinese alike in dense, allegorical prose. Shen told with a penetrating voice of the quandaries of love in a

195

starkly formalized society, of families who lived on riverboats, of villagers and banditry and the mysteries of Chengzhou magic and the jinxes of witchcraft. Of his hometown, he wrote:

"This lonely border town with its round city wall of big, solid, rough-hewn stones, is encircled by over five hundred Miao villages with garrisons between them. There are also approximately five hundred forts and two hundred barracks. . . . This was according to a master plan drawn up one hundred and eighty years ago to cope with the Miao tribesmen driven back to that territory, who often revolted. . . . Now, all this has changed. Most of the forts are in ruins, most of the barracks are occupied by civilians, and half the minority people have adopted Chinese ways. But at sunset or dusk, if you climb a height in that town which stands impressively alone surrounded by mountains, gazing at the ruined forts near and far, you can still conjure up a faint picture of the past when bugles, drums, and torches raised an alarm."

Much of Fenghuang remains as it was a century ago, a town of narrow alleyways, paved with large flat flagstones, which slip along the edges of the River Tuo, impassable to vehicles and sandwiched between houses of ash-gray granite and tobacco-colored wood. More modern streets surround the old town, with cement buildings in loud pastels and new metal shutters. Down the alleyways, the wood houses, their planks stained deep mocha from tung oil, teeter gingerly over the currents of the Tuo, their floors balanced precariously on wooden stilts like spindly stork legs. From time to time, a wooden bucket on a rope tether drops suddenly to the muddy river to haul water to the house above. The houses are piled upon one another like shaken building blocks, their roof beams never quite level and their wall posts askew under the strain of age. Many window frames still yawn with hand-carved wood latticework that filters stone-brushed light into the dim interiors of the old houses. Other houses, built with blocks of the abundant granite that makes up the surrounding hills, crouch heavily along the alleys, their walls deeply cool to the fingertips. Like sheets of dried fish scales, roofs of charcoal-gray baked tiles hang heavily in overlapping layers, brooding over the dark-walled houses. Along the south bank of the Tuo, the old city wall rises thick and ominous as it marches ponderously from the city gates. About midway between the town's two bridges, one of these old gates, its wooden tower somewhat reconstructed, pokes above the muddle of houses and the wall itself, its river face incised with the ideograms *bihuimen,* or Shining Screen Gate. Broad stone steps slip from the gate to a flat slab along the river, where boys and young men come to fish and women can be seen washing clothing, beating the garments with thick, flat wooden paddles.

It is beyond the city wall and the new, electrified parts of Fenghuang, up in the rocky hills, that the Miao live. As the old Shanghai car I had rented struggled into the mountains, I could see an outcropping here and there of the crumbling stone foundations of the forts where Qing-dynasty soldiers had once been garrisoned in efforts to subdue Miao rebellions. Once the hills were dense with cypress, China fir, scholar, and poplar trees, but a voracious appetite for fuel, ceiling poles, and building beams has reduced the forests of western Hunan to stubble; the last recorded sighting of a tiger, animals that had roamed the forests from time immemorial, was in 1964. Crescent-moon paddy fields tumbled down hillsides like glittering staircases in a Busby Berkeley musical, and from time to time I could hear a farmer shouting, "Shhhyouuu," swatting the flank of his water buffalo as it pulled a primitive wooden plow. It was a Friday and a market day on the lunar calendar. Along the road, a narrow sliver of asphalt, and on paths winding from the hills, Miao women in embroidered turquoise tunics and black cotton trousers, their heads wrapped in swollen turbans made from ten or fifteen yards of black gauze, padded toward the market in Ala town. The saying here is "The bigger the hat, the richer the woman." They carried thimble-shaped knapsacks of woven bamboo, or garishly clad infants in bamboo-frame chairs strapped to their backs. For more than two decades, until 1980, almost all Miao customs had been banned, including the traditional forms of adornment favored by women. With the relaxation of the more onerous forms of repression, many Miao women wore heavy necklaces and bracelets of intricate hammered silver, jewelry that clinked softly as they walked.

I visited Ala and some of the other surrounding villages, trying to get a sense for how the Miao have endured. I was squired about by Wu Songzuo, the director of the Fenghuang County Minority Affairs Commission, who was, of course, not Miao but

Han Chinese. Wu was supposed to "guide" my observations, but, in an unintended way, he revealed the extent of the erosion of the Miao way of life. I stopped to talk to a local Communist Party secretary, Long Yunbang, who was also not a Miao, and he told me that only one of the fourteen villages in the district had electricity, a significant measure of the region's considerable poverty. For the entire county, he said, there was only a single primary school. I asked him what language the children were taught in. "The lessons are in Chinese," he said, and, after a pause, "but the teachers explain in Miao." My escort then jumped in: "The Miao language is not popularized now. For a time in 1956, they tried to popularize Miao as a written language, but it was suspended. After 1982, the campaign to study written Miao was restarted. They use an alphabet, not Chinese characters." Wu admitted that he had made no effort to learn the written language himself but, he conjectured, "As far as I know, the language is easy to use and master. The students can become literate after only three months of study."

I pressed Wu to take me to the primary school, and several days later was driven to Tangjiaqiao, a village near the border of Guizhou Province. The schoolhouse, fashioned of red clay block, was built in a small clearing on a hilltop. There was one classroom full of students the day I came, and though the single book on each child's desk seemed pristinely new, there were no pencils or pads of paper to be seen. The teacher had written a stanza from a Tang dynasty poem in Chinese on a cracked blackboard and was explaining each line in Miao to his pupils. Then he asked several children to write the poem on the board in Miao, a task they executed with some difficulty. While there were posters written in Chinese hung along the walls, I saw nothing written in Miao. Later, the head of the school told me that, until 1986, there had been no books in the school at all. The books I saw on the students' desks, he told me, "had just arrived."

There is as yet no dictionary of the Miao tongue, no books in written Miao, no collections of the abundant folktales, songs, and rites of the Miao people. Wu Housheng, who edits a compilation of official reports on local minority affairs in Fenghuang, explained to me that the provincial leadership regards Miao as "an experimental language." He went on: "If the leadership does not provide enough money, it will be difficult to develop the written language." I asked if any of the Chinese population in the area, whether officials or civilians, learned Miao. "No," he said sharply, "certainly not." I questioned him as to whether, given the degree of official neglect, the language would eventually be displaced by Chinese. "It's hard to tell," he replied. "It's hard to tell."

For the two decades following 1959, virtually all manifestations of Miao culture were banned. Miao festivals, the singing and dancing that was a central feature of courtship, traditional wedding rituals, burial rites—all were forbidden as expressions of "feudalism and superstition." But with the general relaxation of political controls in Hunan Province since 1980, some of these practices have reappeared, particularly the important lunar New Year festival, which conjointly celebrates the heroism of a Qing dynasty Miao rebel who led a successful campaign against Chinese armies. Before the advent of communism, the Miao used to hold the Nuoyan, a religious rite of symbolic sacrifice conducted every three years to ensure good harvests, the welfare of families, and escape from calamity. This ceremony, so fundamental to the culture, "was prevalent before Liberation," Wu Songzuo informed me, "but it is banned now because it is considered a kind of superstition." Also prohibited was the mournful funeral rite common among the Miao. But this the authorities have not been able to stop, he said. "We forbid it," he said, "but it still goes on. It is much simpler than Nuoyan, just within the family, so we let it go."

I tried repeatedly to meet with provincial officials in the area to get some feeling for the full scope of provincial policy toward the Miao, but was rebuffed in each instance. "Why don't you visit the local waterfall?" was one retort. "They are all out inspecting damage from a storm," came another, and, finally, "There is one official here, but he refuses to see you." By sheer luck, though, I stumbled across a journalist from a newspaper in Beijing, Gu Chengwen, who was spending a year in western Hunan compiling a series of reports on the region. Among everyone I met there, he was the only person who was clear-eyed and candid about the devastating poverty and the cultural annihilation that was occurring. I told my watchdog from Changsha (who had clung to me like a leech since I left the capital days earlier), much to his visible displeasure, that I would meet him later, and Gu and I retreated to a sidewalk dumpling house to talk.

"It's forbidden to talk about all this," he said, obviously relaxed now that my minder had been dispatched. "This area is among the poorest in China. I have been in places where people have only enough food for half the year, where two people have to share one quilt at night. I've talked to many officials and they all are very pessimistic about the future of the area. They think this place has no future. It is just too poor." I pushed Gu to talk about the Miao as a distinct culture. "In my opinion," he answered, "the Miao will die out. It is taboo to say this, but this is my view. The younger generation are being forced to speak Chinese. They don't want to wear traditional dress; they don't know their own traditions. They are being made into Chinese. That is the policy. Nobody says so, but that is the policy. Have you ever seen an official, a single official, in traditional dress? Not once."

There are occasions, I reminded Gu, such as national conferences in Beijing, where deputies can be seen garbed in a panoply of distinctive ethnic dress, from Mongolian to Tibetan, Miao to Hui. "Ah yes," he replied, "but that is the capital, and those are stage settings. They are told to wear those costumes."

Gu is right, of course. People like the Miao are battered daily by the inevitable sweep of Han culture, no less so than the Indians of the Amazon rain forest who wilt under the pressure of white development or the aborigines who succumb to the pizza parlors and beer halls of white Australia. Platitudes about cultural diversity and the rights of national minorities mouthed by party officials in Beijing or in provincial capitals cannot obscure the reality of policies actually designed to homogenize culture in China. From the vantage point of Beijing, a modern nation can only exist if there is a common tongue, common points of cultural and political reference. The official from the capital who makes his inspection tours of the hinterland expects to be able to communicate with the locals; that is a measure of national integration, of modernity itself.

Chinese sensitivity to the appearance of heavy-handedness in its dealings with these minority cultures is acute, but it is a sensitivity of image, not of substance. One summer I visited Hainan Island, a dollop of land that drips from the southern coast of Guangdong Province and home to China's nine hundred thousand Li people. Like the Miao of Hunan, most Li live in villages without electricity, without schools, in a subsistence poverty. But on the main north-south road that bisects the island, there is a model Li village, a Potemkin settlement where tourists, most of whom happen to be from Hong Kong, can buy tribal trinkets and have their photographs taken with a young woman in exotic headdress, the quintessential happy native.

TIBET, HOWEVER, is where Chinese policy has exacted its highest price, where it has systematically and violently assaulted a coherent, thriving, and unique culture. In the latter part of the 1980s, for the first time in the three decades since the Chinese army crushed an independence rebellion in 1959 (and nearly four decades after the first Chinese soldiers marched into the Himalayan country), Tibetans staged a series of increasingly violent protests against Chinese rule. On each occasion, the Chinese responded in fury, mobilizing thousands of armed police to subdue maroon-robed Buddhist monks and lay Tibetans protesting China's occupation of their homeland. Hundreds, perhaps thousands—no one besides the Chinese authorities knows the real numbers with any certainty—were arrested, dozens more shot to death.

China's formal nomenclature for the area is the Tibetan Autonomous Region, a designation that belies Tibet's real status. Tibet is run by Communist Party officials dispatched from Beijing, whose authority is enforced by Chinese troops. The economic infrastructure, such as it is, is dominated by Chinese who have been settled in Tibet by the Beijing government. China defends this arrangement by citing what it contends are historical antecedents for Chinese sovereignty over the region. Among historians—that is, among historians whose work is not molded by political considerations—the complexity of Tibet's relationship with dynastic China precludes simplistic claims of Chinese sovereignty. What is unmistakably clear, however, is that from the early nineteenth century on, China's Qing dynasty ceased to exercise any real authority over Lhasa. In the twentieth century, until Mao's armies arrived in Lhasa in 1951, Tibet was effectively an independent country.

Despite a newly emerging economic structure which has enhanced regional autonomy for swathes of coastal and southern China, Tibet, if anything, has been sewn more securely into the fabric of the Chinese state. The independence from Beijing exhibited by provinces like Guangdong, Fujian, or Zhejiang, disturbing though it may be for China's leadership, is a consequence of economic, not nationalistic, forces. Tibet, precisely because of an imbued nationalism fired by an intense religious and cultural identity, has proved more threatening to the Chinese authorities. The winds of change that roused much of the rest of China in the 1980s have soughed but faintly in Tibet.

In the spring of 1981, party leader Hu Yaobang visited Lhasa and declared that he was appalled at the poverty and backwardness of Tibet, conditions that had been imposed by the reigning Communist Party officials. Hu fired Tibet's Communist Party secretary, appointed a successor (an army political commissar who had participated in the Chinese invasion of Tibet in 1951), and ordered a series of policy changes intended to lift the most oppressive aspects of Chinese rule. Among the measures Hu approved was permission for the Tibetans to resume growing barley, the traditional grain crop of the region, instead of winter wheat, a grain more suited to Chinese tastes than barley. Hu's visit, the first by a senior member of the party since the Chinese invasion, was intended to demonstrate a new leniency toward Tibetans and to go some distance in bolstering the prestige of the party in the region.

By then, however, such extraordinary devastation had been committed by the Chinese in Tibet that no effort by Beijing stood any chance of winning Tibetan hearts and minds. It was apparent during my first visit to Tibet in the spring of 1987 that hatred of China and the Chinese was pervasive among all sectors of the Tibetan population. For its part, Chinese propagandists churned out piles of pamphlets, magazines, and books depicting happy Tibetans joyfully working for the greater good of the motherland. I accumulated quite a collection of these documents while in China; the baldness of their propaganda was quite distinct from the generally more sophisticated descriptions of China's economy and society. From descriptions of China's invasion of Tibet in 1951, invariably referred to as "the peaceful liberation of Tibet," to the heralded "forty-three government sponsored construction projects" of the mid-1980s (a scattering of hotels, gymnasiums, a bus terminal, and a handful of hospitals, all for an area the size of Western Europe), Chinese suzerainty has been portrayed as consistently beneficial for the grateful Tibetans. As one enthusiastic Chinese writer tellingly put it: "The light of hope has risen over the Tibetan plateau. It inspires the Tibetan people and makes overseas Tibetans long to return to their homeland. We are sure that more and more overseas Tibetans will come back. Tibet is thriving and prospering day by day. Its tomorrow surely will be better than today."

Beijing's propaganda, not surprisingly, is dismissive of the more than two decades of calamity experienced by Tibetans at the hands of the Chinese: the destruction of monasteries and temples, the imprisonment and murder of monks, the machinegunning of herds of wild yaks by Chinese troops, the bludgeoning of traditional agriculture, arts, and music. In the words of a typical Chinese screed, "During that period, the party's national, economic, religious, united front, and cadre policies were annulled, and Tibetans suffered the consequences with all the people of China." That is all. China's act of cultural genocide is reduced to "consequences" of bad policies, mere "errors," as common characterization has it.

I visited many of the consequences of these errors in the spring of 1987. One in particular will forever remain fixed in my mind: the remains of the monastery at Ganden, about thirty miles east of Lhasa. Ganden was founded in 1409 by Tsongkhapa, a formidable religious teacher who, as abbot of the fledgling monastery, set forth the tenets of a new Buddhist sect, the Gelugpa, or, as it is more widely known in the West, the Yellow Hats. It was, along with Sera and Drepung in Lhasa, one of the "Three Pillars of the State," a central place of learning for Tibetan Buddhist monks, and a monastery known for its fierce sense of purpose and independence.

The narrow gravel road from Lhasa to Ganden meanders along the southern bank of the Kyichu River, creeping into the heartland of Tibet. There is a primitive desolation about the Tibetan countryside, a stillness that somehow seems to echo in the searing wilderness. Against the rim of Tibet's central plain, mountains loom, scrub-covered foothills edging forward first, and, behind them, raw, fractured, snow-dipped peaks. We drove thirty miles along this road, a trip that took nearly two hours, skirting occasional rock slides, squeezing past two army trucks that had collided head-on. At about the thirty-mile point, the driver swung south on a still narrower, dusty track and into a corral of mountains. The driver then tacked onto a thread of gravel that wound up the side of a mountain, a path we shared with the occasional mule, huddles of peasants treading toward the summit, some spinning hand-held prayer wheels. After some time, the driver shifted into four-wheel drive, to more safely negotiate the climb, I hoped. Then, as we swung around an obtrusion of granite, Ganden monastery appeared, suddenly, in an amphitheater of rock.

But it was not the Ganden of history, the seemingly endless tiers of whitewashed stone buildings, traditionally thicker at the base than at the roof, crowded together in a dense jumble that gave a sense of ordered chaos. What I saw, what I knew I would see, was a scene from hell, a Dresden at fourteen thousand feet. Collapsed stone walls, the crumbling foundations of abbeys, the ruins of a fifteenth-century masterpiece that until a mere two decades before had been one of the most important sites of religious learning in the world, were spread across the apex of the mountain like bleached bones on a killing field.

It was not easy for the Chinese to pulverize Ganden. The massive walls of the monastery, the tabernacle where Tsongkhapa was buried, the columned prayer halls did not yield willingly. Using field artillery and dynamite, the Chinese pummeled Ganden to rubble, but only after first burning the monastery's vast collection of ancient scriptures, melting down its religious statuary, defacing its murals, and imprisoning its monks. The might of the Chinese army, the hysteria of Communist politics, silenced the thump of the monk's drum, the drone of chanted prayer, the tangle and wisdom of stylized doctrinal debate—for a time.

We stopped the Land Cruiser where the road widened at the mountain's summit. My driver went off in search of tea and my interpreter (whose name I shall withhold out of concern for his safety) and I descended toward the gutted monastery. Some reconstruction amid the ruin has occurred; a handful of new buildings rising from the weathered carapace of the old monastery, spindly scaffolding of tree limbs spiderwebbing over excavated building sites. My interpreter talked quietly with a few monks while I took photographs—what I later realized was more than two rolls of film of the devastation that lay before me. After a time, my interpreter motioned for me to follow him, and we climbed through a maze of stone steps, toward a restored cloister where we were greeted by an old monk, stooped, it seemed, under the very weight of his roughly woven robes.

The monk scoured the passageways with his eyes, a practice I would see repeated many times before I interviewed someone in a monastery, and then invited us into his chamber. A sourish, oily aroma clung to the walls of his cell; traces of the scent of the yak butter votive candles that burn by the thousands in the prayer halls, an odor that lacquers everything in a Tibetan monastery. The old monk sank onto his pallet and proffered cups of yak-butter tea poured from a dented aluminum thermos. Along the wall, under the cell's sole window, lay a few scriptures, the sheaf of long, narrow pages bound between thin wooden covers. A framed photograph of the Dalai Lama, draped in the traditional white gauze scarf of honor, was propped up on a small shrine. I asked the monk about the monastery's religious library and the books used by Ganden's monks.

"The Chinese burned all the scriptures," the monk explained. "All the scriptures we have are new. There is nothing old. Now, we have the scriptures printed in Lhasa." The printing of scriptures, now permitted by the Chinese, has enabled some monasteries to begin to recreate the core texts of the Buddhist faith, but the ancient volumes, akin to the illuminated, hand-penned medieval Bibles, were destroyed. "Before the Chinese destroyed Ganden," the monk told me, "there were thirty-three hundred monks here. When the Dalai Lama came to Ganden to give instruction, there were five thousand monks. After the Chinese invaded Tibet, they put some monks in prison; some were put in villages, some went to live with relatives, some eventually got married. I was here when they destroyed Ganden. All the monks tried to flee. I was very afraid, and I ran away too."

The old monk struggled to his feet and lifted the heavy padded cloth flap from the doorway of his chamber to peer about. "Chinese tour guides spy on us. We have to be very careful. The Chinese army comes to spy on us too. They come as tourists to the monastery, but they spy on us." He lowered the flap and returned to his pallet.

"I became a monk when I was eighteen. Now, I'm sixty-two years old. I came back here in 1980, when the Chinese allowed us to return. The high lama asked me to come back because I was an old student and he wanted me to teach the new students. But there are only thirty-eight old monks left. The rest of the monks are new. The Chinese determine how many new monks we can accept. If a boy wants to become a monk, he has to register at the religious office. The Chinese only allow fifteen or twenty new monks a year. If the office gives the stamp, then the young man can wear the robes. We cannot accept people without permission, without the stamp. The Chinese come to see if all the monks have a permit. We ask for more monks, but the office does not allow it. There were monks who wanted to come back, but the Chinese did not allow them back."

I asked the old monk if he would show us around the rebuilt parts of Ganden. Beneath his window, as we left his chamber, I could see young monks in a walled courtyard engaging in a boisterous scriptural repartee, a patterned series of pointed questions and answers on theological issues punctuated by rhythmic clapping that is a feature of the young monk's education. "We are going to rebuild," the old monk said, as we moved outside, "but it will take many, many years. We are still collecting wood and sand and stone. It will take very long." We walked into the main prayer hall, a cavernous room perfumed with the thick odor of burning yak butter candles. Tibetan pilgrims shuffled from one image of Buddha to another, spooning globs of yak butter from hand buckets so that the flames never die again. "All the statues were smashed or stolen by the Chinese," the old monk explained, gesturing toward the immense Buddhas in the room. "These are all new, made from clay and just painted gold." As we moved clockwise around the circumference of the room, I could see dozens of postcard-sized pictures of the Dalai Lama tucked in front of the Buddhas.

We met another ancient monk as we walked along, and were introduced to him. Unlike the first elderly monk, he said he was afraid to take us to his living chamber. "We should walk around," he cautioned, "so that the Chinese can't spy on us. There are sometimes people from the Religious Affairs Office here, and they spy on us. There are Tibetans in the office, but even those Tibetans are Chinese." We trooped up zigzagging stone steps toward what was once an immense room, now a gutted shell. "This was the chanting hall where all the monks would pray," the elderly monk told me. "Five thousand monks could chant here at the same time." The center of the wrecked hall was filled with rocks and cracked timbers, a crater amid hundreds. As my eyes drifted over the shattered walls, across the panorama of the mountain and the ruins of the monastery, it seemed as if I were gazing over the ruins of Rome or Athens, the remains of a civilization dead thousands of years.

I told the monk that as one drives around the Lhasa area, and on the road to Ganden, one sees prayer flags, in vivid yellows, blues, reds, and whites, fluttering from poles, roof peaks, fences. Were these, I asked, a sign of religious fervor? "No," he retorted abruptly, "the Chinese had them put up to deceive the world. From 1980, the Chinese ordered us to put the prayer flags up, when the foreigners began to come. Really, prayer flags should only be on hilltops, not on houses. We put them up here, on the *tarchen*"—and he directed his crooked index finger toward a prayer pole swaddled in thick layers of prayer flags and wrapped with yak-hair rope.

"When I walked along here," he said, "there used to be so many monks; many, many monks. Now, I don't know if we'll be independent. I don't know if ever that will happen. The Chinese have so much propaganda now. They tell young people, don't be a monk, don't be a Buddhist, don't practice religion. Still, the young people want to be monks." The elderly monk moved slowly down the stone steps, his right hand touching the stone walls for support as he moved. Young monks scampered by while we edged downward, toward the entrance to the monastery where the buses of pilgrims, and some tourists, were parked. As one of the young monks climbed by, his robe flying out behind him, my elderly guide gestured for him to stop. The young man came over and, urged on by the old teacher, told me why he was at Ganden. "I am seventeen," he said. "I came here four years ago, when I was thirteen. I saw a lot of killing when I was a child, and I wanted to become a monk. It was what I wanted to do. I still have seven more years of study." And when he was not studying? "I build. I help rebuild Ganden."

At Ganden, and at more than a dozen other monasteries I visited, I saw photographs, postcards, and small cloth replicas of

207

the flag of free Tibet, a yellow sun radiating twelve rays rising over a snow-covered mountain, before which two snow lions hold the three jewels of Buddha. The flag has been outlawed by the Chinese authorities. Displaying it, even possessing it, is grounds for immediate arrest. Sometimes a monk would slide a portrait of the Dalai Lama away from the wall of his cell to reveal the flag. Elsewhere, the flag would be tucked next to a huge Buddha in a prayer hall, camouflaged from casual glances by the profusion of butter lamps, white honorific scarves, pictures of the Dalai Lama and his predecessors. It was a small but danger-ous sign of resistance to Chinese rule. At Sera monastery, one of the major lamaseries in Lhasa proper, I visited a younger monk in his living chamber, on the wall of which were stenciled large Chinese ideograms, *"Gongchandang wansui"*—"Long live the Communist Party." He lifted a pillow and showed me the snow-lion flag.

Only in meandering bicycle rides does the full dimension of the Chinese presence in Lhasa become apparent. The center of Lhasa, a warren of traditional, thick-walled buildings radiating from the Jokhang Cathedral (the holiest of Tibetan Buddhism's religious sites), is dense with market stalls, pilgrims, and Khampa herdsmen, their unshorn hair wrapped in red cloth ties, long knives strapped to their waists, haggling over the price of saddles. Directly across from the Jokhang is a police station, staffed by Chinese and Tibetan officers, although all the com-manders are Chinese. Looming above the old city is the Potala Palace, the former residence of the Dalai Lama, a massive com-plex of conjoined buildings for living quarters, prayer rooms, kitchens, corridors, and winding staircases that seems to rise from the very rock of the mountain itself.

But beyond the old city core, in walled and gated compounds, are the Chinese living and working units. The buildings them-selves, the typical drab socialist architecture that has trans-formed China's own cities, are a jarring contrast to the ponder-ous grace of Tibetan structures; grotesquely visible reminders that Tibet is occupied by foreigners. It is in more than their buildings, however, that the Chinese dominate Lhasa. I talked with a Tibetan cook in a restaurant that supposedly serves Ti-betan food. But the cook, Tsering Ngodup, admitted that what he prepared was more Chinese than Tibetan. "Cooking used to

208

be very different," he acknowledged, "but now it's more similar to Chinese-style cooking. Young people want Chinese-style food. It's the influence of the Chinese here. They have the money. They control things." Before the Chinese came, Tsering said, he had worked for a wealthy family, making indigenous dishes like *bobi,* a kind of flat, round bread filled with vegetables, but no longer. "I like to cook that," he said, "but I don't now. I don't know anybody who does."

Even far from Lhasa, in the mountains where nomads tend yak herds, the Chinese influence has penetrated. I trekked for most of a morning with my interpreter, guided by the son of a maker of coracles, the clumsy, pillow-shaped boats fashioned from stretched yak hides that ferry about the rivers of Tibet. We walked into the mountains, the altitude and scarcity of oxygen pounding my lungs. After several hours, I was stopping every fifteen minutes or so to recover, much to the amusement of my interpreter and our guide. In the distance, on a pancake of grass wedged in the crook of some mountains, I detected a dark black tent, smoke puffing from its peak. An hour later, we arrived.

Two women, a mother and daughter, greeted us, almost as if visitors dropped by this remote place regularly. Far up the mountains, like a handful of coffee beans spilled on brown carpet, black long-haired yaks grazed. The mother, who gave her name as Choden, invited us into the tent, a dwelling crafted of thick strips of yak-hair carpet supported in the center by poles surrounding an adobe stove. From the tent poles hung blackened pots, two yak-hair slingshots, and some rags. Two wooden butter churns, banded in copper and with long wooden handles, stood next to the stove, where a fire of round yak-dung cakes roared under a sooty kettle. We sat on mattresses that hugged the tent's walls, and the daughter, who remained silent and unnamed, served us yak-butter tea, making sure the level in our cups never fell more than an eighth of an inch.

"We are nomad people," Choden said, after a time of silent tea-slurping. "So wherever there is much grass, we go for the animals. We have seventy yaks and more than twenty sheep. In the winter, when the snow comes, we go down to the village." Choden said that she thought she was sixty-eight years old, but it was hard to judge accurately; her face of weathered wrinkles suggested age less than a reserve of harshly tempered experience. "I've been a nomad all my life," she said. "My father was a nomad. We always came into this valley. In 1969, the Chinese army came into this valley and ordered us to leave. The army is gone now."

Choden did not respond easily to questions about her life, as if she felt that in a sense there was no other way of life, nothing with which to compare it. "So-so," she said carefully, "not so good, not so bad. Sometimes a yak disappears in the mountains and we have to go search for it. We get sad and scold each other." How, I asked, did her family decide when it was the proper time to leave the village for the mountains? "My husband learned from his father, and he from his father. He reads the scriptures and he watches the sun and the stars. If it seems right, then we go to the mountains. It takes four days to come up here." During my first trip to Tibet, the Chinese were engaged in a small border skirmish with India, news of which had even filtered to this nomadic tent. "Are the Chinese losing?" Choden asked. "I hope the Chinese lose. Before 1949, we were independent. We were free to go where we wanted. Now the Chinese stop us from going where we want. They don't want us nomad people going to Lhasa. Before, we couldn't pray. Now we can pray and read scriptures. I'm getting a bit old now, so I don't want to go to Lhasa. When I was young, though, I used to go there for the big festivals, like Monlam."

FOR TWENTY-SEVEN YEARS after the 1959 independence rebellion was crushed by Chinese troops, Tibetans were forbidden to celebrate Monlam Chenmo, the Great Prayer Festival, a three-week celebration ceremony around the Jokhang Cathedral. Monlam Chenmo is a time when monks debate and sermonize in public, when the people parade, horses are raced, and thousands of monks and laypeople flood the streets of Lhasa to dispel the old and embrace the new. Above all, it is a festival thoroughly Tibetan, one grounded in the culture and religion of Tibet, untinged by Chinese influence. For this reason, as well as the patronizing Chinese view that Monlam encouraged superstition within Tibetan Buddhism, the Chinese government prohibited the festival. In the early spring of 1986, when it seemed to the Chinese that the Tibetans had been sufficiently tamed, the festival was again allowed. It was celebrated tentatively, with a caution bred of memories of the past and fear of the future, but it was held.

In 1987, the Monlam festival was again celebrated, this time with more exuberance. But the following autumn, three decades of contained rage, of suppressed aspirations, of desperation and hope, exploded in a week of demonstrations and violence against Chinese rule. At this time I was in Beijing, and the first news reached my colleagues and me by telephone from tourists who had witnessed the march of monks and local people around the Jokhang, a traditional devotional circuit; but instead of prayer, slogans for Tibetan independence were shouted, and the Tibetan flag was defiantly carried through the streets. It was October 1, China's national day.

That evening, as news from Lhasa trickled into Beijing, a small gathering of reporters were at a dinner with Shivshankar Menon, the second-ranking diplomat at the Indian embassy and, without question, the most knowledgeable and acute observer of China among the senior diplomatic corps. He also, we discovered, just happened to speak Tibetan, and he discussed the events in that region with astonishing prescience and sophistication. We talked anxiously of the looting and burning we were slowly learning about, and speculated on Beijing's response. Menon expressed apprehension about a draconian Chinese reaction, and, while some of us felt the same way, his view carried an authority, a feel for China's attitude toward that battered region that none of us possessed. At dawn the next day, most foreign reporters in Beijing sped through empty streets to the airport to catch the first flight to Chengdu, and from there the flight to Lhasa. Tensions among the usually amiable press corps were high, because everyone was flying standby and the chance of being left behind engendered Damoclean anxieties. My driver, a man of remarkable resources and schemes, talents that would eventually bring him to Canada, managed to secure boarding passes for a colleague and me, to the dismay and anger of some other reporters, who rightly believed we had circumvented the formal queue for standby seats. It was, I am afraid, one instance in which my normally subdued competitive instincts succumbed to a measure of unbecoming rivalry. In the end, of course, everyone made the flight.

In Chengdu, where we were forced to spend the night before

catching the morning flight to Lhasa, we rushed about town buttonholing tourists arriving from the Tibetan capital to find out what had happened. A picture unfolded of the most serious outbreak of anti-Chinese sentiment since 1959, a sudden and intense rebellion against China's occupation of Tibet. Tourists spoke of children throwing stones at the police, mobs overturning police vehicles, the rattle of automatic weapons.

A first demonstration had materialized on September 27, as groups of monks making ritual rounds of the Jokhang Cathedral began chanting slogans for Tibetan independence. At least two dozen monks from that protest were yanked from the growing crowd by green-uniformed police and jailed. I was told by several foreigners who witnessed the scene that the monks were beaten with shovels by the police while they were being dragged into the police station next to the Jokhang. In the days that followed, frantic meetings among monks at Drepung and Sera monasteries, two enormous ecclesiastical institutions, the most important in Lhasa, went on late into the night to decide what action should be taken next. A supportive letter from the Dalai Lama, who was in Washington, D.C., at the time, was also somehow smuggled into the monasteries.

Early on the morning of October 1, monks from the two monasteries began parading around the Jokhang, chanting, "Dalai Lama, come back to Tibet," "Chinese out of Tibet," and "Free Tibet." Two Americans, Dr. Blake Kerr and John Ackerly, appeared in the crowd with copies of the Tibetan flag, and were instantly mobbed by people begging for the small banners. Meanwhile, the mass of people swelled into the thousands, all shouting as they swirled around the walls of the Jokhang. When the police appeared, young monks and lay Tibetans began pelting them with stones. Many women crouched in front of the Jokhang and began breaking apart paving stones, the small fragments of which they then passed forward to the stone throwers. Armed police and soldiers arrived in groups at the square in front of the Jokhang. One Chinese soldier charged into the crowd waving an AK-47 assault rifle and was immediately hit on the head with a rock. As he fell, a young boy dashed over and grabbed his rifle and made off into the crowd. The soldier was stoned to death.

A huge crowd gathered in front of the police station across

from the Jokhang, chanting for the release of arrested monks. The crowd began rocking several police cars and a motorcycle parked in front of the stone-walled police station, then tipped them over. Gasoline spilled from their tanks, coursing through the cracks in the pavement toward the station. A small boy darted over and lit the rivulet of fuel with a wooden match; almost instantly, the police station erupted in flames, sending thick clouds of black smoke spiraling into the sky. Even as flames leaped from the charred lower windows, about ten young monks smashed through the front door to rescue some twenty monks who were being held there. An older monk emerged from the inferno, crawling from a window, his face black from severe burns, shouting for Tibetan independence. The crowd cheered as he stood up. And then he was carried away on a table to be treated for his injuries. Another monk came out, his hair singed by the flames. Many people in the crowd were weeping.

A Dutch tourist, Wytze Bakker, described what he saw next. "Suddenly police came up a side street. There were about eight of them. I had a feeling there were more behind them, but I couldn't see them. They were carrying small pistols and they were shooting up in the air. Afterward, they were shooting low, and you could hear the bullets hitting the wall and the ground. One man was shot dead in front of the police station—a Tibetan, not a lama. A fire truck came onto the square, and there were police running after it, shooting in the air. There must have been three hundred soldiers on the square by then. The crowd came by me with a body on a stretcher. He had a piece of cloth on his head. The people removed the cloth and asked me to take a picture. He was dead. The police started heaving tear gas and smoke grenades into the crowd. People were running away."

It is impossible to know for sure, but it appears that about nine Tibetans, including some children, were killed that day, many from gunshot wounds, and dozens more arrested. Six police were also killed, one of whom reportedly shot himself to death accidentally.

THE PLANE TO LHASA on October 4, an aged, creaky Boeing 707, was packed with senior Chinese army and police officials. Scattered through their ranks was the Western press corps. We arrived to find the People's Armed Police occupying the city in force, with armed troops posted atop buildings and at road junctions. As we pulled into the city from the airport, it was easy to sense the fear and tension that permeated the capital. I immediately went to the Barkhor, the alleyway that surrounds the Jokhang Cathedral, where I saw freshly printed signs, in Chinese and English, which were pasted on the stone walls and which read: "Foreigners are not allowed to crowd around watching and photographing the disturbances manipulated by a few splittists and they should not do any distorted propaganda concerning disturbances that is not in accordance with the facts."

Many wounded monks were being secretly treated by Dr. Kerr, who was being harried by the foreign reporters as well as by the lack of medicines and bandages for his patients. Ackerly passed around a brass cartridge from a Chinese gun, the numbers "31" and "66" stamped on its base; I traced the outline of the shell onto a page in my notebook. Both men had been detained after the big riot at gunpoint by the police for possessing Tibetan flags, but were quickly released. "We had to write a self-criticism," Ackerly told me. "They accepted the first one. We said we did not intend any unfriendly acts and we did not mean any harm."

Public loudspeakers over the square broadcast warnings in Chinese and Tibetan, which echoed against the stone walls of the surrounding buildings. One announcement declared: "Those who were involved in the demonstration should confess at the police station and those that do so will get lenient treatment. Those that do not will be treated seriously. The deadline is October 15." Other broadcasts urged the populace to "increase vigilance" against "a handful of separatists" who sought to create chaos and instability. Armed police occupied the entire third floor of the Jokhang, while also commandeering a building on the square and converting it into a temporary police headquarters.

A letter in Tibetan addressed to the United Nations from the monasteries of Drepung, Sera, and Ganden was circulated to the correspondents. The epistle called on the world body to denounce the Chinese occupation of Tibet and to recognize the right of Tibetans to independence. A group of us who were collaborating on gathering the strands of the story spread out to different monasteries to talk to monks. At Nechung monastery, the former residence of the State Oracle, the agent of mystical prophecy in Tibetan Buddhism, a monk told me that the police had come and posted a notice instructing the monks not to talk to foreigners. In one room off the central courtyard, a Chinese official in a blue Mao suit was haranguing an assembly of young monks. "One of the comrades," the monk told me, "is lecturing the students on the history of Tibet. He kicked out the monk who was teaching scripture." The monk spat derisively at the word "comrades." Then he turned to me and said, "The people of Lhasa are very happy that the Dalai Lama went to the United States. The people of Lhasa can't fight the Chinese alone; we're like mice against an elephant."

On October 6, a procession of about one hundred monks from Drepung walked slowly toward the government offices, down People's Avenue, chanting, "Free the imprisoned monks," and "Independent Tibet." They were mostly young and all had newly shaven heads, a sign either of penitence or of recent incarceration in a Chinese prison. A dozen army trucks roared down the street, some with machine guns mounted on tripods atop the driver's cab. Soldiers and police armed with assault rifles, pistols, and clubs surrounded the monks and halted the procession. The monks were herded onto the trucks as police video cameras recorded the scene and each monk had his photograph taken. A crowd began to gather, and when a policeman whipped a monk on the head with a leather belt, the crowd surged forward, angry, shouting. Instantly, the soldiers wheeled their rifles around and waved them at the Tibetans, screaming for the crowd to disperse.

At noon the following day, a convoy of open-backed army trucks crawled menacingly through the heart of Lhasa. Standing at attention in the back of each truck were twenty-five soldiers in ranks of five, all carrying AK-47s with mounted bayonets. Silently, Lhasa's residents watched this display of Chinese might, an unmistakable message that China's leaders would not tolerate the slightest opposition to its rule in Tibet. The only sound was the clatter of steel shopfront shutters slamming shut in advance of the convoy. Again, I returned to a monastery, one I shall not name here, to talk with the monks. It was a small monastery, just a couple of hours from Lhasa, where I met two elderly monks. Their bitterness permeated their words.

We sat on the usual padded sleeping pallets, and the monks talked freely, without any prodding, their words driven by the emotion of the past week. "I spent six years in prison," one monk said, banging his wrists together as if they were hand-cuffed. "Countless monks were there. I would give my life for the Dalai Lama." The second monk, also quite elderly, inter-rupted. "The Dalai Lama is the only religious and political leader for us. The Chinese government says the Tibetan people don't want independence. But everyone loves the Dalai Lama." Both monks scoffed at the suggestion that their lives were better since 1980, since the introduction of Deng Xiaoping's liberal-ized economic program. "Most of these kinds of people don't like us monks. Deng Xiaoping is the same as Mao Zedong. They're all the same. Now there are Tibetans in the army and Tibetans are killing Tibetans. The Dalai Lama says, 'Never kill people; never kill even a flea.' "

"The Chinese government is always telling lies," the first monk continued. "All lies. They're trying to make fools of the Tibetan people. Even young children know the Dalai Lama's name and chant it. Everyone loves the Dalai Lama. I myself am working for Tibetan independence. Now there are thorns all around us. If the Dalai Lama were here, it would be all flowers."

For two days, the foreign reporters in Lhasa had been able to send their stories, detailed reports of the first public resistance to Chinese rule in nearly three decades, to their newspapers. The post office in Lhasa, realizing that it stood to profit hand-somely from the deluge of correspondents who were spending thousands of dollars in telex fees every day, installed three extra telex machines to cash in on this bonanza. But even as we were frantically sending stories, Chinese officials in their command posts were trying to stanch the flow of news from Lhasa to the outside world. I was sitting at one of the new telex machines in the post office, frenetically banging away at the keys, sending a story to New York, when suddenly the red light indicating a connection with the newspaper's telex machine went dark; the police had severed Lhasa from the outside world.

Two days later, at twelve minutes past midnight, all the for-eign reporters were summoned to a conference room, where we were confronted by a grim-faced official from the foreign affairs office, a man named Deng Zhu. Surrounding him were officials

216

from Beijing, an interpreter, and a note taker. Deng sat at a long table facing the weary reporters, and read a statement declaring that our presence in Tibet violated an obscure regulation issued by the Foreign Ministry, what he described as sections sixteen and twenty-one of this newly discovered rule. "Your activities for press coverage in Lhasa," he then announced, "have violated the aforesaid regulations and are illegal. Therefore, you are forbidden to use communication facilities." He went on: "I therefore demand all foreign correspondents to leave Lhasa and Tibet within forty-eight hours." It so happened that Raymond Burkhardt, the senior political officer from the American embassy in Beijing, was in Lhasa and attempted to intervene on our behalf with Deng. Burkhardt was rebuffed.

With less than two days left to work, we fanned out around Lhasa, talking to as many Tibetans as possible. Adi Ignatius of *The Wall Street Journal* volunteered to leave Lhasa a day early carrying a pool report that he would transmit for those who remained behind when he reached Chengdu. The evening before we were to be expelled from Tibet, we all gathered in my room at the Lhasa Hotel to discuss what we had seen and to celebrate our expulsion over a few beers. The hotel's management, executives from Hong Kong and Germany, as well as two American diplomats and one from Canada, joined us for the evening, as we watched Chinese television's version of events and strained to hear staticky shortwave reports by the British Broadcasting Corporation and the Voice of America. Throughout the evening, we were harassed repeatedly by plainclothes security police who lurked outside the room and by repeated telephone calls from officials attempting to learn the identity of those who were there. At one juncture, I stuck my head out of the door and snapped a picture of the secret police in the hallway. Instantly, the police rushed the room, demanding the film, demanding me. Two or three of the heftier journalists and diplomats yanked me back into the room and barricaded the doorway with their bodies. A shouting match ensued, with neither side giving way until the manager of the hotel somehow persuaded the police to leave. Because I feared the police would return that night, I slept in the room of *Der Spiegel's* Stefan Simons.

The following morning, the group of reporters catching the

first flight to Chengdu took the bus to the airport. After we had weathered the check-in procedures at Lhasa airport, Stefan and I were comparing notes as we waited to board the plane. Suddenly, a policeman appeared in front of us and demanded that I go with him. Stefan insisted that he accompany me. The officer refused, and in a matter of moments we were surrounded with green-uniformed police. I was led away and taken to a police interrogation room at the airport. I was seated behind a wooden desk. Across from me, standing against the wall, were about a dozen uniformed police as well as some of the plainclothes secret police, each in an unbuttoned trench coat, who had been in the hallway the night before. Whatever bravado I may have possessed until then oozed away. I was, if not frightened, quite worried.

One of the policemen began addressing me in Chinese, reading from a piece of paper. "I'm sorry, I don't understand," I said, feigning incomprehension, a tactic most journalists in China adopted in tight situations, believing that it creates more difficulties for the Chinese authorities and may ultimately render the whole affair too troublesome to bother with.

"We were told you spoke Chinese," the policeman retorted, in good English.

"You were told wrong," I said.

The officer then proceeded to read a charge sheet which accused me of "beating up a man," the victim never being identified, but, obviously, given the presence of the secret police in the room, it was connected with the previous night's encounter. As he read this charge sheet, a policeman took endless photographs of me while another officer held what proved to be my arrest warrant next to my head. The evolving Keystone Kops quality of the proceedings did much to erode my apprehension. I tried to take notes as the officer read the charge against me, but to this day I cannot locate them. It makes no difference; the incident remains permanently etched in my memory.

"For this action," the policeman continued, "you are given a serious warning." He then handed me the warrant, a document in both Chinese and Tibetan, covered with impressive round red stamps.

I stood up from the desk. "I would just like to say that these charges are completely false," I said. "That man in the corner"

218

—I pointed to one of the police officials in a trench coat—
"attacked me and several people who were in my room last
night. I deny these charges completely. There were several diplomats in the room last night, one from the Canadian embassy
and two from the American embassy, and both will testify to the
facts in this matter. I intend to report this incident to the American ambassador when I return to Beijing."

With a contemptuous flick of his hand, the presiding officer
indicated I was dismissed. I walked from the interrogation room
and noticed that my hand, holding the warrant, was shaking.
Less than an hour had passed. I submitted to the security search
again, and rejoined Stefan in the waiting area. The flight was
called and we flew to Chengdu, and from there to Beijing.

The arrest warrant, elaborately framed, now hangs in my
home.

IN THE WEEKS THAT FOLLOWED, the Chinese government issued a
series of denunciations of the Dalai Lama and even accused him
of instigating acts of sabotage. Doje Cering, a Tibetan who is the
equivalent of the region's governor, appeared at a press conference in Beijing. "In 1985," Doje declared, "the Dalai Lama sent
people to conduct explosions. In 1986, the Dalai Lama sent back
people to engage in assassinations in the Lhasa municipality."
While he refused to say more about these charges, he insisted
that these actions were the prelude to the demonstrations of the
past month. "We have conclusive evidence to show that the
Lhasa riot early this month was instigated and engineered by the
Dalai separatist clique," Doje said, offering no further support
for his contentions.

Meanwhile, China's newspapers and magazines were filled
with reports on how the government had enhanced the lives of
Tibetans. Endless interviews with happy Tibetans appeared,
each recounting the oppressiveness of their lives before Chinese
troops "liberated" them from serfdom. A woman named Qu Ni,
who is married to a Chinese, was quoted as saying, "Things are
going so well in Tibet now, it's just impossible to believe that
things like that could happen spontaneously, without outside
planning and instigation. . . . [I]t would be quite impossible
for the Hans in Tibet to get together and oppress the local
people." Lhagba Puncog, a former serf who now heads the

Tibetan Academy of Social Sciences, told Chinese reporters, "Today, to make sure that Tibetan culture prospers, we must study the good points from the culture of other Chinese nationalities, especially that of the majority Han, and also the merits of foreign cultures. Only in this way can we give our own national culture greater vitality."

Reporters in Beijing were effectively prohibited from returning to Lhasa. I tried repeatedly to obtain permission to return to Tibet, but it was denied. The Chinese airline, CAAC, refused to sell tickets to passengers who were not on a group tour, and the Foreign Ministry threatened to expel any reporters who traveled to Tibet without permission. Independent information about Tibet was almost impossible to get. Trickles of news appeared in Beijing. There were reports of extensive political indoctrination in monasteries. The Tibet Office, a group representing the views of the Dalai Lama in New York, issued a report of one session at the Sera monastery on the northern edge of Lhasa.

"In Sera monastery, the monks were divided into two categories, those who have to attend daily 'advice' sessions and those who had to attend only one session. Some sessions were held in large groups and others were individual with perhaps one or two officials and two monks. These were held in the afternoon at about 3 P.M. and lasted for two to three hours. The officials were in some cases Chinese and in some cases Tibetan. Some were attended by police officers. In Sera the main line was that China and Tibet were one and that they had been so since the time of the fifth Dalai Lama," or since the seventeenth century.

As best we could discern from Beijing, the Tibetan capital crackled with tension. In February 1988, two journalists were invited to watch the Monlam Chenmo festival, an occasion that seemed most likely to trigger a new burst of anti-Chinese protest. Throughout the festival, according to Patrick Lescot, a reporter for Agence France Presse who was permitted into Lhasa, the mood of the monks and pilgrims grew increasingly angry at the presence of two thousand armed Chinese soldiers on the streets of Lhasa. Then, on the final day of the ceremony, a solitary monk stood up in the Jokhang Cathedral and began chanting independence slogans. He was joined by about three hundred young monks who took up his call, "Long live His

Holiness the Dalai Lama" and "Liberty for Tibet." Hordes of undercover Chinese police who were monitoring the festival rushed the first monk and dragged him off. Instantly, thousands of Tibetans began stoning the police and police video-camera crews. The crowd, which Lescot estimated at twenty-five thousand, spilled through the streets of Lhasa, looting and burning Chinese shops. The police fired tear gas in an effort to restrain the enraged mass of people, but there were too many Tibetans and they were too angry to be stopped.

After the Chinese troops restored order, they announced that one policeman had been killed and another three hundred and nine injured. The Chinese provided no information on the number of Tibetans killed or injured, but Lescot and other foreigners said that five Tibetans had been shot to death by the police. A young monk in his mid-teens was shot point-blank in the face, according to a foreign witness. As in October, it was impossible to contact Lhasa by telephone or telex and Patrick Lescot was expelled from Tibet immediately.

In the months that followed, only slivers of information about Tibet and the monasteries in Lhasa reached Beijing. Compulsory political indoctrination classes were conducted in the monasteries by innocuously named "affairs units," armed troops patrolled the streets of the capital, and arrests of monks and civilians who participated in the riots continued. The Chinese refused to permit foreign reporters into the region, a decision that enabled the crackdown on dissidence to go unchronicled. Before October 1, China's national day, the people of Lhasa were told by their "neighborhood committees" that if they demonstrated that day in the capital they would be shot down in the streets. On December 1, the Communist Party announced the summary dismissal of the region's party secretary, Wu Jinghua, a member of the Yi minority, and the appointment of Hu Jingtao, a Han, as his successor. Wu's failings, which were never publicly explained by the central party apparatus, were apparent; he had failed to inculcate a respect for and devotion to communism among the fiercely religious people of Tibet.

Hu's appointment, however, did nothing to dampen the spirit of rebellion among Tibet's religious and civil population. Ten days after he took over Tibet's party apparatus, a parade of demonstrating monks and nuns, marching on International Human Rights Day, was raked with gunfire in front of the Jokhang Cathedral by troops of the People's Armed Police. A Dutch translator, Christa Meindersma, was wounded. Meindersma, who had lived in Tibet for fourteen months and was one of just a handful of foreigners to witness the shootings, described the political mood among Tibetans: "Since these first protests, Tibetans have found themselves subjected to political indoctrination sessions, arrest, torture, and interrogation. This has led them to start thinking more pointedly about the meaning of independence, as well as of political terms such as freedom, democracy, human rights, and socialism."

Three months later, fully three decades after Chinese troops invaded Tibet to put down a rebellion for independence, the people of Lhasa rose again in protest against their Chinese masters. Spontaneous pro-independence marches flickered for several weeks in February 1989, growing in size as time passed. Then, on March 5, a small parade of thirteen Buddhist monks and nuns mushroomed into a march by hundreds of people. Hundreds more tried to storm the government and party headquarters in central Lhasa. Armed troops in battle dress opened fire, killing as many as two hundred and fifty Tibetans and wounding hundreds more. For three days, Tibetans rampaged through the streets, smashing Chinese-owned shops, glass-enclosed traffic police huts, and official cars and trucks. From alleyways and shaded windows, Tibetans with slingshots fired rocks at the troops. The central government in Beijing reacted swiftly by imposing martial law over Lhasa, giving the police and army sweeping authority to conduct arrests and searches, as well as to suppress expressions of anti-Chinese sentiment by any means necessary. Parades and strikes were banned, foreigners were expelled from the region, and Tibet was closed to the outside world. Police swarmed through the city, smashing down the doors of Tibetan homes and dragging those they arrested off into the night, according to tourists who were in the city before being forced to leave.

Once again there was silence from Tibet. There were sporadic accounts of renewed arrests, trials, and imprisonment, but no detailed reports on the effect of martial law on the people of Lhasa. There also was little response from the world community to the violent repression of the Tibetan people. Indeed, just one day after the shooting of monks and nuns in Lhasa, a senior White House official assured the Senate leadership that the position of the United States and China on the human rights situation in Tibet remained the same.

So overwhelming is the presence of Chinese military might in Tibet, so draconian is the government's response to any suggestion of opposition to Chinese rule, that there is no real hope for meaningful autonomy or independence for the Tibetan people. They are destined, as they learn with each bullet and each truncheon blow, to be trampled upon by the Chinese and ignored by the world. Even among thoughtful Chinese, among those Chinese who so forcefully focused the world's attention on the lack of genuine freedom and democracy within China itself during the spring of 1989, the Tibetan people and their demands for freedom were never mentioned.

As CHINA ENTERS THE 1990s in the grip of fierce political repression and economic retreat, China's minorities are doomed to the role of bit players in a tragedy of enormous dimensions. Always an irritant to the government—they really are not Chinese, after all—China's minority peoples can only expect greater cultural and economic devastation. With the Communist Party and the government absorbed with the tasks of extirpating Western ideas and values from Chinese society and extolling the virtues of socialist puritanism, the fragility of societies and cultures whose survival is at odds with the pervasiveness of Han culture becomes apparent.

The Miao in Hunan, or the Tibetans on the vast Himalayan plateau, will survive only if China can accommodate difference, only if China is comfortable with cultures that derive their strengths from nonideological roots. This possibility seems increasingly remote. Conformity—in politics, in thought, in behavior—has once again become the central feature of Chinese society. The unrelieved destitution of the Li of Hainan Island, for example, fades in significance, even as a public relations problem, for a Beijing consumed with reasserting the virtues of socialism. Tibet, a colony no different from Europe's conquests in Africa in the nineteenth century, will be brought to heel by the sheer might of the Chinese army. Offered to the world in the past decade as a delightful and exotic culture, the last great tourist adventure, it is apparent that what matters to Beijing is not the preservation of Tibetan culture, but the preservation of Chinese power over the area.

A twenty-two-year-old Tibetan shopowner in Lhasa told me about his desperation, and that of his people, in October 1987, before the heavy blanket of repression settled over this land. "The Chinese have eased up for a while," he said, as I glanced over his thin stock of trousers, shirts, and jackets, "but in two or three years, they will crack down again. The Chinese want to give the impression that things are very free, so that Tibetans in exile will come back. If all Tibetans were here, and not in exile, they would keep us all as slaves."

TEN

Mandarin Machinations

ON JUNE 9, 1989, five days after the Chinese army thundered into Beijing spewing machine-gun fire through the city's streets, slaughtering citizens, students, children, the evening television news presented the country with the face of China's new leadership. At the head of an oval table sat Deng Xiaoping. Half of the twenty men with him at the table were military commanders, all of whom sat at the far end of the table. To Deng's left and right sat nine men, the victors in the power struggle that had sundered the upper ranks of China's Communist Party. Five of these nine men at the table were well into their eighties, an age shared by Deng as well. Six of them held seats neither on the party's Politburo nor the Central Committee. Neither, indeed, did Deng himself.

It was these elderly (and, to some eyes, palsied) men, ruthless, steel-fisted Leninists, who had emerged victorious after a vicious fight for control of the party and the nation. They were the men who sent the army into Beijing. They were the men who were to guide China into the next decade.

225

There is much that will never be known about the battles fought inside the Zhongnanhai compound during April and May 1989. But what is visible—the public pronouncements, the occasional leaks from secret party meetings, and the outcome itself of this internecine warfare—says much about China's Communist Party, its real centers of power, its resistance to change, its future. The outcome of that power struggle reveals as well the vast chasm between the goal and purpose of the party, and the hopes and dreams of the people it rules over.

IF CHINA'S LEADERS needed to be told that the ideological pap periodically fed the Chinese people was unpalatable, they had only to look out the windows of their guarded, secretive offices during the month of May 1989. On some days, there were one million or more of the capital's citizens marching or riding in the back of trucks, brandishing banners denouncing the country's rulers, calling for them to step down, demanding democracy, freedom of expression, and an end to privilege. Forty years of Chinese communism, of preaching the verities of Marx and Lenin and Mao, and none of it had been digested.

For China, the 1980s had meant two things: increasing living standards, and relief from the tom-tom beat of political indoctrination. Even within the party, especially among the generation of post-Cultural Revolution party members, the chores of studying politics and ideology were performed perfunctorily, a bit the way Catholic-school children zip through compulsory rosaries. But, for the older men of Deng Xiaoping's generation, the generation who had fought the Japanese and the Kuomintang, ideology had always been the binding force, the fiber in the tapestry of communism.

During the first decades of the People's Republic, ideology molded policy. To be sure, ideology was shaped and reshaped by Mao Zedong, but it remained the core of policy-making. The concentration on heavy industry, the scattering of factories across the country regardless of access to raw materials or transport lines, the collectivization of agriculture during the first decade; all these policies were guided by principles set forth by Mao. The catastrophes of the Great Leap Forward were ordained by Mao's ideological predilections, and even the Cultural Revolution, a political movement aimed in part at destroying the party structure, was driven by Mao's grab bag of increasingly deranged ideological precepts.

Upon his return from political oblivion in 1977, Deng Xiaoping perceived clearly that the wildly mutating scope of political principle, as well as the grinding preoccupation with ideological rectitude, had undermined not only the party but the nation as a whole. As he established his control over the party and government at the onset of the 1980s, Deng, who was approaching his own eightieth year, was intent on designating successors who could oversee the ideological tasks of the party and manage the restructuring of China's economy. Succession, a process never orderly or institutionalized in Communist societies, remained, for Deng, an enduring concern.

The slightly younger men whom Deng chose to execute his vision commanded growing respect within the party and were known for innovative approaches to party and economic life. Hu Yaobang, named general secretary of the party in February 1980, was credited with reviving the party's Youth League, the breeding ground for future party members and a testing ground for ideological leadership. To him, Deng assigned the task of instilling confidence within the party about its mission and reviving respect for the organization among the vast population of the country. Hu was to maintain the fine balance between an ill-defined ideological orthodoxy and the nationwide desire to forget about politics for a while, perhaps forever. Hu also was to convince doubters within the party as to the wisdom, and political correctness, of the emerging economic order.

To Zhao Ziyang, appointed prime minister in September 1980, fell the staggering labor of giving form to Deng's vision for an economy starkly different from conventional socialist notions of economic order. Zhao, who himself had pioneered many similar ideas in the southwestern province of Sichuan, embraced his mission with verve, each year gaining in confidence and determination. He established a welter of think tanks to funnel ideas to policy-makers, establishments that wrestled with problems as diverse as the future of family farming, the role that commodities trading could play in stabilizing prices for agricultural products, and the development of a national governmental civil service.

As the decade progressed, Hu and Zhao increasingly defined

the future that China was headed toward, a future whose groundwork was laid by Deng, but which became bolder each year, as Hu and Zhao pushed for more and faster change. In early 1985, there were rumors within the China-watching community that Hu was trying to nudge Deng toward something more than de jure retirement. At the same time, Deng, who continued to express confidence in his protégés, was regularly confronted with the growing restlessness of the party's old guard, the men of Deng's generation who had fought the guerrilla wars and had led the country before the Cultural Revolution.

One of these men, Chen Yun, himself physically enfeebled by the middle of the decade, doddered painfully through public occasions such as major party meetings, gatherings at which his presence became briefer as the years wore on. Yet Chen, whose contributions to the revolution were unquestioned, maintained enormous authority, repeatedly forcing compromises on policy issues and consistently pushing forward men of his choosing into the councils of power. During the 1950s, Chen had overseen the construction of China's economy along Soviet lines. He was a man wedded to the virtues of central planning and central management, not only because he believed that these methods worked—he could point with some pride to the economic growth of the 1950s—but because it was an approach that embodied the doctrines of socialism.

Again and again during the 1980s, Chen urged restraint, arguing that socialism required an adherence to clear theoretical principles. "We are Communists. Our goal is to build socialism," Chen told a party conference in 1985. "In terms of the country as a whole, the planned economy's primacy and the subordinate role of market regulation are still necessary. Of course, planning consists of both mandatory and guidance planning. . . . [M]arket regulation involves no planning, blindly allowing supply and demand to determine production." His allegiance to Deng (for it was Deng who brought Chen and hundreds of other senior party members back from exile imposed during the Cultural Revolution) tempered his public comments, but within the conclaves of the Politburo, Chen drove hard for promoting men more sympathetic to planning than markets, to state-owned industries rather than free enterprise.

228

One of the men he propelled forward was Li Peng, an electrical engineer with two modest claims to fame. One was that he had kept Beijing's electricity supply going even during the worst ravages of the Cultural Revolution. The other was that he was a foster son of Zhou Enlai and his wife, Deng Yingchao.

Other old-guard party members were equally reluctant to step aside, to let Hu and Zhao gradually expand their power and influence, to dominate party and government life. These elderly veterans saw no reason why they should be denied a voice in the leadership simply because of their age. They were, after all, the men who had fought to create the "New China." Many of them had participated in the Long March, the extraordinary tactical retreat from southern to northern China in 1936 which had given new life to Mao's Red Army. It was their sweat and blood that had brought the People's Republic into existence, and they were not to be denied a role in guiding its future now that stability had been reasserted. But even within this old cadre of leaders, there were still widely varying views about the country, the party, and policy.

Some, like Yang Shangkun, an old political commissar who ran a drama troupe during the years of guerrilla fighting, witnessed the pounding the Chinese army took at the hands of the Vietnamese in the border skirmishes of 1979. In the mid-eighties, the size of the army was slashed from four million to three million, munitions factories were transformed into plants producing radios, fans, refrigerators, and myriad consumer goods, and army funding was being redirected into joint-venture projects like hotels, including the luxurious Palace Hotel in the heart of Beijing. Meanwhile, army salaries remained stagnant, and the military's reputation, once glorified in propaganda everywhere, had sunk so low that luring recruits was becoming a serious problem. Military parades, a habit copied from the Soviets, were abandoned in 1984. The party's model Communist and soldier, Lei Feng, a fictional soldier who supposedly devoted himself wholeheartedly to the cause of the people, helping old ladies across the street and fixing the shoes of old men, was derided as a fool by the public. Worse, the military's presence in the uppermost ranks of the leadership was dwindling steadily; its representation on the Central Committee plunged between 1978 and 1987. Yang and other aging generals bemoaned this erosion of the army's stature and influence, and resisted Deng's efforts to give either Hu or Zhao any real power in the military establishment.

Other elderly leaders busied themselves with what they saw as the corruption of artistic and intellectual life. Revolutionary themes, once the staple of films, plays, and novels, were ignored or radically reinterpreted in the 1980s, something that these aged party leaders found reprehensible. Men like Wang Zhen, Bo Yibo, and Hu Qiaomu railed against the infiltration of Western ideas in art and literature, against the permissiveness encouraged by the aping of Western culture, against the collapse of revolutionary ideals. The rapid growth of underground, gray-market publishing undermined the party's monopoly over the printed word. These men continually battled to reassert control, demanding the closure of illegal or unauthorized presses, prohibitions on using official presses to print "obscene" literature in off-hours, and restrictions on the import of foreign books, periodicals, and movies.

Deng, who retained his veto power over all government and party decisions despite his nominal retreat from daily affairs, realized that the obstructionist machinations of his elderly colleagues were also beneficial at times. Especially in moments of political restiveness—during the Democracy Wall movement of 1979, the campaign against "spiritual pollution" of 1983, the "anti-bourgeois liberalization" campaign of 1987—the old guard brought moral authority to their denunciations of political deviance. Deng tolerated this because he regarded stability, political and social, as the single most important prerequisite to successful economic development.

Although Deng relied on economic mechanisms rooted in the capitalist economies of the West, he did not countenance a concomitant political liberalization. Rather, Deng looked to the authoritarian capitalisms of South Korea, Taiwan, and Singapore, newly developed economies that thrived despite repressive political orders. What Deng's older colleagues could ensure, he believed, was the useful memory of the recent revolutionary past. They could tout the values of "hard work and simple living," values annealed during the guerrilla campaigns of the 1940s. They could also intimidate wayward intellectuals. Wu Zuguang, a playwright known for his disdain for the imperious-

ness of party officials, loves to recount how Hu Qiaomu tried to
bully him by ordering him to resign from the Communist Party.
"Old Hu climbed five flights of stairs," Wu told me one day in
1987, "came in, and sat on the chair you're sitting in right now.
He said, 'We think you should resign from the party. If you don't
resign, you'll be dismissed.' Well, I laughed at this. I told him
that I never wanted to join the party in the first place. If they
wanted me to resign, I'd be happy to resign.

"In the last few years, I've felt discouraged," Wu went on. "I
feel that the Communist Party should have confidence in itself. I
feel that it lacks confidence. It's coming closer to alienating itself
from intellectuals; objecting to them, incurring their enmity,
and crushing them. This hasn't caused a great loss to my freedom because I have a lot of support at home and abroad. Instead
of me, it is the party that has suffered the loss."

For their part, Hu and Zhao found the activities of these old
men at best meddling, and at worst seriously damaging to the
process of economic reform. The two men quietly pressed Deng
to demand the retirement, the real retirement, of the old guard.
It would then be only a matter of time before Deng too slipped
into the background. The first move in this direction was taken
in 1983 when a new party organization, the Central Advisory
Commission, was created. This body was to be made up of
senior party veterans, moving them out of the mainstream of
policy-making but giving them an institutional presence through
which they could make their views felt. But few party elders
elected to join the new commission that year, and the victory Hu
and Zhao had hoped for was put off.

Instead, the old guard retained its hold on the Politburo and
its Standing Committee, the latter body being where most party
decisions are made. Deng remained on the Standing Committee, along with three other elderly veterans, Chen Yun, Li Xiannian, and Ye Jianying, who was to die shortly afterward. A modest effort was made to include some younger faces on the
Central Committee; what amounted to a token gesture, given
that body's relative powerlessness. According to the party's own
constitution, Hu's position as general secretary made him the
most powerful man in China. However, real power remained
with Deng.

In the wake of the student protests of December 1986, the

elders of the party found their opportunity to eliminate one of Deng's successors. Hu Yaobang had reacted to the demonstrations with some nonchalance, preferring to downplay their importance rather than viewing them as a significant attack on the political system itself, an attitude that mirrored his, in general, somewhat tolerant disposition, as well as his broader view that the limits of permissible public political discussion were too arbitrarily narrow. To party elders, Hu's attitude reflected an indifference to ideological issues, which in turn had encouraged the wave of national protest and rendered Hu unsuitable as the leader, putative or not, of the Communist Party. Deng Xiaoping, himself severely disturbed by the protests, agreed with the elderly mandarins and decided to sacrifice Hu, both to placate these veterans and to send a stark message to the party's forty-six million members. As Deng lectured his colleagues in the leadership, "This is not a problem that has arisen in just one or two places or in just the last couple of years. It is the result of failure over the past several years to take a firm, clear-cut stand against bourgeois liberalization. . . . There is no way to ensure continued political stability and unity without the people's dictatorship. People who confuse right and wrong, who turn black into white, who start rumors and spread slanders, can't be allowed to go around with impunity stirring the masses up to make trouble." Following Hu into disgrace were dozens of his supporters: editors of magazines, cultural figures, young inner-party staff.

But what was truly significant about Hu's dismissal was the tremendous hidden strength of the old guard. Hu, who was enormously popular among a vast swathe of younger provincial party officials, many of whom had matured politically under his stewardship of the Youth League, was unable to survive, despite his formal position, despite his popularity. What mattered, in the end, was the ability of this coalition of elderly veterans to move swiftly against him, forcefully presenting the case to Deng that Hu no longer possessed the ideological backbone to lead the party. In the slipstream of their success, they waged a six-month campaign of intellectual terror, cowing writers and artists, railing against the infiltration of polluting Western ideas, and beating the drum of Marxist-Leninist orthodoxy. Many China watchers, particularly among the American diplomatic community, dismissed this terror as simply the growing pains of a maturing polity. And indeed, the anti-bourgeois liberalization campaign did fizzle out by the late summer of 1987. It was said then that the old men had played their hand and lost.

To be sure, the polemics of orthodoxy fell dissonantly on Chinese ears more attuned to new expectations and new values created by the changing economic order. More, the stultified language of the hard-liners contained no alternatives to the economic changes pursued by Hu and Zhao. Indeed, Deng insisted throughout the campaign for renewed political orthodoxy that the country's basic economic course would not be altered; that only the continued restructuring of the economy offered hope for genuine modernization. In the south, in places like Fuzhou and Guangdong, the campaign was hardly noticed. The culture of money-making had taken such firm root that the politics of the past seemed at best a distant memory. Reviving those memories only produced mocking laughter. A typical remark I heard during trips to Guangzhou during the height of the anti-bourgeois liberalization campaign was "That's Beijing. We do things differently down here."

Zhao stepped into the vacuum left by Hu's demise, and was named acting general secretary of the party. He was, however, openly uncomfortable with the idea of taking the new party post. In conversations with several foreign visitors, he pointedly noted that he preferred to retain his job as prime minister, for which he felt better suited. Although he never said so publicly, he was also acutely conscious of the precariousness of party leaders in post-Cultural Revolution China: two of his predecessors, Hua Guofeng and Hu Yaobang, had both been stripped of their posts after losing power struggles. Even worse, to be party chief was, in many senses, to be a king with no clothes.

As prime minister, Zhao could wield the reins of government at some distance from the supervision and advice of the old guard. While broad policy is determined by the Politburo and its Standing Committee, its implementation during the 1980s has been the province of the prime minister. Under Zhao's stewardship, the role of government had been dramatically enhanced. He had created a nationwide network of advisers, think tanks, and semipublic development corporations all geared to implementing his economic designs. He had proposed accelerating central elements of the reform program, radically shifting the country's system of pricing away from any dependency on planning to pure market forces, and proposed the rapid development of China's coastal areas, even if it meant that other parts of the country would lag behind. Zhao, in short, was more comfortable crafting economic strategy than in tending the party's ideological garden, more competent to reorganize the government's enormous, arthritic bureaucracy than in policing the boundaries of political orthodoxy.

It was not to be, however. At the Thirteenth Party Congress, held in October 1987, Zhao was named general secretary in his own right. Many other things occurred at that meeting as well, some of which seemed to suggest that the older party veterans were finally being pushed from the rooms where the real power lay, but there was less behind this impression than it seemed. The entire older generation, led by Deng Xiaoping, retired from the Central Committee. Nine members of the Politburo retired, including the country's president, Li Xiannian; the chairman of the country's nominal parliament, Peng Zhen; and the hard-line economic planner, Chen Yun. Three of the men most prominent in fanning the flames of the anti-bourgeois liberalization campaign, Bo Yibo, Hu Qiaomu, and Deng Liqun, also left the Central Committee. Fully one third of the faces on the Central Committee were new, and the body's average age plummeted from 64.1 years to 55.2. On the surface, it seemed like a party rejuvenated, a party that had finally passed the scepter of leadership to a new generation.

But a closer examination of the new leadership revealed that the tendrils of the old men snaked unmistakably into the corridors of power. The Standing Committee of the Politburo, reduced to five members, was tilted heavily toward the views of the old guard, despite the face of novelty and unity Zhao Ziyang attempted to put on things. Apart from Zhao, the only member who was distinctly enthusiastic about the country's economic reforms was Hu Qili, then fifty-eight, a veteran of the party's youth wing and a protégé of Hu Yaobang's. The other three members owed their allegiance to the old guard. Senior among them was Yao Yilin, at seventy the oldest member of the Standing Committee. Yao had cut his teeth as an economic manager under Chen Yun when the cumbersome machinery of state planning was put together in the 1950s. He shared Chen's predilection for careful central control and consistently sought to temper the pace of reform.

Li Peng, another of the Standing Committee members, was also one of Chen's protégés. Li rose through the party ranks despite the concerted efforts of Hu and Zhao to stop him. In 1981, when Li was named to his first ministerial post, Chen gloated publicly that he was responsible for the promotion. Li, who had been trained in the Soviet Union in the late Stalin years, spoke frequently of the need to reassert central controls over the economy while relegating market forces to a largely tangential role. The final member of the Standing Committee, Qiao Shi, had emerged from the ranks of the security and intelligence forces, a man who exercised control over the forces of repression. From the start, then, Zhao was outnumbered in his new job.

As for Deng, a party spokesman described the implications of his formal retirement in an artful understatement: "The leadership role that has been played by Comrade Deng Xiaoping has not been determined by his post. Though he has left the party Central Committee now, his prestige and wisdom will ensure him a major role in the work of both the party and the state." A Soviet diplomat named Alexandre Pichugov, who had made it his business to keep tabs on me while I was in Beijing, put it less deftly: "Even if Deng was voted street sweeper, he'd still be calling the shots in this country." The Party Congress compliantly changed the party constitution so that Deng could retain the chairmanship of the Central Military Commission, a public admission that the old army brass were unwilling to submit to the authority of Zhao Ziyang.

The old guard scored an even greater victory in their rigged game of musical chairs, because Zhao's elevation to the party's highest post forced him to relinquish the prime ministership. The man they positioned to step into Zhao's shoes was Li Peng. Where Zhao had promoted free markets, private entrepreneurship, embryonic stock markets, and foreign investment, his hard-line opponents spoke incessantly of inflation, unemployment, corruption, spiritual pollution, and the erosion of revolutionary principles. The old guard saw greed where Zhao saw incentives, profiteering where Zhao saw the ebb and flow of supply and demand, the undermining of party authority where Zhao urged competence.

More, Zhao Ziyang's attitude toward proliferating social evils, increased crime rates, rampant corruption within the bureaucracy and party, and prostitution infuriated the party elders. Zhao argued—both within the councils of power and, more obliquely, outside—that these were all transitional phenomena, evils that necessarily accompanied such a monumental enterprise as remolding China's economy. Zhao pointed to the transformation of the countryside from rock-hard poverty to emerging agricultural abundance, to a nascent revitalization of industry, and, above all, to a vastly better-educated, well-informed Chinese nation, but the hard-liners could not, and would not, accept such placating. For them, these evils represented the reemergence of aspects of prerevolutionary China they had fought to exterminate. Not only was the party losing its total control in an economy that slid toward free markets, but it was losing control over the behavior and thinking of the Chinese people. This, the old guard determined, they would never permit.

Relegating Zhao to the job of party general secretary effectively removed his hand from the whole process of reform. He was hemmed in on the Politburo Standing Committee, and economic policy was turned over to Li Peng and his cadre of cautious bureaucrats. To be sure, Zhao was not exiled from the political landscape. He could and did speak his mind. He traveled widely throughout the country, encouraging party members to remain committed to the complex, frustrating, and slow process of modernization. He spoke frequently of the need to open the political process, to give the Chinese people a greater voice in their own governance, to free the press from ideological shackles and censorship. He quietly encouraged prominent academics to push beyond the bounds of economic and political discussion.

Zhao's economic policies were supported by two pillars: first, a sweeping program of price reform, and second, a fundamental change in the country's system of ownership. Zhao's proposals, formulated by his economic think tanks, were predicated on the contention that the initial steps in the process of economic reform had largely run their course. Distribution of land, free agricultural markets, and the introduction of management expertise instead of party control in industry had produced what benefits they could, and it was time, he argued, to move to the next stage of the reform process. To do this, Zhao and his theoreticians maintained that all central control over pricing had to be phased out. China's economy, still a pastiche of free and fixed prices, had developed a two-tier structure of prices that had introduced growing irrationality into the distribution of goods and services, as well as engendering mushrooming corruption as state-owned enterprises illegally sold state-allocated materials with low, fixed prices for enormous profits on the free market. Clearly, they said, the continued distortions of centrally controlled price fixing were warping economic growth.

Even more radical was Zhao's proposal that the traditional pattern of ownership, whereby the state owned everything in the country, from land to factories, department stores to restaurants, should be gradually dismantled. The Zhaoists maintained that genuine economic efficiency was unattainable unless producers, be they farmers or basket makers, taxi drivers, or bankers, had a stake in their enterprises. Reforming management practices alone could not revitalize state industries. Only by cutting the umbilical cord to the state treasury and transforming these dinosaur-like enterprises into stock-owned companies would genuine productivity and profitability, the only meaningful measures of modernization, be achieved.

Zhao was hobbled in moving the country to this second, and vastly more difficult and risky, stage of the reform process because of his new mission in the party, a pulpit from which he could do little more than preach. Li and the elders he represented as prime minister were galvanized not by the urge to move forward but by the need to stanch the flood of problems that threatened to overwhelm the nation. Inflation, which until 1987 had remained trivial, was now rampaging in urban areas at official rates of 25 percent and unofficial rates of 50 percent or more. Urban workers, whether in offices or factories, were struggling to get by on fixed government incomes that failed to keep pace with the staggering increase in prices.

True to their leader's approach to economic policy, Zhao's advisers insisted that inflation was not inherently bad and that price controls were more damaging to the economy in the long run than the sudden surge in prices. Indeed, some inflation was inevitable after decades of artificial pricing. Moreover, insisted the Zhaoists, consciously invoking Milton Friedman's theoretical tenets, inflation was in the end a monetary phenomenon that could be managed only by effective central bank controls over the country's money supply, an argument that at once demanded a strong and relatively independent central bank and an economy based on free market pricing.

To the hard-liners, this was dangerous apostasy. Li and his backers saw inflation as symptomatic of economic policy gone wrong; it attested not only to the rapaciousness of private entrepreneurs, but more soberingly, to fatal flaws in the reform strategy itself. Worse still, in their view, were the potential political threats posed by sharply rising prices. They remembered graphically the participation of Shanghai's workers in the student protests of 1986, and they contemplated with dread the spectre of widespread urban unrest as city dwellers took to the streets to voice their growing discontent. Already the level of vocal discontent was ballooning. Newspapers were filled with man-in-the-street stories of people complaining about the price of everything from cooking oil to eggs, shoes to sugar. And this dissatisfaction was compounded by the emergence of visible income disparities between those who worked in the private sector or with foreign enterprises and those who were chained to state jobs. Resentment against the newly affluent was becoming more common in cities.

Within the party, the Zhaoists fought a battle they were destined to lose. Their ammunition of analytical and intellectual forcefulness was outgunned by the hard-liners' relentless focus on the political dimensions of policy. For Li and his faction within the party, the preservation of party control and what they defined as social stability were the preeminent considerations in any policy-making. During a heated confrontation in August 1988 at the leaders' summer resort at Beidaihe, the party leadership voted to shelve Zhao's program of price reform and to halt any further moves toward expanding the role of market mechanisms in the economy. In addition, the rationing of basic commodities, items such as cooking oil, pork, and eggs, was reintroduced in several cities as a way of dampening consumer discontent. Zhao, after less than a year in his new post, had lost a critical fight, an indication then that he would no longer be a significant voice within the leadership.

The final pillar of Zhao's economic program was razed in March 1989 when the leadership decided to abandon discussion of changing the state's monopoly of ownership. With prices still climbing unabated despite the government's moves to contain them, Li and his wing of the party saw no virtue in loosening controls over industry through some as yet undefined method of privatization. That decision effectively ended the process of economic reform.

LI PENG'S INTENTIONS, never disguised throughout his career, were to reimpose greater centralization over the economy, to rein in growing regional autonomy, and to reassert some of the traditional socialist economic methods. This flowering of antireform sentiment was not unexpected. To the hard-liners, both of Zhao's fundamental programs, the adoption of a market-driven economy and the gradual privatization of the state sector, undermined the very principles on which Chinese socialism is based. State dominance of production and distribution were at the core of socialist economic theory. To jettison dominance in both these areas would raise inevitable, and appropriate, questions about what the real nature of the Chinese polity is. And those were questions so uncomfortable, so challenging, that the leadership simply could not address them except in the conventional vocabulary of the past.

That same month, Li made a direct public attack on Zhao and his policies at the annual meeting of the National People's Congress, an assembly created to ratify party decisions as government policy. Li spoke for two and a quarter hours of the economic difficulties facing the nation, particularly the unrelenting pace of inflation. He told the Chinese people that they must be prepared for "several years of austerity" if the country were to overcome its economic problems. And then, in a direct allusion to Zhao and his programs, Li said that the government had made mistakes in the past, most of which were due to "the tendency of some people to want quick results." Li then outlined a program of vigorous economic retrenchment, including sharp cutbacks in capital spending and a restriction on the autonomy of provinces to make major financial and economic decisions. It was, unmistakably, a move toward enhanced central control. It was the voice of the old men who stood offstage, behind a screen.

WE WILL NEVER KNOW, but it must have been clear to Zhao as he heard Li's words that he had lost the struggle for control of the party and its policies. His accomplishments were now blamed for the host of problems besieging the economy, his solutions dismissed as posing even further danger. All that was left was for Zhao to be forced from his leadership of the party, a demise that began its slow, painful unfolding less than a month later.

On April 15, 1989, Hu Yaobang died. His disgrace in being dismissed as party chief in January 1987 was conveniently forgotten in the profusion of obituaries in the official press, including the *People's Daily,* hailing his contributions to the great Chinese revolution. Only in death was Hu resurrected politically, by then a concession easily made. To China's people, however, and its students in particular, this hypocrisy was gallingly transparent. They began marching, first by the thousands, then by the tens and hundreds of thousands, to pay homage to a man they respected, whom they believed had been treated badly at the hands of the party's fossilized leaders. Those memorial marches blossomed into broader demonstrations for democracy and freedom, leading inexorably to the massacre that incinerated the hopes and dreams of China's people.

The demonstrations, which built into the largest spontaneous expressions of political discontent since the establishment of the People's Republic, created the ideal pretext for the old guard to make its move against Zhao. Zhao reacted erratically to the sudden protests, failing at every juncture to see that he would be blamed, that he would perish under the onslaught of resurgent hard-line orthodoxy. From the steady trickle of inner-party documents, we have a window on how the old men won this final struggle, how they perceived the threat to their power and how they organized themselves to subdue it.

On April 26, eleven days after Hu's death, the old men published their assessment of the protests in a harsh, uncompromising editorial on the front page of the *People's Daily.* The editorial, it was made clear, was the voice of the party. It also revealed starkly the unwillingness of these leaders to countenance dissent or free discussion, and betrayed the inability of these men to surmount the primitive political impulses by which they lived.

"After the memorial meeting," the editorial said, "an extremely small number of people with ulterior purposes continued to take advantage of the young students' feelings of grief for Comrade Hu Yaobang to spread all kinds of rumors to poison and confuse people's minds. Using posters of both big and small characters, they vilified, hurled invective at, and attacked party and state leaders. Blatantly violating the constitution, they called for opposition to the leadership by the Communist Party and the socialist system. . . . Flaunting the banner of democracy, they undermined democracy and the legal system. Their purpose was to sow dissension among the people, plunge the whole country into chaos, and sabotage the political situation of the stability and unity. This is a planned conspiracy and a disturbance. Its essence is to once and for all negate the leadership of the Chinese Communist Party and the socialist system. This is a serious political struggle confronting the whole party and the people of all nationalities throughout the country. . . . All comrades in the party and the people throughout the country must soberly recognize the fact that our country will have no peaceful days if this disturbance is not checked resolutely. This struggle concerns the success or failure of the reform and opening up, the program of the four modernizations, and the future of our state and the nation."

The students on the square reacted to this editorial with horror and outrage. It said to them that nothing had changed in their country, that nothing could or would change. It said to them that the leadership refused to recognize the need for a decisive change in the political structure of the nation, one that would truly represent the needs and aspirations of the people as well as reflect the diversity of opinion that lay restively beneath the party's efforts to jerry-rig a facade of national unity. Beijing's students immediately staged marches through campuses across the city, and many visited factories where they solicited donations for their cause. To the anger and alarm of the hard-liners, the city's workers dug into their pockets, already parched by roaring inflation, and gave heavily to the students. And the protests continued.

Unknown to most students, Zhao sharply attacked the *People's*

Daily editorial upon returning from a quick trip to North Korea on April 29, assailing its assumptions and rhetoric during a meeting with the senior leadership. The demonstrations, an angry Zhao told his colleagues, were not a riot; they were not intended to displace the leadership of the party. They were, he insisted, patriotic expressions of the people's will. He demanded that the Central Committee retract the editorial and recognize the legitimacy of the student movement. He was overruled.

On May 3, to commemorate the anniversary of the student demonstrations of May 4, 1919, which had first propelled China toward a modern, nationalist consciousness (spawning in its wake the fledgling Communist Party), Zhao spoke to the people of China, and to the demonstrators on Tiananmen Square in particular. Unlike the *People's Daily* editorial, Zhao was more conciliatory toward the student demonstrators, more discursive and more intent on touching the areas of commonality between the students and the party, or what he wished those areas to be.

"In a large country with a population of 1.1 billion," Zhao said in his address, broadcast on local radio, "we should, in all aspects of social life and all our reform and construction work, carry on the spirit of democracy, build up a system of democracy, develop a scientific spirit, do everything with a scientific attitude in the light of the actual conditions, and gradually and greatly promote science and education. Without democracy and science, we will not have socialism and socialist modernization. . . . On the issue of stability, which is related to the entire situation of the country, we must have a common understanding and work in full cooperation and with unity of purpose. This is not an easy thing. When people are living in a state of stability, they sometimes do not realize the importance of stability. However, if one day stability disappears, it will be too late to repent. We will not be able to accomplish even one of the things desired by all of us. Even our achieved results will be lost in one day. If we destroy stability, what do we have? Can we win democracy and achieve progress in science? Can we enjoy the fruits of reform and construction? Can we revitalize the motherland? No, we cannot do any of this."

In sharp contrast to the editorial of April 26, Zhao's appeal for stability, for an end to the demonstrations, did not threaten; it did not bludgeon with the thuggish political rhetoric of the old men. Instead, it sought to persuade, to reason with the students. It was a mark of Zhao's political mien, his belief that modern China would have to rest on a foundation of consensus, not *diktat;* freedom, not repression. But it also came across as a plea for an end to the protests; a plea, unheard by the students, that if they did not end, Zhao's vision of the future would careen toward extinction. Zhao knew it. The students refused to accept it.

Through inner-party documents leaked on the square, foreign reporters learned later that a group of the old guard had told Zhao, before he gave his May 4 commemorative address, that he was to include criticism of "bourgeois liberalization," the pernicious influence of Western culture and ideas. Yang Shangkun described the confrontation during a meeting of senior officials later in the month: "Comrade Li Peng gave me the revised version and I told Zhao that quite a few comrades held this opinion and that he had better add this to his speech, but he still did not agree."

The following day, Zhao met with the members of the board of governors of the Asian Development Bank, which was meeting in Beijing. Zhao explained his view of events on the square and predicted that there would be no riots and that eventually the demonstrations would dissipate. "I am very confident of this," Zhao told the governors. But even as he spoke, protests were spreading across the country, with students marching in dozens of cities, including Shanghai, Hangzhou, and Guangzhou. And as Zhao met with the bank governors, more than a hundred thousand people were camped out on Tiananmen Square.

The elderly hard-liners were incensed at Zhao's conversation with the bank governors and a summit meeting was called for the leadership, plus some of the old guard, at Deng Xiaoping's house. Yang Shangkun recounted the meeting this way. "Comrade Xiaoping raised a question: 'If a retreat is made, where should we retreat to?' I said that this is the final dike against the floods and if we retreat the dike will immediately collapse. Comrade Xiaoping said: 'I know that there are different opinions among you, but this is not the time for debating about this or that matter. Today, we only decide whether or not we should retreat.' Comrade Xiaoping said that we cannot retreat and that the problem exists inside the party. He also said that it was necessary to declare martial law."

According to Yang, Zhao retorted to Deng's demands with a simple declaration. "I cannot implement this policy," Zhao said. "I have difficulties."

"Then the minority should submit to the majority," Deng demanded. The meeting was then adjourned until eight o'clock that evening.

Zhao opened the discussion at the evening session. "My duty has come to an end today and I cannot continue to work because my opinion is different from yours and you form the majority. I am not convinced, and as general secretary, how can I perform my duty? If I cannot implement the decision, I will cause difficulties for you in the Standing Committee. Therefore, I must resign from office."

Yang Shangkun shot back angrily, "Comrade Ziyang, your attitude is not good. We should maintain unity now, but you are trying to quit at this moment." Zhao then wrote a letter to the Politburo declaring his intention to resign his post as general secretary and restating his view that the editorial of April 26 should be retracted.

A few days later, Deng lectured Zhao on his failings. "Comrade Ziyang, your speech to the Asian Development Bank officials on May 4 became a turning point, because after that the students created more serious disturbances." Yang joined the attack, haranguing Zhao for a lack of will. "If you resign from office, first, how can you justify yourself to the whole country? Second, how can you justify yourself to the whole party? Third, how can you justify yourself to the Politburo? Fourth, how can you justify yourself to the Standing Committee of the Politburo? And fifth, and most important, how will you treat Comrade Xiaoping?"

In the days that followed, China's newspapers, radio stations, and television broadcasts reported the events on the square and in Beijing mostly accurately and with little or no political slant, although there was no news of the conflict within the party. It was the first time in the four decades of the People's Republic that its media had approached the standard of objective reporting generally seen as the role of the press in democratic societies. For China's reporters, many of whom marched for a free press in the parades to Tiananmen, carrying banners reading "News Must Speak the Truth" and "Defend the Constitution and Freedom of the Press," it was a moment of great liberation and jubilation. For the people of China, at least those who did not follow events through the shortwave broadcasts of the BBC or the Voice of America, it was a jarring journey into reality, one that presented a picture of events that unwrapped the easy packaging of propagandists, that was riveting in its challenge to the petrified ideas about the mood of the Chinese people. And, on May 12, when the leadership refused to respond to a demand for discussions issued by the student leaders, several thousand university students began a hunger strike, an action that mobilized hundreds of thousands of Beijing's citizens in marches of support.

ON MAY 14, Mikhail Gorbachev arrived in Beijing, his visit intended to heal a three-decade rift between the two Communist giants. Despite warnings and pleadings to end their protests, the students continued their occupation of Tiananmen Square and the official welcoming ceremony for Gorbachev had to be shifted to the airport from the eastern steps of the Great Hall of the People, the usual site for such occasions. Other events, including a wreath-laying ceremony at the Monument to the People's Heroes, were moved or dropped because of the mass of demonstrators that clogged Beijing's streets and continued to occupy the square. Gorbachev took the disruptions in stride and good humor, an attitude not shared by the hard-liners, who were enraged at what they considered an affront to the Soviet leader. Even worse, these old men believed that the events on the street showed them to be ineffectual leaders, unable to control the people on this most historic of occasions. They had lost face.

Again, Zhao tempered his comments on the protests, insisting that the leadership would listen to the student demands and opinions and that the government would "propose and adopt concrete measures to enhance democracy and law, oppose corruption, build an honest and clean government, and expand openness." As the nominal leader of China's Communist Party, Zhao likewise spoke candidly in his conversations with Gorbachev, jesting and trading stories with the man from Moscow with a casual familiarity. In the course of these meetings, talks that both men seemed to enjoy thoroughly, Zhao spoke about his party and its experiences, mentioning in an almost off-the-cuff way that though he held the senior post, in reality it was Deng Xiaoping who remained the controlling force in party and governmental affairs, that all major decisions had to be approved by a man who was supposed to be in semiretirement.

On the square, students followed the discussions with Gorbachev with their usual carefully tuned political antennae. It became clear to them that Zhao represented but one faction within the party and that a monumental struggle for control of the party was occurring. What they did not know was that Zhao was being regularly outvoted on the Politburo and that he was being methodically pushed from the center of power by the old guard and their younger surrogates.

The Politburo met repeatedly to discuss the situation, to decide how to respond to the student protesters. On May 19, presaging the oncoming storm and his own demise, Zhao made a tearful appearance on Tiananmen Square to address some of the protesting students. "We are here too late," he said, his eyes watery, his voice choking. "We are getting old and don't count for much. But you young people have a long way to go. You should take good care of yourselves." Even as he spoke, tens of thousands of troops were moving in force toward the city in preparation for the declaration of martial law the following day. A council of war held by party elders that night to plan for martial law was boycotted by Zhao. He was placed under house arrest the next day.

A remarkable speech by Yang Shangkun on May 24 to the Central Military Commission, leaked by supporters of Zhao to the students on the square, described in detail how the elderly hard-liners maneuvered against Zhao and took control of the party. Photocopies of Yang's talk circulated swiftly on the square, and I was given a copy of the original document Yang read to his colleagues; it had extra-large ideograms so that they would be legible for an old man with bad eyesight. Martial law had been in effect for four days, although the people of Beijing had stopped the troops from entering the city. Demonstrators continued their sit-in in front of the gates of Zhongnanhai, and Tiananmen Square was a sprawling encampment of tents and people. Yang painted a portrait of a city and country on the brink of anarchy.

"Beijing is out of control," Yang told the military commanders. "Moreover, for a time it was calm in other provinces, but now trouble has been stirred up again there. There is now trouble in almost every province and city. In short, every time we take a step backward, they take a step forward. At present, they are focusing on one slogan, namely, 'Down with Li Peng.' This is what they have decided internally, and they have discarded other slogans. Their objective is the overthrow of the Communist Party and the present government.

"Why has this situation emerged?" Yang continued. "Some time ago, some old comrades of noble character and high prestige, such as Comrade Chen Yun, Comrade [Li] Xiannian, Comrade Peng Zhen, Comrade [Deng] Xiaoping, Comrade Wang Zhen, and Sister Deng Yingchao, were very worried about this and asked why the situation had developed to such an extent. After analyzing the development of things, they drew this conclusion: the events are happening among the students, but the root is in the party. That is to say, there are two voices, two different voices in the Standing Committee of the Politburo." In other words, Zhao Ziyang was the cause of China's current unrest.

Yang went on to describe a series of meetings held by the Politburo at which Zhao maintained that the students were patriotic in their actions. "Even when Comrade Xiaoping attended the meeting," Yang told the military commission, "he still stuck to his view, saying that he was unconvinced and that on the question of the nature of the student movement, he could not maintain unanimity with the arguments of Comrade Xiaoping and other comrades of the Standing Committee. He therefore asked to resign, saying that he could no longer work. Later, I told him that the issue was so great that if [our characterization of the movement's] nature was changed, we would all collapse." Yang also told Zhao that the situation on the streets of Beijing resembled that of the Cultural Revolution, of students taking independent political action and challenging the legitimacy of authority.

"This was the first time that these octogenarians had got together to discuss central affairs in many years," Yang explained. "Xiaoping, Chen Yun, Peng Zhen, Sister Deng, and Wang Zhen all felt that there was no way to retreat, because a retreat would indicate our collapse and the collapse of the People's Republic of China, and this would mean a comeback for capitalism. . . . Comrades in Beijing clearly heard what Comrade Ziyang said on the morning of May 19 when visiting the hunger strikers on Tiananmen Square. Any sensible person could discern that his words were unreasonable. First, he said that we had come too late and then he began to cry. Second, he said that events were very complicated and that many things could not be solved at that moment, but that things could eventually be solved in time. He told the students that they were still young and had a long way to go but that we are old so it does not matter. It was a low-key speech full of compunction. It seemed that he had a great deal of pain and difficulty that could not be expressed clearly. After hearing what he said, most cadres in Beijing said that he simply had no sense of organization or discipline."

Then, Yang revealed to the generals what was by then all but public knowledge. "The central comrades," Yang said, a reference not to the constitutionally designated party Central Committee but to the old men led by Deng Xiaoping, "have considered again and again and found that it is necessary to change the leader, because he has refused to implement central instructions and has stuck to his own ideas." Yang, cognizant of the irregularity of the action, defended the legitimacy of the party elders. "The many old comrades enjoy the highest prestige inside the party, because they have the highest seniority in the party and have made major contributions to the party and the state. . . . At such a critical juncture of the party and the state, how could they remain silent? They could not just sit there and see our state being brought to the verge of destruction."

The turmoil within the Communist Party, however, was never as important to the Chinese people as the forces at work within society. Because of its increasing irrelevance to people's lives as the decade wore on, as well as its internal corruption and decay, the party had ceased to shape society; indeed, at every turn, throughout the 1980s, it was always the party that scrambled to keep abreast of the changes within society. And while it was the constellation of a decade's changes that led to the night of June 4, 1989, it was activities of a young electrician eleven years earlier that had begun everything.

ELEVEN

Democratic Stirrings

ON DECEMBER 5, 1978, a twenty-nine-year-old electrician named Wei Jingsheng plastered several densely written paper broadsheets on a seven-foot-high gray-brick wall on Xidan Road, a bit west of the Forbidden City in central Beijing; what the world came to know as Democracy Wall. "The leaders of our nation must be informed that we want to take our destiny into our own hands," Wei wrote. "We want no more gods and emperors. No more saviors of any kind. We want to be masters of our own country, not modernized tools for the expansionist ambitions of dictators. Democracy, freedom, and happiness are the only goals of modernization. Without modernization, the four others are nothing more than a newfangled lie."

A few months later, in his illegal independent journal *Explorations,* Wei pursued this theme. "Everyone in China is well aware that the Chinese social system is not democratic and that this lack of democracy has severely stunted every aspect of the country's social development over the past thirty years. In the face of this hard fact there are two choices before the Chinese people:

either to reform the social system if they want to develop their society and seek a swift increase in the prosperity of their livelihood and economic resources; or, if they are content with a continuation of the Mao Zedong brand of proletarian dictatorship, they cannot even talk of democracy, nor will they be able to realize the modernization of their lives and resources." Wei called his notion, this novel idea of democracy, the fifth modernization; what he believed was an essential precondition to the Communist Party's official program of economic development, which it had dubbed "the four modernizations," referring to the process of modernizing the country's woefully obsolescent industry, agriculture, military, and scientific and technological establishments.

Deng Xiaoping at first tolerated the wall; it was a phenomenon he could exploit while consolidating his power over the still-fractured Communist Party. Once secure, however, he ordered the imprisonment of Wei Jingsheng and the other poster-writers who made the wall China's first example of free expression in more than two decades. The brush-stroked pleas for basic rights were ripped down and the country's constitution rewritten to prohibit the right even to pen such posters. A few other rights, those of "speaking out freely, airing views fully, holding great debates," were also expurgated from the constitution.

At his trial in October 1979, Wei uttered these final words in defense of his beliefs: "The debasing of the concept of revolution—to label the will of the people in power as forever revolutionary, to wipe out all divergent views and theories, and to think of power as truth—was precisely one of the most effective tools used by the Gang of Four in the past twenty years and more to suppress revolutionaries and the people. . . . The current historical tide is a democratic tide, one which opposes feudal fascist dictatorship. The central theme in my articles such as 'The Fifth Modernization: Democracy and Others' is that without democracy, there can be no four modernizations. Without the fifth modernization—democracy—all modernizations are doomed to failure. How can such a central theme be counterrevolutionary? People and things that oppose it should be justly included in the realm of counterrevolution.

"It is the right of every citizen to criticize any unreasonable people or thing that he sees," Wei told the judges who were to convict him. "This is also a responsibility which he cannot shift. Nobody and no organization has the right to interfere with this sovereign right. Criticism cannot possibly be nice and appealing to the ear, or all correct. To require criticism, to be entirely correct, and to inflict punishment if it is not is the same as prohibiting criticism and reforms and elevating the leaders to the positions of deities." For this crime of counterrevolution, Wei was sentenced to fifteen years in prison; others, like Wang Xizhe, Liu Qing, and Xu Wenli, for somewhat lesser terms. The Democracy Wall Movement was crushed; simply, swiftly, mercilessly.

"What would have happened if we had continued to allow such posters to be put up without restraint?" Deng asked a gathering of Central Committee members in 1980. "One must not take such things lightly, thinking that they won't cause disturbances. Even a handful of persons could undermine our great undertaking. . . . Under China's present circumstances it is clear that without stability and unity we have nothing."

At the end of the Cultural Revolution, China was, simply put, a police state in which the Chinese people had no individual rights, no control over their lives, over what they could read, where they worked, where their children went to school. Worse, the state sought to control the very substance of what people thought. The error committed by Wei Jingsheng and his comrades was to believe that the end of the Cultural Revolution and discussions about the tentative loosening of economic controls would extend into other aspects of Chinese life, into the essence of society itself. Neither Deng nor any of China's Communist leaders were willing to tolerate independent voices, voices that ultimately challenged the dominance and legitimacy of the party itself.

That burst of genuine democratic yearning, the passionate conviction that three decades of intellectual and political repression could be swept away in the exhilarating atmosphere of liberation that came at the end of the Cultural Revolution, was in the end very limited in its scope. Only in a few cities, Shanghai, Hangzhou, and Guangzhou, did the appeals of Beijing's dissidents resonate, and even then in a significantly more subdued manner. The feverish enthusiasm of those days in the capital, those weeks when hopes soared and when there was a sense that

popular aspirations would finally help shape the style and direction of Chinese governance, were described in copious reports
by European and American journalists, who themselves were
often unsure what they were seeing, what it really meant.

The young men and women of this movement (although there
were far fewer prominent women than men) were an eclectic
cross-section of society. There were workers ill at ease with the
complexion of life after three decades of Communist rule. There
were university students and academics tired of the mayhem of
the Cultural Revolution who wanted something approaching an
unfettered intellectual life. There were Communist Party members who felt that the party had betrayed both itself and the
Chinese people. There were, later on, even peasants by the
thousands, who came on foot and by donkey cart to petition the
country's leadership over grievances against tyrannical local officials.

These democratic stirrings, the proliferation of irreverent
journals published by sinitic Tom Paines, struck the Communist
Party leadership like a sledgehammer. While the hold of the
Communist Party on the reins of government was never in danger, Deng and his colleagues immediately recognized the implications of the small democracy movement. The Communist
Party, whose stature had been skewered during the Cultural
Revolution and whose pronouncements were received by most
people with an ingrained cynicism, was valiantly trying to bur-
nish its image, to project itself not as the cause of the Cultural
Revolution but as the sage victor in its defeat.

The skeptical Chinese people were told that, yes, the Communist Party did commit mistakes, but the party itself resolved
those mistakes. Only with the leadership of the party could
China move forward out of poverty toward prosperity. The Cultural Revolution was a catastrophe, but it represented not the
essence of the party but an aberration from historical truth. The
Communist Party overcame that debacle, and others before it,
and now, in 1980, was firmly on the correct path.

China's democratic activists had challenged these proclama-
tions. They asked not why did the Cultural Revolution happen
but was it not the very nature of the Communist Party that had
inexorably led to such catastrophe? They asked not why was
China socialist but why was it so impoverished—materially, in-

tellectually, morally? They asked not whether the party was legitimate but above all whether the people of China should have a say in their own future.

Although the bands of democratic pamphleteers, poster-writers, and public orators never sought to wrest power physically from the Communist Party, they nevertheless believed that the issues themselves, the questions they posed, would strip bare the pretenses and injustices perpetrated by the party. They believed that a democratic process, the genuine expression of popular will, would bore away at the party's innards, leaving a brittle shell that would crumble of its own accord.

Deng, however, would have none of this. Neither he nor any of his fellow party leaders could countenance even the appearance of a challenge to their right to rule. In a tough speech to Communist Party theoreticians, the bureaucrats that devise the propaganda campaigns intended to justify and promote party policy, Deng demarcated the line over which no Chinese could ever cross. He declared that there were four immutable truths, principles on which the People's Republic was founded and which would remain the pillars of the Chinese state. These "four cardinal principles," as he called them on March 20, 1979, were sharply etched: "We must keep to the socialist road. We must uphold the dictatorship of the proletariat. We must uphold the leadership of the Communist Party. We must uphold Marxism-Leninism and Mao Zedong Thought." This formula was accorded near-talismanic power and would be invoked by party leaders whenever discordant voices were heard during the 1980s.

MANY DEMOCRATIC ACTIVISTS, to this day no one knows how many, were imprisoned. The magazines—*Explorations, Beijing Spring, Today, Enlightenment, Autumn Fruit*—were shut down. Street cleaners in Beijing were dispatched to the gray-brick wall on Xidan Avenue, where they scrubbed away the posters. But as hard as they scrubbed, as many people as were jailed, the ideas that bloomed in those four months in late 1978 and 1979 lingered in the air like the scent of fine perfume.

In a real sense, much of what happened in China during the 1980s revolved around the question of putting this genie of freer thinking back in the bottle of greater control. Instinctively, the Chinese Communist Party sought to stifle any form of expression that provoked genuine inquiry into the nature of the Chinese polity and society. But a combination of indigenous democratic urges and the relentless influence of foreign ideas began to permeate virtually every segment of intellectual and artistic life, leaving the party increasingly and repeatedly on the defensive. The tactics of the past—threats, beatings, jail, banishment—were no longer viable in a country that was trying to project an image of civilized tolerance. Alternatively, the ideological claims of the party, increasingly irrelevant in the economic life of the country, were seen as equally barren by young artists and writers, filmmakers and academics.

As easy as it had been for the party to suppress the overtly political polemics of the Democracy Wall period, it proved impossible to restrain the flood of literary creativity, held back by the dam of the Cultural Revolution, that inundated the terrain of formal and informal culture. Three of China's most important contemporary poets saw their first works roughly pasted to that brick wall on Xidan Avenue; only later would they be hurriedly and amateurishly bound in the journal *Today,* the most significant of the literary periodicals from that period. They wrote what became known as the "literature of the ruins." Their ideological critics called it *menglong shi,* obscure poetry.

The editor of *Today* was Zhao Zhenkai, a young former construction worker whose steady gaze and hollowed cheeks lent to his seriousness an edge of severity. Despite his initial enthusiasm for the Cultural Revolution in its early years (he was a Red Guard), Zhao developed a deep-seated loathing for what the chaos of that time had done to China, and had abandoned politics in favor of writing poetry and short stories. Under the pen name Bei Dao, he established himself as the foremost voice of the new generation of poets. Until *Today* was forcibly shut down by the Public Security Bureau in August 1980, his work appeared there regularly. It was, like much written by the new young poets, as much a forceful rejection of the claims of the political order as a clarion for a rejuvenated literary climate. His poem "The Echo" suggests the pessimism that underscored the mood of the time:

you can't get out of this valley
in the funeral procession
you can't let go of the coffin by yourself
make peace with death, or let the autumn
continue to stay at home
stay in the tin can beside the stove
and bear infertile buds
the avalanche has started—
the echo seeks the mental connections
between you and others: good fortune
lasts, good fortune lasts until tomorrow
but joins tomorrow's
sunbeam, coming from
a jewel hidden in your breast
an evil jewel
you can't get out of this valley, because
the funeral is yours

Even more despairing is his poem "A Blank":

poverty is a blank
freedom is a blank
in the sockets of a marble statue:
victory is a blank
black birds pouring from the horizon
reveal tomorrow's age spots:
despair is a blank
at the bottom of a friend's cup
betrayal is a blank
on the lover's photograph:
disgust is a blank
in the long-awaited letter:
time is a blank
a swarm of ominous flies
settle on the hospital ceiling:
history is a blank
a running genealogy
where only the dead are recognized

There were many other voices; poets like Shu Ting, Gu
Cheng, and his father Gu Gong, short story writers and novelists

like Shi Tiesheng, Dai Houying, Zhu Lin. These authors sought to understand how the People's Republic, a nation that had been born with Mao's assertion that the Chinese people have "stood up," had sunk so low; how it had turned on itself in such a vengeful and murderous fashion.

Gu Cheng, a carpenter by trade and one of the most poignant of the young poets, would write in 1983, "We have paid an enormous price, and we have begun to understand that neither politics nor materialism can substitute for everything. If a nation wants progress, it needs more than electronic technology and scientific management; it needs a highly advanced spiritual civilization, and that includes the creation of a modern, a new aesthetic consciousness. Beauty will no longer be prisoner or slave, it will shine with as much light as the sun and the moon. It will rise high in the heavens to drive away the shadow of evil. Through the windows of art and poetry it will cast light on the hearts of both the waking and the sleeping."

The Communist Party reacted swiftly to the new literary storm. Unlike all previous literature written during Communist rule, the new poetry, short stories, and plays did not tread the familiar track of socialist realism. The good guys were not snow white, the bad guys coal black. There were no heroes vanquishing despicable, oppressive landlords. There was no celebration of the Communist Party's glorious achievements in liberating the people of China. Instead, there were more questions than answers, more imagination than formula, more doubt than certainty, more ambiguity than conviction. These young authors explored relations between human beings as imperfect, confused, and troubled, not as idealized projections of a politicized harmony.

Ironically, it was Hu Yaobang, at the time the head of the party's propaganda department, who led the official onslaught against the new literature. In a rambling, six-hour speech to a convention of playwrights in February 1980, Hu spelled out the precise limits of artistic freedom and the contours to which artists had to conform in describing Chinese history and society. Hu—who himself was to be seen in a few short years as a defender of intellectual freedom—told writers in no uncertain terms what was expected of them: they were to describe the "lovable" People's Liberation Army, to embrace the "great and lovable" Communist Party, to show the "bright side" of society. And if literary works of tragedy were to be published (because it was inevitable that authors would write of the evils of the Cultural Revolution), "What we want to prevent is the writing of tragedies that just go on being tragic forever without any future, giving people a feeling of destruction. This kind of tragedy is not in accord with the development of history, is not realistic."

But despite Hu's injunctions, despite the herculean efforts of the reconstituted official writers' associations, the new literature kept appearing, some in underground journals, some on stapled-together mimeographed sheets, some even in semiofficial periodicals. It was, however, not a young, iconoclastic writer who triggered the first post-Cultural Revolution political campaign against intellectuals, but a fifty-one year old Communist who had fought in Mao's guerrilla army, named Bai Hua. In 1958, Bai had been a victim of a pogrom against intellectuals, the so-called anti-rightist campaign, and was banished to a labor camp. After the Cultural Revolution, when he and many older writers who survived were allowed to resume their work, Bai again set his pen to paper and wrote a long play called *Bitter Love,* verse that was to excite younger writers and enrage party autocrats.

Written in a chaotic, jumpy style, *Bitter Love* tells a highly symbolic story of the artist-intellectual in modern China; the dashed hopes, betrayal, exile, and finally death in a snowy wasteland. Produced as the film *Sun and Man,* Bai's work was denounced repeatedly by the nation's party newspapers and later by the party hierarchy, including Deng Xiaoping himself. Deng accused Bai of giving "the impression that the Communist Party and the socialist system are bad. [The film] vilifies the latter to such an extent that one wonders what has happened to the author's party spirit. Some say the movie achieves a fairly high artistic standard, but that only makes it all the more harmful. In fact, a work of this sort has the same effect as the views of the so-called democrats."

Deng was, of course, correct. What the wall poster writers of Xidan Avenue had done for political discourse, Bai had encouraged for artists and writers. The Communist ideological establishment lashed out at Bai, denigrating his work, eventually bullying him into submission. The acting minister of culture, Zhou

Weizhi, summed up the problem with people like Bai Hua: some people, he said in September 1981, "hold that creation is solely the self-expression of writers and artists; they deny the need to take the social effects of literary pieces into consideration. This reflects the fact that a small number of people in the art and literary world crave 'absolute freedom' and extreme individualistic 'rights,' that they want to get rid of party leadership, depart from the socialist road and go in for bourgeois liberalization. The scenario *Bitter Love* is an example of this and so should be criticized seriously." Thoroughly cowed, Bai confessed his sins in an official literary magazine, promising to reexamine his approach to writing and, in a pathetic exhibition of his own humiliation, thanked his attackers for their gentle criticism.

ALTHOUGH THE PEOPLE'S REPUBLIC had had sporadic contacts with Western culture, particularly in the 1950s when Russian novels, films, and music constituted the lighter side of fraternal cooperation with the Soviet Union, the Chinese people knew virtually nothing of the West; its politics, its literary life, its artistic accomplishments. That changed dramatically in the years after 1979, as China's leaders began actively seeking substantial foreign investment and technology.

And the foreigners came, in the hundreds of thousands. Some were investors. Others were language teachers, writers, academics, journalists like myself. Foreign movies, foreign novels, and foreign manners pushed into China in a fashion not seen since the era of the treaty ports. For China's literature-starved people, it was as if they were thrown the keys to all the candy stores on Main Street. As quickly as a new novel was received it was translated, usually hastily and poorly, and published in Chinese. Authors like Joseph Heller, Saul Bellow, and Kurt Vonnegut joined Shakespeare, Balzac, and Flaubert on Chinese bookshelves. Foreign videotapes were copied and circulated hand to hand. Rock'n'roll cassette tapes were pirated and sold in the remotest corners of the country. Dance halls and discos, deemed the excrescence of a bourgeois society during the Cultural Revolution, opened in every city in China.

China's intellectuals, its artists and poets, its philosophers and playwrights, were swept up in the swirl of new ideas that crashed over the decaying walls of habitual xenophobia. Notions of social alienation, the role of humanism, Freudianism, Darwinism were suddenly the currency of intellectual debate. Yet, because every statement, every idea, every discussion is invariably tinctured by political hues, in the end, no one could speak without courting reprisal.

Wang Ruoshui, a senior editor at the *People's Daily,* a man whose job it was to oversee the theoretical orthodoxy of the paper's output, triggered a vigorous, and later virulent, controversy in early 1983, when he wrote that "a spectre is haunting the Chinese intellectual world—the spectre of humanism." Wang was no wild-eyed wall poster writer; he was a stalwart of the Communist establishment, a man entrusted with molding the mind of China.

"In the present period," Wang wrote, "when we are constructing socialism and modernizing our country, we need socialist humanism." By this, Wang meant "the determined rejection of the 'total dictatorship' and cruel struggles of the Cultural Revolution . . . the sanctity of personal freedom and dignity . . . demanding that people should really be seen as people, and that individuals should be judged by what they are in themselves, not on the basis of class origin, position, or wealth . . . it means valuing the human factor in socialist construction; giving full play to the self-motivation and creativity of the working people."

Wang's heresy provoked an outcry from the party mandarins. Hu Qiaomu, one of the most rigid of the leadership's hard-line Marxists, retaliated with a blunt denunciation of Wang's view, and, as with earlier ideological ripostes, quickly pinpointed the threat Wang posed: "Sloganeering about humanism will only encourage all kinds of unrealistic demands for individual well-being and freedom, and create a false impression that once the socialist system is established, all personal demands will be satisfied—for otherwise, the socialist system would be proven 'inhumane.' "

Humanism was just one of the philosophical perspectives that filtered into China from the West. Sigmund Freud's approach to the study of personality and neuroses attracted considerable interest, particularly in its more vulgarized form, concentrating on the role of sexuality. Abstract painting, a radical departure from both the socialist realism of the Cultural Revolution and the more refined tradition of scroll painting, exploded across the paper and canvas of young artists as experimentation replaced propaganda as the current métier.

Party leaders surveyed this intrusion of new ideas, the easy rejection of the canonical values of hard work, self-reliance, and simple living they still cherished, values cultivated during the years of revolutionary war, and saw a need to fight back. The leadership recognized the need for the populace to absorb foreign learning, technology, and investment, but they resented their inability to filter out the unwanted side effects of these foreign contacts. More, they began genuinely to fear the loss of national direction and spirit. Responding in the only way they knew, they instigated a political campaign, this time against what they called spiritual pollution. Deng Xiaoping was the driving force behind the new movement, and he outlined the themes of the new campaign at a meeting of the party's Central Committee in October 1983: "What attitude should we take toward the bourgeois culture of the modern West? We keep our doors open, but we are selective. We don't introduce anything without a purpose and a plan and we firmly combat all corrupting bourgeois influences. . . . In learning things in the cultural realm, we must adopt a Marxist approach, analyzing them, distinguishing the good from the bad, and making a critical judgment about their ideological content and artistic form. There are quite a few honest, progressive scholars, writers, and artists in the West today who are producing serious and valuable works, which of course we should introduce into China. But some of our comrades rush to praise to the skies all trends in the philosophy, economics, socio-politics, literature, and art of the West, without analyzing them, distinguishing the good from the bad, or exercising any critical judgment.

"There has been such confusion in the import of Western academic and cultural things that in recent years we have witnessed an influx of books, films, music, dances, and audio and video recordings that even in Western countries are regarded as pernicious junk. This corruption of our young people by the decadent bourgeois culture of the West is no longer tolerable. . . . Spiritual pollution can be so damaging as to bring disaster upon the country and the people. It blurs the distinction between right and wrong, leads to passivity, laxity, and disunity, corrupts the mind and erodes the will. It encourages the spread of all kinds of individualism and causes people to doubt or even reject socialism and the party's leadership."

The new campaign burst beyond the bounds of esoteric discussions over humanism. Young men with long hair were rounded up and given haircuts. Bell-bottom pants were banned. Rock 'n' roll music was roundly denounced for its mind-altering influence. Wealthy farmers were hounded by politically driven cadres who now felt free to persecute obvious practitioners of capitalism.

But then again, these were not the years of the Cultural Revolution. The injunctions of the leadership, once issued with the expectations of old imperial decrees that concluded, "Let all tremblingly obey," did not evoke old fears. Certainly there was enhanced caution, the momentary holding of the tongue, but even by then there was a momentum toward more affluence and toward a greater personal independence. By 1983, the average personal income in rural areas was three hundred yuan a year, more than 130 percent higher than a mere five years before. And in the cities, average annual earnings jumped more than 65 percent, to five hundred and twenty yuan. However small this amount seems, it was enormous to the Chinese, and the frugality and hard living of the past gave way to the newly discovered pleasures of consumption. And with that, came the sense of liberation from the endless impoverishment that had imprisoned body and spirit.

One jolt came as summer began clamping down on China in 1984, a season that became known as "the tornado of the skirt." City women, usually those under thirty, decided in virtual unison to abandon baggy cotton pants. Suddenly, the drab gray city streets were bustling with a vivid chromatic fabric panorama of women wearing skirts—pleated, straight, mini, balloon. Even the official clerical garb, the two-piece high-collared Mao suit (actually a modification of a dress style pioneered by Sun Yatsen) uniformly worn by male officialdom, gave way to a preference for tailored Western business suits. Zhao Ziyang had presaged this sartorial sea change in 1982 while on a visit to Japan, but by 1984 many of the second generation of the leadership had forsaken their Mao suits. Still, the older party leaders, men like Deng Xiaoping, Chen Yun, Li Xiannian, Peng Zhen, men whose ideological predilections found comfort with the older revolutionary ways, always appeared in public wearing the familiar Mao jackets, except in the summer months, when short-sleeved open-necked white shirts were acceptable. As with everything else in the People's Republic, habiliments are not without political weave.

The following year, two writers, Zhang Xinxin and Sang Ye, stirred attention about the new aspirations of China's people in a remarkable collection of interviews with average citizens. For the first time, people were able to read opinions that reflected their own, that understood the pains and frustrations of daily life as well as anticipation for better things to come. The volume, *Beijing Man,* was excerpted in five national major literary magazines which sold out as soon as they hit the bookstores.

A NINETEEN-YEAR-OLD MAN in Nanjing blurted out his frustrations: "If you've any guts, record what I say and print it! Let people judge for themselves. In China, in Nanjing, why can't Chinese go to places where foreigners go? The Dingshan Hotel, The Shuangmenlou, and the Jinling . . . all keep us out; even the bloody curio shop serves foreigners only . . . it doesn't make sense. My dad's a party member. I ask him, 'Is this in line with the Marxism-Leninism you believe in?' He acts dumb."

An old man named Zhang gave his view of Beijing: "In those days there was plenty of housing and not many people. If you wanted to buy or rent a house you could take your pick. Despite all the big blocks they've put up now, there's still a housing shortage—too many people. . . . As for prices, that depends on how you look at them. In the old days everything was very cheap except calico, grain, and foreign oil—what's called paraffin these days. A one-way tram ticket cost three coppers and the circular round the city five. You got five hundred coppers for a silver dollar. Now it costs five fen to get on a bus, and how many five-fen coins are there in a yuan? . . . Things are really more expensive than they were. But the standard of living has gone up in the last few years and everyone's got things like televisions, refrigerators, and electric fans. That's good."

A young woman in a silver lamé dress who sings in a hotel nightclub spoke earnestly: "We're very professional about our singing, 'cause if you're slack the audience will hiss you. A lot of them really know their music and they're out there listening to see if you sing the song right or not. If you're only out one note or get something wrong, the band can tell immediately and they tick you off at the end of the performance. . . . There was a while there before the law campaign when Guangzhou was in a real bad way. Someone from the band had to see us home after the performance every night. And if anyone sleeps around then they're criticized by the others. . . . We don't dare look at the audience too much—people say we're trying to manipulate them if we do. Then we'd get into trouble. You can't let yourself dance around the stage too much either as you'd be accused of being lewd and they'd make things hard for us."

THIS WAS THE STUFF of daily life. There was nothing here to shock, nothing extraordinary, just the quotidian expressiveness of the Chinese nation. What was riveting, what was so fresh, was the gritty realism, as opposed to a fabricated socialist realism, of these two authors' work. As Zhang Xinxin put it in the epilogue to the book, "Half an hour's talk, or a few hours' talk, gives you a story, a whole human life, a sculpture that needs no reworking. A few thousand words can express it all. Pull it apart, knead it to pieces, and the flavor disappears."

To be sure, as the young singer intimated, there were limits, but what those limits were, how they were drawn, and how one found them grew increasingly difficult to ascertain. Even as the local newspaper of Guangzhou, the *Yancheng Evening News,* wrote about the "six new crazes" of Guangzhou's youth in 1985— "reading, dancing, traveling, music, calligraphy, and photography"—the *People's Daily* bemoaned the fact that only popular music by Hong Kong and Taiwanese singers was available on cassette tapes, and that nowhere could one buy copies of the Internationale or the national anthem. And the *Nanfang Daily News,* while bragging about the wonderful service of the stewardesses on the super-deluxe Guangzhou to Hong Kong rail line, also noted that they "are always on guard against the corrosive influence of capitalism." The American film *First Blood,* a saga of Rambo's decimation of the American Pacific Northwest, played to packed houses, while the movie *Superman* was hurriedly withdrawn from theaters. The *Beijing Evening News,* providing murky explanation, warned that the Caped Crusader was "a narcotic the capitalist class gives itself to cast off its serious crises," while his acrophobic flights around the Statue of Liberty, the paper continued ominously, "blatantly exposes the director's intentions."

It was amid this atmosphere—a time of cultural and intellectual expectancy, growing anxiety within the party, underlain by remarkable economic expansion—that the first serious political challenges to the party's monopoly on ideas and power were heard.

TWELVE

Students Rising

By 1986, THE CHILL of earlier years had given way to an atmosphere of pronounced optimism. Talk among the country's intelligentsia hovered around the question of whether there would be a return to the heady but brutally truncated days of 1956, when the party "let a hundred flowers bloom, a hundred schools of thought contend." For a brief time that year, Mao had encouraged the country's intelligentsia to speak out, to illuminate the party's shortcomings and suggest ways to improve the country's intellectual climate. There was, to Mao's distress, not a stream of well-controlled opinion, but a swell of voices in opposition to the party's tyranny. Mao was startled severely by the depth and fury of discontent, and he ordered one of his lieutenants, Deng Xiaoping, to direct the crackdown on the country's outspoken intellectuals who had been assured that they could speak and criticize freely. Thousands upon thousands of professors, writers, artists, musicians—anyone who had accepted the party's challenge to speak out—were shipped to labor camps and a reign of full-fledged intellectual terror descended upon the country.

In 1986, though, many of the new generation of thinkers and writers, those who had seen what the West offered and what China lacked, as well as those who had suffered in Mao's labor camps, began tentatively discussing the germination of a new "Hundred Flowers" period. Even the *People's Daily* quoted the leader of the party's propaganda apparatus as urging "the propagation of independent thinking and the discussion and contention of different viewpoints." A month later, the paper editorialized that "the people are masters of a socialist country. Only when their function as masters is truly developed in political life, economic life, and the whole spectrum of social life will the enthusiasm of the people break out."

Heralding this new mood was a man still unknown in the West, although his was a familiar name on campuses across China. An astrophysicist whose academic work had won him some note in international scientific circles, he was the vice-president of the country's foremost institution for the study of science, the University of Science and Technology in the city of Hefei, in Anhui Province. His name was Fang Lizhi.

In mid-November of 1986, he traveled to Shanghai, where he gave a rousing speech to college students jammed into an auditorium on the campus of Jiaotong University. Although he was fifty years old, Fang possessed a boyish, buoyant air that made him seem younger. A shock of unruly black hair fell over his forehead, which he would brush back periodically with a careless sweep of his hand. His eyes were intent and careful behind thick black-framed glasses. At Hefei, he was known for his jocular manner, biting wit, and merciless skewering of Communist shibboleths and pretensions. His speech in Shanghai, one of many he delivered around the country—his iconoclastic views made him a sought-after speaker on many campuses—exuded the confidence and expectations generated by the newly felt sense of intellectual liberalization. He talked not about science but about democracy.

"Everybody says it is extremely difficult to practice democracy in China," Fang told the spellbound students. "Democracy has been called for ever since May 4, 1919. Years have passed, yet up to the present there are many undemocratic practices in the society. Why is this so? . . . [Y]esterday, someone mentioned that a jingle has become popular lately that implies that although democracy has not yet been practiced to the same extent as in the West, there are emerging signs of democracy. The jingle reads: 'The east wind blows, the war drum alarms; now no one can intimidate anyone else.' To some extent, this is indeed the case. No one is scared of others. On many occasions you don't dare to do certain things; but once you did them, you would discover that others dared not bother you. Democracy can be achieved only gradually through consistent effort. There is nothing to be afraid of. For instance, criticizing government leaders is a symbol of democracy. I hold that we may criticize leaders. . . . Democracy does not mean I will impose my views on you. Democracy means I am allowed to express my views.

"Students in China have long been a force of democracy and progress. In our times, students have pounded at the society to move forward step by step. . . . I have always been opposed to the view that Marxist philosophy should become the sole theoretical guidance of everything. . . . We have finally realized that the guidance can only lead to erroneous outcome. It has never produced correct results. . . . It is said that reforms in China depend on the resolve of the top leadership . . . the problem is that by relying only on the resolve of the top leadership, China cannot hope to become a developed country . . . if the democracy we are striving for remains one that is granted only from the top, then the democracy that is practiced in our society is not true democracy.

"Human rights as a term is taboo in China. In fact it is a very popular term. It simply means that men are born with rights to live, to marry, to think, to receive an education, and so on. . . . We should think of human rights, liberty, equality, and love as a positive historical legacy and then strive for democracy. Until then there is no true democracy. We should not place our hope on grants from the top leadership. Democracy granted from above is not democracy in a real sense. It is relaxation of control."

His words reverberated through the auditorium the way soft spring thunder augurs the oncoming storm. This man was deeply embedded in the academic establishment. He was a member of the Communist Party and a senior administrator at one of the country's most prestigious institutions of higher learning. And yet, here he was extolling the virtues of free choice and human dignity, of independent judgment and personal liberty. These were ideas of more than heresy; they were spiritual weapons pointed at the soul of the state and the Communist Party itself.

Three days later, Fang again took the podium, this time at Shanghai's Tongji University. He was even blunter on this occasion. "Socialism has failed," he declared before the wildly cheering students. "I am here to tell you that the socialist movement, from Marx and Lenin to Stalin and Mao Zedong, has been a failure."

It was not long, less than three weeks, before students at his own school embraced Fang's call, and on the evening of December 9 more than three thousand students poured from the campus and paraded out onto the streets of the provincial capital. They carried banners on which were drawn silhouettes of the Statue of Liberty, and they shouted slogans demanding the postponement of student elections to the provincial legislature, which they said were being rigged by the local authorities. They slathered the walls of university buildings with big-character posters reminiscent of the heady days of the Democracy Wall.

"For thirty-six years since liberation," one poster read, "Chinese people have never really exercised their political rights, they have only performed their obligations to the 'state.' The Chinese people have not become masters of the state, but have been dominated by a few politicians." Another poster read, "It's still a fresh memory that over ten years ago people were savagely killed in demonstrations in Beijing. There always has been pseudodemocracy and true tyranny. Could we ask how long the senile leaders will still hold their positions."

One poster, written in English, quoted Abraham Lincoln's address at Gettysburg: "Democracy is government of the people, by the people and for the people." And yet another turned to Patrick Henry, in large letters proclaiming: "Give me liberty or give me death." Still other posters decried the less weighty, criticizing the cafeteria's bad food and the miserable conditions in the student dormitories.

China's central leadership dispatched Wan Li, a vice-premier thought by many students to share a more liberal political perspective, to Hefei to try to get things under control. He came too late and offered too little. Already, word of the Hefei demonstrations had spread to campuses in Shanghai, Nanjing, Guangzhou, Wuhan, Chengdu, Hangzhou, and Beijing, and the hesitation of the leadership only fueled the sense that times had changed once and for all. Far from banning the protests, the police in Hefei helped clear traffic along the route of the students' march. Indeed, a local official of the Foreign Affairs Bureau, the government bureau responsible for funneling sanitized information to foreign journalists, told inquiring reporters who called from Beijing that no demonstration had occurred at all. It was, he explained, merely a rally "intended to publicize the electoral law under the constitution."

Ten days later, as the student demonstrations spilled onto the streets of other cities, the leadership in Beijing still had not responded definitively to what was happening. But there appeared a hint that perhaps the students enjoyed some high-level, although unspecified, support. In an interview with the government news agency, an unnamed "leading official of the higher-learning department of the State Education Commission" voiced what many students, as well as most of the foreign reporters in Beijing, believed was the government line: "It's true that some college students in Hefei, Wuhan, Shanghai, and other cities have held demonstrations recently. But according to our country's constitution, Chinese citizens have the right to hold demonstrations."

The official maintained that the root cause of the protests was discontent over living conditions on campus and "on certain problems in some grass-roots units concerning the selection of delegates to local people's congresses." Only when pressed, however, did this anonymous official admit that wider political demands, calls for genuine democracy, were also part of the demonstrators' objectives. "One of the most important planks of the restructuring of the political system is to expand socialist democracy," was the way this official put it. "It is understandable that college students should be concerned about the restructuring of the political system and hope to express their views on these issues."

Meanwhile, several posters appeared at Beijing University proclaiming the need for China to adopt more democratic ways.

Even on more out-of-the-way campuses, such as Wuhan University in Hubei Province, similar posters were cropping up. But in Shanghai, at the campuses where Fang Lizhi had spoken, and at the prestigious Fudan University, a blizzard of posters swept through the college grounds, and again the theme was democracy. This was the first concerted public discussion of democracy since the Democracy Wall period eight years earlier. At the time, to those of us who were trying to understand this extraordinary outburst of political expression, it seemed a spontaneous eruption of sentiments more deeply held than we had thought. We learned later that a rapid network of communication among campuses had emerged, with student activists making the most use of limited telephone lines, telegrams, and frequent rail trips throughout the country.

It was obvious to us in Beijing that Shanghai would be the site of the largest demonstrations. The city's history of radical activism during the Cultural Revolution and its general sense of superiority over other cities ensured that its students would be the vanguard in this new explosion of political will. We all rushed to the airport to try and get on a flight to Shanghai. A group of us cooled our heels for hours trying to go standby even as thirty-five thousand Shanghai students were tramping through the city's streets. Some of us never made it that day and were frustrated trying to write about events occurring a thousand miles to the south. True to form, the diplomats at the American embassy once again proved themselves incapable of not painting China in the rosiest of shades. More, it maintained that Deng Xiaoping was using the demonstrations as a weapon in an internal power struggle. That scenario was so bizarre that none of the resident correspondents even bothered to report it.

In Shanghai, more than ten thousand students staged a sit-in in People's Square on December 21, 1986, in front of the building where the rubber-stamp city council met. On the Bund, another group of students sat down outside of City Hall, once the headquarters of the Hong Kong and Shanghai Bank, and demanded to see Mayor Jiang Zemin. The mayor, evidently believing he could defuse the mounting protest, allowed student representatives into the gray granite building and talked with them until three o'clock that morning. The students brought with them four demands: greater democracy, freedom of the press, guarantees for the safety of the protesters, and a statement from the mayor that the protests were legal.

The students who emerged from the building in the wee hours of the morning seemed somewhat mollified; the mayor had agreed the demonstrations were legal and he had personally guaranteed the students' safety. But three hours later, squads of police who had been lurking on the edges of People's Square charged into the crowd of students and broke up the sit-in. Witnesses spoke of police using karate kicks and punches against the student protesters, more than three hundred of whom were dragged away. Toward midday, new waves of students rolled toward the square and, beyond that, the riverfront. Nanjing Road was packed with demonstrators surging slowly toward the Bund and City Hall. By then the ranks of protesters had swollen to more than thirty thousand, and foreigners who were there estimated that another forty thousand people crowded the sidewalks, simply watching the first public politics the city had seen in a decade. Only if they had marched in silence would they have heard the faint strains of the big-band tunes being pumped out by the aging jazz musicians inside the Peace Hotel.

City officials, apparently acting on directions from Beijing, reversed themselves on the following day, December 22, and issued a sharply worded attack on the student tactics, a statement presaging a new mood of intolerance. "A tiny number of people are attempting to disrupt stability and unity, derange production and social order by taking advantage of the patriotic zeal of students and their longing for democracy." Still, the students paraded, and this time there were more than fifty thousand. Huge white banners, held aloft on bamboo poles, bore slogans like "Law, Not Authoritarianism" and "Long Live Democracy."

I wore a blue baseball hat that day with the words "The New York Times" plastered across the front in large white letters, a purposeful declaration of my intent. All the foreign reporters who plunged into the crowds of students were mobbed; the students wanted to know what was going on in other cities, they wanted to know how many students had been arrested in Shanghai, they wanted to tell us why they were marching. As I was swept along by a swirling knot of two or three hundred students, a young medical student, who was sage enough not to give his name, shouted his reasons for being there: "We are calling for democracy, for freedom of the press. We want freedom of expression and the freedom to publish." At one point on People's Square, the crush of enthusiastic students was so intense that I and two other reporters had to clamber to safety over a chain-link fence, behind which several hundred police stood around watching. A CBS camera crew managed to get over the fence and moments later were in position to film the police clubbing demonstrators who had stumbled onto their cantonment.

Rumors of arrests swept through the marchers. Someone here said that two hundred were arrested. Another insisted that the number was closer to five hundred. "I heard that on Saturday," the student maintained. Still another claimed that forty students had been beaten up by the police the day before. Shanghai's newspapers and radio and television stations were silent about the demonstrations that gripped the heart of the city, a silence that only fueled even more rumors. Sheets of three-by-five-inch tissue paper were passed through the crowd, a mimeographed manifesto. "To our countrymen," the flimsy document read; "Our guiding principle is to propagate democratic ideas among the people. Our slogan is to oppose bureaucracy and authoritarianism, and strive for democracy and freedom. The time has come to awaken the democratic ideas that have long been suppressed."

Skirting the edge of the demonstrations on the way to meet another reporter, I found, only a block away from the main core of demonstrators, a city evidently indifferent to the tumult nearby. Couples were strolling hand in hand, window shopping for down jackets, washing machines, Seiko watches. Gray and white buses crept down the street, unruffled by the commotion. In the distance, I heard a loudspeaker booming through the night air: "Go home, you're disrupting traffic."

The next morning, the twenty-third, the wrought-iron gates of City Hall were wrapped with thick chains and locked, soldiers with automatic weapons standing nervously on the front steps. Policemen in groups milled around, smoking but not talking. Plainclothes police with video and still cameras filmed the crowds from rooftops and the street while the students gathered a few dozen yards from City Hall, holding their banners, shouting, but not moving toward the fortified building. That day, local newspapers began publishing statistics about the "damages and losses" caused to the city by the protests, including information that the city's buses had traveled eighty-five thousand fewer kilometers during the first three days of protest than on an average day. A student holding a banner that said he was from the Institute of Machine Engineering commented to me that "They're treating these demonstrations like they're legal and illegal at the same time."

On the campuses, freshly brushed big-character posters were pasted like wallpaper onto bulletin boards. "We can't wait ten thousand years for something to happen," read one. "Fellow students, we have not achieved our goals. We must be persistent" went another. In front of the posters, students stood reading the text of posters into small tape recorders. Later, the tapes would be transcribed, run off on rudimentary mimeograph machines, and sent to other schools around the country. One poster, the transcript of a Voice of America broadcast describing the demonstrations, had drawn a clump of students; the station's shortwave broadcasts were a principal source of information about the nationwide protests.

In part, it was the onset of university examinations that began to temper the Shanghai marches. In part, it was the threat of violent action by the police. Even so, the newspapers and the government in Beijing, while discouraging the protests, still seemed unsure how to react. The *People's Daily,* in an elliptical front-page editorial, declared that living standards had soared in recent years and that "socialist democracy and legality are being improved." The paper went on to instruct that "It is our firm and unshakable policy to keep on the road of socialism with Chinese characteristics. The party and the government welcome suggestions and criticisms. But radical action can objectively affect unity and stability and also hinder the freedom of work and study, and the lives of others." The capital itself had been generally quiet. Occasional wall posters had appeared on notice boards at Beijing University and Beijing Normal University, but there had been no marches. But that changed suddenly, and I and every other foreign reporter in Shanghai flew back on the evening of the twenty-third to witness the final act in the student upheaval.

273

At Beijing University, known by the more colloquial appella-
tion of Beida (shorthand for Beijing Daxue) the school's officials
had issued warnings that protests would not be tolerated. The
branch of the Communist Youth League loyally tried to prevent
any marches on the scale that had occurred in Shanghai. And at
Qinghua University, a school devoted primarily to scientific and
technological higher education, wall posters appeared on bulletin boards across campus. By now there had been two weeks of
protests in more than a dozen Chinese cities and there had still
been no demonstrations in Beijing. There was a real sense
among the capital's university students that somehow they were
being left behind in the rising national tide.

On the night of December 23, several thousand students burst
through the gates of Qinghua University into below-freezing
temperatures, carrying banners and shouting slogans for more
democracy in their lives and in that of the country. I accompanied them as they marched past Beida and then south, down
snow-covered streets lined with the leafless, stark trees of winter, toward Beijing Normal University. From time to time, clus-
ters of a hundred or a hundred and fifty students would break off
from the march and, pressed into a tight huddle, engage in
vigorous and often heated discussion of why and what they were
demonstrating about. I spun off with one such satellite group
and talked to one of the students.

"We're trying to discuss what is going on in Shanghai," he
told me, declining, like many students, to give me his name;
wariness is a well-honed tactic in times of political instability in
China. We bounced up and down on our toes to keep warm as we
talked. "We were all called by the authorities and warned. Here
in Beijing, the pressure on us is much greater than elsewhere.
They tried to keep the university gates closed and only under
pressure from several thousand students were they forced to
open them. I think really we're here to support the Shanghai
students, their call for freedom of speech, democracy, the freedom to publish. We also want a fair assessment of the student
movement." I asked him about the *People's Daily* editorial. "It's
all rubbish, a pack of lies," he shot back. "They depicted the
movement as caused by the agitation of a small number of people. In fact, it has been something to express ideals."

Why, I asked, had Beijing's students, who pride themselves on their cosmopolitan and progressive outlook, been so slow in joining what seemed to be a national expression of discontent? "Because there was an information blockade," he answered. "Also, the pressure from the authorities has been very great. Anyway, today's action was spurred by official reaction. That editorial distorted facts. It's only cosmetic. We think it's only the top leaders who are calling in a big way for democracy. However, there has been no response from the middle-level cadres. They don't allow the grass roots, like the students, to say anything."

Another student had joined us, barging into our conversation, his words exploding in little clouds of steam. "Should democracy be from the top to the bottom or the bottom to the top," he lectured. "We think democracy is not something given, it is something achieved and fought for. We believe it should start from the bottom with the people, because the bureaucracy is the antithesis of democracy. It's very unrealistic to expect the bureaucracy to grant democracy."

Methodically, the national press began building its campaign against the students, and more important, against the ideas they were advocating. The *Beijing Daily,* a hard-line paper controlled by the most rigid Marxist-Leninists in the leadership, threatened the students: "Anyone who instigates the overthrow of the proletarian dictatorship and the socialist system with counterrevolutionary slogans and leaflets shall be sentenced to five years' imprisonment, forced labor or deprived of political rights." The *Workers Daily* condemned the students for advocating "total Westernization," which, the paper explained, "means opposing socialism and advocating capitalism. History and reality tell us that the capitalist countries are not paradise on earth. The purpose of opening windows is to let in fresh air, not to welcome flies and mosquitoes." Wang Zhen, one of the hard-liners in the leadership, delivered a tough attack on the students, laden with rhetoric typical of the emerging intolerance: "We should heighten our vigilance against a small number of people who have ulterior motives and always oppose the four basic principles. Otherwise we shall be divorced from the broad masses and will be unable to lead the masses in marching toward our set, great objectives."

The mood on Beijing's campuses, all of which are located in

Haidian district in the northwest section of the city, was tense. The students were beginning to feel the hovering forces of repression, yet they were determined that they would be heard, that they could truly infuse some basic freedoms into the country's stultifying political atmosphere. A march by students from all the campuses to Tiananmen was planned for New Year's Day, a march that would carry the message of democracy to the heart of the capital. There was a sense of hesitation among the students, a fear of repercussions from university authorities, from the police. No one knew what to expect. While they hoped for the best, they began to fear the worst.

On January 1, 1987, the *People's Daily* signaled the sharp swing toward intellectual repression and political orthodoxy. "The democracy which the Chinese people need today can only be the socialist democracy known as the people's democracy, rather than the individualist democracy of the bourgeoisie. We must never forget to struggle against the handful of people who are hostile to and are sabotaging China's socialist system, and under no circumstances shall we lay down the weapons of the people's democratic dictatorship. Adherence to the four cardinal principles makes it imperative to oppose bourgeois liberalization by taking a clear-cut stand. Taking advantage of reform and the open policy, some people in ideological and cultural circles during the past few years have aired opinions that run counter to the four cardinal principles, thus spreading the trend of bourgeois liberalization in some sectors . . . we must not allow such a situation to continue."

What we suspected (but did not know the details) was that a fierce battle within the leadership had erupted, one that was not to be resolved publicly for two more weeks. But the tenor of the *People's Daily* editorial, combined with the rapid announcement of new regulations governing public gatherings in many cities, indicated that the student protests would no longer be permitted, even if it meant violent action by the police. The city of Hangzhou banned all public demonstrations, outlawed any publication that was not registered with the city's propaganda departments, and forbade "contacts and ties between different organizations or between different localities." The police in Shanghai, in a blaze of publicity, arrested a lacquer worker named Shi Guanfu and charged him with counterrevolutionary activities for aiding the student protesters. In Hefei, two railway workers were arrested, accused of inciting students to demonstrate. The cities of Zhengzhou, Nanjing, and Beijing issued regulations outlawing any demonstrations without police permits.

Posters on Beida's campus reflected apprehension. "These days, we are overwhelmed by the commentaries in the *People's Daily* and the *Beijing Daily* saying that students don't understand reform, that we disrupt social order and create disorder in people's thoughts," one poster writer despaired. "We are not disruptive. We take to the streets because we are concerned about the reforms." And then, in an explicit allusion to the official party slogan, "Without the Communist Party, There Is No China," the poster's author had written in huge ideograms, "Without Democracy, There Is No China."

Shortly before dawn on New Year's Day, blue and white water trucks appeared on Tiananmen Square and city workers hosed down the concrete expanse, creating a vast sheet of ice that was obviously intended to deter demonstrators from assembling there. But the students came anyway. They dribbled into the square, in twos and fours, in small and large groups, flowing into winding rivers of humanity that washed over the icy pavement. Hundreds upon hundreds of police in long files girded the square. Tension crackled in the bitter cold.

The crowds surged across the ice, at one point moving toward City Hall, which lies just off the square. Banners, some on cloth, others on white perforated computer paper, were unfurled with slogans: "Oppose Conservatives and Reactionaries," and "Support Deng Xiaoping and the Four Modernizations." The interplay of slogans reflected the continuing belief among the students that Deng could be relied on to support their cause and embrace the need for political reforms. Many students, while professing their desire for broad democratic goals, remained convinced that the "liberal" wing of the party, in which they still placed Deng, would steer the country toward a less authoritarian political order. Deng, the architect of economic reform, would also be the master planner for democratic change. This trust in Deng, they would soon learn, was badly placed.

Later, the students regrouped at Beida, surrounding the home of the university president, Ding Shisun, to demand the release of twenty-four arrested students. He told the students through a megaphone that he would answer them in two hours. But the students would not wait. Once again, some three thousand of them started marching toward Tiananmen. A university vice-chancellor tried to head them off by announcing through a police car's public address system that the arrested students were being released. "There is no need to go on," the Beida official said. "Please go back to the school. Please don't go forward." The students cheered, but moved on under their banners—"Long Live Democracy," "Long Live Freedom," "Long Live Deng Xiaoping."

The drama of the student demonstrations was nearly over. A few days later, about five hundred students, chanting "Burn, burn," set fire to copies of the *Beijing Daily,* a paper they regarded as unalterably hostile to their goals, but the action was no more than the dimming embers of the student movement, extinguished in the end by winter's cold, rapid police action, and an avalanche of propaganda in the nation's press.

As the fire of protest died out, an eerie calm descended on the political scene, and the nation held its breath waiting for the leadership to respond. The Japanese news agency Kyodo, which had always had good contacts within the Communist Party, reported a bitter fight among the seven members of the Standing Committee of the Politburo, what it described as an "ideological confrontation." The American embassy, for its part, continued to downplay the import of the protests. One of the senior political officers insisted that the demonstrations "did not constitute a major challenge" to the political order. Meanwhile, the country's newspapers all began running front-page editorials declaring that a new struggle was needed to combat "bourgeois liberalization." Several of the most outspoken newspapers were suspended from publication so that party officials could evaluate the ideological tenor of their work.

On January 12, Fang Lizhi was expelled from the Communist Party and fired from his post as vice-president of the University of Science and Technology. In its report on his expulsion, the Anhui provincial party committee indicted Fang on five counts: "(1) He made public speeches saying that Marxism-Leninism was outdated and negated its guiding role. (2) He negated the socialist system and called for 'total Westernization' and following the capitalist road. (3) He openly called for 'changing the true color of the party' and negating the party's leading role. (4) He advocated that universities should eliminate the party's leadership and called for 'total independence.' He incited dissension between the intellectuals and the party and government. (5) He advocated bourgeois 'democracy' and 'freedom' and instigated students to make trouble, thus damaging the political situation of stability and unity."

It was soon clear that no less a figure than Deng Xiaoping himself had ordered the expulsion of Fang, as he would that of the muckraking reporter Liu Binyan and the Shanghai satirist Wang Ruowang, both outspoken critics of the government. "When necessary, we must deal severely with those who defy orders," an enraged Deng told the Politburo's Standing Committee during the heat of the student demonstrations. "We can afford to shed some blood. Just try as much as possible not to kill anyone. Look at Wei Jingsheng. We put him behind bars and the democracy movement died. We haven't released him, but that didn't raise much of an international uproar. These few years, we have been too lax in curbing the tides of bourgeois liberalism. Allowing some rightist influence is essential and correct, but we have gone overboard. We cannot continue to make concessions in the face of current student troubles. The battle against bourgeois liberalization must continue for at least twenty years."

Four days after Fang's ouster, and one week after the Kyodo report of strife within the leadership, as well as after a full week's worth of torrid editorials condemning "total Westernization" and "bourgeois rights" in the nation's major newspapers, the American embassy told a group of reporters that at best China was entering a period of what it called "ideological chill."

That evening, on Chinese national television, a dour young man in a gray Mao suit announced that Hu Yaobang, the second-most-powerful man in China after Deng Xiaoping, had been toppled from his position as general secretary of the Communist Party. Very rapidly, the new political and intellectual climate took shape, a climate of fear and retribution. Hu's protégés in the party were demoted and transferred, beginning with Zhu Houze, whom Hu had installed as chief of the party propaganda department. Liu Binyan and Wang Ruowang were duly expelled from the party and, like Fang, they disappeared into political black holes from which they could neither defend nor explain themselves. But more important, China's intellectuals retreated into their shells in yet another desperate effort at self-preservation.

James Schiffman, a colleague of mine from *The Wall Street Journal,* interviewed several dozen students during these early January days, none of whom would allow their names to be used in his articles. One student expressed the fear that he would be banished to a mind-numbing job in some distant backwater if it was discovered he was even talking to a Western journalist. Another student told Schiffman, "We feel much pressure on us. Maybe the government will do something terrible to us." Again and again, this tale was told. My own Chinese friends suddenly were "ill," or "busy," or "it is not convenient just now."

On a bitterly cold February day when the haze of coal dust had contracted visibility to a block or so, I drove to a small dumpling restaurant to meet a Chinese reporter who worked at a magazine in Beijing. All foreigners are given special license plates for their cars so the police can easily identify them, but there are now so many foreigners living in Beijing, about ten thousand, that a car with the black foreign plates is not unusual even in a back alley. My friend arrived on his motor scooter, which he parked away from my car, and we met inside the restaurant, a dingy, not very clean room that reeked with the thick clouds of acrid Chinese cigarette smoke. We ate greasy dumplings, complained about our editors, and talked about the prevailing atmosphere of fear. It was not meant to be an interview, just a chat about the vagaries of life. I later learned that my friend had been approached by the security officer at his magazine and interrogated about why he had been talking to a foreigner. As it turned out, I had been followed that day and my friend had been seen, his license plate number taken and his identity established. We didn't see each other for a long time after that.

As if rising from the crypt, the elderly party hard-liners who had swung ideological cudgels against artists and writers during the spiritual pollution campaign of 1983 suddenly reappeared in public prominence. Deng Liqun, Bo Yibo, Wang Zhen, Hu Qiaomu—all men with straitjacket views of political and cultural life—wrested effective control of the newspapers and the party's propaganda apparatus from Hu Yaobang's supporters. Deng Liqun called for stepped-up "ideological work" in universities, what in practice became a greater number of political meetings for the students, so that, as he put it, "We can guarantee college students and future students become fine elements in the process of socialist construction." And to instill a proper sense of discipline, compulsory military training was instituted for all university students.

The newly confident ideologues, aware that the student protests had handed them an opportunity to exert control once and for all over the cultural and intellectual life of the country, quickly defined what was now acceptable. Deng Yingchao, the widow of Zhou Enlai and a soulmate of the hard-liners, declared that political rectitude was the essential prerequisite to a happy married life. Li Xiannian, China's doddering President, revived a slew of Maoist slogans in doing his part to whip up enthusiasm for the suppression of iconoclastic ideas. The Chinese people, Li said, should move forward "in a spirit of self-reliance, hard work, plain living, and building China thriftily," all phrases aimed at derailing the thrust of Deng's economic reforms, which had been fired by slogans like "to get rich is glorious." In Henan, the provincial party secretary solemnly ordered that all peasants, "especially the young peasants," should "boycott bourgeois liberalization spontaneously." In Guizhou, the local party secretary frantically instructed that "efforts should be made to strengthen workers' immunity from bourgeois liberalization."

Red Flag, the party's monthly devoted to Communist theory, issued a hysterical attack on Freud, citing Chinese intellectuals' interest in his work as an unadulterated example of their bourgeois tendencies. "Besides his absurd and inappropriate over-emphasis on the unconscious," *Red Flag* maintained, "Freud's greatest error in his view of art is his undue exaggeration of the role of sexual desire in artistic creation. He makes sexual desire the perpetual theme of artistic expression. Freud's view of art not only negates objective reality, but rejects the social nature of art."

Acting General Secretary Zhao Ziyang attempted to confine the burgeoning campaign to the forty-six million members of the party. But even Zhao was swamped for a time by the momentum generated by the hard-liners, and at one point conceded that "opposition to bourgeois liberalization is a long-term and sustained effort." Liberal editors at newspapers across the country were fired. In Guangxi Province alone, thirty-nine periodicals were shut down for "straightening out." And Liu De, an editor at the tiny journal *Jiannan Literature* in Sichuan Province, was sentenced to seven years in prison because he "desperately pursued and preached so-called 'democracy' and 'freedom' of capitalist countries" and because he "uglified the socialist system."

So that there would be no uncertainty in the mind of any writer or artist, He Jingzhi, the number two official in the Central Committee's propaganda department, announced what the new campaign was about. "The purpose of opposing bourgeois liberalization is to rectify the orientation for literature and art," he said. "This struggle is a great event of prime importance not only to the future of the state but also to the future of the literature and art circles, as well as to the future of the writers and artists themselves." And to drive home his point, he stated explicitly what he and the party expected. "We favor artistic works with socialist rhythm as well as good works that are understood and welcomed by the people."

Many of China's best writers simply left their manuscripts on their desks, rather than send them to certain rejection, or, worse still, publication. Many writers believed that the appearance of even an ideologically innocuous essay would imply their assent to the new intellectual crackdown. Wang Zengqi, a protégé of Shen Congwen's and the father of Searching for Roots, an emerging literary movement that explores the cultural underpinnings of Chinese behavior through the fiction and poetry of daily life, shared this attitude.

A close friend took me to see Wang one day. Then sixty-six, Wang lived in a book-stuffed apartment on the top floor of one of Beijing's monotonous concrete apartment blocks. Newspapers, magazines, sheafs of tissue-thin rice paper covered with his strong, fluid brushstrokes, rough sketches for his paintings, were piled in corners and on desktops. Wang sat easily in the wicker chair, and explained how he was responding to the atmosphere of repression. "Some people will not publish for some time," he said. "They write what we call 'drawer literature.'

Basically, there are some younger and more radical people who have said things that are explosive or near-explosive. Secondly, there are the elderly writers, like me, who have always been careful. And thirdly, there are the orthodox writers who feel they were oppressed before, when everyone else was writing. Me, I won't write any fiction this year. I'm doing some travelogues about Yunnan Province. I'll also rewrite some ghost stories. My stories are one hundred percent safe."

For Wang, the new crackdown seemed like merely another of the periodic turns of the screw, which had turned perhaps less tightly this time than in the past. During the savage anti-rightist campaign of 1957, Wang was sentenced to two years of forced labor in the countryside. "I painted pictures of Chinese potatoes," he said, laughing quietly at the distant memory of those harsh years. "Then at the beginning of the Cultural Revolution I was persecuted again. But Jiang Qing liked my writing, for some reason, so I was elevated to become a court writer. I wrote the librettos for some of her model operas. It was pointless."

Wang's own attitude toward the new generation of writers, however, was not entirely without criticism, although he was reluctant to voice it for fear of appearing to side with the political attacks raging outside his door. "I know some of these young writers," he told me. "And they want to say things that are new and different, and they compete with each other to do so. But you know, they also want to win applause. Some of these young people are attracted by Western ideas they do not understand. But this doesn't mean they should be attacked." Was there any hope, I asked, for China to break out of the seemingly endless cycle of repression, liberalization, and repression? Wang turned gloomy. "I don't think it's easy to get out of this pattern. This is China, after all."

Many younger Chinese felt, and had felt for some years, that there was a widening lacuna in sensibility and intentions between the elderly party leaders closeted in their Zhongnanhai compound and the younger generation of post-Cultural Revolution artists and intellectuals. Indeed, during the student street marches in December, a frequently reproduced banner read, "The Future Belongs to Us." I spent a lot of time on China's campuses in these months, trying to get a feel for the mood of China's best and brightest in what seemed very dark days. One professor, who became a good friend, handed me a sheaf of student essays from one of his classes. He said they were the most succinct statements on the current atmosphere on campus he'd found.

"Old people," one student wrote, "on account of their deep-rooted conceptions and former experiences, tend to have fixed ideas about things and sometimes cannot adjust themselves to the changing world. They are more stubborn and conservative. Many things which are considered as good and right are regarded by them as evil. They often fail to make the young believe." Another student wrote that "In China, tradition is much more respected than novelty. Those who prefer novelty are thought to be bad and are often criticized. But in my opinion, the revolt of youth is a cure, more than a cancer, for present-day China."

For six months, the ideologues within the leadership maintained their grip, pummeling what they regarded as liberally oriented publications, intimidating writers and artists. As a professor of literature who was a close friend told me at the time, "The literary garden will probably have a lot of plastic flowers in it." But despite the oppressiveness of the hard-liners' assault, there remained a feeling in the artistic and literary community that there would never be a return to the bleakness of earlier years. In part, this feeling stemmed from generational vigor, a basic optimism bred of youthful aspirations. The older generation of intellectuals, those who had been in the labor camps and the villages, instinctively ducked their heads. The younger painters and filmmakers, poets and playwrights, some of whom had been tossed about as teenagers in the tempests of the Cultural Revolution, simply looked for ways around the new ideological strictures, all of which would soon pass, they were convinced.

Wang Ping, a sculptor whom I knew, put on an exhibit of abstract art at the staid and official Chinese Art Gallery in downtown Beijing in the midst of this artistic freeze. She looked much younger than her thirty-two years, her nearly round face etched by severe bangs with a long ponytail of Blackglama hair hanging nearly to her waist. Wang's work—strange shapes of glazed mud, mottled brown faces, ghost-faced ceramic children, grotesquely carved masks—was scattered through the central gallery of the museum. She told me that she was not bothered by the outbursts from the party mandarins who lived just a short distance from where her work was displayed. "Sometimes when you do abstract art, some people automatically say it is Western. But you know, our folk art contains lots of this. Even our traditional Chinese painting has this. What I'm really trying to do is put together the old and the new and come up with a style of my own. They don't oppose modernization per se, but it must be a Chinese or Asian modernism."

But because the potential for the ideologically suspect lurks everywhere, the museum brought in its artistic watchdogs to scrutinize Wang's works before the exhibit opened. She laughed easily about the old men drifting through the gallery, peering at the distorted clays and warped wooden visages. "Before the exhibit," she said, "a group of older artists were called in to go through my work. They said it was great. Not a single piece was removed from the exhibit."

Gradually, throughout 1987, the hard-liners' appeal to socialist purity in intellectual and artistic circles clanged more and more hollowly, and their efforts to extend it into other spheres of life withered. By the end of that summer, the campaign appeared to have run its course. Hu Yaobang remained in oblivion, as did many of the party members who had owed their jobs to him, but new poetry magazines, exploratory films, and intellectual journals began once again to test the limits of expression. Within a year, the first Chinese translation of George Orwell's harrowing portrait of totalitarian society, *1984,* was published, after being held up by wary censors.

The man who, at least in the minds of China's leaders, had instigated the campus turmoil had been silenced by the government. Fang Lizhi was not permitted to see foreign reporters and could not be quoted in the Chinese press. In the summer of 1987, he was allowed to visit Italy to attend a meeting of the International Center for Theoretical Physics in Trieste. There, he was interviewed by Tiziano Terzani, a correspondent for *Der Spiegel.* The interview, the first with Fang since his expulsion from the party, showed him unrepentant and unswerving in his beliefs. "Without democracy there can be no development," Fang explained. "Unless individual human rights are recognized there can be no true democracy." Although he also had been invited to attend a second physics conference in Cambridge, England, commemorating the three hundredth anniversary of the publication of Isaac Newton's *Principia,* the Chinese government ordered him home.

Despite his silencing at home, Fang's popularity on the campuses of Beijing continued to grow. An effort to have him elected to the local consultative people's congress, obviously a direct affront to the authorities, was quashed from above, but his wife, Li Shuxian, who is also a physicist, ran in his stead, winning overwhelmingly. Fang was muzzled for another six months.

The following February, I met Fang and his wife at one of Beijing's international restaurants. I had been introduced to the physicist by a friend who taught in one of the city's universities, and we met for a long lunch to discuss what was beginning to appear to be a return to an easier intellectual climate. Fang, who had just been promoted from a "fourth-rank" professor to a "second-rank" professor, a decision he dismissed as "just propaganda," was scornful.

"On the surface, there is more tolerance," he said, "but this is not so in reality." He derided the tendency of many American and European China specialists to see a liberalizing of the controls over intellectual life. "They're deceived," he said bluntly. "Power is still held by Deng and the older generation. Zhao is number one in principle, but when they talk about who will talk with Gorbachev, it is Deng. It is clear who is in charge." At the time, Fang was waiting to learn whether he would be permitted to spend a year at Cambridge University. Twelve months later, he was still waiting.

Unlike Fang, Liu Binyan, who was never able to speak to foreign reporters after his expulsion from the party, was permitted to leave China to spend a year at Harvard University. On his way to the United States, Liu stopped in Hong Kong, where he gave a remarkably candid interview to *The Nineties,* a political magazine banned in China because of its regular and detailed exposés of conflicts within the leadership. Throughout his career as a writer and journalist, Liu had drawn the wrath of the party hierarchy. His reporting, often composed in a semifictional reportage style, focused repeatedly on corruption within the party, corruption both material and spiritual. In sharp contrast to Fang Lizhi, Liu was reluctant to renounce either the utility of Marxism or the role of the Communist Party. What he rejected was slavish idolatry to party leaders, from Mao Zedong on, and the transformation of the party into an avenue for personal gain. While Liu's muckraking reporting about tyrannical and corrupt local officials has brought him a wide and admiring readership, his continuing belief in the basic goodness of the party has afforded him a less generous hearing among the intelligentsia and the artistic community. He remains, though, the preeminent witness to and chronicler of the party's inability and unwillingness to reform itself. In his discussion with *The Nineties*, he brooded about the ebb and flow of repression, and the implications of the campaign that had brought his expulsion from the party for the second time.

"It was an obvious attempt to stifle freedom," he told the Hong Kong magazine. "In addition, it set back the relative openness seen in the summer of 1986. We had just recovered from the spiritual pollution campaign, developed a little hope for the political situation, and were feeling enthusiastic. Then, again the intellectuals were targeted and initiative crushed. . . . Look at what Gorbachev has been doing and you will not blame the students for taking to the streets."

As for his own prospects, Liu was equally pessimistic. "I will disappear from journalism and the literary world. Readers will not be able to read my things. I once said to an author, in order to be able to write, 'I will do my best to control myself, not to go over the boundary. But I will not easily throw away my freedom. I will exert my greatest effort to use my freedom, to push hard against that boundary.' This way I continued to write. But there will come a day when they will not allow me to write. When they do not want me to write, then I might as well not write."

Liu Binyan did not consider himself a dissident; Fang Lizhi did. Each remained convinced, however, that something was desperately wrong with the existing political order, which sought out and crushed all attempts to question the status quo. In periods of both Maoist terror and Dengist reform, Fang and Liu, and thousands upon thousands of other intellectuals, suffered.

Wang Ruowang, the third of those tossed out of the party in January 1987, acerbically assayed their plight. "We often use the terms 'reining in' and 'letting out' to describe the political climate in China," he told an interviewer from *The Nineties*. "The fact is that what we mean by 'letting out' is lifting up the bird cage cover, and what we mean by 'reining in' is lowering the same cover."

The hand that raises and lowers that cover belongs to the Communist Party, and to the party alone. The voices of Democracy Wall, of the new literature and art, of people like Fang Lizhi, all test the resolve of the party, as well as its continuing viability. For the party leadership, of course, there was no question about surrendering authority and power to the demands of this fringe, as they saw it. As Premier Li Peng put it in the closing months of the decade, "Democracy is a good thing, but it must arise from the conditions within a country."

As many people in China came to see it, in 1989, the conditions were right.

THIRTEEN

Tiananmen Days, Tiananmen Nights

IT HAD BEEN FIVE MONTHS since I completed my term as *The Times*'s Beijing correspondent, and I was in my study in New York when the BBC news came on the shortwave radio next to my desk. It was April 17, two days after the death of Hu Yaobang, the politically banished former party leader. Tim Leward, the BBC's Beijing correspondent, reported that ten thousand students had marched from the university district in mourning for Hu. They were also chanting slogans for more democracy. A poster at Beijing University declared that the wrong man had died.

As the days went by, ten thousand became twenty thousand, and then forty thousand. It was clear that I would have to go back to China for what would be the closing chapter for China in the decade. As usual, my pessimism ran ahead of the din of optimistic reporting that began roaring out of Beijing, pessimism born of my belief that China's Communist Party is fundamentally incapable of change as long as it is dominated by leaders whose political instincts were honed in the guerrilla campaigns of the 1940s. Before I went, though, I stopped in Bolinas, California, to attend a small conference on the problems of democratic ideas and ideals in China, a gathering attended by some of China's most prominent writers, filmmakers, journalists, and democratic activists.

Every evening, people at the conference were on the phone talking to friends in China about the mushrooming crowds on Tiananmen Square, about the promise for change. One evening, Liu Binyan hovered over the telephone receiver shmoozing with Fang Lizhi. Shortwave radios were tuned to the BBC, and there was discernible excitement and jubilation among the two dozen or so attendees. One of the Chinese invited to the conference, Liu Xiaobo, a gifted young writer, decided abruptly to return to China to join the movement on Beijing's streets, forgoing the pastoral pleasures of California's coast. Shortly afterward, I too returned to China to write a magazine piece about the resurgent student movement. I was hoping for the best but expected far less.

IT WAS NOT HU YAOBANG the party leader who galvanized the students of Beijing, but Hu Yaobang the victim of Deng Xiaoping's arbitrary power. The hypocrisy of the eulogies to Hu on the front page of the *People's Daily* was transparent to everyone. Hu's death, though, was little more than a pretext for the protesters.

Even before Hu's funeral on April 22, students had been raising fundamental questions about the political status quo. On the night of April 18, tens of thousands of university students marched to the Zhongnanhai compound, chanting "Down with dictatorship," "Long live democracy," "Down with corruption," and "Down with bureaucracy." In Shanghai, university students were marching, and soon virtually every city in China would see protesters swirling through the streets.

The expectations raised by ten years of economic liberalization, the confidence that political changes appropriate for a free market economy would finally propel China into the modern world, had permeated the consciousness of a vast segment of China's population. Free speech and expression, a democratic political order, the right to demonstrate publicly; all these were seen no longer as forbidden fruit, but as the natural rights of a modernizing people. There were, as well, the thorns of corruption, nepotism, and official venality, which angered most Chinese, from the farmer who could not get fertilizer from corrupt local bureaucrats to students incensed at the children of senior party officials who used their connections and influence to enrich themselves. And, economically, China was stalling in midflight, a consequence in part of the policy battles that Zhao Ziyang had lost the previous year; inflation was rampaging and the incomes of the urban working classes were falling farther and farther behind the relentless march of prices.

What had brought the thousands, and later millions, of students and citizens onto the streets of China's cities in the spring of 1989 was, very simply, a decade of waking up from past nightmares.

DAY AFTER DAY, the number of students grew. By May 4, the seventieth anniversary of the 1919 student protests that were, arguably, the final rupture with imperial and traditional China, and that led to the founding of the Communist Party, there were more than a hundred thousand students camped out on Tiananmen Square. As the size of the protest increased, so did the confidence of the young students who were thrust into leadership positions. It seemed, for a time, as if by sheer numbers the people could bend their leaders to their will.

The students wanted more. They wanted to present their case to the leadership. The leaders, remote and severe, deigned not to reply. The students went on a hunger strike to demand what they called a "substantive, concrete, and equal" dialogue with their rulers. "In this sunny, brilliant month of May, we are going on a hunger strike," declared the students' *Hunger Strike Manifesto*. "During this most beautiful moment of youth, we have no choice but to put the beauty of life behind us. We do not want to die. We would like to lead a good life, because we are in the prime of our lives. We do not want to die. We would like to study hard. Our country is very poor. We will be leaving our country behind if we die. Death is certainly not our goal. But if the death of one person or a group of a few would ameliorate lives of a larger group of people and succor the prosperity of our country, we would not have the right to escape death." Within two days, two thousand students were on hunger strike.

291

As a state visit by Mikhail Gorbachev approached, the leadership pleaded with the protesters to leave the square so that this historic reconciliation of the world's two largest Communist powers could proceed smoothly. It was not to be. Not only was Gorbachev's schedule disrupted, but the enormous potential significance of the trip itself was also rendered meaningless by the events on Beijing's streets, by the tent villages on Tiananmen Square.

Finally, on the day Gorbachev flew back to Moscow from Shanghai, Prime Minister Li Peng acceded to the protesters' demands and invited some of the student leaders into the Great Hall of the People. Under the lenses of live television cameras, however, the prime minister chose not to listen but to lecture. Visibly seething at even having to be present for the meeting, Li told the students that Beijing was in anarchy. "I hope you students will think for a moment what consequences might be brought about by such a situation," Li said ominously. Two days later, he declared martial law.

IT WAS A SULTRY DAY in late May. Beijing had already been under martial law for ten days. Hundreds of thousands of troops, armed with assault rifles and machine guns, tanks, and armored personnel carriers, ringed the city. Tiananmen Square, the center of the capital, had for more than a month been a sprawling encampment of China's students and Beijing's workers in tents, lean-tos, and cotton mattresses in the open air. There had been weeks of marches, rallies, sit-ins, and hunger strikes by the people of the capital; its grandmothers and high school students, its shopkeepers and professors, its college students and steel workers. At times, as many as a million citizens clogged the streets of the city, marching for a real say in their own lives, for genuine freedom of speech and expression. They marched under banners announcing their weariness with the corrupt, geriatric mandarins who ruled over them.

But the jubilance of those marches had waned as the army took up positions on the city's periphery, fueling foreboding rumors which swept across town, unsubstantiated yet unrefutable, and all uncontrolled. The government and the Communist Party had begun issuing a stream of threats against the students, against anyone who offered support to this people's movement for democracy. The mounting tension was taking its toll. In dribs and drabs, students and their supporters had begun trickling out of the square, some frightened by visions of impending violence, others exhausted by a vigil of protest that seemed not to have borne fruit. Where just a week before it was difficult to move across the square, on this day there were expanses of empty concrete littered only with the debris of an abandoned village.

Toward evening, I wandered across the square, stopping at a few tents to talk to students whom I had befriended over the previous weeks, picking my way past piles of garbage, through the passageways that snaked between tents. As darkness fell, I walked toward the Monument to the People's Heroes, a squat cenotaph set on a stone frieze of idealized revolutionary scenes, which had become the headquarters of China's democracy movement. Student marshals stopped me, as they did everyone who tried to climb the steps to the monument, until I showed the blue plastic press pass issued by the Foreign Ministry which I had used as *The Times*'s correspondent, a document six months expired but still authoritative-looking. In the chaos of those days, there was no way, or need, to obtain official press credentials.

On the stone esplanade at the base of the obelisk, students moved about desultorily. Spirits were low. The talk was of troops forcing their way into the city, of the wisdom of surrendering the square and returning to campuses. Even the student press, a battery of stencil machines under a canopy at the base of the monument, was silent that evening. As darkness enveloped the square, it seemed that the exuberant movement for democracy that had galvanized this city and the world was now disintegrating.

Then, in the northeast corner, amid a tide of humanity that spilled onto the square, I could see a procession of flatbed tricycle carts crawling forward, on the lead cart the luminously white head and torso of a woman holding a torch aloft. Behind that cart, three others bore still more pieces of the immense sculpture. Bathed in the dim yellow sulfur lights of the square, the throngs of people parted to allow the carts passage. Clanging cymbals and the *bomph-bomph-bomph* of drums heralded the arrival of this massive figure. White pops of flashbulbs and the

293

glare of television lights pinpointed the statue's slow progress. On the Heroes Monument everyone—students, journalists, hangers-on—watched silently, marveling at this apparition.

Suddenly, over the jerry-rigged loudspeaker system the students had strung throughout the square, the opening strains of Chinese national anthem blared, a revolutionary brass fanfare. Then clapping, isolated at first, built into a wave of applause that swept over the square as everyone realized that a new symbol of the movement, a monument of their own, was being brought into Tiananmen Square, the heart of the capital, what a student friend called "the throat of democracy." Firecrackers sounded, welcoming the statue in a traditional Chinese salute, one which, lore has it, scares away lurking ghosts as well. And then Eugène Pottier's anthem of the Paris Commune of 1871, the Internationale, boomed over the speaker system. It was, it seemed then, a moment of resurrection, of revival, of reigniting that vast popular movement for freedom and democracy, for openness and hope, and the banishing of the fear and oppression which has been such a staple of Chinese life.

As the night wore on, students from the Central Academy of the Arts erected a rickety scaffold of bamboo poles catwalked with frail planks at the head of the square, directly across from the immense portrait of Mao Zedong that hangs over the Gate of Heavenly Peace. Slowly, precisely, the students set the statue's base on a platform of boards, then fixed the middle sections, and, by morning, as dawn first glimmered, the statue's head and arms. There, in the oranges and pinks of the first sun, rose the image of a woman, her hair puffed slightly as if by a brisk breeze, her left knee pushing forward through a flowing gown. Above her right shoulder, her two arms held a solid torch, its flame swollen as if newly fired. The students called their creation *minzhu zhi shen*, the Goddess of Democracy.

From her head, the students draped a few streamers of red and black, covering the statue's features. At its base were placed crimson school banners, pots of flowers, and two red fire extinguishers. The new day broke and blossomed, bringing with it thousands of people to the square to see this great new monument unveiled, the symbol of their movement. At noon, as mothers snapped photographs of their children before it, some students pulled the cloth streamers from the visage of the statue, baring it for China and the world to see. The statue stared across Chang'an Avenue, toward the Gate of Heavenly Peace, at the portrait of Mao, the man whose vision had created modern China and whose madness had brought it down. The students who cheered the unveiling of the Goddess were, in a real sense, his children, for they were spawned by his political legacy.

With a mixture of admiration and apprehension, I watched the Goddess of Democracy unveiled, a statue that to many eyes mimicked the idea, if not the form, of the Statue of Liberty. Consciously, however, the artists who fashioned the plaster and polystyrene monument had chosen a figurine of an Olympic athlete holding a torch as the model from which to work, convinced that China deserved its own emblem of freedom. They labored, though, knowing acutely that the statue in New York Harbor bears heavy symbolism not just for the people of the United States but for the people of the world. Their monument, they hoped, would generate similar associations, similar pride.

Almost instantly, screeds denouncing the Goddess gushed from the country's controlled media, which the central government had by then wrested from editors and reporters sympathetic to the students and workers in Tiananmen Square. A radio broadcast heard by many people baldly displayed the shock and disgust of Communist Party hard-liners over this new symbol: "The statue of the so-called Goddess of Democracy at Tiananmen Square should be dismantled, and all one-sided glorifications of bourgeois democracy and freedom must stop . . . China is not America!"

This was much of what the people of Beijing were hearing during the last days of May and the first of June. Still, they came by the thousands, mothers pushing perambulators, couples holding hands, fathers carrying children on their shoulders, to have their photographs taken before this new monument, the first erected by the people themselves on Tiananmen Square. In the days that followed, I often strolled by the statue to talk with people about the Goddess of Democracy, or just to watch people's expressions as they surveyed the new addition to the square. "What do I think?" an ice-cream seller in a white cloth hat said as she dipped her hand into her ice chest to serve a customer. "I think it's a good thing. I don't have a high cultural level so I don't know much about these things, but I think it is good. It looks very good here, this goddess. It should be here. This is our place, you see," she waved a chubby hand toward the tent cities on the square. "The square belongs to the people. We have the right to put up our own statue. It should stay here."

Even as the protests on Tiananmen Square unfolded, student activists were visiting hundreds of factories, big and small, throughout the capital, encouraging workers to join them in their demonstrations. For Beijing's workers, indeed, for all manual laborers in China, discontent had been smoldering for a long time. Roaring inflation had hacked away at workers' wages, while endless stories of corruption within the party, and within the management of their own factories, in some cases, had bred widespread resentment over their inability to alter their lives. Official unions, designed more to ensure tranquility in the work force rather than to voice the complaints and demands of their members, had long since lost credibility.

There was, in many ways, little common ground between the students and the country's working class. For their part, the students were consciously fleeing the prospect of a life of factory drudgery by attending college; once there, they cultivated the arrogance that many of the educated possess toward manual workers. The workers themselves were largely unmoved by the students' and intellectuals' cry for freedom of expression, for a democratic polity. But what drew both together was the common enemy: a party and government that viewed dissent anywhere as counterrevolutionary, as destabilizing, as inimical to China's future.

On the day the statue was unveiled, May 30, bright red banners with white ideograms appeared on the exteriors of the city's major hotels. The Beijing Hotel, a shabby state-owned institution with a panoramic view of the square, led the way with streaming banners declaring, "Long Live the Great, Glorious, and Correct Chinese Communist Party" and "Clearly and Resolutely Oppose Bourgeois Liberalization." Shortly after the banners were unfurled from the hotel's top floor, a small parade of journalists marched by, coincidentally, it seemed to me, with a sign reading, "Long Live Democracy, Long Live Freedom." Even the foreign-managed hotels were not exempt from the impromptu exercise in the government's propaganda counterattack. As the manager of one of the foreign hotels told me after the banners were hung from the roof of his establishment, "Better red than dead." He didn't smile when he said it.

It was clear to me, as well as to several other journalists with whom I was working closely, that the situation in Beijing was approaching its finale, one that, I argued, not always persuasively, was likely to be extremely harsh. During the height of the demonstrations, when most of America's China experts and journalists seemed suffused with the enthusiasm and hopes fired by Beijing's massive street marches, by the sheer, intense righteousness of the student hunger strikers, I could not help feeling a sense of looming disaster.

The fall of China's government, predicted at the time by so many of these experts, people with good hearts and great expectations, seemed to me a fantasy based more on desire than on reporting or understanding. I wrote several long articles for the *Los Angeles Times* opinion pages during these weeks, suggesting that there was no happy ending to what we were witnessing, that China's Communist leadership, men like Deng Xiaoping who really controlled the party, would in the end react with tremendous repression. I failed to see in Deng's past, or in his writings, any suggestion that he harbored any patience for substantive dissent from Communist Party fiat. Without hesitation, he had shipped tens of thousands of intellectuals to forced labor camps in 1957. He had savagely suppressed the Democracy Wall movement. Throughout the past decade he had repeatedly warned against the erosion of ideological will. At every juncture in the history of the People's Republic, Deng's instincts had been repression, not tolerance; dictatorship, not democracy. This was not a man, I was convinced, who was inclined to loosen the reins of party control. No one, though, Chinese or foreigner, could have anticipated the extent of the repression to come.

FOR SIX WEEKS, Beijing was controlled not by the city government but by its own people. Students and ordinary citizens directed traffic on those days when vehicles could pass through the city. Mail deliveries were sporadic and public transportation had slowed to a virtual halt. There had even been some disruption of the city's food supplies. Later, I learned that the hardliners within the party who had won the internal battle for power had stopped food shipments in order to aggravate conditions within the city while simultaneously blaming the ongoing protests for interfering with food deliveries. The government was to cite this state of affairs as one reason for the need to force an end to the demonstrations, to the occupation of the Tiananmen Square.

Within the country's leadership, the tremendous and vicious battle for control of the Communist Party (described in Chapter Ten) had been fought behind the scenes. In the days following Zhao's last public appearance on May 19, some party officials allied with him sowed misinformation among foreign journalists suggesting that Zhao was winning a power struggle within the leadership, reports that received wide play abroad. My contacts within the party center, ever cautious, scoffed at these reports. "It's over, don't you see," one of them told me. "Zhao lost. He's finished. His people are finished." The old veterans, hard-line Leninists enraged at the mass expression of popular opinion around them and eager to seize this chance to stanch the tide of economic reform that was sweeping their socialism out to sea, knew that this was their last chance. The mouthpiece for the old men was Li Peng, the country's prime minister and a man long known for not only his intolerance of political dissidence but his unease at the rapid pace of economic change. On May 20, the day after Zhao's nocturnal visit to the square, Li ordered most of Beijing placed under martial law and commanded that the People's Liberation Army be deployed throughout the city and that the square be cleared.

On national television, Li delivered his speech ordering martial law to an auditorium filled with senior party and military officials. "The situation in the capital is quite grim," Li said, his face bathed in sweat, stumbling in the harsh staccato delivery of his orders, "The anarchic state is going from bad to worse. Law and discipline have been undermined . . . more and more students and other people have been involved in demonstrations. Many institutions of higher education have come to a standstill. Traffic jams have taken place everywhere . . . it has become clear that very, very few people"—in Chinese, *"jishaoshu, jishaoshu,"* a phrase that was to be chanted again and again by tens of thousands of demonstrators—"who attempt to create turmoil want to achieve, under the conditions of turmoil, precisely their political goals, which they could not achieve through normal democratic and legal channels, namely to negate the leadership of the Chinese Communist Party and to negate the socialist system. . . . Comrades, our party is the party in power and our government is a people's government. To be responsible to our sacred motherland and to the entire people, we must adopt firm and resolute measures to end the turmoil swiftly, to maintain the leadership of the party, as well as the socialist system."

But the army sent by the leadership was halted in its tracks. For more than ten days, the people of Beijing—railroad workers, old men with wooden canes, swaggering young taxi drivers, aproned shop girls, grandmothers with gray hair in buns, college students in T-shirts emblazoned *"jishaoshu, jishaoshu"*—had stopped the Chinese army from entering their city. They swarmed over the columns of green canvas-backed trucks, arguing, cajoling, pleading with the soldiers not to advance, not to raise their weapons against their own people. There was a palpable sense of exhilaration on Beijing's streets, a mixture of surprise and pride in actually having prevented these heavily armed troops from occupying the city. Wherever I walked during those days, past food stalls, through department stores, in simple four-table dumpling houses, everyone was chattering about the army's defeat, about the people's victory. Strangers talked animatedly with one another. Street corners became congregating spots for political seminars and lectures, places where a construction worker would harangue the crowd over corruption within the party and a graduate student in political science would discourse on the need for a representative democracy. In one local bar, a rowdy, late-night gathering spot for young men with shady incomes, where hookers cruised by flicking their skirts, the mood was jubilant. "It's not most of the people," a tough-looking fellow with a mustache told me after I'd asked if the majority of Beijing's people supported the protests on the square, "it's ninety percent. Ask anybody."

I spent most of my time on the square, talking with the young people camped out in the squatter settlements of innumerable universities, institutes, and high schools. Flapping red banners daubed with yellow or white ideograms announced the Central Academy of Music, the Institute of International Relations, the Sichuan Foreign Languages Institute, the Petroleum Institute, the Chinese Opera Institute, and a hundred, two hundred more. At a more spacious tent of army-green canvas toward the edge of the square, I became friends with a young student whom I visited every day, to talk, to joke, to reflect on the meaning of the momentous events around us. When I first met him, he had already been on the square for two weeks. His clothes were wrinkled and needed a wash, his glasses never seemed quite straight. He was fatigued, yet somehow buoyant.

He invited me into the tent, as always lifting the strand of twine that demarcated the inner sanctum of his university's encampment. Gingerly, we stepped around the soiled padded mattresses and patterned cotton quilts, finding our way to two low three-legged stools in a back corner of the tent. "We have to overthrow this feudal system," he began, lighting one of his habitual cigarettes with a borrowed match. "Our leaders are like feudal kings. Our people are like serfs. We must establish a democratic system and that is very difficult because of our country's long history of feudalism. We have a lot of work to do because the level of consciousness of the people is very low. We know that people's conditions of living, their ordinary lives, are very hard. But we students have to teach the people that they are the owners of the country. We are the safeguards of the democratic movement."

As we talked, students drifted in and out of the tent, some carrying sheaves of announcements and tracts from the movement presses, others lugging cases of soda, a carbonated orange concoction that had become the principal beverage of China's democracy movement. A few others simply sat and listened to our conversation, nodding now and then. "Our socialist system is rooted in feudalism," he went on. "Capitalism is a great gap for China. We have to fill that gap. Our leaders have to be elected by the people. In Western countries, the leaders are elected by the ordinary people. In China, they're elected by a few people. We want free elections." I suggested that this process could not happen overnight. "Yes," he replied, "this will be a long course, maybe twenty years, maybe fifty years."

Was there, I pursued, any real expectation for change under the continued rule of the Communist Party? He paused, not only because this had become a critical issue for the students, but also because we had not known each other long, and criticizing the party, even on Tiananmen Square, brought with it potential danger, potential reprisal. "Well," he said, sucking his cigarette to a pinched butt, "I think the Communist Party is the shadow of feudalism. They say they want to get rid of feudalism, but feudalism is deeply rooted in their minds. They will never compromise with the students. That is why the government may win. They have military power. They have the guns." He looked at me carefully, and then very deliberately said, "If the party does not reform itself, it will be overthrown by the people. A lot has happened in the last ten years. The Chinese people have grown up."

I drifted over to the tent used as the headquarters of the Beijing Autonomous Workers Union, an encampment on the northwest edge of the square, which had become something of a public forum for the non-student protesters. The tent had its own broadcast system, and, every day, one worker with a gift for mimicry would regale huge crowds with tales of the leadership, parodying the voices of Li, Deng, and others. The workers' mood was much sterner than the students', perhaps because they were older, they were less idealistic, they knew better the risks they took. I sat and spoke with a worker who had been selected as one of the leaders of the union. He sat on a box, bouncing his son on his knee. His face was dusty, his hair shooting off at all angles. He explained why the city's manual workers had joined the students.

"From the viewpoint of the workers," he said, "the students' initial demands were not high at all. They opposed corruption among high officials. So do we. But I think inflation is a big reason most of us are here. What we could buy for one thousand yuan just a few years ago now is three thousand yuan. Salaries have gone up a little, but prices have gone up more. There's a direct connection between official corruption and inflation. We've become much poorer." Why, I asked him, was it necessary to organize their own union? Didn't the workers already have unions? "Hah," he spat, "those are government unions. This is our union. With this organization we can express our own opinions, not what they tell us to say. The government must recognize this is a democratic, patriotic movement." I asked him what he thought would happen. Were not he and his friends afraid of what might happen? "From my point of view we're within the law," he replied, his voice gruff. "We're not afraid of anything. There's a possibility that the army will come, of course. But we will protect the Goddess of Democracy."

As May became June, tensions in the city grew, daily, hourly. The martial law authorities, unnamed forces outside the city, issued strings of orders. Strikes, protests, speeches, and leafleting were banned. Foreign reporters were ordered not to engage in "demagogic reporting," and were forbidden to speak to anyone anywhere without the approval of the martial law command. Menacingly, the martial law orders declared that "public security personnel, armed police units, and the People's Liberation Army on duty are authorized to adopt any means to forcefully handle the situation." All this was ignored, but the level of apprehension within the city mounted. Across the capital, at main roads and critical intersections, barricades of red-and-yellow public buses, blue-and-white-banded water trucks, garbage and coal trucks blocked the army from marching into Beijing—a city it had taken without firing a shot in the autumn of 1949.

On the square, student leaders debated tactics at the base of the Heroes Monument, some advocating enduring until the end, come what may, others proposing abandoning the square to prevent any possibility of bloodshed. Periodically, the government-controlled loudspeakers on the square would broadcast denunciations of the student protesters, ordering them to leave the square and return to their campuses. In reply, the student public address system, a Rube Goldberg assemblage of high-tech amplifiers and primitive cone speakers provided by Hong Kong supporters, would roar into action with songs, speeches by student leaders, announcements about the goings-on elsewhere in the city. By then, the stench of sun-baked, rotting garbage was so strong that student organizers marshaled garbage trucks to collect it. Disinfectants were sprayed on the square by public health trucks, and fresh water supplies were delivered by city water trucks.

On Friday, June 2, I returned late to the place I was staying, the apartment of Robert Delfs, the correspondent of the *Far Eastern Economic Review* and one of the most careful observers of the Chinese political scene I knew in Beijing. We sat up until well past midnight, sipping scotches and thrashing out the latest rumors on army movements, factional debates among the students, and the implications of the consolidation of power by the grizzled Leninists within the leadership. Robert probed for spots of brightness in the darkening landscape. There were few to be found, and we retired at 2 A.M. with more foreboding than ever. Minutes later, the phone jolted me awake. It was another reporter excitedly shouting that troops were on the move from the east into the city's center. I banged on Robert's door, phoned two other American journalists and told them to meet us at the car, and dashed down seven flights of stairs to the car. We screeched out of our diplomatic residential compound to try to catch the army.

In soft-soled boots, the soldiers moved almost silently, with just the thump of rubber on the asphalt of Chang'an Avenue, the six-lane road that slices Beijing in half from east to west. They wore white shirts and green pants, and carried small backpacks and round metal thermoses. It was two-thirty in the morning, yet somehow the people of Beijing were materializing on the streets. Wild young men on bicycles whizzed up the avenue, windmilling their arms as they rode, raising the alarm like frenzied Paul Reveres. From the hutong, the alleyways that burrow into the old residential areas of the capital, men and women rushed into the street, some still clad in pajamas or nightgowns. I was in a car full of journalists, and we raced ahead of the jogging troops, squirting down the bicycle lane, trying to outrun the column, to witness what we believed would be a major confrontation. We skidded into the parking lot of the Beijing Hotel ten minutes or so ahead of the column of soldiers.

I bolted from the car. Looking east down Chang'an Avenue, I could not see the soldiers we had passed. At the western edge of the hotel, on the last cross street before Tiananmen Square, Donganmen North Street, a convoy of coal trucks, water trucks, and buses commandeered by the people roared up, horns blaring, to block the width of the boulevard. A swell of applause surged over the rapidly filling streets, and bare arms sprouted above the sea of heads, fingers forked in the sign of victory. Then, as if on a whispered command, students and workers, men and women, perhaps fifty in all, linked arms in a line across the avenue, facing the oncoming wave of troops. I will never forget one young woman in that line. She wore a ponytail and glasses and was crying, large tears dropping darkly onto her

303

pink blouse. A man who put his arm through hers hushed her: "Don't be afraid."

Under the hazy yellow glare of streetlights, everyone was still. At first faintly, then louder, the sound of thousands of pounding feet swept over the crowd. A student shouted through a hand-held battery-powered megaphone, "The whole people have stood up," a paraphrase of Mao Zedong's words when he declared the establishment of the People's Republic some forty years earlier from atop Tiananmen, the Gate of Heavenly Peace. "Let the whole world know," the young man yelled. I circled through the crowds in front of the Beijing Hotel. Cars full of foreign journalists honked and squeezed through the throng, and the lights of television cameras bathed clots of people in eerie white pools. The head of the column came into sight, and the line of people across Chang'an Avenue huddled closer. A chant burst from the crowd: "Go back, go back, go back."

As the troops moved forward, still tightly bunched, five or six abreast, in a moving river of humanity, the crowd pushed against the column, funneling it toward the line of protesters linking arms. Almost instantly, the soldiers were swallowed by the mass of people, surrounded like an invading organism and pushed back. The young recruits grabbed each other, their eyes fearful, astonished, uncomprehending. They stumbled sideways, backward, the column disintegrating into clumps of sweating troops wildly looking about for a place to hide. A soldier fainted next to me, and was caught by two companions before he fell to the pavement. The crowd took up another chant: "Sit down, sit down." Others countercalled, "Down with Li Peng." Then, as if on command, the soldiers hunched down, some on the street, many more on the sidewalks.

Two teenagers, brother and sister, drifted toward me arm in arm, innocence and wonder on their faces. "It's marvelous," the girl said in carefully syllabled English. "The people of Beijing are marvelous. I don't think these soldiers have ever seen anything like this, never since Liberation. It's like the Philippines. It's really people power." The tension of the crowd had dissipated like air rushing from a balloon. It was three o'clock in the morning. Only thirty minutes had passed. Once again the people of Beijing had stopped the army from reaching Tiananmen Square, from moving against the students who protected the

Goddess of Democracy. Everywhere, soldiers crouched on sidewalks or in front of buildings, and people talked softly to these frightened youngsters in uniform. "Don't be afraid of the people," someone said. "With the people, the country has hope. The people don't want you to hurt them." Some soldiers cried, wiping their eyes with the backs of their hands. "They're not from Beijing, you know," a man pushing a bicycle told me. "They're from Liaoning. They know nothing. They don't even know why they are here."

Popsicle vendors maneuvered their wheeled ice chests through the crowds, crying, *"Binggunr, binggunr"*—"Popsicles, Popsicles." Two young women shoved a wad of bills into the hands of one vendor and marched off with two cartons filled with Popsicles, which they began passing out to soldiers huddled along the east side of the Beijing Hotel under a propaganda banner reading, "Firmly Oppose Turmoil. Maintain Order and Stability." Gradually the young soldiers rose to their feet, urged on by the people, and began straggling back east along Chang'an Avenue. I walked with a group of soldiers for the first mile, tracing my route home, their ragged retreat cheered by the bystanders who lined the sidewalks in the predawn hours. Rhythmic clapping and laughter carried the soldiers on, out of the heart of Beijing, away from Tiananmen Square, away from "the throat of democracy."

I returned to the square toward noon to find my friend, to recount the events of the previous night. He was in his school's tent, more despondent than I had ever seen him, and he greeted me with an air of weariness, of brooding concern. We made our way to the back of the tent, to our accustomed conversation pit. Outside the tent, a middle-aged man in an open-necked blue Mao jacket took some pictures of us with a Nikon camera. Other students chased him away, he protesting that he was a journalist, we certain that he was a police agent. No one cared at this point. Near us, a circle of students sat on quilts, silently playing cards, the soft slap of cardboard on a makeshift table somehow audible through the din of loudspeakers in the square. My friend lit a cigarette from a package I pushed toward him, and exhaled a cloud of bluish smoke, sighing slightly. We sat quietly, both of us exhausted, gnawed with uncertainty as we waited for the forces of the state to act.

I asked him about his parents, what they thought of what he was doing. He laughed softly. "My parents?" he replied. "My parents want me to stay home. They support me, but they worry." I described to my friend what I had seen the night before, news of which had already swept the square, but he found the details interesting. "I think the soldiers will follow orders," he said. "But if they are allowed to talk to the people, they will be educated." Did not the wave of soldiers, I suggested, erode some of the students' determination to remain in the square? "Tiananmen is very important to us," he said. "It's the heart of China and the throat of democracy. If this throat is cut, there will be great repression. I think most of the people in China think a great movement is going on. But the aim of the government is to create a sense of despair for the students and to separate the people from the students. Our government's propaganda always says something on behalf of the people, but in fact, it is simply to tell the people how to think."

Beyond the shadowed cool of the tent, shimmers of heat, like crinkled cellophane, rose from the baked concrete expanse of the square. About one hundred feet from where we sat, the Goddess of Democracy stood amid a small sea of blue and red nylon igloo tents, supplied by Hong Kong supporters. I asked my friend about the statue, what it had come to mean in the five days it had dominated the square. "Many people have come to see the statue," he said. "I think when they see it, they understand. This statue is a symbol against feudalism, against antidemocratic tendencies. It is face-to-face with the portrait of Mao Zedong. That picture is the face of tyranny. The statue represents the mass image of the people." We sat a bit longer, until it seemed time to leave, to let my friend return to the meetings of the students' leaders. That night, the army came, with tanks and guns. I never saw my friend again.

I walked away from the tent, and walked toward the leadership's compound at Zhongnanhai to check on the demonstrations outside the front gate. As I moved past the Great Hall of the People, a pink-columned edifice where China's nominal parliament gathers annually, I saw that a contingent of five thousand soldiers armed with AK-47 assault rifles was surrounded by singing, chanting, hectoring crowds. Some soldiers passed their canteens to protesters to have them refilled. Others accepted proffered sticks of ice cream. An officer stood and tried to lead his troops in song, a futile effort to drown out choruses of the Internationale from the crowd. A student orator lectured the troops. There was no sense of crisis, of impending cataclysm. It was, as far as I could tell then, another in what had become a series of routine nonviolent victories over the army.

When I returned to the diplomatic compound, a colleague with better sources in the Chinese military than I told me that the military was likely to move against the students later that night. She also mentioned a menacing broadcast she had just heard on Beijing's local radio station, of an "urgent notice" issued by the martial law headquarters. "We solemnly declare," the broadcast warned, "that nobody may use any excuse to lawlessly intercept military vehicles, obstruct and besiege the Liberation Army, and obstruct martial law units from carrying out their duties. . . . If there are people who refuse to listen to admonitions, act willfully and defy the law, then the martial law units, the public security personnel, and the armed police force have the right to handle the situation by force."

EVERY EVENING POSSIBLE, a group of us would gather to watch the news, which provided us with some feeling for the government's mood. Only a month earlier, the national news, in a startling rupture with its usual approach, had reported on the demonstrations, hunger strikes, and occupation of Tiananmen Square in a reasonably fair fashion. Now, however, the broadcast had returned to its usual ways, denouncing the demonstrations and issuing thinly veiled threats against the students and people of Beijing. At precisely seven o'clock that evening, June 3, the news opened with a dour-faced Li Peng, oddly attired in a Western jacket and tie, reading a bizarre speech about global environmental problems. All of us were flabbergasted, totally at sea as to the import of Li's incongruous address at this moment of national crisis. Even as he spoke, we would know later that evening, armored vehicles were grinding into Beijing from the west.

As darkness crept over the city, the streets and boulevards teemed with restless, skittish streams of bicyclists and pedestrians. By eight-thirty, the inner city—what was once contained by the old city wall—was electric with tension. I walked outside the

307

compound to talk to people pedaling west, toward the square. "There's been shooting at Muxidi," someone said, referring to one of the outlying western districts of the capital. Truckloads of workers in yellow hard hats—looking tough, alert, and confident, to my eyes—sped down the Second Ring Road, on their way to man the people's roadblocks, I figured. At the Jianguomenwai Bridge, I watched a procession of about forty canvas-backed army trucks lumber north, jolting to a halt at a roadblock, where they were swallowed up by chanting crowds waving fists and V signs. "This isn't the people's army, it's a traitor's army," a man shouted as he pounded on the fender of an army truck. These troops clutched rifles between their legs. At one point, a group of workers burst from the crush around the truck waving steel helmets and bandoleers taken from one of the trucks.

At midnight, I got another phone call. A reporter yelled into my ear, "The army's moving in from the west. They're shooting." I immediately called Sandra Burton of *Time* magazine, who had a Toyota sedan. "Let's go," I shouted. "They're moving on the square. They're firing on people." I rushed around collecting my camera and notebook. I stuck a flask of scotch in my back pocket, thinking it might serve as a last-recourse antiseptic if someone was shot. Robert Delfs and I sprinted down seven flights of stairs, taking the steps three at a time. It was impossible to drive across the city on Chang'an Avenue, now a sea of barricades, so we sped north and west on the Second Ring Road, careening through roadblocks, with a sign in our window reading *"jizhe"*—"journalists." As we circled the center of the city and headed south toward the Fuxingmen Bridge, the commotion on the streets was intense. Bicyclists, who in Beijing usually crawl sedately along the road, were tearing along the highways and down side streets in packs. People were running away from the bridge. Finally, we rounded a curve that brought it into sight.

A wall of flaming buses down the entire length of the bridge lit the sky like day. Sandra slammed on the brakes, sliding the car into the curb along the highway. We ran, crouched over, toward the on-ramp that led to the inferno. Sandra and Robert then hung back, talking to a group of people at the base of the ramp under a light pole. The stutter of automatic weapons crackled in the air, mixing with the low *whoomph* of a bus's exploding gas tank. As I got closer, I could see a column of armored personnel carriers crashing through the flaming blockade. "They're firing at children," someone hollered at me as I ran past. People were lying next to the hedges that lined the bottom of the ramp, but I couldn't tell whether they were dead or alive. A man who had followed me up the ramp, screamed, shaking in anger, "Kuomintang fascists!" The gunfire was too intense for me to get closer, so I retreated to where my two friends were waiting. A man, almost hysterical, said that he had seen thirty people shot —"Old people, young people."

"Are you a journalist?" a woman asked, her words clutching at me in despair.

"Yes, yes, I am," I said.

"Thank you," she exhaled. "Thank you."

I could see the alarm and shock on my colleagues' faces. They said they had been told that people who had been killed were brought down the ramp just before we got there. We stood for a moment behind a telephone pole, stunned, peering at the column of armor roaring over the bridge. It was simply too dangerous to stay where we were, so we jogged back to the car. The Beijing to which we had become accustomed was never more than a gray, placidly boring city where people's public emotions were confined to drinking games and cooing over babies. The 1986–87 student protests had petered out when the government merely shook the fist of repression. It was inconceivable that the army would actually fight its way into Beijing. We decided we had to get to Tiananmen Square before the first assault troops. We were scared, but we only talked of that much later.

We wound east through the inner-city streets dense with people. At one roadblock, we slowed to weave through barricades lined with thousands of people. Suddenly someone pointed at our "journalist" placard and started clapping. Then another, and another. Applause swept us along. V signs were waved in front of our car. The people of Beijing wanted us to record that night. "God, I can't believe it," said Sandra, who had reported the demise of the Marcos regime in the Philippines three years earlier. "I can't believe it." She said it again and again as we drove toward the square. A reporter on a motorcycle roared up alongside our car and handed me a soldier's hat. "Hang on to this for me," he shouted. I stuffed it under the front seat as he pulled away. Days later, the cap, long since forgotten, was discovered under the seat. It was splashed with the dark stain of blood.

We parked the car just north of Chang'an Avenue, next to Zhongnanhai, a couple of blocks west of the square. Hurrying toward Tiananmen, we were ahead of the army. The next day, I learned that many people had died at Xidan Road, just to the west. We ran toward the square, rushing along with a tide of retreating people, some on foot, others pedaling furiously on their black bicycles. Breathing heavily, unsure of escape routes, Sandra, Robert, and I stopped under the portrait of Mao. We agreed that if we were separated, we would meet by one of the stone lions that guard the archway to the Forbidden City. As I looked east, thirty or forty yards away, I could see an armored personnel carrier ablaze. I ran over to take some pictures. People were heaving boxes and blankets on the searing metal surface. I could see the fractured silhouette of a fifty-caliber machine gun pointed crazily into the starless sky.

"They killed too many people," cried a young girl who grabbed my sleeve as I scribbled notes. "We hate them. We hate them." It was 1:30 A.M., June 4. Still the army had not made it to the square. Then, loudspeakers on the massive floodlight stanchions edging the square blared to life. "A serious counterrevolutionary rebellion is taking place in the capital tonight," a voice echoed. "Rioters have furiously attacked soldiers and stolen their weapons and ammunition. . . . The counterrevolutionary rebellion must now be resolutely counterattacked. . . . Residents should strictly abide by the specific regulations as provided by the martial law. . . . Safeguard the constitution and defend the security of the socialist motherland. . . . The personal safety of anyone who ignores this warning cannot be guaranteed."

I wandered along the northern edge of the square. Buses were on fire, their window frames white with flames that billowed from the vehicles' innards. Nearby, the Goddess of Democracy flickered with each surge of fire. A bus rocketed through the crowd on Chang'an Avenue, its driver wrestling with the huge steering wheel as he pointed it at the main gate of the Forbidden City. The bus sliced through the gate, jackknifing across the

310

inner entrance in what seemed to be an effort to block soldiers from charging through. Over the heads of the horde of people, blue flashing ambulance lights spun as the white vans crept toward the square from the east. A woman with long black hair, wearing a white satin dress, clacked past me on white spike heels, swinging a white patent-leather purse. I watched her for a moment, arrested by the sight of her effortless saunter, her studied obliviousness to the building storm.

To the west, I heard the thunder of engines and the churn of tank treads; the crowd turned to watch as a wave of closely set pairs of headlights came into view. I looked at my watch. It was one forty-five. Dozens of tanks, the barrels of their cannons almost parallel to the ground, shuddered to a halt about a hundred yards from the western edge of the square. I heard the sporadic crack of rifle fire. Behind the headlights, through my binoculars, I could make out the shadows of troops, thousands of steel helmets glinting faintly in the darkness as the soldiers moved behind the tanks, running toward the wall of the Forbidden City. I hurried to where my two colleagues were to meet me. They were not there.

People walked or ran aimlessly through the square, across Chang'an Avenue, as if they did not know where to go. I trotted toward the lights of the tanks. There, about one hundred yards from the wall of armor that spread across the avenue, not more than a hundred people formed a thin line, not linking arms but standing quietly. I ran up behind them. I wanted to see their faces, to look in their eyes, to see these people who stood unarmed in front of the Chinese army. The people, baby-faced students and weathered workers, gazed toward the army that had come for them, some vacantly, some worried, some, it seemed, without fear. Suddenly there was a sharp popping sound, then a rattle, like firecrackers going off in a neighbor's backyard. Some people in front of me fell to the ground, awkwardly, as if broken apart. I dove onto the pavement and began crawling backward. I bumped into another American journalist, John Schidlovsky of the *Baltimore Sun,* who was also on all fours, holding his mountain bike upright. The bicycle seemed to tower over us, a target for the bullets flying above our heads. I suggested that he abandon the bicycle, that perhaps we needn't draw attention to ourselves. "It's not your five-hundred-dollar bicycle," he shot back.

311

The crowd retreated, some running bent over, some crawling. Two young men ran by me, furiously pushing a bicycle cart. On the flatbed of the cart, a man lay bathed in blood. More people ran by, carrying a woman whose shoulder was soaked with red. There was little screaming that I remember. Instead, there was a silent anger, and a frenzy to move the wounded to the ambulances. A chant of *"jishaoshu, jishaoshu"*—"very, very few"— erupted from the mob, which regrouped in straggly lines of forty or fifty to face the troops. Again, a wave of people moved to meet the army, and again the rifles cracked. More people fell. I ran farther east, past the edge of the square. Behind me, helmeted troops ran around the line of tanks, whose engines thundered as they crept forward. Another bus sped through the retreating crowd, the young men leaning from the windows waving bamboo poles fixed with crimson flags; the driver, in a snow-white headband, barreling suicidally toward the oncoming tanks.

"Ba gong, ba gong, ba gong," the crowd chanted. "Strike, strike, strike."

People swarmed by me, some moving toward the square. Many were weeping. By then the sound of gunfire was almost continuous. Filaments of yellow light shot from the southern edge of the square, machine gun tracer bullets, I later learned. I stopped a young man to talk for a moment. "I don't believe it," he said, his voice shaking. "How is this possible? How could we prepare?" He stopped abruptly as another young man, lying facedown on a cart, blood seeping through his clothing, was pushed past us. The first young man put his hands on his face. "You must support the Chinese people," he said, turning to me. "You must go to your country and support the Chinese people."

"Siduole, siduole"—"Many are dead, many are dead"—I heard this again and again as the crowd fell back under the crackle of gunfire, retreating eastward, down Chang'an. I was caught between my desire to see what happened on the square and the gunfire from the troops pressing down from the west. I ran, then walked with the throng, too frightened to figure out how to get back to the square. John Schidlovsky came by, weaving his bicycle through the crowd. I hopped on the back and we rode east, back to the diplomatic compound.

I learned what happened later at Tiananmen Square by talking with students and the few foreign reporters who stayed till dawn. As the avenue on its north side emptied of people, a strange quiet enveloped the square. Bicyclists circled over the expanse of concrete. In the tents that had been set up earlier to treat hunger strikers and ailing students, doctors in stained white coats worked furiously. Students filtered out of their tents, away from the edge of the square where the growling armored personnel carriers were assembling. In some tents, I was told, despite the gunfire, the roar of tanks, students slept. I could only understand it as a response of catatonic, paralyzing fear. Near 3:30 A.M., the Taiwanese rock singer Hou Dejian, who was on a hunger strike at the Heroes Monument, walked over to the row of soldiers at the north end of the square. There, I later learned from several eyewitnesses, he managed to negotiate time for a retreat for the thousands of students still huddled on the steps of the monument and in the tents scattered across the square. At four o'clock, the floodlights on the square were doused and only the headlights of the APCs and an occasional television light pierced the darkness. A wave of soldiers spewed from the Great Hall of the People and marched onto the southern half of the square, their rifles, bayonets fixed, pointed before them. Twenty minutes later, the lights came on again.

"I remember the APCs moving," a Western reporter told me days later. "It was eerie; the dark outlines of the APCs against the floodlights, the elongated shadows stretching into the square." As the APCs churned over the northern edge of the square, a column of students started pouring toward the southeast corner through a gauntlet of student marshals holding hands, forming a tunnel to apparent safety. It was 5 A.M. Five minutes later, the first soldier was on the monument. Five minutes after that, the Goddess of Democracy toppled forward, ground under the tracks of an APC.

What happened in the next sixty minutes may never be fully known. The next day, many students told of APCs rolling over tents filled with students, grinding their bodies to a pulp. The American ambassador, James Lilley, said later that many students were crushed to death. There have been dozens of first-hand accounts of bodies being burned on the square with flame-throwers, of soldiers shoveling bodies into piles, "like cordwood," one Chinese told me. There is, too, a tale, perhaps apocryphal, of students standing to protect the Goddess of De-mocracy. In the days that followed, as I visited university campuses, I heard the story over and over: a dozen students had linked arms around the statue, facing the armor that would devour them. "They were run over," a student said, tears streaming down his face. "They were all killed."

Somehow, though, the students who retreated south escaped the square unharmed. A Western reporter who walked the last yards with the students said that he saw no one shot during the withdrawal, that even the last stragglers made it off the square alive. "I was impressed by the calm," he said, "indeed, the serenity of the students." Meanwhile, the Chinese army fanned out across Beijing, the rattle of machine guns and automatic rifles filling the air. A huge group of students who had just left the square and were retreating west and north, trying to work their way back to their campuses, were slaughtered as they attempted to cross Chang'an Avenue. Tanks pushed through the streets, bashing through barricades, retaking the city from its own citizens.

In the days that followed, many, many more people were killed. The city was a war zone, with gutted tanks, armored personnel carriers, and buses clogging the streets like the rotting shells of huge beetles. Road barriers pretzeled across scorched macadam. Broken glass, toppled light poles, bicycles flattened like freshly rolled dough littered every thoroughfare. I bicycled through city neighborhoods, talking to people huddled in small groups fearfully scanning the road for truckloads of soldiers. In one neighborhood near the Forbidden City, a woman pointed to a dark stain on the cement sidewalk. "An old man was shot here," she said, "in the head. He was just standing there." I asked who he was but no one knew, or they were too afraid to say.

I was in shock for days at what I had seen and what I had been told. I still find the crack of firecrackers unsettling; their sound is so similar to that of an AK-47. While many of us felt Deng Xiaoping was capable of great repression—certainly, he had shown his willingness to imprison tens of thousands of intellectuals in the past—no one, not the journalists in Beijing, and certainly not I, and, more important, none of the hundreds of Chinese I had spoken to in those weeks, believed he would slaughter his people on the streets of the capital.

FOURTEEN

China Elegy

THE MORNING SUN climbed through a gray-brown haze on June 4, 1989. It brought no solace, no hope to the city. Columns of oily black smoke spiraled from the smoldering tanks and buses that clogged Beijing's main avenues. The clatter of sporadic gunfire jolted me awake, a jarring reminder of the savagery I had seen only hours before, and a sobering indication of what was still taking place on the streets below the apartment where I was staying. I called John Schidlovsky, and we talked about returning to the streets, a dangerous course but one we felt we had to follow, to see for ourselves the aftermath of what was clearly one of the most brutal displays of repressive power by a Communist regime since Soviet tanks roared into Budapest in 1956.

We rode bicycles, gingerly weaving past crushed concrete street dividers pulverized by tanks the night before, past flattened bicycles and steel garbage cans, the windowless shells of scorched and gutted buses that had been futilely pulled across intersections to block the army's advance. We headed toward Tiananmen Square, the sound of an occasional gunshot echoing

315

down the avenue as we rode. At the mouths of hutong uncoiling from old residential neighborhoods, people gathered in small clumps staring at the wreckage of their city. A few other bicyclists ventured out onto the streets. One, a tough, street-wise youth, pumped his bicycle next to us. "It's dangerous," he informed us. "Aren't you scared?" I assured him that I was.

We did not see what happened next, just the results. But numerous eyewitnesses at the Beijing Hotel watched in horror. Beginning about 10:25 A.M., a frail line of about sixty protesters, unarmed, walked slowly past the Beijing Hotel toward the army, pleading with their eyes to stop the slaughter. Rifles chattered. Dozens of people slumped to the pavement. Another line of people pushed toward the wall of soldiers, and again the rifles crackled. More people fell, blood spreading across their chests, some wounded, some dead. In all, more than fifty people were killed or wounded over the next two hours.

"They just stood there and died," Louise do Rosario, a reporter for the *Far Eastern Economic Review,* told me later. "The first time the troops started shooting, it lasted for sixty seconds. I was looking at my watch, counting the seconds." There were four lines of protesters and four fusillades before the suicidal effort was extinguished. John and I pedaled up to the Beijing Hotel just after the slaughter. There were still bodies on the street, some being hoisted onto bicycle carts, others just lying there. We hurried inside the hotel, took an elevator to the top floor, and ran down the hallway straining to find a vantage point onto the square. We tried one locked door after another. Finally, one yielded, and we barged into an office full of Chinese security officers with walkie-talkies. We rushed toward the balcony, pushing past the startled Chinese, but they forced us back. Racing back down the hall, we found a stairwell to a fire escape that led to the roof. Shoving aside planks that had been piled across the exit to block access, we ran to the edge of the roof. Chinese security people on another corner of the roof began moving toward us. We stared for a minute, no more, toward the square, the scene of the previous night's carnage. There, on the vast expanse of gray concrete, like a piece of chalk ground beneath a boot heel, was a stain of white, the shards of the Goddess of Democracy.

In the days and weeks and months that followed, China's

police-state apparatus, which had always lurked just below the surface of economic modernization and reacquired civility, lashed out at the voices of dissent, the voices that spoke of what China could be, not what it had to be. Swarms of secret police descended on neighborhoods, factories, and university campuses across China, rounding up tens of thousands of people, men and women, young and old—all for having expressed a desire for a more democratic country, a country where people would live not in fear but in the security of basic rights. In Shanghai, three young workers were manhandled into a courtroom for a brief show trial. Accused of setting fire to a train—unsaid was the fact the train had run over six protesters sitting peacefully on the tracks—the three were sentenced to death. Two weeks later, they were executed when a soldier fired a bullet into the back of each of their skulls. That same day, seventeen more people were sentenced to death. Fang Lizhi and his wife, Li Shuxian, fled to the safety of the American embassy, where they were given refuge. In all public places—restaurants, subway stations, neighborhood bulletin boards—huge white posters urged the citizenry to inform on anyone they knew had aided or supported the "counterrevolutionary rebellion."

Within days, mug shots of twenty-one student leaders were broadcast on national television, with the picture of twenty-one-year-old Uerkesh Daolet (an ethnic Uighur who is known in Chinese as Wuerkaixi), one of the three most prominent student organizers, leading the list. University campuses in Beijing were becoming ghost towns as the students fled in fear. Every day there were rumors that the army was about to occupy the campuses, but even though there were extensive troop movements throughout the city, the army never took control of any university; the secret police did.

A few days after the massacre, I visited several campuses with Adi Ignatius of *The Wall Street Journal,* our feeling being that there was more safety together than alone. We went first to Beijing University, a place normally crowded with bicycles and pedestrians, vibrant with the hum of conversation, the echo of radios in dorm rooms. It was starkly silent as we strolled through the campus. While we walked down the main campus road, a young man stopped momentarily at a cement light pole. When he pedaled off, I saw that he had left a small, mimeographed poster pasted around the pole. Within minutes, a gray-haired, severe-looking man in a Mao suit came by on a bicycle, braked, and began tearing at the poster, stuffing it into his pocket. He rode off under the glare of a handful of students. It took all my powers of will to restrain myself from screaming at the man, cursing him for his complicity in what was happening.

Adi and I decided to talk to some students, a delicate exercise in these days of mounting fear, so we sat on a low stone wall near what had been the main gathering area for protests in the past, watching bicyclists and the occasional student on foot go by. After a time, a young man stopped his bicycle next to us and introduced himself. He was wearing a T-shirt, the front reading "Democracy Movement '89," the back "Liberty or Death." I asked him whether he knew who was famous for the saying on the back of his shirt. He didn't, so I explained briefly who Patrick Henry was. We asked him about students who had been killed. He told us of three he knew at Qinghua University, and said that the university had erected a memorial to them. He said that the police had been on campus the night before and had arrested twelve people. "I'm not too frightened," he said. "I'm not going home because I want to see what's going on. It's important to do that."

As we left Beijing University, workers with fire hoses were blasting and scrubbing away the "big character" posters that had been glued to cement walls and to the brick sides of buildings over the previous six weeks, effacing any signs of the movement that had gripped the minds and bodies of the country's college students. We drove toward Qinghua University, a school famous for its training of engineers and scientists. We were not stopped as we sped through a side gate, although one of the guards looked quizzically at us as we went by. Several times we stopped and asked people where the memorial shrine to the students was. Finally, a faculty member riding his bicycle volunteered to show us the way, although it was clear that he was scared to be seen talking to us. As we wheeled onto the concrete plaza before the square-pillared Stalinist administration building, our guide glided away in a slow arc, his hand flicking a silent wave.

We walked up the flight of stone steps and stepped into a cavernous, gloomily dark foyer. Across the polished floor, be-

318

yond the lobby, a central antechamber was crowded with white floral wreaths, each bearing the photograph of a murdered student. Above the wreaths, eight ideograms cut from white cloth were fixed to a banner of black: "Mourn our students. Mourn our China." Two T-shirts, each printed with a V sign and the flag of Qinghua University, were draped over a small wooden casket. Behind a slender cord strung between the columns draped in black bunting, a few students stood silently. I snapped some pictures just as a couple of university officials descended on us and told us we were not allowed to see the shrine. "You cannot be here," they said, almost panic-stricken. "You have to leave. Please go now." It seemed we were being told to leave not out of hostility, but out of concern that it was dangerous enough for the university to sponsor such a memorial without foreign journalists advertising the fact. We left quietly.

Once more we headed for another campus, this time Beijing Normal University. Adi parked the car on a cement badminton court, and we made for some student dormitories. In one dormitory, room 400, which had been a student headquarters and the room where Uerkesh Daolet had spent the early days of the movement, was sealed with a paper strip signed by the physics department. Adi and I wandered through the silent hallways, past locked doors. In a stairwell, we bumped into a student and stopped to talk. He gestured at us to be silent and ushered us down the hall, past the empty bathrooms and showers, into a crowded room. There he introduced us to two of his roommates, one of whom lounged on the bottom bunk reading a ragged paperback kung fu novel.

"Last night," one of them told us, "forty or fifty police came, about twelve-thirty. They were searching for students, but I don't know if anybody was arrested. Both plainclothes and cops in uniforms. They didn't search our room. Someone said they were looking for guns. Some students were supposed to have taken guns from the army on June 4 and 5." The room was strung with drying clothes on sagging bamboo poles, piles of books, desks wedged in corners, a metal thermos on the floor. "I was at Tiananmen Square," one of the students continued. "I escaped in a Red Cross vehicle. You can't say the democracy movement is repressed. It's just not in the open now. It is certain that the movement will rise again, certainly after Deng Xiaoping dies. No matter what, though, we're not afraid."

Down in the courtyard, we had passed a new poster on a brick wall. It read, "Departing students, do not forget your responsibility to persist until the end. The people must triumph." It was signed by Uerkesh Daolet. I asked the students about the poster. "None of us know where he is," one said. "But that is his signature. Now the movement will go on, but who knows what we will do next. The student movement will not fail. The army can't suppress the students forever. China has hope because the people stood up. If the economy gets worse, certainly the people will rise up again. The average person understands democracy and freedom only a little. But they do understand quite clearly prices. They do understand corruption. They do understand official profiteering."

We left the dormitory and as we approached the badminton court, we noticed about half a dozen middle-aged men, tough-looking, some smoking cigarettes, standing around the car. Adi moved toward the driver's side, and the men rushed toward him and started pulling at his clothes. "Eh, eh," they shouted, "you come with us." Adi elbowed one of the men and I sprinted to the passenger door. Five of the toughs descended on me and started shoving me, grabbing at my shoulder bag, trying to drag me away. I knocked a couple of them down, hammering all the while on the window for Adi, who was frantically trying to start the car, to unlock the door. Somehow I managed to get the door open, fling my bag on the seat, and get in. I slammed the door, missing one man's fingers by millimeters as he yanked them away. As Adi revved the engine, one of the thugs smashed the outside mirror. Another karate-kicked the side of the car, caving in the passenger door. Adi left a trail of rubber on the court as we screeched toward the university's gate. Once through the gate, we laughed aloud at our close call with police obviously intent on finding out whom we'd talked to, laughter that camouflaged our genuine anxiety.

Night after night, the national news broadcasts showed parades of brutally beaten people arrested for participating in the demonstrations around China. "Thugs" and "evildoers" they were called, again and again. A news clip showed laughing and clapping soldiers being given food by civilians. A soldier was shown helping an old couple cross the street. And a bit of film pirated from an ABC satellite, showing a man being interviewed by an American reporter, flashed by with subtitles asking the viewing public to tell the police where this "rumor monger" could be found; he was turned in a few days later and was hurriedly sentenced to ten years in prison. A sister was shown explaining why she had informed on her brother, the student leader Zhou Fensuo. The message was clear to the people of China: the government is everywhere; only criminals participated in the events of May and June; the army loves the people.

In the countryside around Beijing, the government's propaganda was seen with less cynicism than in the capital itself. About a week after the massacre, I drove, again with a few reporters, to Tailing, a village near the tomb of the Ming emperor Xiao Zong, who died in 1505. The edges of the macadam road were carpeted with drying grain. A threshing machine clattered away nearby and a solitary tractor chugged through a distant field. I sat at the base of the stone stele mounted on the back of a stone tortoise, chewing on a piece of straw, asking some of the farmers about the year's crop. After a while, the conversation turned to the events in Beijing. "We're farmers," an older man said. His words, thick with the rural patois of the area, resonated with the current line: "We want peace. We don't want disorder." Some younger villagers sidled up and one offered a view shaded a little differently. "We don't know anything. We're peasants. We're out here." I asked him if he believed the government's accounts on television, whether he thought the people who demonstrated in Beijing were *baotu*, "thugs." "I'm not sure if they're baotu," he admitted, dragging on a cigarette. "Not everything on Chinese television is true. But not everything on the Voice of America is true. The students are against corruption. I'm against that too."

Control of the media, China's leadership knows, is essential to controlling the people. In early May, as the democracy movement soared on heady expectations of making history, transforming history, the country's newspapers and television shrugged off the weighted hand of imposed and self-censorship. Accounts of the demonstrations on Tiananmen Square were accurate, informed, detailed, nuanced; they were not propaganda, they were news. That alone, something remarked on by

321

Chinese everywhere during May, helped shred the government's effort to instruct the populace as to the "true" nature of these events. Li Peng understood this all too well. Ten days after the bloodshed on Beijing's streets, he restated in the starkest terms what the Communist Party expected of the country's journalists, many of whom had been fervent participants in the protests. "Because of mistakes in the guidance of media work by a small number of comrades in the central leadership who have departed from the stand of the Communist Party, it got to the point that some media organizations, in the work of suppressing this rebellion, have given incorrect guidance to public opinion. It should be said that this is a result of the free spread of bourgeois liberalization over a long period. The guidance of public opinion is extremely important. We earnestly demand that the media immediately adopt the viewpoint of the party and the people."

Swiftly, the police moved against China's best and brightest. The Twenty-seventh Army, the unit that led that murderous onslaught at the square, occupied the Chinese Academy of Social Science, the umbrella body for many of the research institutes that were home to the country's most imaginative thinkers. Secret police moved methodically through the research offices, searching files, carting away books, interrogating faculty and students. Some of those academics who were on the government's most-wanted list managed to escape to the West. Others were not so lucky and waited in fear. "Everyone is too afraid to talk, too afraid to do anything," said a foreign scholar who, until the massacre, had been working at the academy. Cultural critics, poets, journalists, scholars were rounded up, some arrested publicly, others spirited away in secret.

The police executed dozens of industrial workers, arresting and imprisoning thousands more, for having defied the party's claim to be the sole representative of the proletariat. But for the intelligentsia, arrests and imprisonment were not enough. Against these people, the broad spectrum of Chinese who used their minds—moviemakers, entrepreneurs, literary critics, think-tank theorists, Marxist scholars, journalists—the party's propaganda apparatus erupted in an orgy of denunciation, a relentless drumbeat of excoriation intended to depict these people as the enemies of China, as manipulators of innocent young minds, as the font of all evil.

MORE THAN THE SHEER NUMBERS of demonstrators themselves, staggering as they were for the Chinese leadership to witness and contemplate, it was the constellation of ideas, the mélange of economic, political, and cultural views that challenged the party's monopoly on discourse, that provoked such virulent fury from the party mandarins. In the manner of their crudest imperial forebears, the aged hard-liners who had triumphed in Tiananmen sought to cloister China from the free exchange of ideas. These leaders, accustomed to issuing mandates to be carried out without discussion, accustomed to defining China for the world, were enraged that they had been forced to engage these intellectuals in dialogue, in debate.

One of the most gripping moments in the history of the People's Republic had occurred on May 18, at the height of the student hunger strike. Prime Minister Li Peng was forced to meet with a group of student leaders, a confrontation broadcast on national television. For the first time, the Chinese people watched as normal people talked to and challenged one of the country's senior leaders—without stilted prepared texts, without artificial formality. For Li, and for the men he represented, it was the closest they would permit themselves to come to engaging in genuine discussion with the people they rule.

The meeting took place in the Great Hall of the People, on the edge of Tiananmen Square. Li, imperious in manner and speech, declared that only one subject would be discussed, that of how the hunger strike was to be ended. Uerkesh Daolet, in an act never before seen by the Chinese people, interjected himself into Li's lecture. "Premier Li, if we go on like this, it seems we won't have enough time. We should have substantial talks as soon as possible. Just now you said we would discuss only one thing, but in fact it was not you who invited us to be here; rather, it was so many people on Tiananmen Square who asked you to come out and talk to us." Then the twenty-one-year-old student ticked off a list of demands: that Li and Zhao Ziyang go directly to talk to the students on the square, that the *People's Daily* editorial of April 26 be retracted, and that an apology to the people of China be issued by the leadership.

It is difficult to describe the significance of this interchange; a malnourished, charismatic, pajama-clad Uighur college student rebuking one of the country's most powerful leaders, ripping from him the aura of authority conferred by a practiced remoteness from the Chinese people. China's leaders, fond of proclaiming on behalf of "the people," in fact no more engage their subjects than did the doddering, corrupt Empress Dowager Ci Xi. Never do the leaders speak to the Chinese people directly over television or radio. Always, they are shown addressing robotic audiences in mammoth halls, or meeting foreign dignitaries. They are never heckled, never questioned. They simply rule. This is why Uerkesh Daolet's words to Li Peng, the words of one man to another, words between equals, were so jarring to China's leadership. Like dragon-robed emperors, Chinese leaders expect heads to bow in their presence. Uerkesh's did not.

I LEFT CHINA in late June 1989, less than a month after the bloodshed on Tiananmen Square. My final week in Beijing was one of anguish and anger. I feared for my friends and despaired for a country that had, at times, seemed to be finding its way.

In those last days, I bicycled through the streets, watching, wondering about the months and years ahead. In the heady days of May, people used to sidle up alongside me and chat about politics, about life. After Tiananmen, though, bicyclists pedaled by deliberately, wrapped in cocoons of self-preservation. It was simply too dangerous to be seen talking to a foreigner. There was shock on the faces of Beijing's citizens in those days, a stunned realization that the country's leaders had actually launched a war against them.

There were instances of instinctive behavior, people performing tasks just, I thought, to be doing something. On one of my bicycle tours, I saw an old man with a hand broom carefully sweeping out the shell of a burned bus that had been thrown across the road to stop the army. He didn't look around as he worked. He just worked his way from the back of the bus to the front, sweeping glass, charred fragments of seat cushions, the debris of fire out the front door. It was a meaningless labor, but one he seemed absorbed in.

Army propaganda trucks fitted with large electronic speakers and manned with helmeted troops fingering AK-47s cruised the streets of the capital, the speakers blaring: "The army loves the people. The people love the army. Salute the martial law troops." The heads of bicyclists remained fixed in front of them, not turning toward the high-decibel abuse. Cranes guarded by troops lumbered through the city, hoisting burned trucks and buses onto the backs of flatbed trucks to be hauled away. Work crews, again watched over by armed soldiers, replaced the steel-gate medians on Chang'an Avenue. Dozens of new monitoring cameras appeared on lampposts across town. It was difficult to recall, amid the sullenness that had descended on Beijing, the ebullience and jubilation of the democracy days. "This is," a university friend told me, "a terrified and terrorized nation."

In the days that followed, the United States and Europe were deluged with accounts of the massacre, of its aftermath. For its part, the Chinese government insisted that no one had been killed. Only in the face of graphic photographs and countless eyewitness descriptions did the government begin to waver in its stand, finally declaring that three hundred people had been killed, most of them soldiers. More important, they insisted, no one was killed on Tiananmen Square itself.

There will never be a full accounting of the total number of deaths on June 3 and June 4 so long as the old men rule China. Still, there were some efforts by foreign reporters to lend credence to the government accounts, including rather clumsy extrapolations of hospital admittances. It was a disgraceful exercise, both because the evidence was so apparent and the government so corrupt in its accounts of events. The day of the massacre, the Chinese Red Cross estimated that twenty-six hundred people were killed by army troops. The Red Cross was forced to retract that estimate when government officials took charge of the organization.

Amnesty International issued a report three months after the slaughter stating that "at least a thousand civilians" were killed by army troops between June 3 and June 9. I regard this estimate as conservative. Following the massacre I talked to two people with extensive contacts within China's security apparatus. Both, without equivocation, insisted that more than twenty-five hundred people had been killed throughout Beijing over that two-day period. Since I talked to them, reports prepared by both American and European intelligence agencies have settled on the figure of three thousand for the number of civilians killed. These reports are based in part on extensive electronic intercepts of Chinese military and police communications during the assault on Beijing and Tiananmen Square.

Even as we in the West struggle to comprehend the dimensions of the bloodshed, it is the Chinese people themselves who are kept in the dark by their leaders. They know that their government lies to them daily, and they know the official accounts are distorted. Deep in their memories are the events of the spring of 1976. They remember the massacre on Tiananmen Square on April 5, 1976, when tens of thousands of mourners who had come to pay homage to Zhou Enlai, who had died three months earlier, were assaulted by club-wielding Chinese soldiers. To this day, China's leaders have never acknowledged the precise number of people who were killed that night, although internal documents that surfaced in Hong Kong speak of as many as one hundred deaths. They also remember that the April Fifth Incident, as it was later called, led to the downfall of a popular leader who had only recently been politically rehabilitated—Deng Xiaoping.

As DECISIVELY AS ANY EVENT in modern Chinese history, the Tiananmen massacre ended a decade of experimentation, a decade of hope for China. There had been ten years of success, of astonishing growth, of new learning, of new experiences. The country's farmers, unburdened of socialist meddling, grew more rice and wheat than at any time in Chinese history. They became richer, better educated, and more confident of their future. In the cities, consumerism was infectious and the decades of material drought were displaced by remarkable abundance. Quick-witted entrepreneurs made money and salaried workers saved for color television sets. Bankers thought about stock markets and political scientists planned for democracy. Writers and artists reshaped the way China thought of itself. Moviemakers probed the ambiguities of the human condition, and musicians learned rock 'n' roll. Everything seemed possible. Tiananmen ended all that.

In the most fundamental sense, Tiananmen represented the inevitable collision of the economic and political forces unleashed by the reform process of the 1980s, with the inherently rigid and intransigent Communist Party ruling the country. Economic liberalization, the process of yielding total control to free decision-makers—a farmer growing his own crops and selling them on free markets, a young man risking all by starting a vial-making factory, a woman staking her fortune on her managerial wits, a banker defying the state to provide money to newborn industries—brings in its churning wake irrepressible demands for a voice in civic life. Basic human and political rights, rights not recognized by the Chinese Communist Party, germinated in the fertile soil of free economic life and the free exchange of ideas. Every time the party tried to stifle the growing clamor for political change, it only grew louder. Every time the party attempted to reassert control, its claim to legitimacy weakened. For every worker shot, for every student jailed, the party's grip on the soul of its subjects weakened.

At decade's end, China's leaders saw everywhere the unmistakable and inexorable reality that awaits them and their party. In Eastern Europe, the Communist Parties of Czechoslovakia, East Germany, Hungary, Poland, and Romania were brushed aside like frail cobwebs in the exuberant sprint toward democracy. In Beijing, the execution of the Ceauşescu was greeted by an audible torrent of excited discussion; glasses of beer were hoisted in great number and the beer bottles smashed in metaphorical vengeance against Deng Xiaoping—*xiaoping* being a homonym for "little bottle." Unable, however, to comprehend genuinely the forces at work in Eastern Europe, China's leaders flailed about for a scapegoat, someone they could pin the blame on for the collapse of the ideology to which they were wed; they latched onto Mikhail Gorbachev.

"Gorbachev," Jiang Zemin, the party's new leader, told a secret meeting of the party's Politburo in late December 1989, "has betrayed the international Communist movement and the Communist Party. He just cannot shirk his responsibility for the currently deteriorating situation in Eastern Europe." Wang Zhen, the most vitriolic of the hard-liners who resurfaced after Tiananmen, assayed the Soviet leader in even more caustic terms. "That Gorbachev fellow is a wastrel," he shouted during a meeting with Beijing's mayor, Chen Xitong, and its party chief, Li Ximing. "What was wrong with Lenin and Stalin? I knew long ago that he was a bad sort. He and Zhao Ziyang are two of a kind."

China's leadership, both the old men who sat behind the curtain of power and the leaders in formal posts, sought to reassure the world that the country had swiftly returned to normal. The Bush administration accepted those assurances and swiftly moved to return relations to their pre-Tiananmen tenor. Even before the last bloodstains had faded from the square, President Bush secretly dispatched emissaries to Beijing, twice in five months, to affirm his administration's commitment to Sino-American relations. Both trips were conducted in secrecy, not from the Chinese but from the American people, whose outrage the President knew he was courting. Yet despite Bush's abject kow-towing, the Chinese leadership made no effort to ease the repression of their people.

Of course, normality, to the Chinese leadership, meant silence. As the leaders' voices echoed through this new stillness, China slipped deeper into economic distress. Instinctively, Deng Xiaoping and the men he chose to run the government and party resorted to the clumsy levers of socialist economic planning and centralization. Millions of private and collective enterprises were closed. Talk of stock and bond markets, of privatization, of the glories of getting rich, ceased.

Systematically, the hard-liners began the process of dismantling Zhao Ziyang's legacy. On June 24, less than three weeks after Tiananmen, Zhao was formally stripped of his position as general secretary and dismissed from the Central Committee. Hu Qili was dismissed from the Politburo's Standing Committee for his support of Zhao. The old men then nominated Jiang Zemin, a colorless, unimaginative sixty-two-year-old man, to head the party. Jiang had been party secretary of Shanghai, and that city's mayor before that. He had failed miserably as mayor, holding Shanghai back as the rest of the coast and other cities south of his sprinted ahead economically. Shanghai under Jiang remained gripped by bureaucratic and ideological infighting. He was widely detested by the people of Shanghai, particularly because of his hard-line attitude toward the student protests of 1986.

As the decade closed, Zhao's followers were arrested or purged. His think tanks were abolished or reorganized. Some of his advisers, men like Yan Jiaqi, who had headed the political science department at the Chinese Academy of Social Science, and Chen Yizi, who headed the State Council think tank on political reform, fled abroad. Others, not arrested, were forced to undergo political reeducation. And on August 25, the *Guangming Daily,* a party newspaper intended for intellectuals, called for the eradication of Zhao's influence on the party and the country, a tacit admission that Zhao's views were widely shared among the people of China. They wrote his political obituary, denouncing him for not "educating, molding, and arming" the people. Instead, the paper scoffed, Zhao Ziyang was guilty of "respecting, understanding, and caring for the people."

Around Deng Xiaoping now hovered a coterie of old men, many of whom held no official party or government post, but who, nonetheless, were very much members of the new ruling coalition. When they gathered around the oval table on June 9, on national television, Deng laid down the new orthodoxy. "This storm," Deng told his aged comrades, "was bound to happen sooner or later. As determined by the international and domestic climate, it was bound to happen and was independent of man's will. It was just a matter of time and scale. It has turned out in our favor, for we still have a large group of veterans who have experienced many storms and have a thorough understanding of things. They were on the side of taking resolute action to counter the turmoil. . . . We still have a group of senior comrades who are alive, we still have the army, and we also have a group of core cadres who took part in the revolution at various times. That is why it was relatively easy for us to handle the present matter."

But even though many of these men had fought side by side in the guerrilla campaigns that brought Mao Zedong to power, even though they shared an unhappiness over the process of economic reform and an aversion to the "polluting" influences of the West, particularly the United States, there still remained stark differences among them. Like carrion birds circling over an aging buffalo, these men gathered around Deng, supporting his political severity but hoping, after his death, to win the battle for his carcass—that combination of power and charismatic authority that would let them rule the party, and China, unchallenged.

In the meantime, they pushed forward policies that attempted to restrict provincial independence. Factory managers were shunted aside in favor of incompetent yet politically proficient party hacks. Price controls were reimposed on a wide range of foodstuffs and manufactured goods. Centralized economic planning, which was being eroded by an emerging market economy, was reimposed with a vengeance. As Jiang Zemin said on October 1, 1989, the occasion of the fortieth anniversary of the establishment of the People's Republic, "Socialism replacing capitalism is the real mainstream of history. We are full of confidence in our socialist cause and we are sure of a bright Communist future for mankind." These were not words of a man just mouthing phrases appropriate to the moment; Jiang and the men he represented profoundly believe them.

I SPENT MANY MONTHS after Tiananmen worrying with Chinese friends who had fled China about the future of their country. In the beginning, many of them cried when they talked about Tiananmen, but as the months passed they dried their tears and grew less somber. Some of them organized overseas students and intellectuals into a worldwide movement of democratic opposition. Others plunged into their new lives as university students. And still others took up their paintbrushes and their writing pens to continue the chronicle of China. All prayed for change.

Some of the student leaders who had managed to escape the secret police dragnet after June 4 surfaced in Europe and the United States. In the glare of sudden, if transient, fame, several of the more prominent leaders signed contracts with Madison Avenue public relations firms, which brought them speaking fees of as much as three thousand dollars. A few student leaders began writing their memoirs. In France, a group of exiled dissidents chartered a ship which they sailed to international waters off the Chinese coast, where they hoped to direct news and opinion radio broadcasts toward the mainland. A plethora of magazines and newspapers devoted to the activities of the democratic opposition sprang up. A computer network devoted to news from China was established, linking Chinese around the world. Two of the most outspoken exiled dissidents, the political scientist Yan Jiaqi and the student leader Uerkesh Daolet, were chosen to head a broad umbrella alliance of opposition groups, its purpose to rally world opinion against the Chinese government and to funnel news secretly into China. Without question, some of the brightest people from China are now in exile, some willingly, many more who had been abroad before the massacre and are simply victims of political events. But from this mass of expatriate intellectuals, some forty thousand in the United States alone, has jelled a powerful voice of dissent. Through faxes, letters, and telephone calls, these Chinese have sought to keep information flowing into China. They have sought to keep the ideals of the spring of 1989 alive.

At the same time, however, the stresses of life in exile, the fractionalization of contending politics and egos, and in some cases the very youth of many of these students (many of the leaders were in their late teens, or barely into their twenties), tended to erode a unified front of the exiled opposition. And while there was support from the overseas Chinese community for these exiles, a significant segment of the Chinese population in the United States and Europe viewed the events of spring 1989 as ephemeral, little more than a passing storm to be weathered, not a cause to be embraced.

The Chinese government railed against the overseas activists, denouncing them as criminals. Official newspapers sought to discredit student leaders, in one case by contending that Uerkesh Daolet would have been expelled from college for low grades even if he had not been involved in the spring demonstrations. And according to Western intelligence reports, the Chinese government also launched a widespread covert intelligence effort against the dissident movement, infiltrating its agents into opposition groups across the United States, and especially in France. A Chinese friend active in exile activities in Boston told me that the dissidents were aware of the spies in their midst, but that it was felt there was little that could be done. "What matters is what we say and what we do," he told me. "Here there isn't anything they can do to us. They can hurt our families in China. That is how they try to intimidate us. But they can't silence us."

As I traveled the United States speaking on China in late 1989, I bumped into many of these students on campuses around the country. They listened to the stories I told about Beijing, and regaled me with tales of their own. I discovered a despair about the present, but a despair alleviated by a profound optimism for the future. How could it be otherwise? For these exiles to go on, for them to entertain any expectation of seeing their homeland again, they could not but retain an undaunted hope for China's future. For my part, I find it difficult, as I write these final words, to envisage how they, a force of such extraordinary intellect and youth, can, in the final analysis, pose a real threat to the forces of power and repression in their homeland. The history of exile movements is not an easy one; the powers these dissidents wielded in China—the ability to present their ideas forcefully, to proselytize within the population, even to lobby and harangue the party itself—have dissipated in the democratic diaspora. Nonetheless, within China, the changes that occurred over the past ten years have been indelibly imprinted on the psyche of the Chinese people. All that remains is for a new generation of activists to give expression to the implications of that change. It will not be swift or easy.

I remember some of the last spontaneous words I heard before I left China, uttered by a university student who braved the stares of other bicycle riders as he maneuvered next to me one afternoon late in June. He pumped his pedals beside me for a while, unspeaking. But when he spoke, his words mirrored the tragedy of China. "There must be blood to have democracy," he whispered hoarsely. "In Chinese history, there has always been blood."

INDEX

Great Wall, 37, 70, 79, 81, 82, 84, 92–93
Guangdong Province, 6, 48, 91, 101, 138, 151, 164, 178, 201, 202, 233
Guangming Daily, 45, 92, 329
Guangong Temple (Lolam), 109–10
Guan Guangmei, 131, 132–36
Guangxi Province, 195, 282
Guangxu (Qing Emperor), 57
Guangzhou (city), xxv, 137, 139, 154, 155, 165, 169, 174, 178, 233, 243, 251, 263
Gu Cheng, 255, 256
Gu Chengwen, 199–200
Gu Gong, 255
Guizhou Province, 198, 281
Guo Moruo, xii
Guo Pu, 120

Hainan Island, 163, 200–1, 223
Halley, Edmund, 81
Han culture, 70, 193–95, 200, 219–21, 223
Hangzhou (city), 243, 251, 276
Hebei Province, 129
Hefei (city), 22, 269, 277
Heilongjiang Province, 163
He Jingzhi, 282
Heller, Joseph, 258
Henan Province, 177, 281
Henry, Patrick, 268, 318
Hicks, Irl R., 8–9, 31
Hinton, William, 147
History of Modern Chinese Literature, The, xiii
Hong Kong, xxiv, 6, 77–79, 91, 101, 137, 142, 155, 156, 161, 164, 201, 302, 306, 326
Hong Xiuchuan, 195
Hou Dejian, 313
Hou Renzhi, 63–64, 66, 69, 70
Hua Guofeng, xvii, xix, xx, 39, 233
Huang Gang, 47–49
Huang Guohua, 147
Huitongsi (Ancestral Temple) (Beijing), 69
Hu Jingtao, 221
Hunan Province, xi, xii, xxiv, 32, 164, 174, 195, 197, 199, 201, 223
"Hundred Flowers" period, 265, 266
Hungary, 327
Hunger Strike Manifesto, 291
Hu Qiaomu, 40, 162, 230, 231, 234, 259, 280
Hu Qili, 24, 234, 328
Hu Yaobang, xxi, xxii, xxv, 40, 55, 170, 229, 230, 231, 235, 241, 281, 285
    background of, xxiv
    death of, 54, 80, 240, 289, 290
    dismissal of, xxvi, 23, 24, 232, 233, 279

on literary limits, 256–57
on Mao Zedong Thought, 45
power of, 227–28
on Tibet, 202
at Twelfth Party Congress, 39

Ignatius, Adi, 148–49, 217, 317–20
India, 193, 210
Institute of Marxism, Leninism, and Mao Zedong Thought, 46
Iran, 25

Japan, xvii, xxi, xxiii, 7, 17, 31, 92, 130, 152, 154, 161, 162, 170, 226, 261, 278
Jia Jing, 62
Jiang Qing, xix, 34, 283
Jiangsu (city), 173
Jiang Xiu'e, 134
Jiang Zemin, 178, 270–71, 327, 328, 330
Jokhang Cathedral (Tibet), 208, 210–14, 220, 222
Joyce, James, 38

Kanghua Development Corporation, 161
Kang Weiying, 180
Kerr, Dr. Blake, 212, 214
Khampa herdsmen, 208
Kinkley, Jeffrey C., xii
Kissinger, Henry A., 5–6, 20, 21
Kong Demao, 82
Korea, 92
    See also North Korea; South Korea
Kunlun Mountain, 121
Kuomintang, xii, xxi, 17, 167, 226, 309
Kyodo (news agency), 278, 279

Lady Chatterley's Lover (Lawrence), 155
Lai Wahfong, 123
Lama Temple (Beijing), 70
Lantos, Tom, 29
Last Emperor, The (film), 47–48, 68
Lawrence, D. H., 155
Lee Chongwing, 110–11, 112, 115, 116
Lee clan, 102–4, 106, 119, 123, 125
Lee Jemcheung, 121
Lee Seegay, 100–2, 105–11, 115, 122–25
Lee Shaywing, 105–6
Lee Waiwing (Mr. Wind and Water), 120–24
Lee Yinfuk, 115–17
Lee Yinsing, 118-19
Lee Yintam, 113–15
Lei Feng, 229
Lenin, Nikolai, 36, 41, 226, 268, 327
Leninism, 42, 53, 225, 298, 303
Lescot, Patrick, 220, 221
Leward, Tim, 289
Lhagba Puncog, 219–20
Lhasa (Tibet), 26, 201–3, 207–13, 215–22, 224

INDEX

Liang Qichao, 62
Liang Sicheng, 61, 62–63, 64
Liaoning Province, 16, 131, 305
Liberation Army Daily, 162–63
Li culture, 201, 223
Lilley, James, 29, 313
Li Ming, 132, 135–36
Lin Biao, 21, 37
Lincoln, Abraham, 268
Li Peng, 15, 24, 55, 240, 243, 247, 301, 304, 307, 322
  background of, 229, 235
  on democracy, 288
  and martial law, 292, 298–99
  and media, 322
  at National People's Congress, 239
  policies of, 236–39
  student confrontation of, 323–24
Li Shuxian, 286, 317
Liu Binyan, 53, 279–80, 286–87, 290
Liu De, 282
Liu Hongru, 137
Liu Huabiao, 146–47, 148
Liulichang (Beijing), 71–72
Liu Qing, 251
Liu Shaoqi, xviii, xx, 107
Liu Xiaobo, 94–95, 290
Liu Xiaolin, 34
Liu Xigui, 131
Liu Zhongtian ("Shotgun"), 14–15, 16
Li Xiannian, 40, 166, 231, 234, 247, 261–62, 281
Li Xiaoyan, 13–14, 15, 16
Li Ximing, 327
Li Zhenyan, 177
Lolam (village), 100–25
Long March, 229
Long Yunbang, 198
Lord, Bette Bao, 19–20
Lord, Winston, 17, 19–22, 24–25, 26, 27
Los Angeles Times, 297
Low Cheunghing, 115
Luo Haigang, 166

Macao, 72
Manchuria, 3, 10
Mann, Jim, 17, 30
Maoists, xxii, xxiii, 12, 18, 73, 147, 281
Mao Zedong, xii, xxi, 4, 37, 38, 40, 41, 47, 52, 59, 76, 79, 86, 119, 131, 216, 250, 256, 268, 287, 329
  armies of, xxiv, 154, 229, 257
  and Beijing, 62–65
  birth of, 32, 33
  death of, xiii, xv–xvi, xvii, xix, 49, 175
  devotion to, xviii, 45, 123, 151
  and factories, 138–39
  glorification of, 35, 89
  and Great Leap Forward, 111–12
  and "Hundred Flowers" period, 265
  ideology of, 42, 226–27

and Kuomintang, 17
labor camps of, 266
legacy of, xx
mausoleum of, 19, 136–37
museum on, 34, 36
and peasantry, 169
and People's Republic, 61, 304
portrait of, 294, 295, 306, 310
statues of, 45–46, 153
successor of, 21, 39, 107
utopian socialism of, 44
and villages, 99
vision of, 42
Mao Zedong Thought, 36–38, 43–45, 53, 253
Marcos, Ferdinand, 309
Market, 162
Marx, Karl, 36, 41, 48, 88, 226, 268
Marxism, 42, 47, 48, 53, 87, 120, 130, 260, 267, 287
Marxism-Leninism, 48, 94, 232, 253, 262, 275, 278
Mauritania, 15, 16
May Fourth Movement, 80
Meindersma, Christa, 222
Menon, Shivshankar, 211
Miao culture, xi, xii, xiv, 195–200, 201, 223
Miaofeng Mountains, 59, 60
Ming, Professor (pseud.), 56–61, 62, 73
Ming dynasty, 62, 68, 94, 195, 321
Ministry of Supervision, 165
Mongolia, 13, 21, 200
Monlam Chenmo (Great Prayer Festival) (Tibet), 210–11, 220
Mount Tai, 75
Mozart, Wolfgang Amadeus, 38
Muslims, 195

Nanfang Daily News, 263
Nanjing, 277
Nationalists, 154, 169
National People's Congress, xxv, 82, 239
NATO, 6
Nechung monastery (Tibet), 214–15
New China News Agency, 130–31
Newton, Isaac, 286
New York Times, The, xiv, xxvi, xxvii
Nicaragua, 26
1984 (Orwell), 285
Nineties, The, 286–88
Ningbo (town), 143, 152
Ningxia Province, 177
Ning Yinghai, 162–63
Nixon, Richard, 5, 6, 8–9
Nixon administration, 5
Northern Wei dynasty, 68
North Korea, 25, 242

337

Obote, Milton, xxvi
Orwell, George, 285

Pang Wengqing, 34–35
Peng Siqi, 67–68
Peng Zhen, xviii, 162, 166, 234, 247, 261–62
People's Armed Police, 17, 90, 213–14, 222
People's Bank of China, 137, 146
People's Daily, 127, 128, 160, 163, 165, 240–42, 263, 266, 273, 274, 276, 277, 290, 323
People's Liberation Army, 11, 160, 256, 298, 302, 307
Phelan, John J., Jr., 136, 137
Philippines, 142, 304, 309
Pichugov, Alexandre, 235
Poland, 26, 327
Politburo, xxiii, 228, 246, 327
  Standing Committee of, 24, 231, 233, 234–35, 236, 244, 247, 278, 279, 328
Potala Palace (Tibet), 208
Pottier, Eugène, 294
Public Security Bureau, 254
Putian (town), 152

Qianlong (Emperor), 55
Qian Qichen, 30
Qiao Shi, 24, 235
Qingdao (port), 7
Qing dynasty, xix, 59, 70, 71, 77, 121, 195, 197, 199, 201
Qin Shihuangdi, 75
Qiu Leimeng, 180
Qi Wenzeng, 127, 128
Qu Geping, 65
Qu Ni, 219

Reagan administration, 22, 25–26, 27
Red Army, 229
Red Flag, 281
Red Guards, xix, 21, 35, 36, 37, 47, 76, 120, 160
Redman, Charles E., 26–27
Religious Affairs Office, 206
"Resolution on Certain Questions in the History of Our Party Since the Founding of the People's Republic of China," 38
River Elegy (Heshang) (TV series), 82–86, 92–94
Romania, 327
Rosario, Louise do, 316

Sang Ye, 262
Schidlovsky, John, 311, 312, 315, 316
Schiffman, James, 280
Sciolino, Elaine, 27
Scowcroft, Brent, 29–30

Searching for Roots, 282
Selected Works (Mao Zedong), 45
Sera monastery (Tibet), 203, 208, 212, 214, 220
Shaanxi Province, 119, 171, 195
Shakespeare, William, 258
Shandong Province, 75
Shanghai, 16, 50, 90, 140, 165, 169, 243, 251, 276–77, 317, 328
  cars in, 186–87
  and Cultural Revolution, xix, 175
  economy of, 173–75, 176–78
  games in, 185–86
  housing in, 179–80, 182, 183–85
  industrial output in, 65
  population of, 171–73
  prostitution in, xxv, 139
  Puto district, 178–79
  restaurants in, 79
  revolutionary history of, 174–75
  stock market in, 128, 137
  student protests in, 168–69, 238, 269, 270–73, 274, 290
Shao Henian, 187
Shaoshan (village), 32–36
Shen Congwen, xi–xv, xxvii–xxviii, 195–96, 282
Shenyang (capital city), 16, 18, 131, 137
Shenzhen (city), 155–56, 165
Shi Guanfu, 276–77
Shi Tiesheng, 256
Shultz, George, 23
Shu Ting, 255
Sichuan Province, 162, 173, 227, 282
Silkworm missiles, 25
Simons, Stefan, 139, 151, 153, 156, 157, 158, 217–18, 219
Singapore, 92, 137, 230
Song (comrade), 177
Song dynasty, 78
Song Lanying, 184–85
South Korea, 8, 137, 230
Soviet Union, 6, 7, 10, 18, 20, 76, 181, 235
  balancing, 22
  culture of, 258
  department stores in, 40
  geopolitical encirclement by, 21
  human rights in, 27
  leadership of, 245, 327
  military aggression of, 315
  military parades of, 229
  as model, 176, 228
  planning of, xxi
  relations with, 31
Stalin, Joseph, 235, 268, 327
Stalinists, 40, 318
State Council, 127, 128, 165
  and housing, 182–83
State Department (U.S.), 26–27, 29
State Economic Commission, 14